ESSENTIAL
HUMAN
ANATOMY
FOR ARTISTS

A Complete Visual Guide to Drawing
the Structures of the Living Form

KEN GOLDMAN

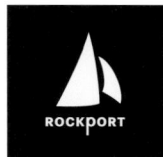

ROCKPORT

Page 2:

Ken Goldman, *Pauolo Cristobal*, oil on canvas,
40" × 30" (102 × 76 cm)
This composition combines anatomical accuracy
with a striking focal point and a simplified
background.

Page 208:

Ken Goldman, *Sketch Group*, watercolor on
toned paper, 9" × 12" (23 × 30 cm) (detail)
Sometimes, during a long pose (2 or 3 hours), it's
a fun challenge to paint not just the model but the
other participants as well.

Quarto.com
© 2023 Quarto Publishing Group USA Inc.
Text, photos, and illustrations (new
content only) © 2023 Ken Goldman

First published in 2023 by
Rockport Publishers, an imprint
of The Quarto Group,
100 Cummings Center, Suite 265-D,
Beverly, MA 01915, USA.
T (978) 282-9590 F (978) 283-2742

Rockport Publishers titles are also
available at discount for retail, wholesale,
promotional, and bulk purchase. For
details, contact the Special Sales
Manager by email at specialsales@
quarto.com or by mail at The Quarto
Group, Attn: Special Sales Manager, 100
Cummings Center, Suite 265-D, Beverly,
MA 01915, USA.

10 9 8 7 6 5 4 3 2

ISBN: 978-1-63159-959-0

Digital edition published in 2023
eISBN: 978-1-63159-960-6

The content on pages 88, 96, 112,
128, 130, 132, 148, 151, and 153 was
previously published in *Drawing: Basic
Anatomy and Figure Drawing* (Walter
Foster Publishing, 2006) by Ken Goldman.

The content on pages 134, 136, 138,
and 140–147 was previously published
in *Success in Art: Drawing Hands & Feet*
(Walter Foster Publishing, 2020) by Ken
Goldman.

Library of Congress Cataloging-in-
Publication Data

Names: Goldman, Ken, 1957- author.
Title: Essential human anatomy for artists
 : a complete visual guide to
  drawing the structures of the living form
/ Ken Goldman.
Description: Beverly, MA : Rockport, 2023. |
Series: For artists series |
  Includes index.
Identifiers: LCCN 2023030303 (print) |
LCCN 2023030304 (ebook) | ISBN
 9781631599590 (trade paperback) |
ISBN 9781631599606 (ebook)
Subjects: LCSH: Human figure in art. |
Anatomy, Artistic. |
  Drawing--Technique.
Classification: LCC NC760 .G677 2023
(print) | LCC NC760 (ebook) | DDC
  743.4/9--dc23/eng/20230727
LC record available at https://lccn.loc.
gov/2023030303
LC ebook record available at https://lccn.
loc.gov/2023030304

Design and layout: Burge Agency
Photography, cover images, and
illustration: Ken Goldman unless
otherwise noted

Printed in China

This book is dedicated to all past and living master anatomists and artists
who have simplified the complex field of artistic human anatomy into
easy-to-understand drawing methods for everyday artists like myself.
In this book, I do my best to further distill and explain their findings.

CONTENTS

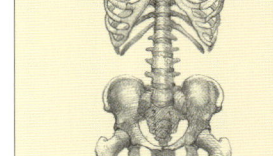
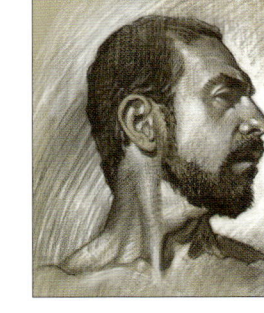
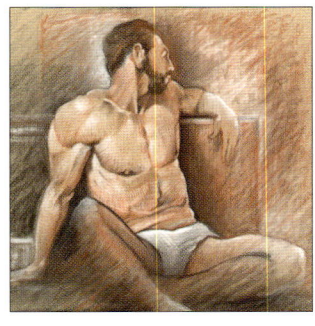

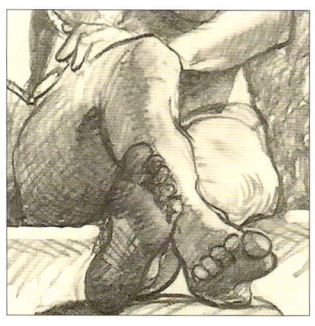

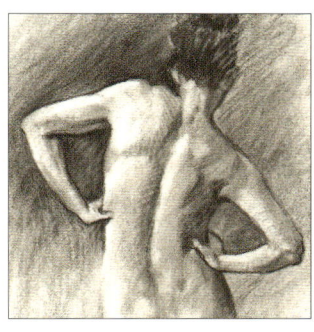

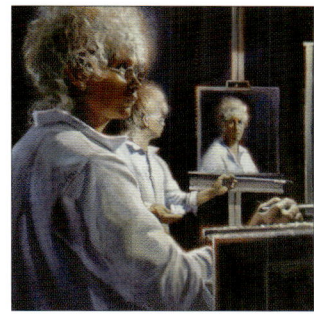

INTRODUCTION

Great artists from the Renaissance on have always included anatomy as a part of their studies because they knew that a thorough understanding of the body's internal structures enhanced their ability to capture form and detail in their drawings and paintings. Today's artists, if they are just as intent on improving their drawing skills as the old masters, also enjoy studying anatomy for exactly the same reasons.

This book is titled *Essential Human Anatomy for Artists* because it includes all the essential bones and muscles artists need to know about when constructing a figure or a portrait. Anatomy is so complex and this book is so short that I've limited my purview to only those muscles and bony landmarks that are easily seen on a model. In addition, whenever adjacent bones look too similar, I color code them to make identifying them easier.

I have strived to make the reading of this book as pleasant and as organized as possible. First, I introduce an illustrated explanation of how to set up a simple home studio, complete with the drawing tools I believe are best to begin with. Then, Chapters 2 through 6 evolve our study of the human form in a very logical way, beginning with the skeleton, without which muscles, nerves, veins, and skin would be no more than blobs

of fibrous tissues lying structureless on the floor. Chapter 7 is a short finale about background strategies and several different types of lighting contrasts that can be used when setting up a portrait composition.

COLOR KEY FOR ANATOMY DRAWINGS
These colors apply to all the anatomy drawings in this book.

▪	Tendons
▪	Carpal and tarsal bones
▪	Proximal phalanx
▪	Muscles
▪	Metacarpal and metatarsal bones
▪	Medial phalanx
▪	Leg/arm bones
▪	Distal phalanx

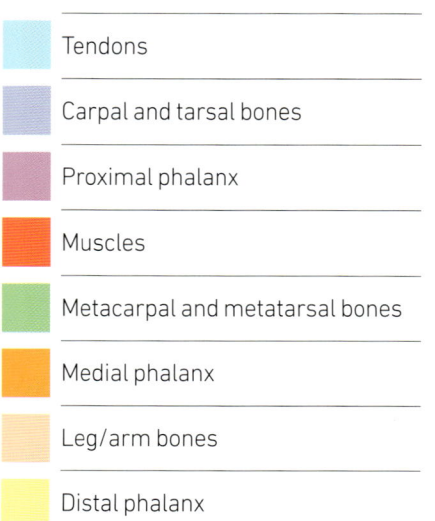

Ken Goldman, *Carlos in Sunlight*, **graphite and watercolor, 30" × 22" (76 × 56 cm)**
Form-following pencil strokes under thin washes of warm transparent watercolor and a cool background amplify this figure's quality of sunlit illumination.

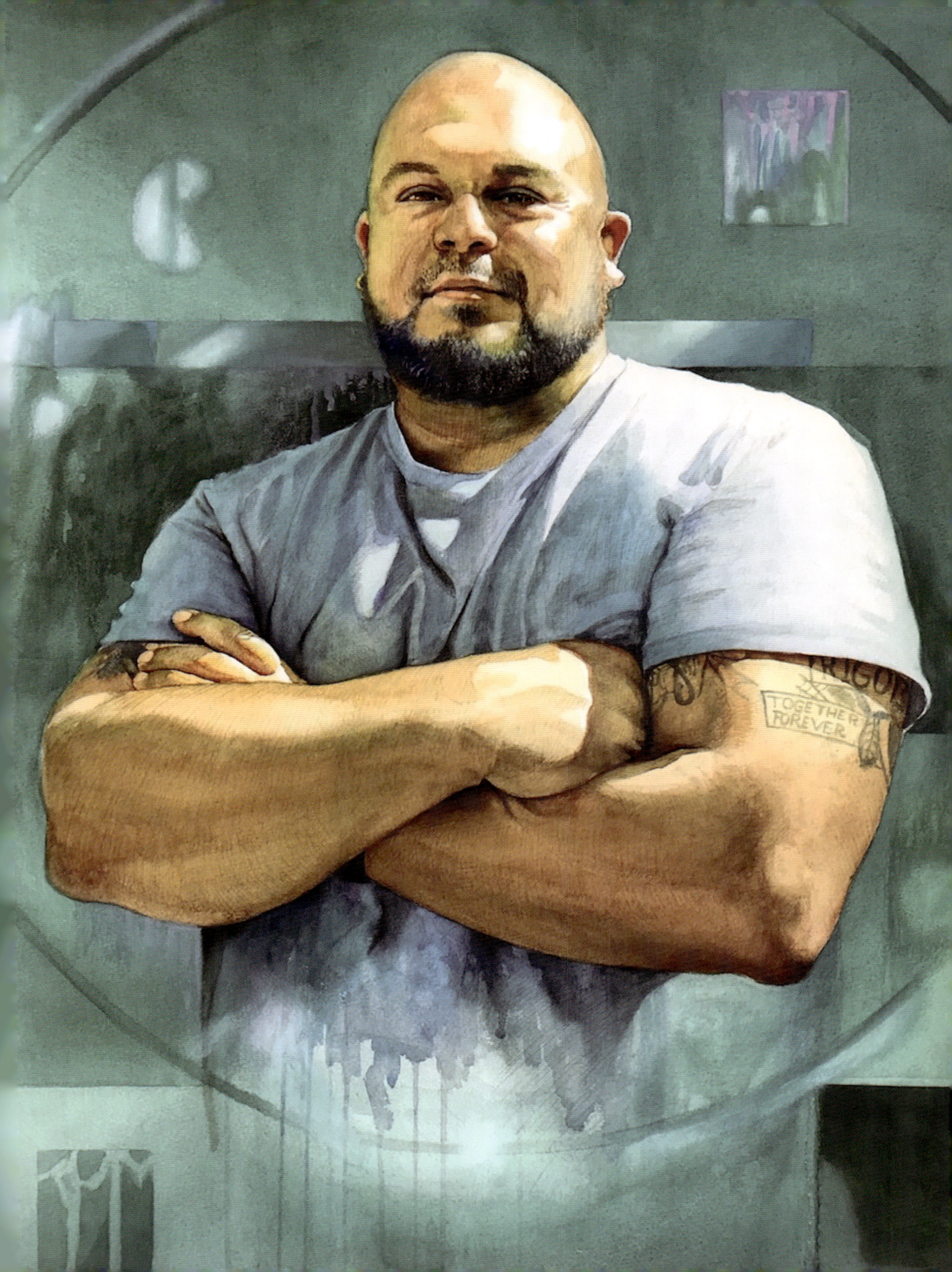

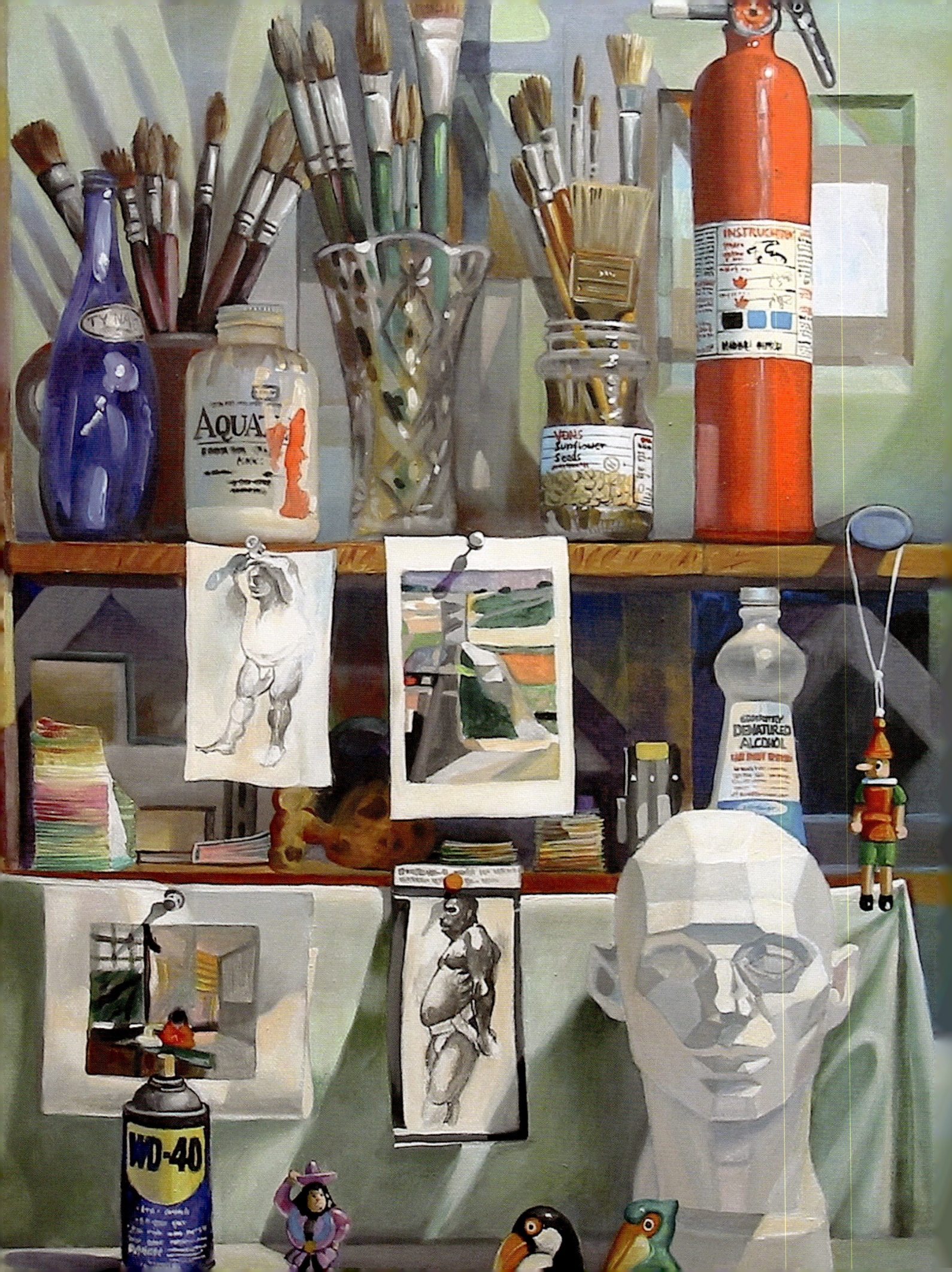

CHAPTER 1

BASIC TOOLS AND TECHNIQUES

This chapter shows how easy it is to set up a simple studio almost anywhere. The tools I recommend are used for all of the drawings in this book. Even at home, when many other tools and materials are available, I favor the following supplies for their compact effectiveness and mobility.

Ken Goldman, *Studio Shelf*, acrylic on canvas, **36" × 24" (91 × 61 cm) (detail)**
The beauty of painting a still life such as this is that it doesn't move, is well lit, and is always available.

DRAWING TOOLS

For quick erasing, try wrapping a small piece of kneaded eraser around the end of the pencil to erase with its side.

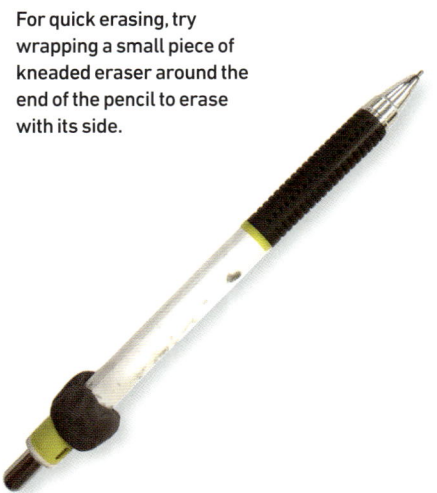

**2.0 mm 4B
Mechanical pencil**

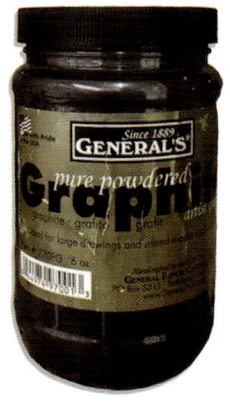

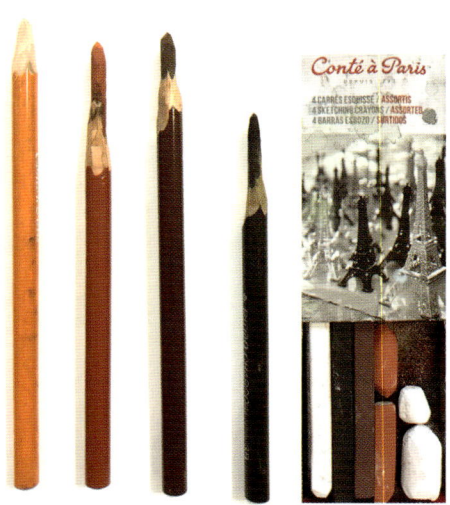

MECHANICAL GRAPHITE PENCILS

A 2.0 mm 4B and .05 mm 2B pencil are essential. The 2.0 mm works best for most of the drawing, while the smaller .05 mm is perfect for final crosshatching and details. Compared to wooden pencils, mechanical pencils are much easier to sharpen with sandpaper and work better for shading large areas with their long-tapered leads.

Many artists also use harder leads such as HB, 2H, or 4H to attain their lightest values. As your drawing progresses, and if you are careful with hand pressure, a 4B not only yields the lightest values but, with increasing pressure, will also deliver rich middle and darker values.

See page 19 for a demonstration.

POWDERED GRAPHITE

For the lift-out technique (see page 22), I use graphite in powdered form, along with an eraser and a paper with a smooth finish.

CONTÉ PENCILS AND CHALKS

My favorite Conté pencils are Conté #630 Blanc (white for toned paper), Sanguine #610, Sepia #617, and Black B #1710 (mainly for line accents and toning).

My favorite chalks are the Conté assortment of four colors: sanguine, bistre, black, and white.

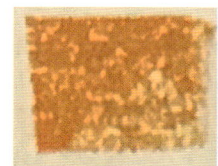

Sanguine

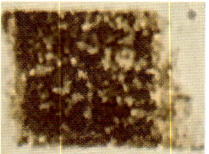

Bistre

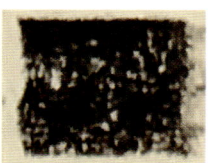

Black

White

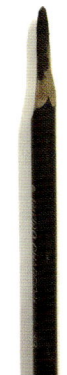

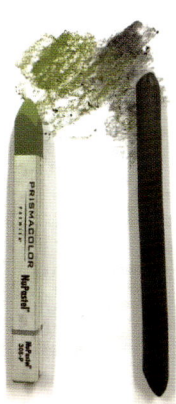

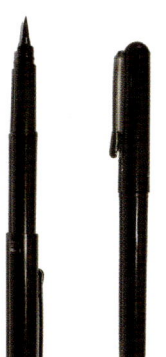

Conté black B #1710

Green NuPastel 308-P
Vine charcoal

CHARCOAL PENCILS

Charcoal pencil lead is a combination of graphite and clay, which provides a unique gliding characteristic. It is available in grades ranging from H to 3B. Soft 3B pencils produce intense lines and rich, dark tones, but they are also difficult to sharpen without breaking. I recommend a B or 2B if you are new to sharpening. Conté, General's®, Prang®, and Ritmo® also make excellent charcoal pencils of varying hardness.

VINE AND WILLOW CHARCOAL

Although both are often called vine, there is a difference between vine and willow charcoal. Vine charcoal (from charred grapevines) is dark gray, while willow is black. Vine and willow are excellent for large drawings but do not work as well for small drawings or final crisp details. I recommend starting with soft vine charcoal for the lay-in and using a charcoal pencil for final details.

GREEN NUPASTEL CHALK

In addition to being a great drawing tool on its own, vine charcoal also acts as a subtle gray toner for various colored pastels such as NuPastel 308-P. Try first massing-in with the NuPastel chalk, and then begin adding vine charcoal shading and linework.

PENTEL BRUSH PEN

This pen is really fun and expressive to use for quick sketching with as few strokes as possible. Lines can be varied from very thin, so initial light guidelines do not show at the end, to very thick. In a sketch group, I seldom use this pen for poses longer than 10 minutes.

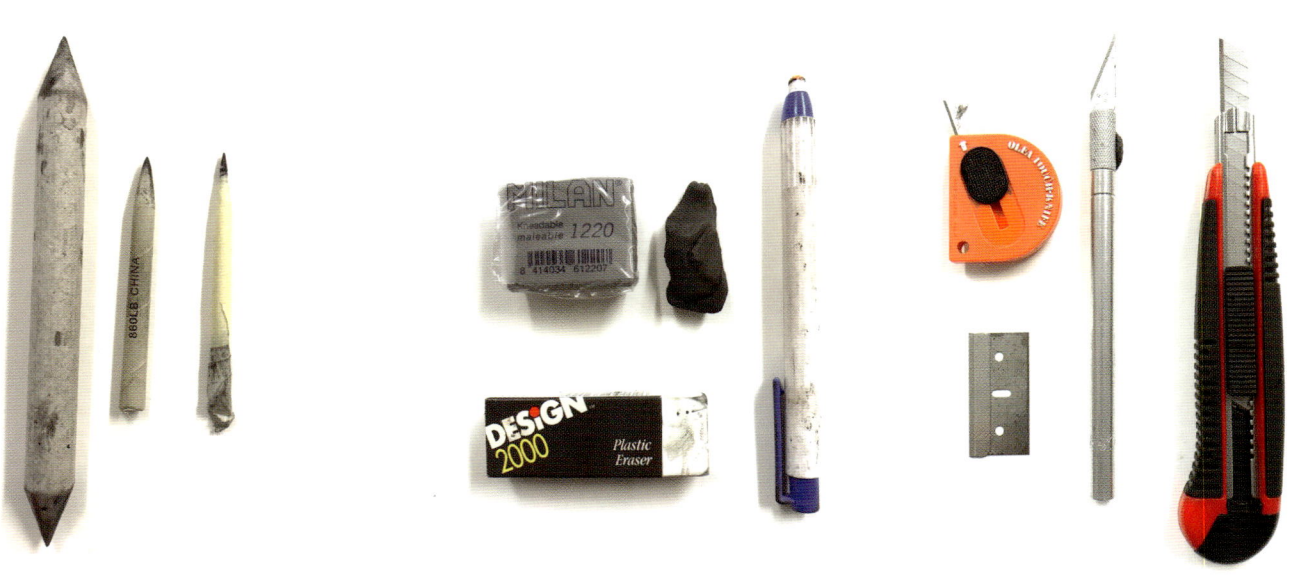

Kneaded erasers
Plastic erasers

BLENDING TOOLS

Large and small blending stumps called tortillons are used to soften or blend large or small areas. Blending to show value transition is a good thing, but sometimes overblending makes a drawing look too photographic. This may be your goal, but if not, the introduction of crosshatched and form-following strokes over the blended areas will help bring back the more spontaneous look of a drawing.

ERASERS

Erasers are not only for correcting mistakes; they are just as effective for creating interesting drawing strokes in toned areas. Kneaded erasers can be molded into any shape, such as a point for picking out specific lights, or can be used bluntly to lighten up an area with tamping. When a kneaded eraser gets dirty, simply knead it until it is clean again.

Plastic erasers are primarily used to add a variety of lifted strokes in toned areas and, in the case of the pen eraser, for erasing in small areas. When the plastic gets dirty and no longer erases, simply cut off the dirty area with a razor blade. Unlike kneaded erasers, plastic erasers leave erasing crumbs, so keep a small, soft brush in your tool kit to gently remove them.

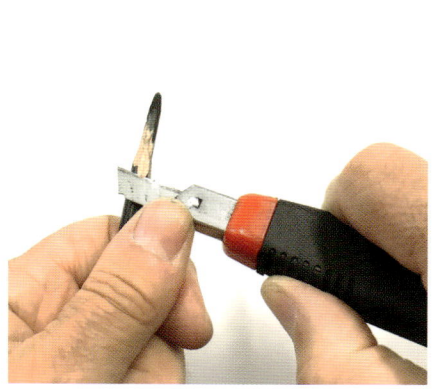
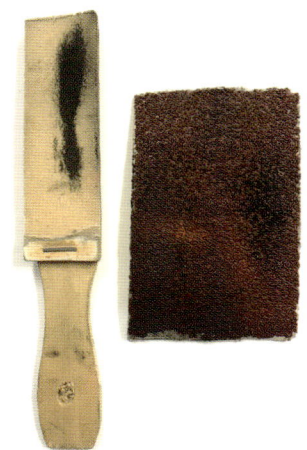
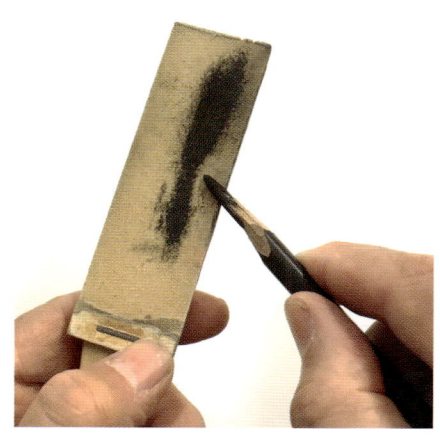

SHARPENING TOOLS

All of these razor blades work equally well for sharpening pencils. The orange touch-blade is my go-to blade for travel. The X-Acto® blade and utility knife are good sharpeners for studio use. When whittling the wood away, always be sure to push the back of the blade with your thumb. This method gives the greatest control and least likelihood of a broken lead or a sliced finger.

SANDPAPER

Use a commercial sandpaper block from the art store or just tear off a piece of regular sandpaper. A very fine 150 grit sandpaper block works well to slowly and carefully shape lead, but it often clogs after several rounds. A quicker alternative is to use a piece of 50 to 90 grit sandpaper, which sharpens pencils quickly and does not clog. When sharpening, hold the pencil as flat as possible and slowly rotate it to keep the tapered lead consistent.

DRAWING SURFACES

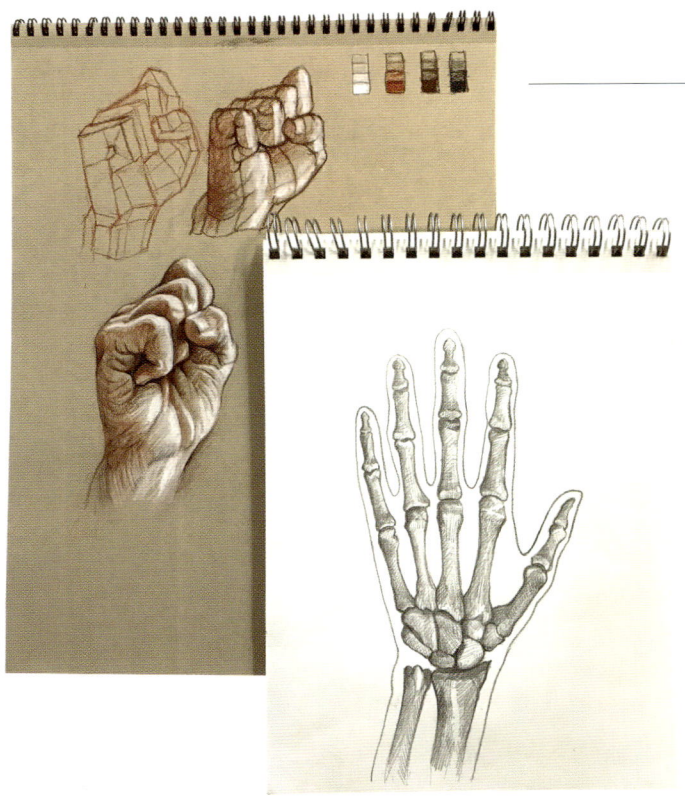

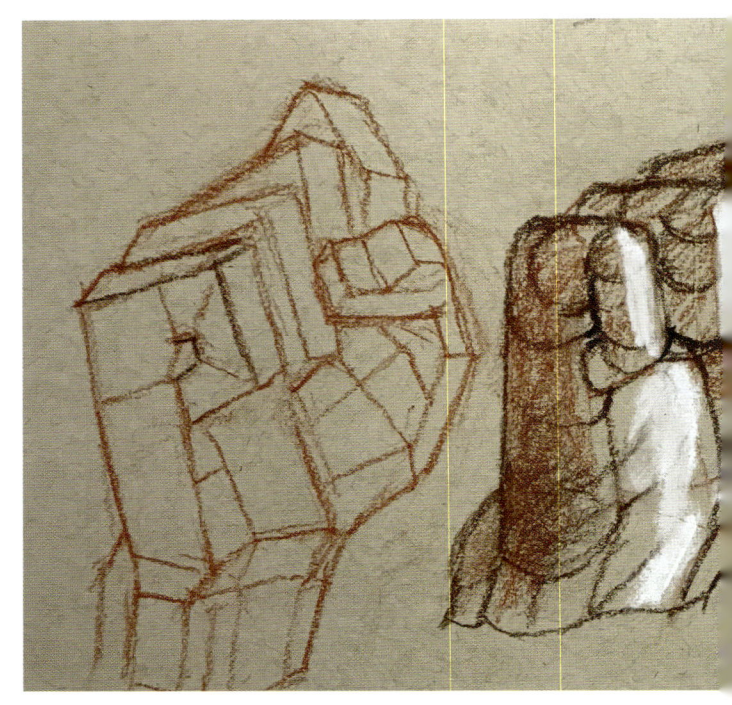

DRAWING PAD
One of the best parts of drawing on a pad is its simplicity. This attribute is especially useful for those who attend life-drawing groups where only a drawing board, pencils, charcoal, and drawing pad are necessary.

If a paper pad does not come spiral-bound (which makes it easier to flip pages), take it to your local office-supply store, where they can quickly convert it for you. Depending on the size of your workstation, pads should be anywhere from 9" × 12" (22.5 × 30 cm) to 18" × 24" (45.5 × 61 cm).

WHITE PAPER
Whether to use white or toned paper depends on your experience level. White paper is a good place to start because it is simple and straightforward. For the sake of economy, a pad of 11" × 14" (28 × 35.5 cm) Strathmore 300 works well for small drawings. As you become more confident in your pencil skills, try the slightly more expensive smooth Bristol series 400, which works really well for graphite.

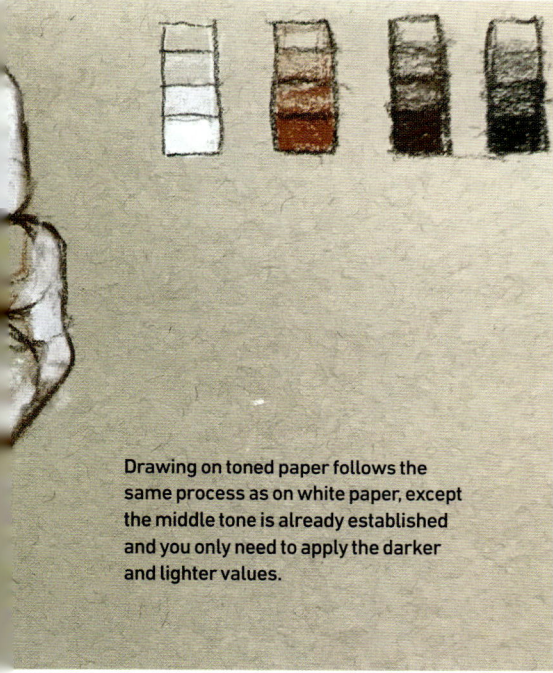

Drawing on toned paper follows the same process as on white paper, except the middle tone is already established and you only need to apply the darker and lighter values.

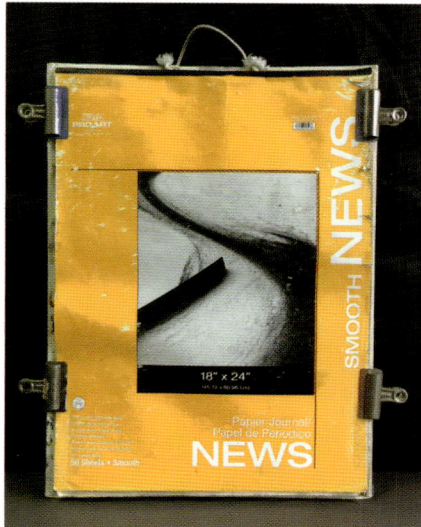

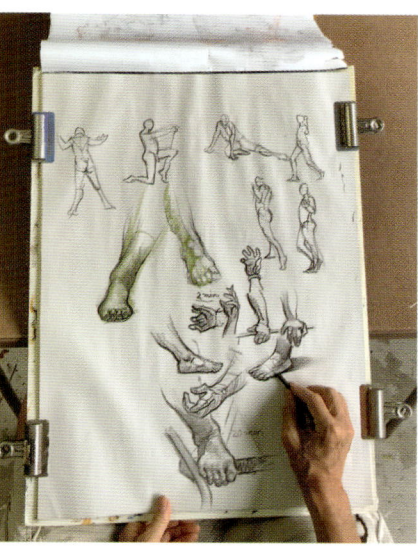

This 24" × 18" (61 × 45.5 cm) newsprint pad is clipped to a homemade ³/₁₆" (4.5 mm) foam-core drawing board with taped edges and a string handle. My regular pad is clipped to another homemade board in the same way. When you go to a sketch group, take two pads: newsprint for practice and good drawing paper for longer poses.

TONED PAPER

Toned paper allows for the addition of white, which creates a dramatic third dimension. Conté pencils, graphite, and charcoal all work really well on toned paper. Strathmore makes both tan and gray pads and also pads in many other colors. Canson makes a wide array of papers in toned colors, too, but if you choose to use this paper, turn it over and use the smoother backside.

NEWSPRINT

Newsprint is a cheap paper-pulp, non-archival alternative to good-quality, acid-free, cotton content drawing paper. Newsprint is primarily used for practicing 2- to 10-minute gesture drawings in a sketch group. Longer poses should be drawn on higher-quality paper. Because high-quality paper does not take charcoal as well as newsprint does, artists sometimes get addicted to newsprint and don't want to move on to better papers. But when work is intended for sale, newsprint is completely useless, as it yellows and deteriorates quickly.

ASSORTED PAPERS

If you are interested in experimenting with other types of papers, buy them as individual sheets and have an office-supply store cut and spiral-bind them into a pad with cardboard backing. In general, a top-bound vertical format is preferable to a side-bound horizontal format, as it can fold back over the top of your board and save space when you are in a sketch group. Shown above are some samples of quick gesture sketches on newsprint and the way a board and paper can be propped up on your lap during a sketch group.

SETTING UP YOUR WORKSPACE

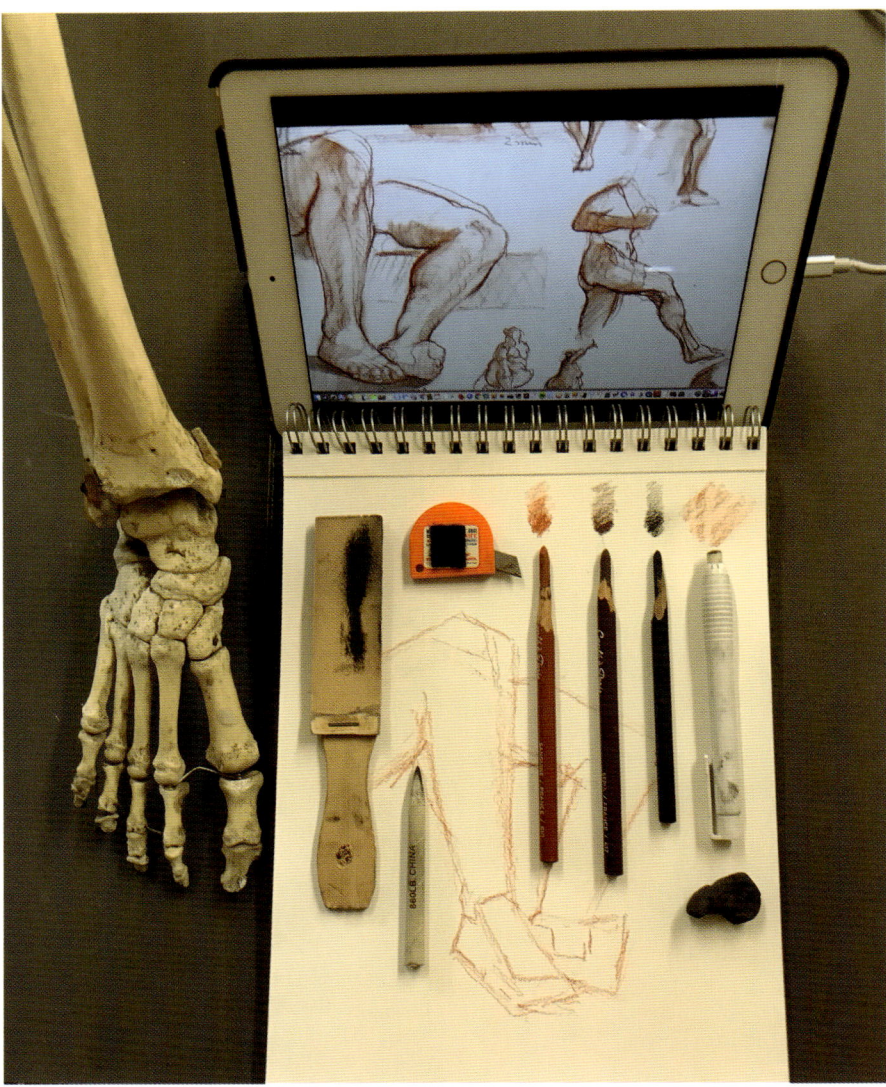

JOIN A SKETCH GROUP
There is no better way to learn anatomy than to draw figures from a live model at a sketch group and then compare and study the anatomy more closely at home from books. You can either stand at an easel or sit at a table, but remember: Seated artists get to sit in the front, where it's easier to see details.

A workspace for drawing can be as simple as a card table with a good light source. If you are right-handed, the light should come from your left so your hand does not cast a shadow on your work. If you are left-handed, the light should come from the right. Drawing tools should be limited to only those you are using and should be kept close to whichever hand you use for drawing.

Place a tablet or smartphone in front of your drawing pad. Devices are often better to work from than books because you can enlarge images quickly, and if you have a question about anatomy, you can quickly find the answer on the internet. If you see something in a book you want to copy, take a picture with your device so you can enlarge it, if necessary, and take it with you to study wherever you go.

If possible, buy a skeleton to draw from. Using a physical skeleton in conjunction with a good anatomy book is a perfect way to further understand the drawings you make from an actual model in a sketch group. I own a real-bone skeleton, but plastic skeletons work just as well and are much less expensive.

BASIC TECHNIQUES AND SAMPLE STUDIES

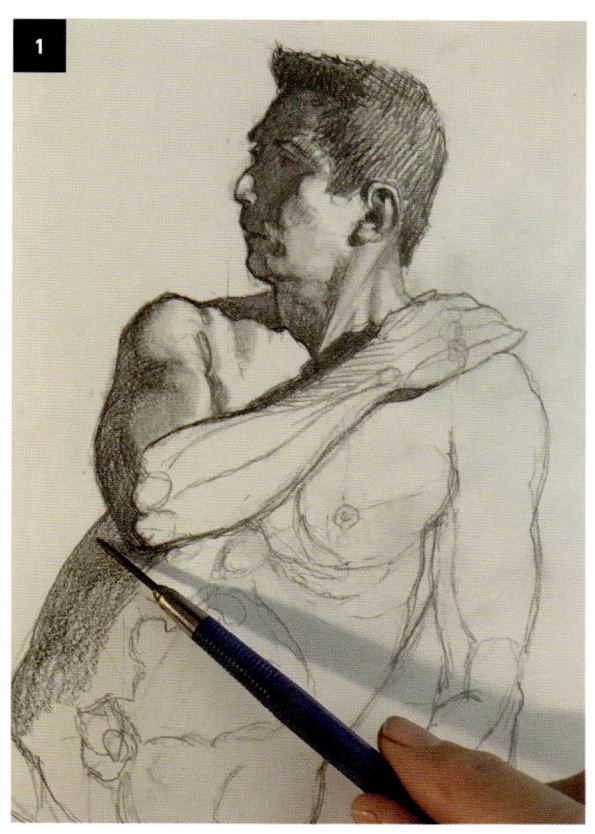

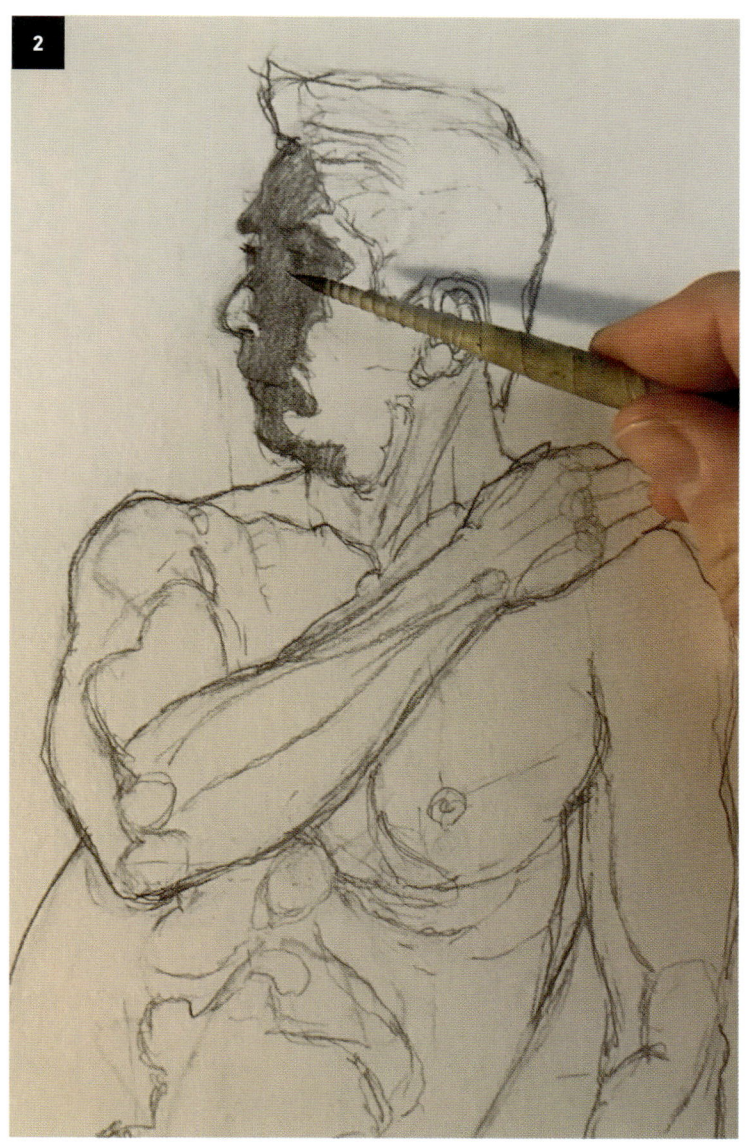

BLENDING WITH MECHANICAL GRAPHITE PENCILS

Sharpened graphite used on its side **(1)** with a blending stump **(2)** is a great way to build up large shapes with any preferred degree of hatching or detail added on top. On the following pages: Crosshatching without blending **(3)**, hatching and blending **(4)**.

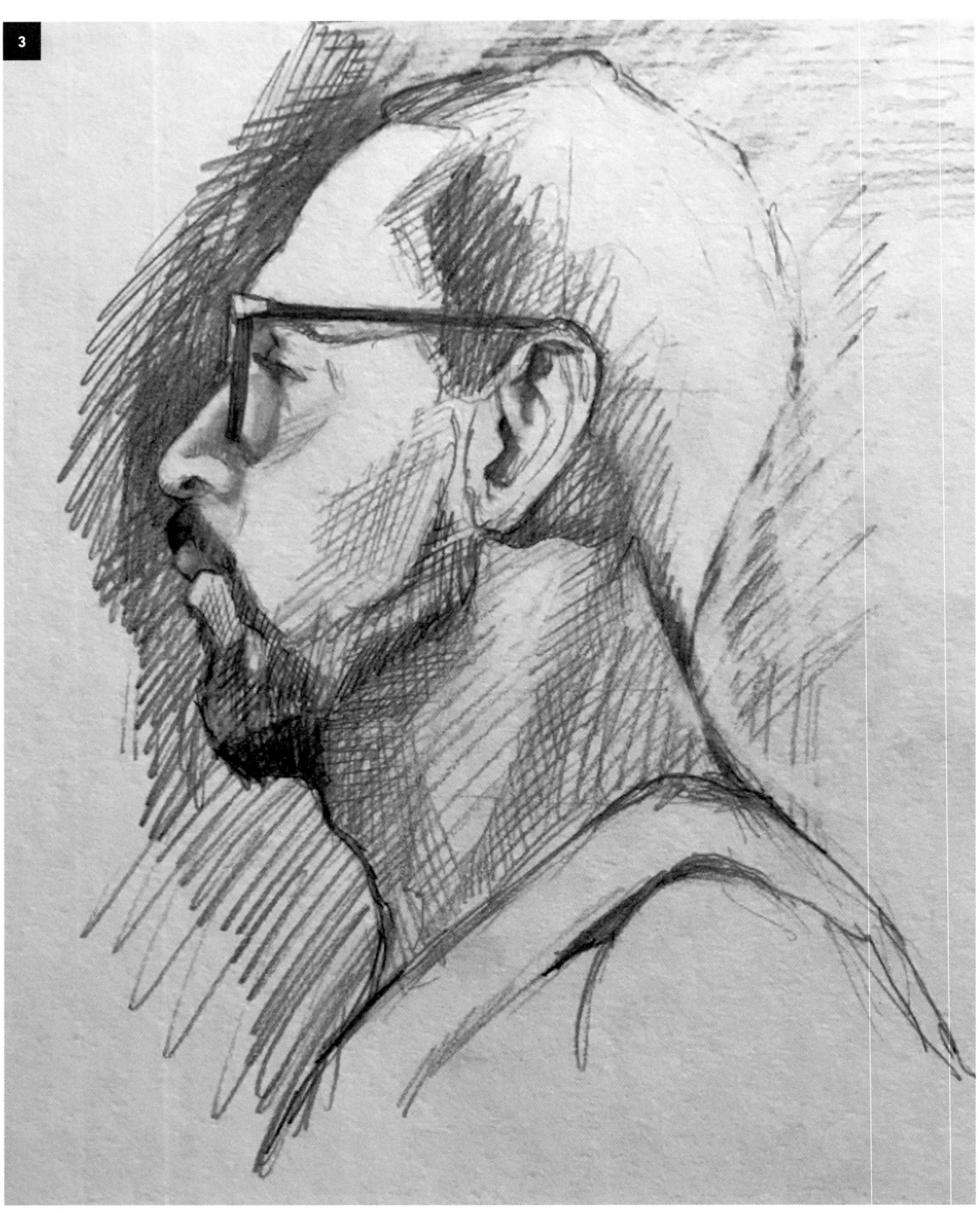

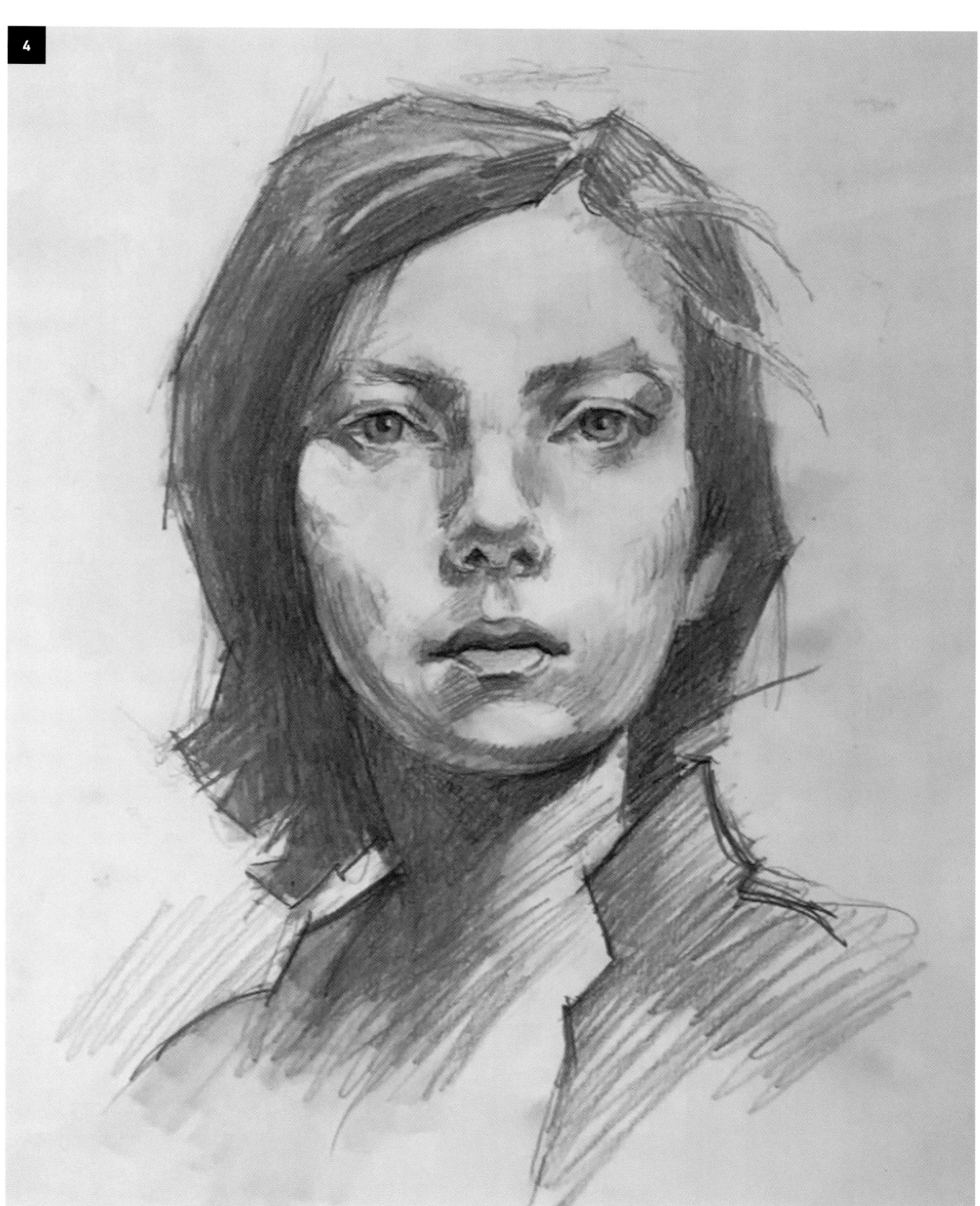

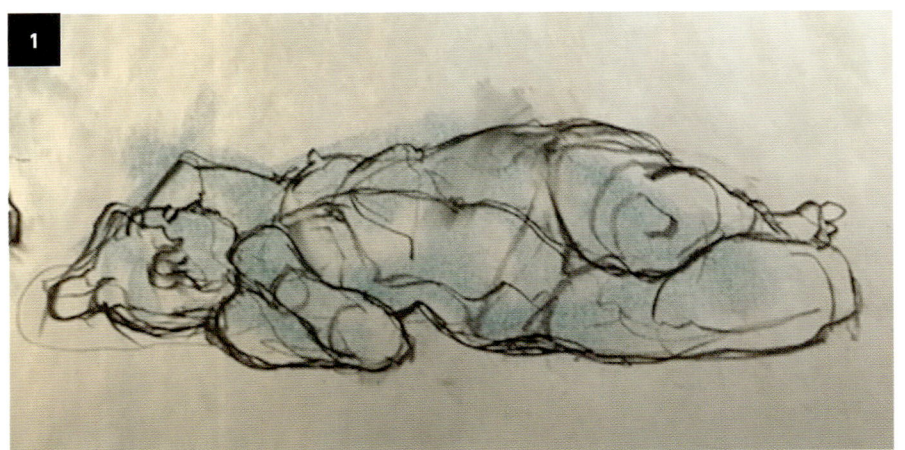

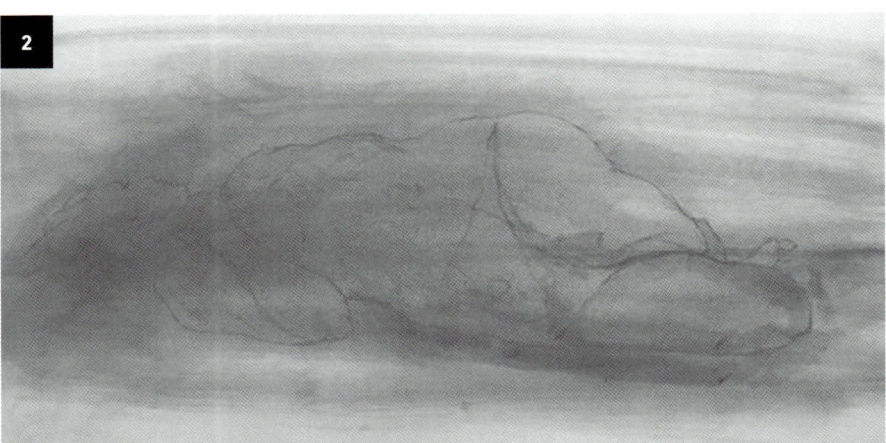

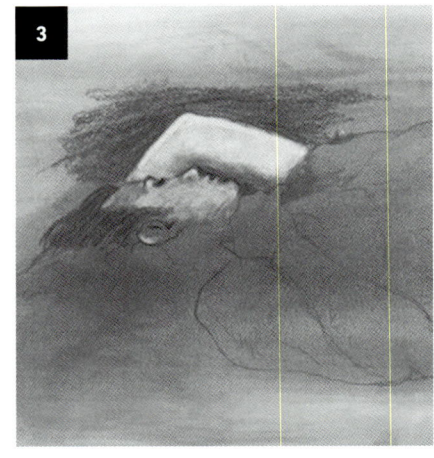

GRAPHITE POWDER LIFT-OUT

This technique requires an understanding of how to see shape relationships as the key to drawing. Although at first it may seem scary to just plunge in with an eraser, this technique is also very forgiving because the smooth paper is highly erasable, and there is always an option to add new lines with the pencil. I typically do a separate drawing first and then transfer it over the applied graphite smear, as you can see in this series of step-by-step illustrations.

The demonstration drawing was begun on a separate sheet of newsprint so I could first become familiar with the critical twist between torso and pelvis (**1**). The newsprint drawing was then transferred onto the graphite smear on the Bristol paper using a graphite transfer sheet (**2**). Lift-outs like these require lots of back and forth between erasing and drawing until an image emerges that is correct enough to call it done (**3**, **4**, and **5**). Patience is a prerequisite!

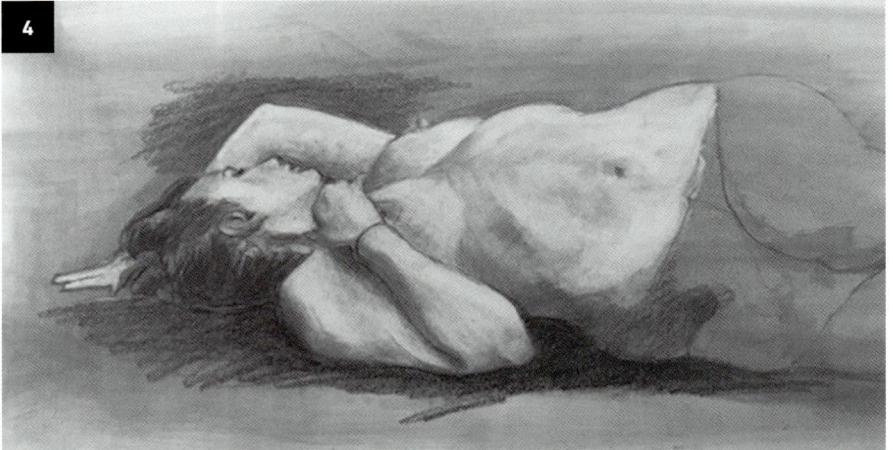

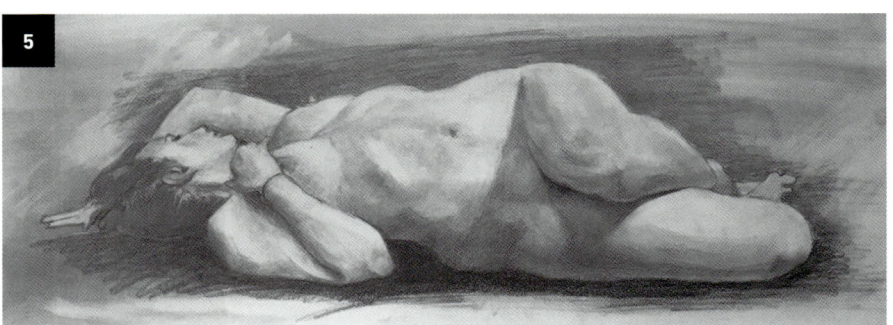

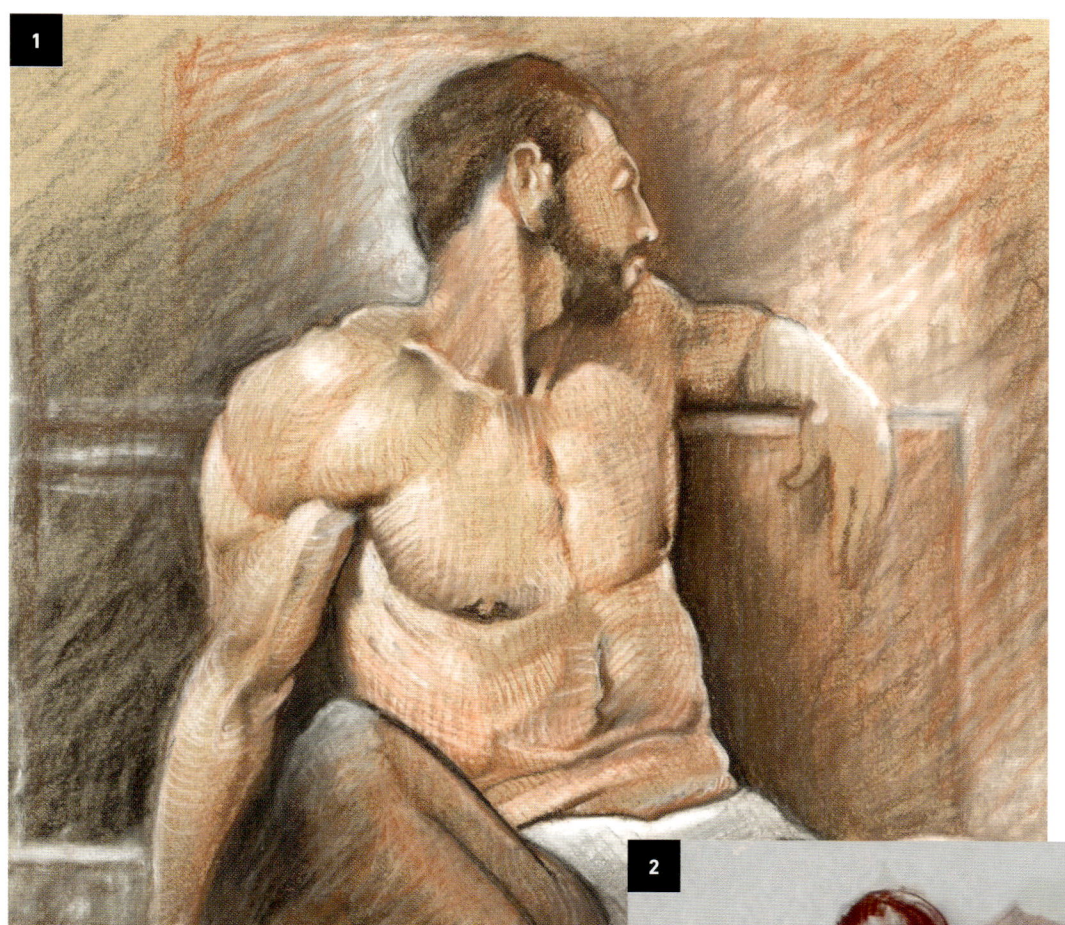

CONTÉ PENCILS AND CHALKS ON WHITE AND TONED PAPER

Whether your paper is toned (**1**) or white (**2**), sanguine is the best color to start with because its textural dryness makes it easy to stay light at the beginning. As the drawing progresses and sanguine starts looking too red, sepia pencil or bistre chalk is the next step for further darkening. Black is mainly used for final accents and overall toning. Conté white is not very bright, so it should only be used for general lightening. To indicate highlights and brighter areas, use a softer white pastel sparingly (see also the drawings on pages 65 and 90).

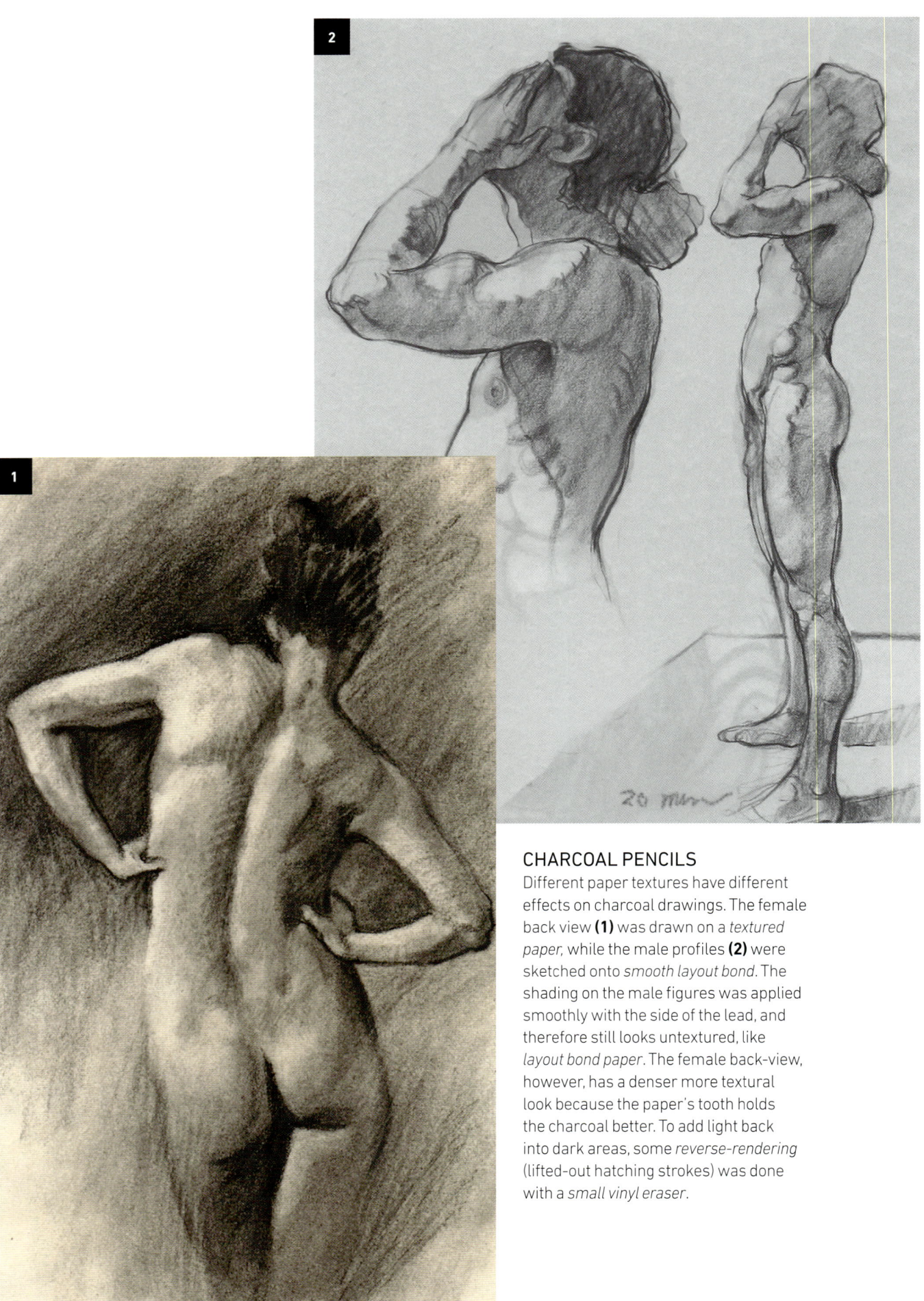

CHARCOAL PENCILS

Different paper textures have different effects on charcoal drawings. The female back view **(1)** was drawn on a *textured paper*, while the male profiles **(2)** were sketched onto *smooth layout bond*. The shading on the male figures was applied smoothly with the side of the lead, and therefore still looks untextured, like *layout bond paper*. The female back-view, however, has a denser more textural look because the paper's tooth holds the charcoal better. To add light back into dark areas, some *reverse-rendering* (lifted-out hatching strokes) was done with a *small vinyl eraser*.

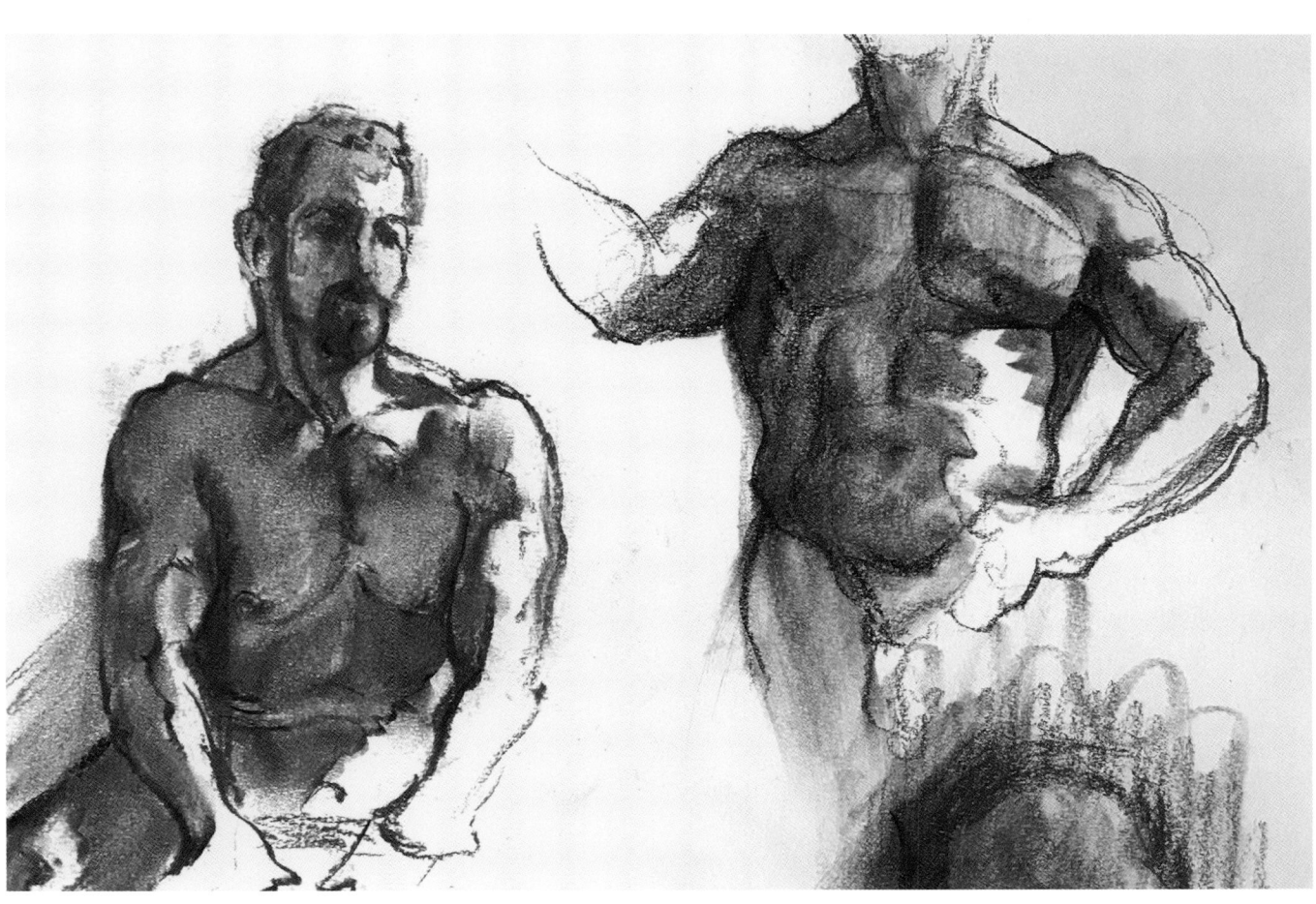

VINE AND WILLOW CHARCOAL

The 10-minute torso studies above were primarily drawn with the side of a ½" (12.5 mm) stick of vine charcoal and rendered with a finger. A kneaded eraser was used to pick out the lights, and a stick of willow charcoal applied the dark accents.

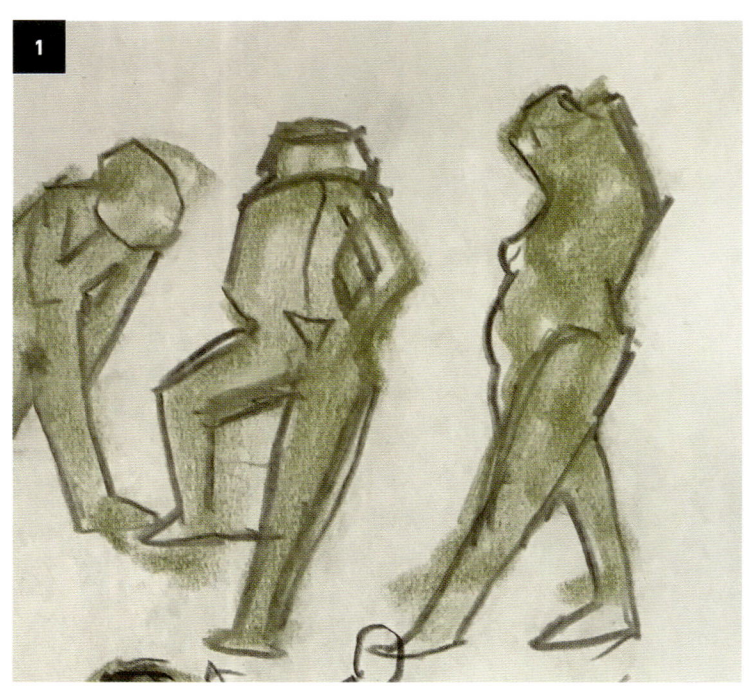

GREEN NUPASTEL CHALK WITH CHARCOAL

NuPastel chalk works well in a sketch group as a quick gestural silhouette of the entire figure can be done in a matter of seconds (**1**). Even though the initial silhouette is seldom entirely accurate, learning to see the negative space around the drawing by keeping the angles straight corrects the inaccuracies.

The 20-minute torso study (**2**) and 2-minute *contrapposto* gesture (**3**) were both begun as quick pastel silhouettes using vine charcoal to create volume and a charcoal pencil for final dark accents.

(For more information on contrapposto, see page 174.)

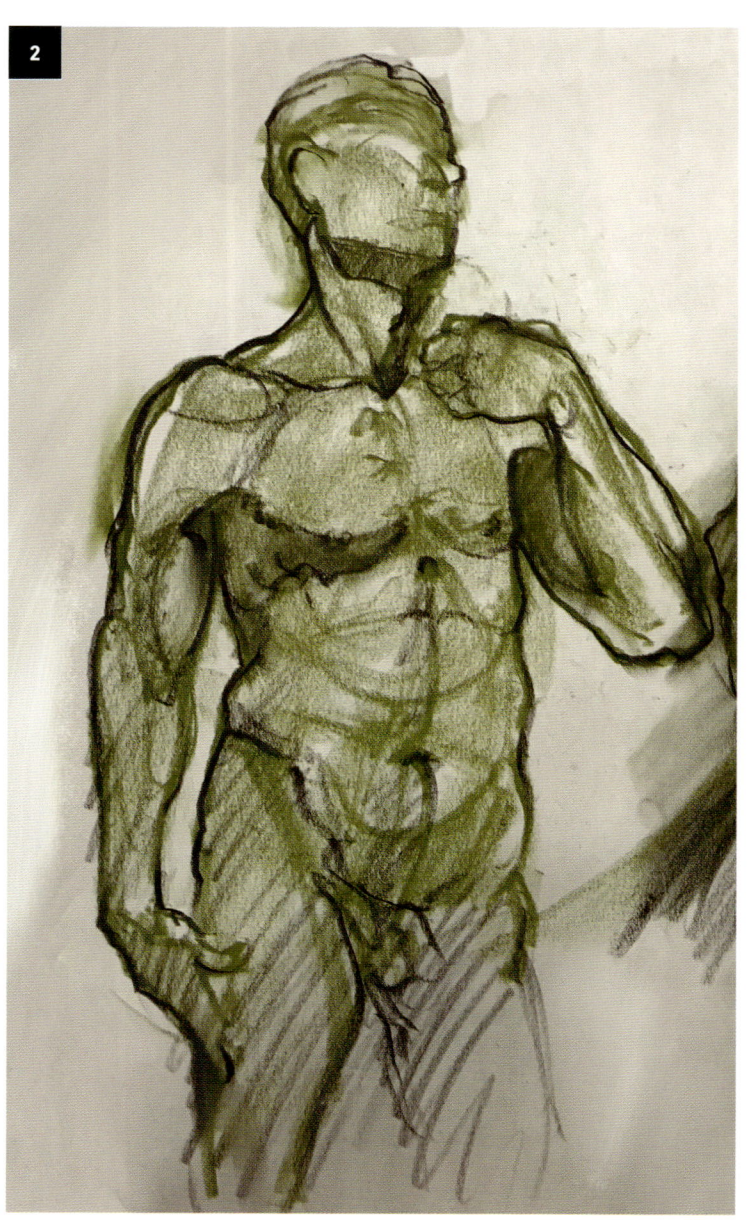

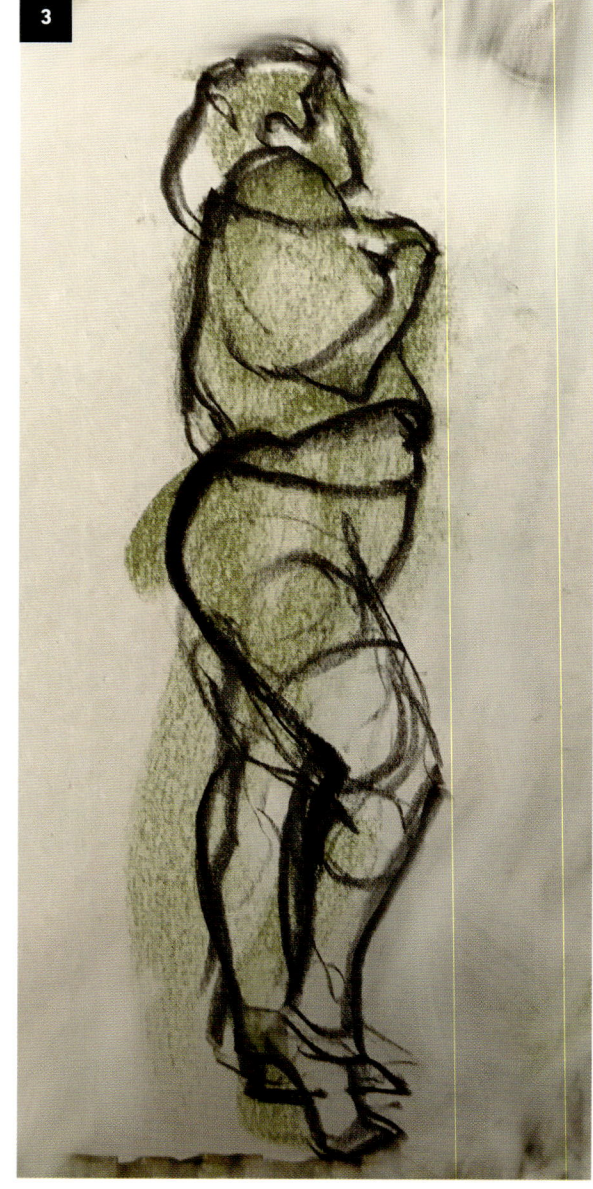

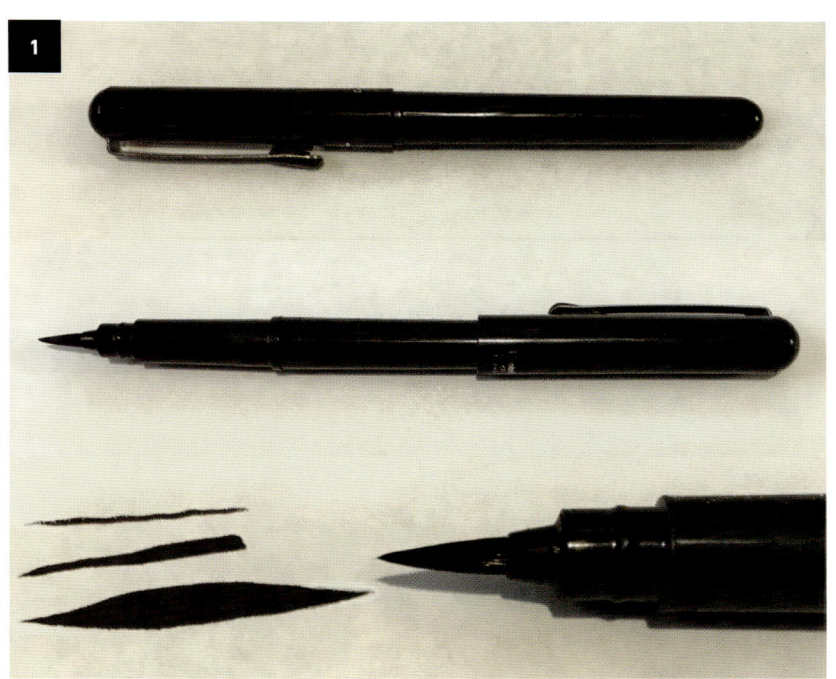

SKETCHING WITH A PENTEL BRUSH PEN

The challenge in using this pen is to see how few strokes are necessary to sketch an accurate but expressive gesture. Marks from this pen are indelible (**1**), so it's a great way to become more thoughtful about where to place each stroke.

The small-hatched internal strokes and overlapping lines within these two life sketches (**2** and **3**) add a third dimension, turning an outlined shape into a 3D form.

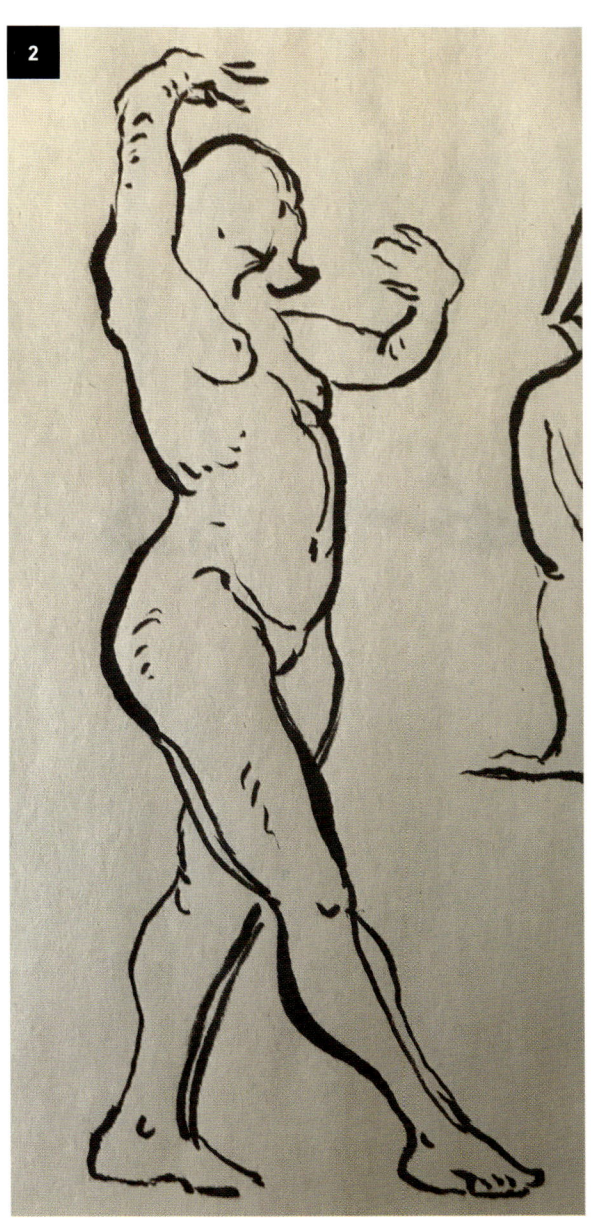

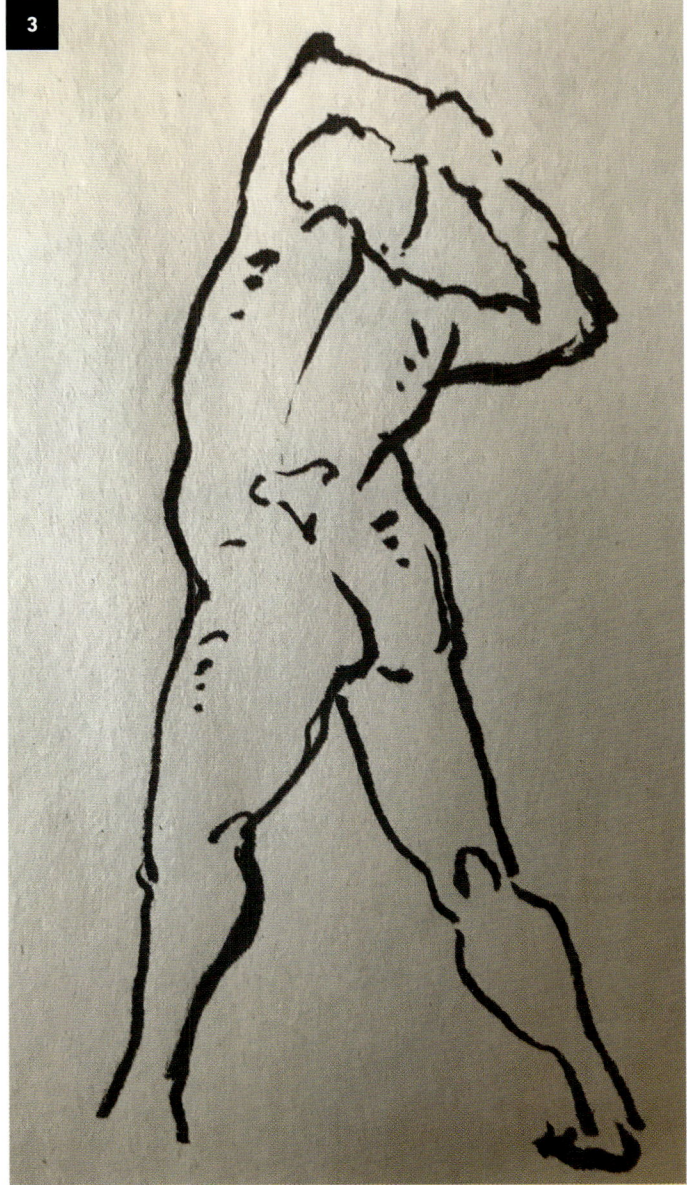

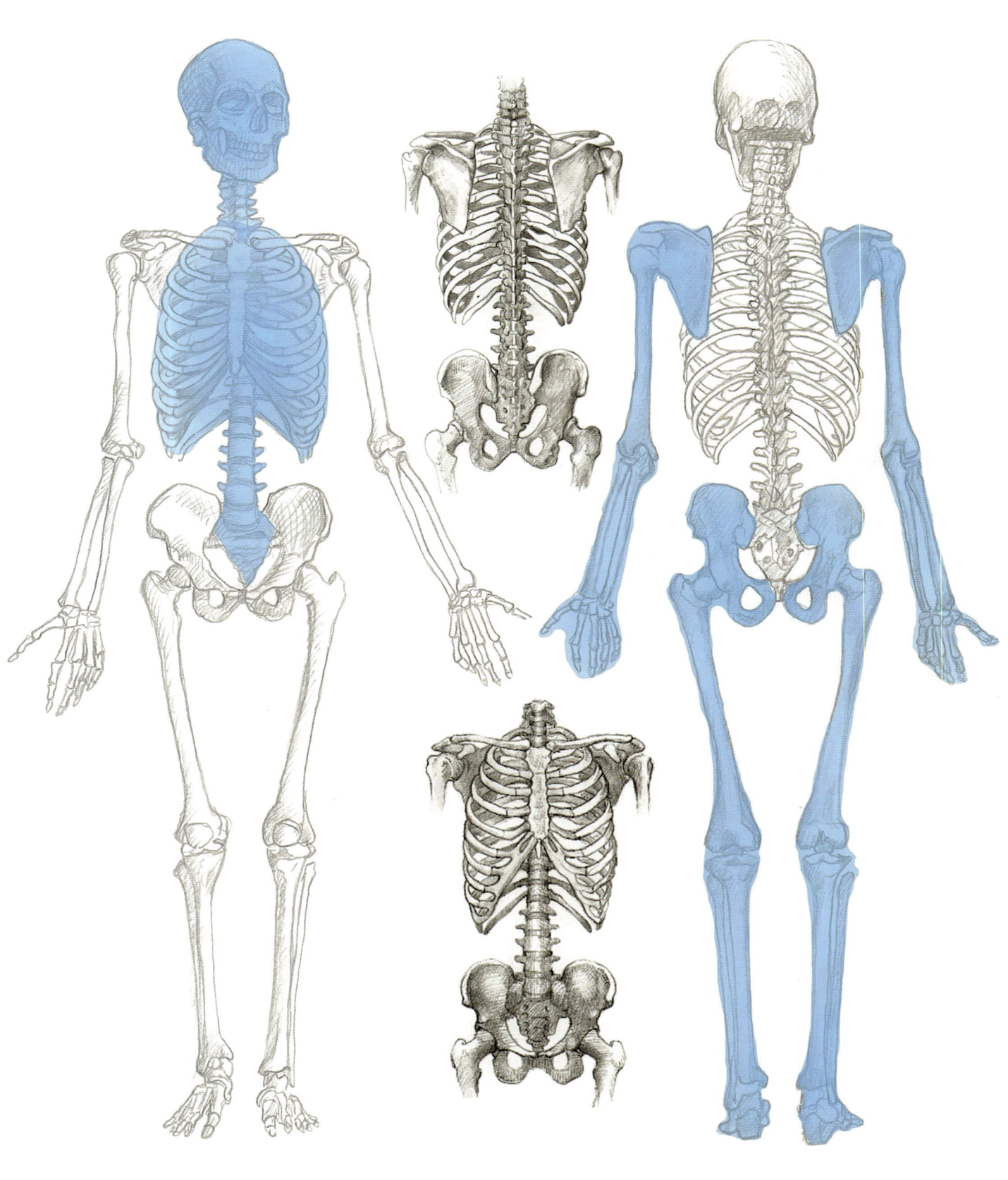

2

THE SKELETON

The human skeleton, with its 206 bones, is the shape-giving framework of the body. Without a skeleton, muscles, nerves, veins, and skin would be no more than blobs of fibrous tissues lying structureless on the floor. *Bones articulate or move against each other at joints and are held in place by strong, non-elastic bands called ligaments. A ligament connects bone to bone; a tendon connects muscle to bone.*

Without the skeleton, muscles, veins, and nerves, the skin would have no recognizable form at all.

SELECTED BONES
OF THE SKELETON

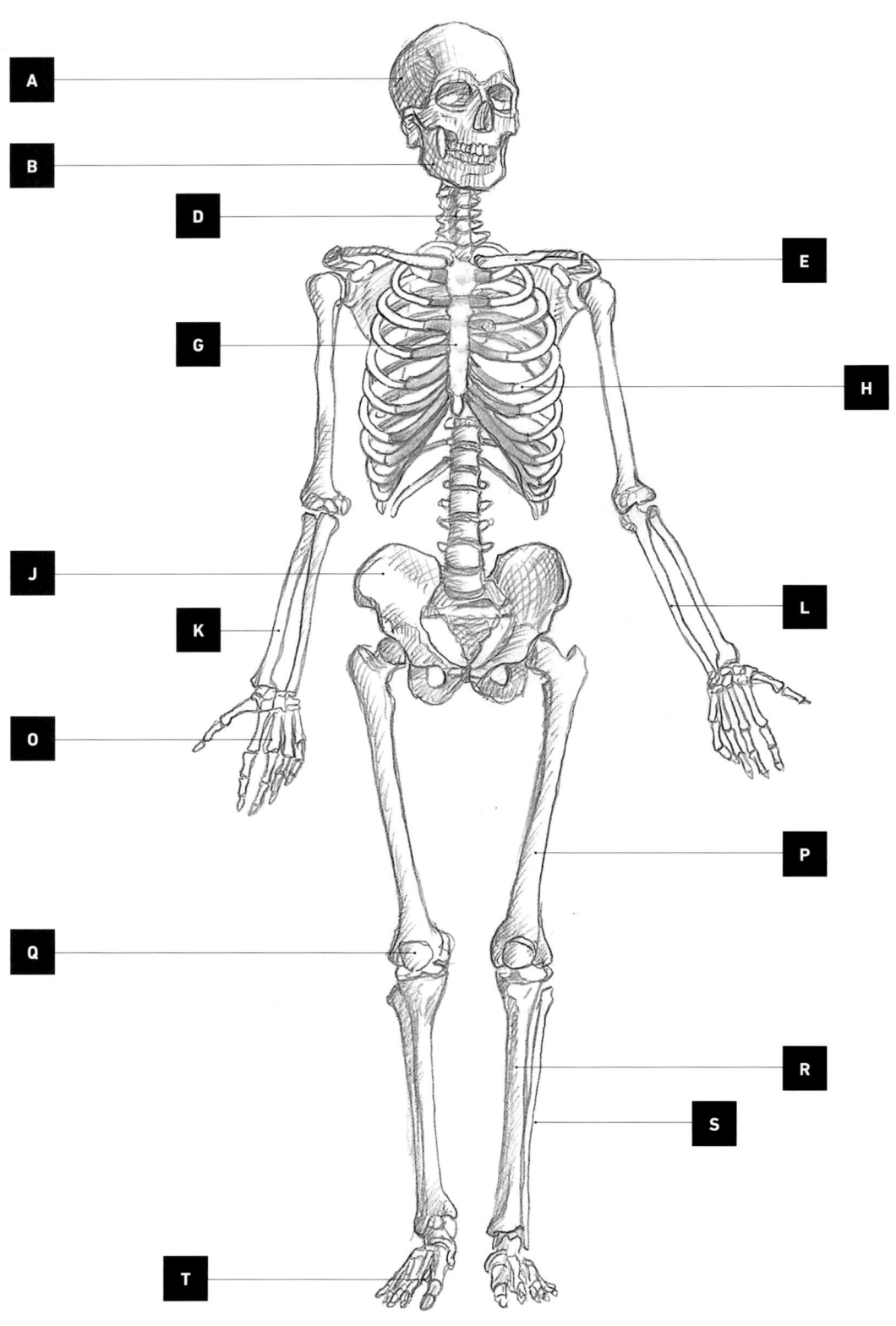

A

B

D

E

G

H

J

K

L

O

P

Q

R

S

T

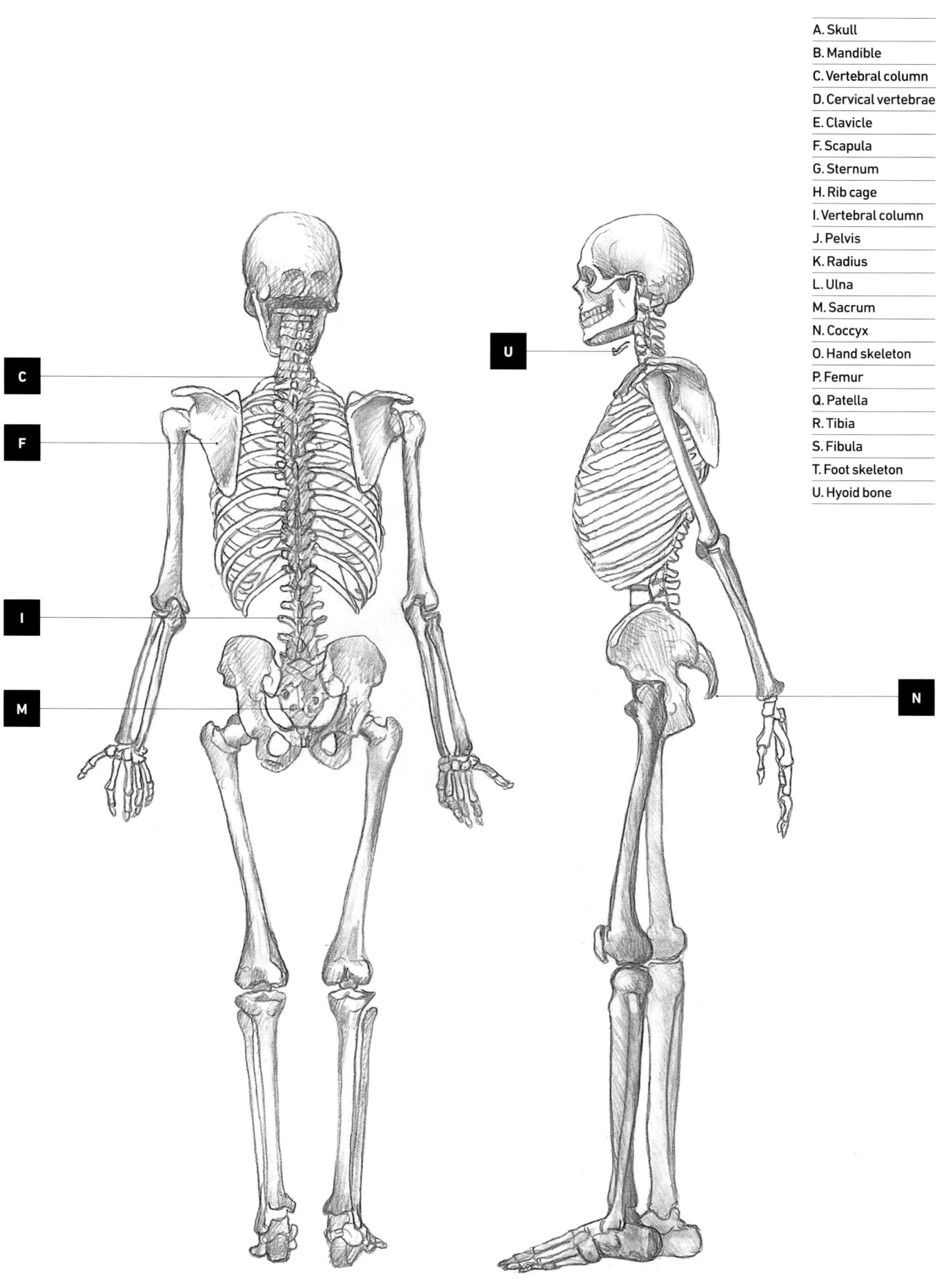

A. Skull
B. Mandible
C. Vertebral column
D. Cervical vertebrae
E. Clavicle
F. Scapula
G. Sternum
H. Rib cage
I. Vertebral column
J. Pelvis
K. Radius
L. Ulna
M. Sacrum
N. Coccyx
O. Hand skeleton
P. Femur
Q. Patella
R. Tibia
S. Fibula
T. Foot skeleton
U. Hyoid bone

The rigid skeleton gives structure to the otherwise formless muscles.

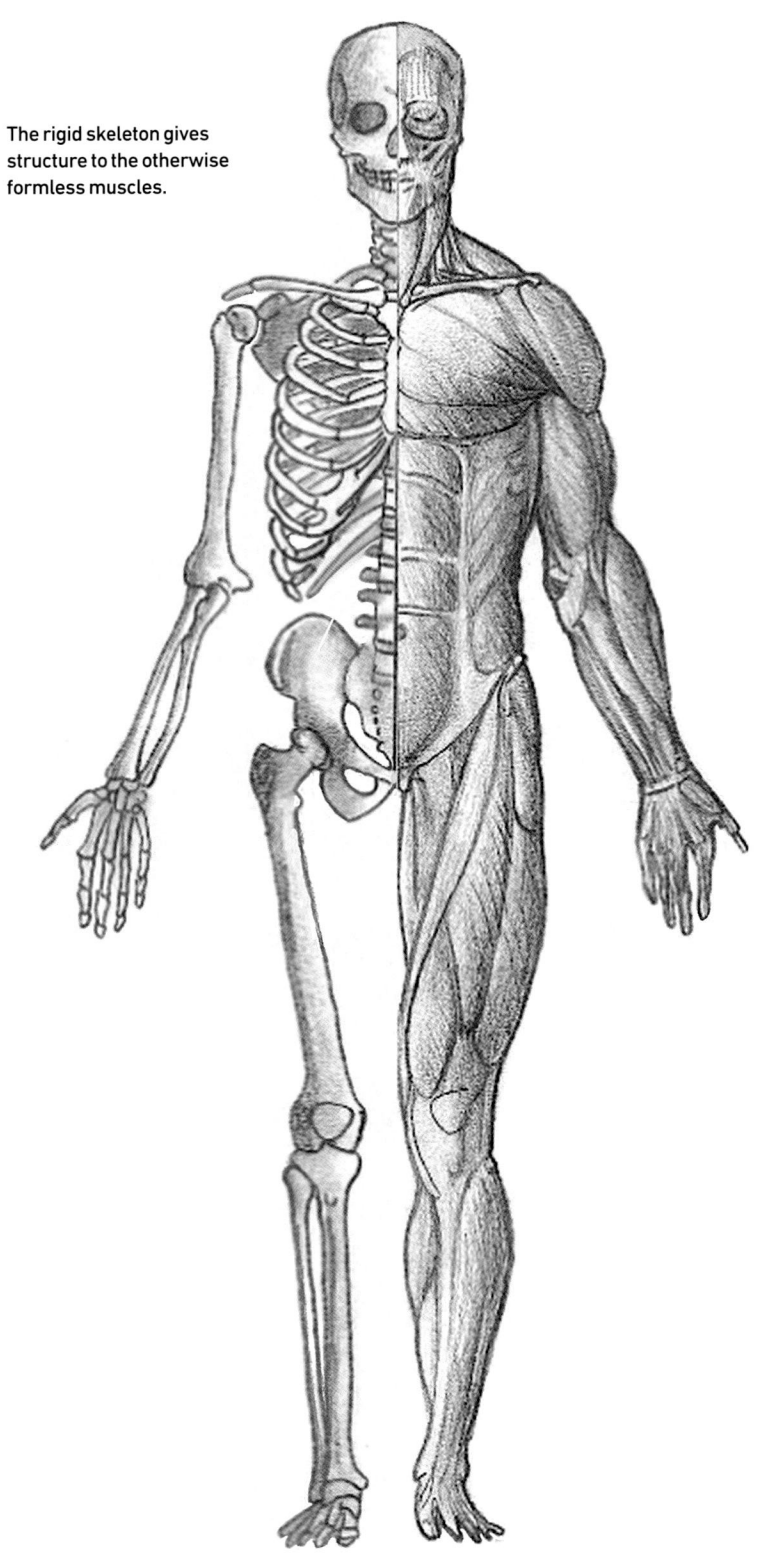

THE AXIAL AND APPENDICULAR SKELETON

The skeleton can be divided into two main parts:

The axial skeleton (below left), consisting of the skull, vertebrae, sacrum, coccyx, and rib cage.

The appendicular skeleton (below right), consisting of arm bones, shoulder girdle, pelvis, and leg bones.

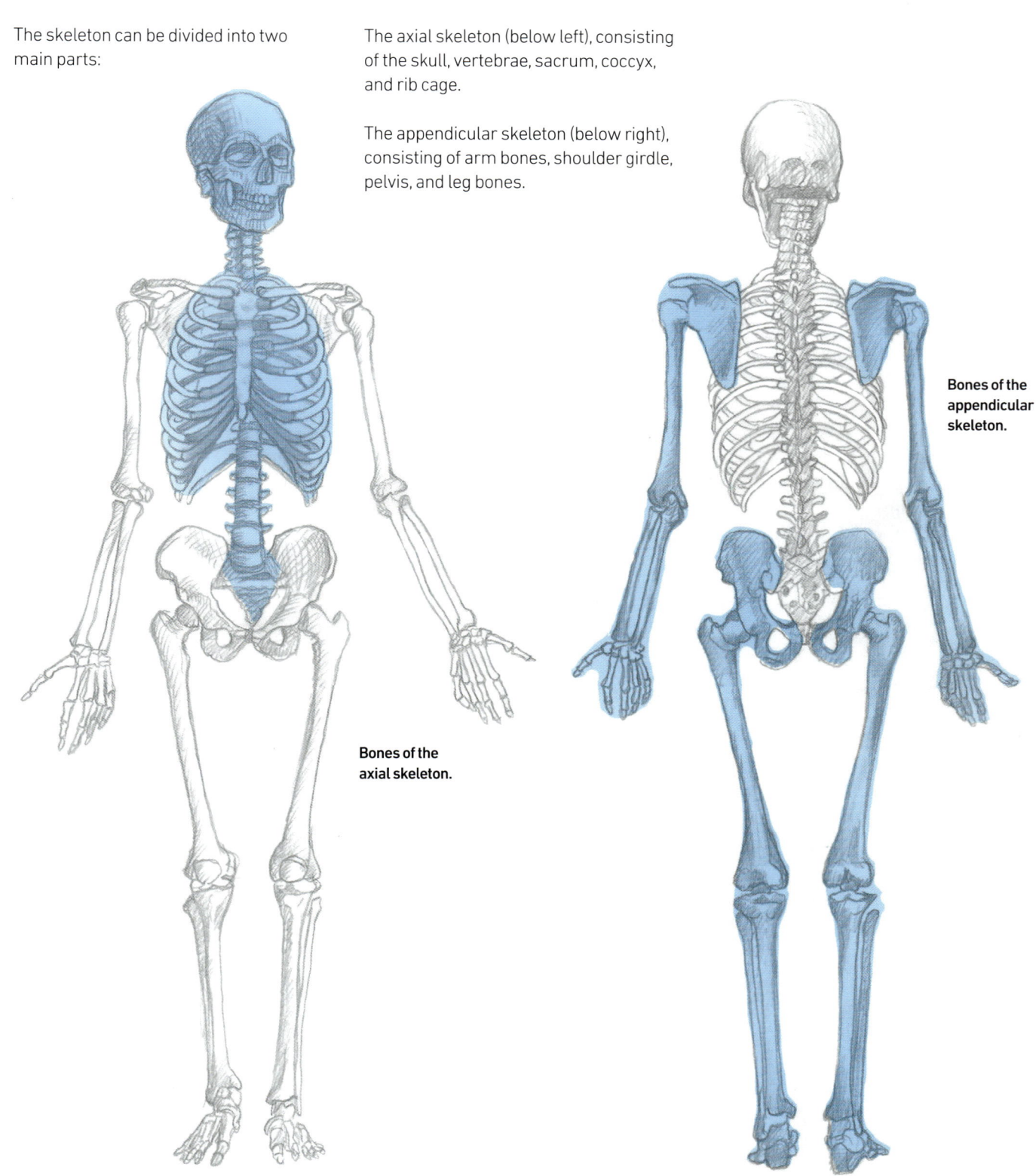

Bones of the axial skeleton.

Bones of the appendicular skeleton.

FOUR BONE CLASSIFICATIONS

There are four main bone classifications in the human skeleton. Each type of bone has a different size and shape based on the specific job it does.

Long bones are longer than they are wide and affect our overall height: clavicles, humerus, radius, ulna, metacarpals, phalanges, femur, tibia, fibula, and metatarsals and phalanges of the feet.

Short bones are equal in width and length and are usually clustered together: wrist (carpals), foot bones (tarsals), and sesamoid bones (patella and metatarsophalangeal joints of the big toes).

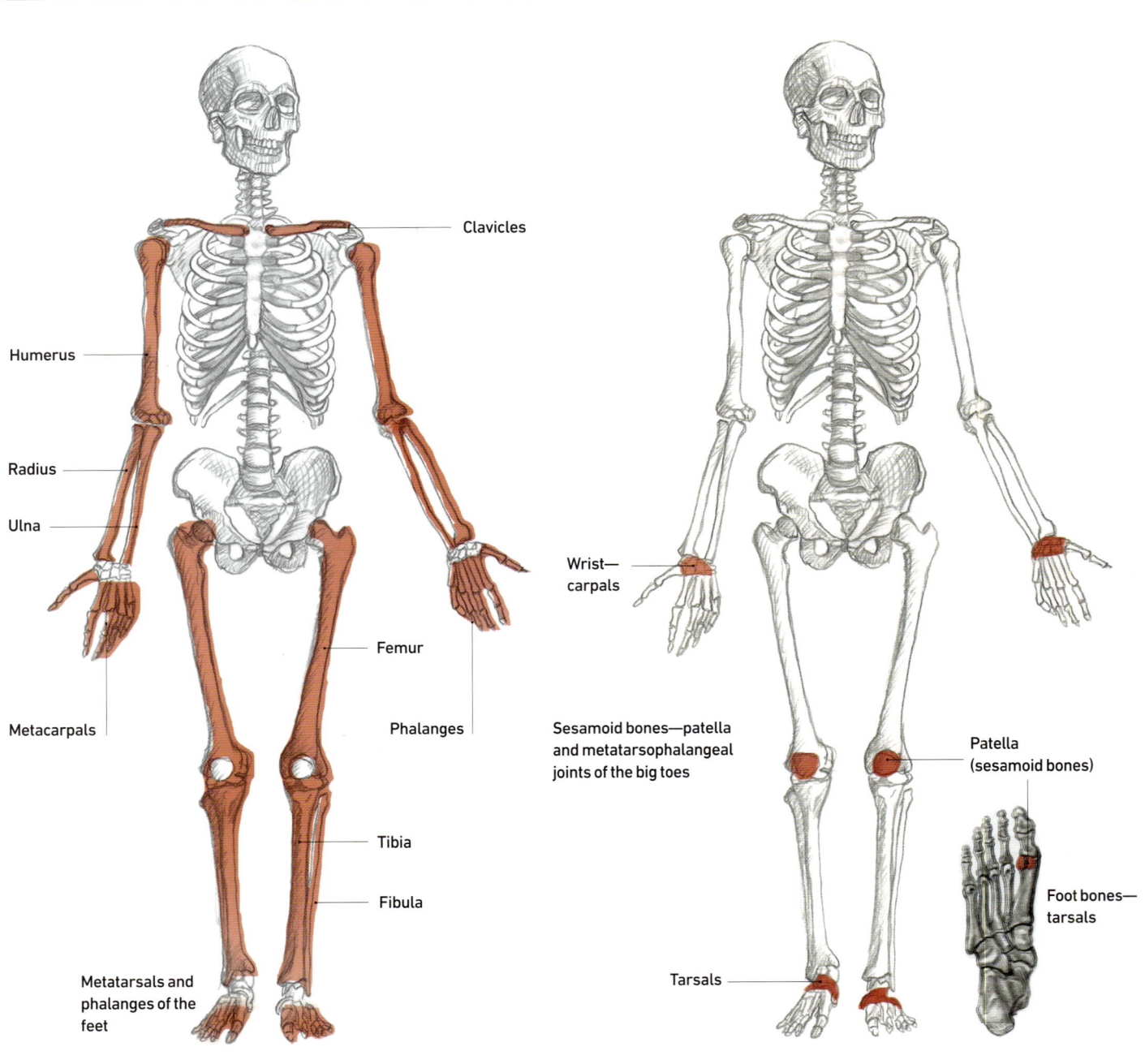

Clavicles

Humerus

Radius

Ulna

Femur

Phalanges

Metacarpals

Tibia

Fibula

Metatarsals and phalanges of the feet

Wrist—carpals

Sesamoid bones—patella and metatarsophalangeal joints of the big toes

Patella (sesamoid bones)

Foot bones—tarsals

Tarsals

Flat bones protect soft organs and are sometimes softly curved: cranial bones, sternum, scapula, ribs, and ilium.

Irregular bones are typically neither flat nor long: e.g., vertebrae and some facial bones.

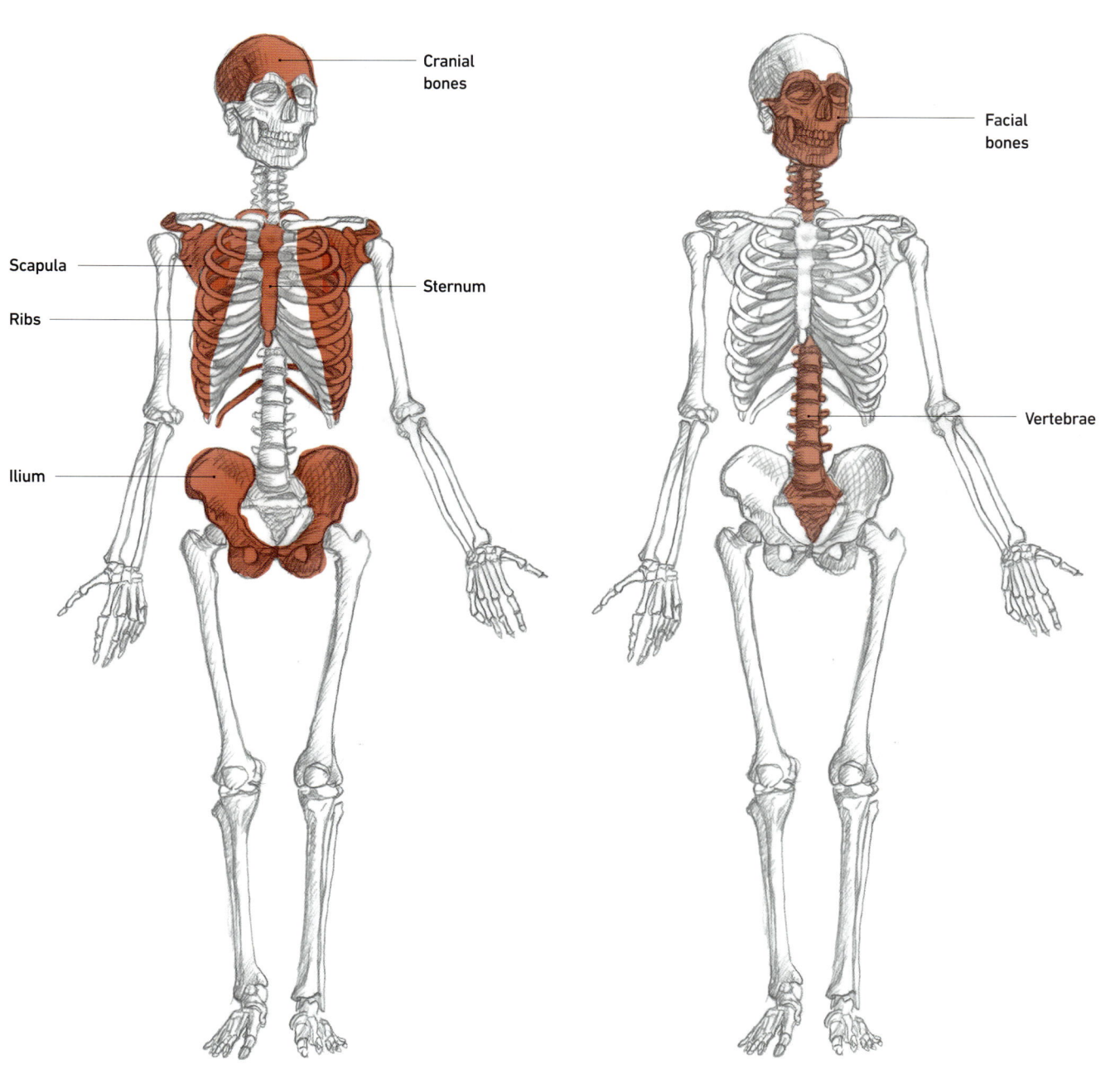

VERTEBRAL COLUMN, RIB CAGE, AND FOUR CURVE DESIGN

The vertebral column houses the spinal cord and supports the weight of the upper body. There are twenty-four movable, or "true," vertebrae and nine fixed vertebrae. They are arranged as follows: seven cervical (neck) vertebrae, twelve thoracic (chest) vertebrae, five lumbar (lower back) vertebrae, five fused sacral vertebrae (sacrum), and four partially fused coccygeal vertebrae (coccyx).

Because human posture is upright, the vertebral column has four curves that enable the body masses (head, rib cage, and pelvis) to achieve balance. The cervical and lumbar vertebrae curve forward (anterior curves); the thoracic and sacrum/coccyx vertebrae curve backward (posterior curves). These four spinal curves are unique to humans.

RIB CAGE

The rib cage protects our vital organs and provides attachments for muscles that allow us to move our arms and to breathe. The first seven pairs of ribs are known as true ribs because they articulate directly with the sternum through their costal cartilages. The eighth, ninth, and tenth ribs are called false ribs because they only articulate indirectly with the sternum via the seventh rib. Ribs eleven and twelve are known as floating ribs because they do not attach to the sternum in any manner.

PELVIC GIRDLE

The pelvic girdle is a very important structure as it carries the entire weight of the upper body. The pelvis is formed posteriorly by the sacrum and coccyx, and laterally and anteriorly by a pair of hip bones. Together, they form a ring which is why the pelvis is often referred to as the *pelvic girdle*. Each hip bone is actually composed of three separate bones: the *ilium*, the *ischium*, and the *pubic bone*. These three bones join with each other to form a socket-like structure known as the *acetabulum* where the *ball of the femur fits into the socket of the acetabulum*.

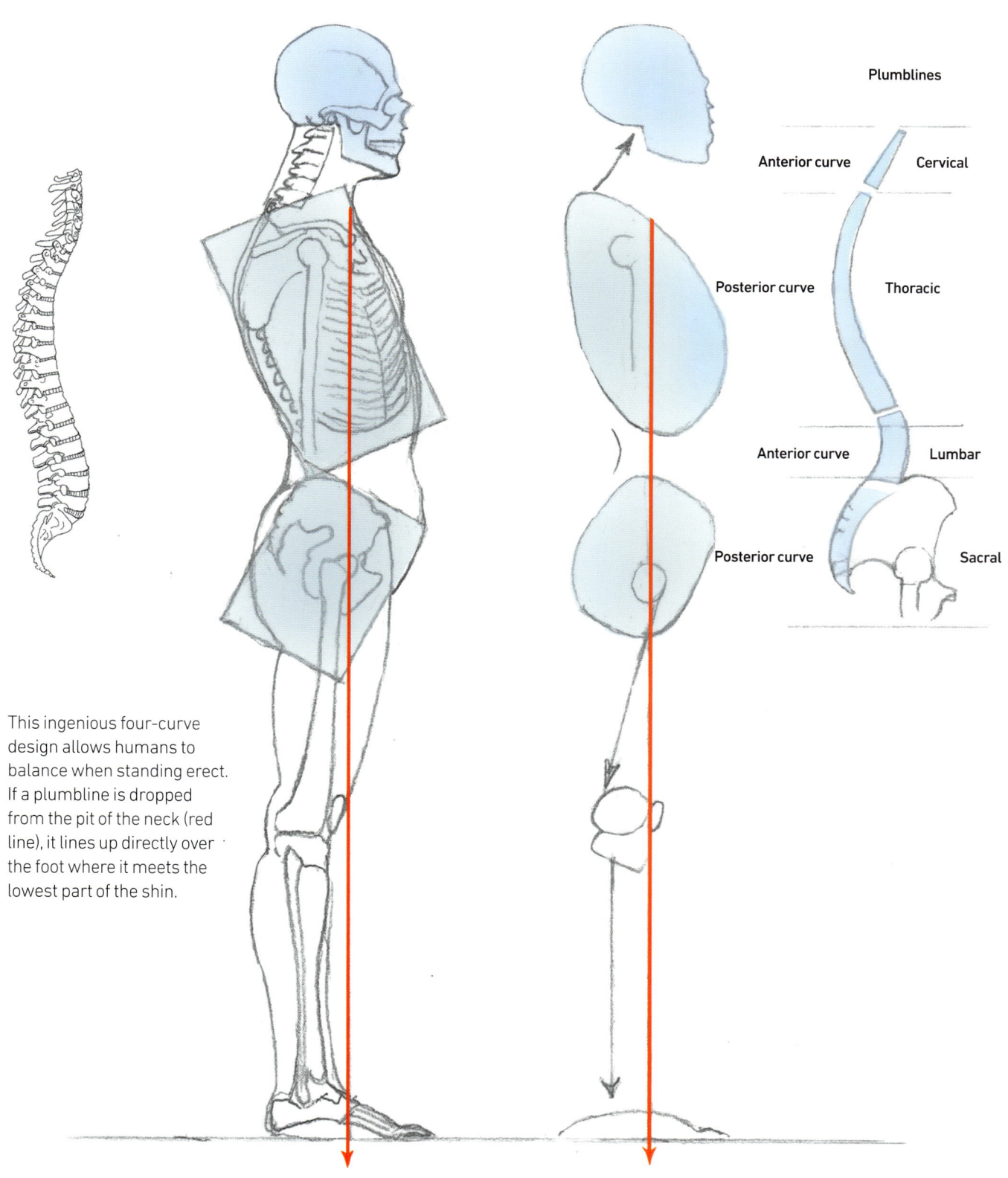

This ingenious four-curve design allows humans to balance when standing erect. If a plumbline is dropped from the pit of the neck (red line), it lines up directly over the foot where it meets the lowest part of the shin.

Plumblines

Anterior curve

Cervical

Posterior curve

Thoracic

Anterior curve

Lumbar

Posterior curve

Sacral

SIMPLIFYING THE RIBCAGE AND HIPS

Experienced artists who know about the details of anatomy ignore them when beginning a figure drawing. They know that major masses are drawn in first and details last. Here are a few examples of ways to visualize the rib cage and pelvic girdles as basic forms:

1. Shows the difference between an anatomical and simplified skeleton.

2. Is a simplified three-quarter view where the pelvic girdle is conceived of as if it were a swimsuit.

3. T U M is a helpful acronym I learned in the 1970s from a book called *Drawing the Figure* by Jack Hamm. I find **TUM** to be very useful when teaching anatomical gesture drawing to beginners. **T** stands for the clavicle, which is basically shaped like a T. The upside-down **U** is a quick way to visualize the top of a ribcage (with the bottom of the **U** representing the 10th rib). The inside of the **M** resembles the inguinal ligament under a belly, and the bottoms of the **M** represents the great trochanter bones (anatomical center of a standing figure).

4. Shows the **TUM** concept put into practice in a gestural way.

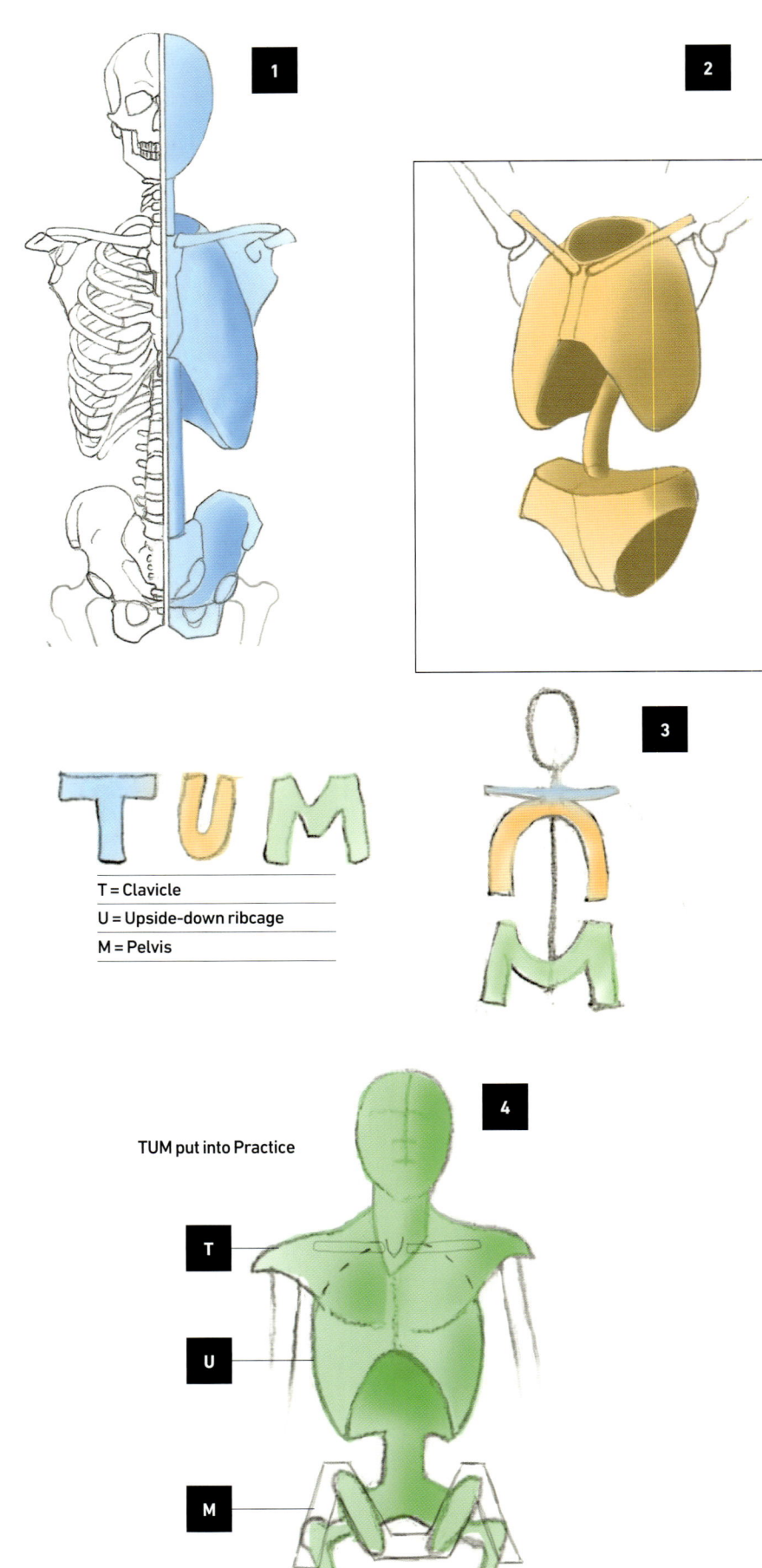

T = Clavicle

U = Upside-down ribcage

M = Pelvis

TUM put into Practice

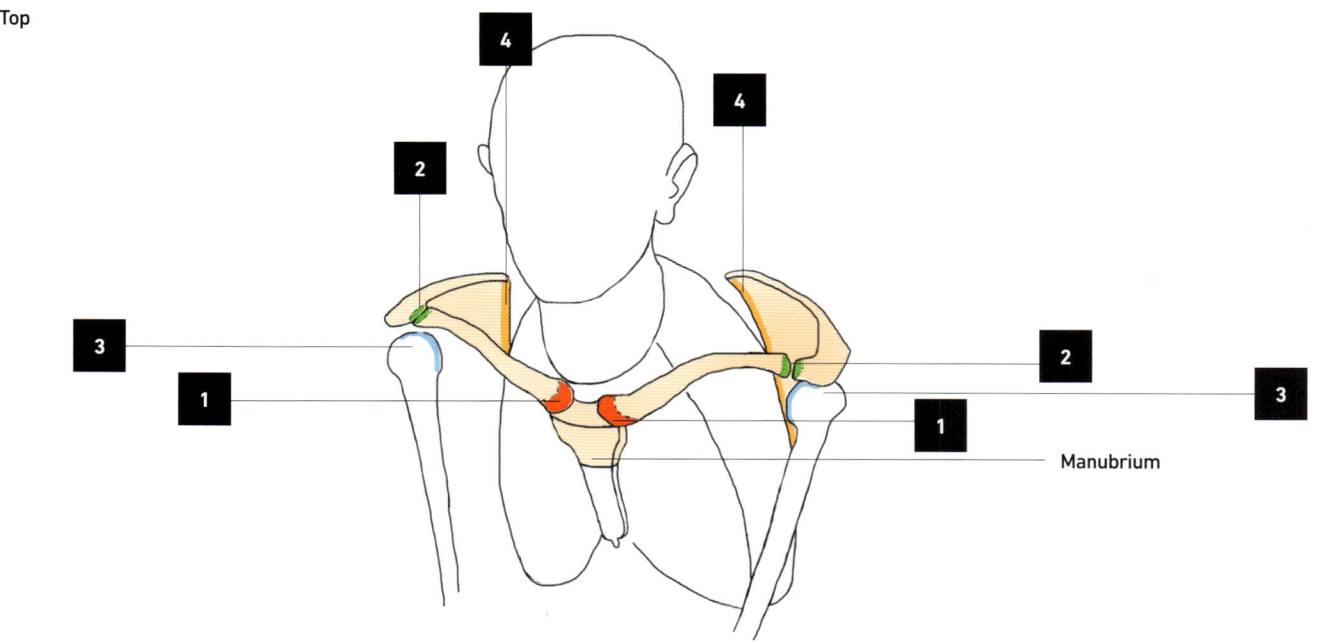

Top

Manubrium

SHOULDER GIRDLE

The shoulder girdle is a bony ring formed by connections between the clavicle, scapulae, back muscles, and the manubrium of the sternum. Where the humerus, scapulae, and clavicles articulate with each other, four joints are formed:

1. The *sternoclavicular (SC) joint* formed between the sternum and clavicle (red).

2. The *acromioclavicular (AC) joint* formed between the scapula and the clavicle (green).

3. The *glenohumeral (GH - shoulder) joint* formed between the scapula and humerus (a very movable ball and socket joint) (blue).

4. The *scapulothoracic joint* formed between the scapula and the posterior thoracic cage (orange).

The highly movable *scapulothoracic joint* on the back is not considered a true joint in the same sense as the other three. Here the scapula glides freely over the ribcage, being controlled by the contracting and relaxing actions of muscles such as the *rhomboideus, serrates anterior,* and *trapezius.* These muscles simultaneously activate and tether the scapula like a boat on the water being pulled or constrained by ropes on all sides. For example: When a boxer punches, it is mainly the serratus anterior muscle, rapidly pulling the scapula forward, that causes the arm (*humerus* enjoined at the *glenohumeral joint*) to project forward into a powerful, quick punch.

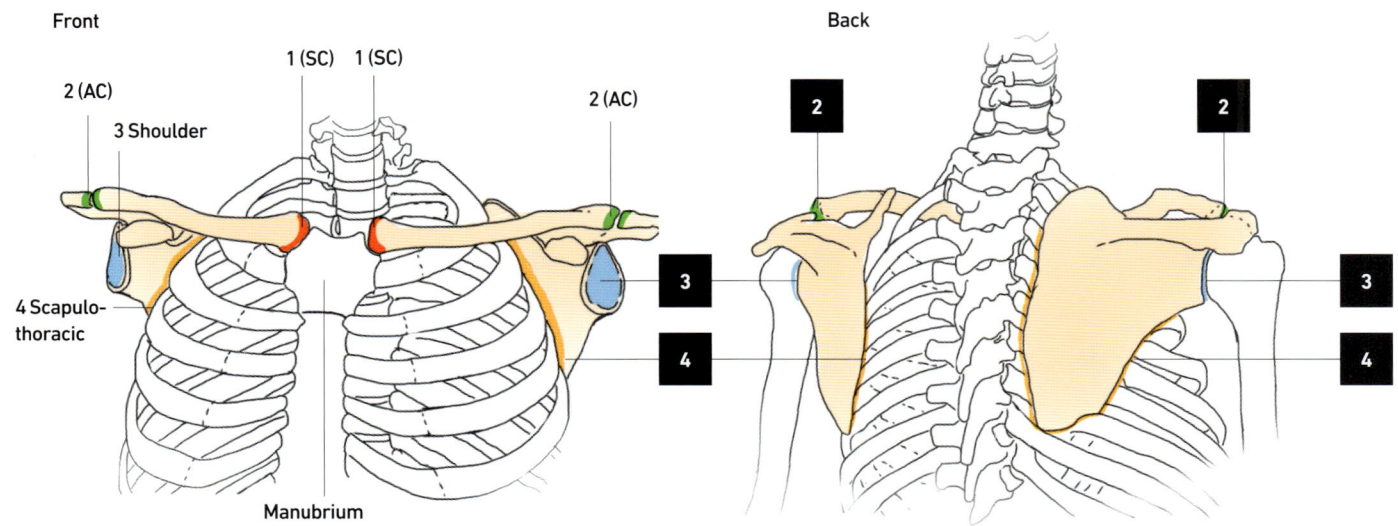

Front

Back

Manubrium

GENERAL TERMINOLOGY

PERTAINING TO POSITION

Midline. Divides body into right and left sides

Medial. Nearer to midline

Lateral. Sidewise, farther from the midline

Superior. Above

Inferior. Below

Anterior. Front

Posterior. Rear

Proximal. Nearer to root of limb

Distal. Farther from root of limb

Palmar. Refers to palm side of hand

Plantar. Refers to sole of foot

Dorsal. Refers to back of hand and top of foot

Supinate. Forearm and hand, turned palm-side upward

Pronation. Forearm and hand, turned palm-side downward

Inverted. Foot turned inward at ankle joint

Everted. Foot turned outward at ankle joint

PERTAINING TO FLESH

Muscle. Contractile organ capable of producing movement

Muscle belly. Fleshy part of a muscle

Flexor. Bends

Extensor. Straightens

Abductor. Draws away from midline

Adductor. Draws toward midline

Supinator. Turns palm of hand upward

Pronator. Turns palm of hand downward

Levator. Raises

Depressor. Lowers

Erector. Draws upright

Tensor. Draws tight

Corrugator. Draws (skin) into wrinkles

Sphincter. Regulates the closing of an aperture

Rotator. Causes to revolve

Origin. Relatively fixed point of a muscle attachment

Insertion. Relatively movable point of a muscle attachment

Tendon. Fibrous tissue securing a muscle to its attachment

Ligament. Fibrous tissue binding bones together or holding tendons/muscles in place

Aponeurosis. Expanded tendon for attachment of a flat muscle

Fascia. Fibrous envelopment of muscular structures

Sheath. Protective covering

BONES

Bone. Inflexible structure composing the skeleton

Cartilage. Substance from which bone ossifies; gristle

Joint. Articulation or connection between bones

Suture. Interlocking of teeth-like edges

Facet. Small articular area; often a pit

Fossa. Shallow depression

Foramen. Hole; perforation

Condyle. Polished articular surface (usually a knob)

Epicondyle. Elevation near a condyle

Protuberance. A protrusion or bump (can be felt under finger)

Process. Projection (can be grasped with fingers)

Spine. Pointed projection or sharp ridge

Crest. Ridge or border

Head. Enlarged knob of a long bone

Neck. Constriction of a bone near its head

Shaft. Longest part of a bone

ANATOMICAL TERMINOLOGY PERTAINING TO POSITION

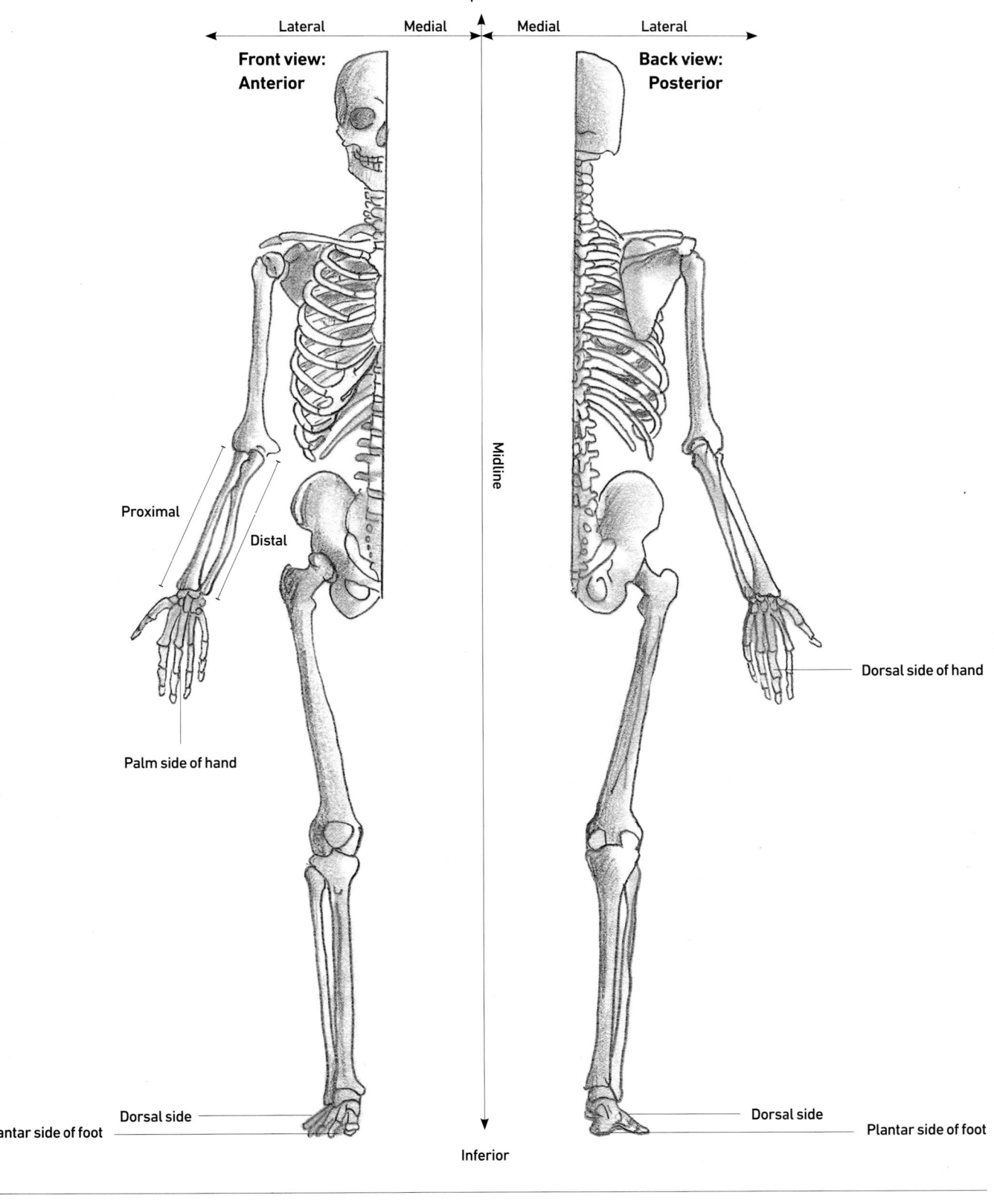

Superior

Lateral　　　Medial　|　Medial　　　Lateral

Front view: Anterior

Back view: Posterior

Midline

Proximal

Distal

Dorsal side of hand

Palm side of hand

Dorsal side

Plantar side of foot

Dorsal side

Plantar side of foot

Inferior

JOINTS

Joints are areas where bones are linked together. To fully understand movement, artists need to become familiar with the mechanics of the joints, which have varying degrees of mobility. Joints are classified into three basic types: immovable joints (cranial sutures), slightly movable joints (intervertebral discs), and freely movable joints (also called synovial joints).

Types of Joints

Immovable joints. These joints have very little or no movement at all. Adjoining edges are held together by a thin layer of fibrous tissue. Example: Distal *tibiofibular joint* (articulation between tibia and fibula in lower leg)—minimal amount of movement. *Sutures* in the skull—no movement.

Slightly movable joints. Example: Joints between the first costal cartilage of a rib and the sternum. Joints between the vertebrae and between the symphysis pubis bones (adhesion by means of *cartilage*).

Freely movable joints. Also called *synovial joints*, they have a tremendous amount of variety in their movements, ranging from extensive (at the shoulder joint) to slight (between some of the carpal bones of the hand). Lubricating *synovial fluid* is secreted within the capsules that surround these types of joints.

The following seven *synovial joints* are classified according to their structure or function:

1. *Plane joints* (e.g., joints of the wrist and ankle bones) glide face to face, limited by their retaining *ligaments*.

2. *Hinge joints* (e.g., joints of the fingers, elbow, etc.) can only swing back and forth (*flexion and extension*).

3. *Saddle joints* (e.g., the trapeziometacarpal joint at the base of the thumb) increase the range of hinge joints by permitting 360-degree motion (but no rotation). The saddle joint gets its name because one part of the joint is concave and looks like a saddle. The other bone's end is convex and looks like a rider in a saddle.

4. *Condyloid joints* (e.g., joints of first row of knuckles) increase the extent of the saddle joint by permitting limited circular movement.

5. *Ball and socket joints* (e.g., hip joint, shoulder joint) add to the wide play of the *condyloid joint* and are the most movable of all. They permit movement in all directions—flexion/extension, abduction/adduction, and rotation.

6. *Ellipsoid joints* (e.g., the oval part of wrist) are a modified ball-and-socket where the uniting surfaces are ellipsoidal rather than spherical.

7. *Pivot joints* (e.g., the atlas and axis of neck, radius and ulna) move within a complete or partial ring in a cylindrical form. Only a vertical axis is present, as in the hinge of a gate.

1. Plane joints

Wrist bones

Carpal bones

Metacarpals 2–5

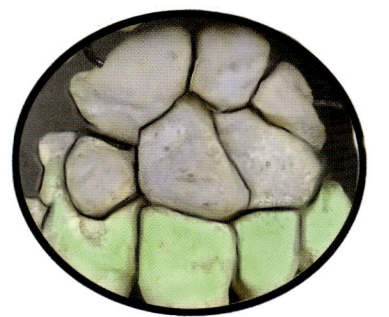

2. Hinge joints

Only swing back and forth

Extensor tendon—typically a pulley system

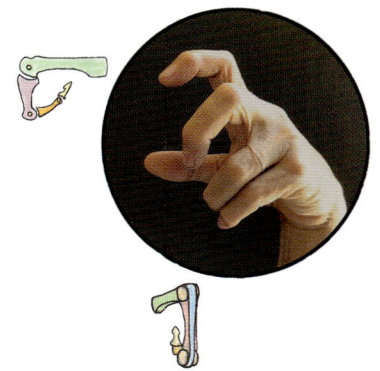

3. Saddle joint

Looks like a rider in a saddle

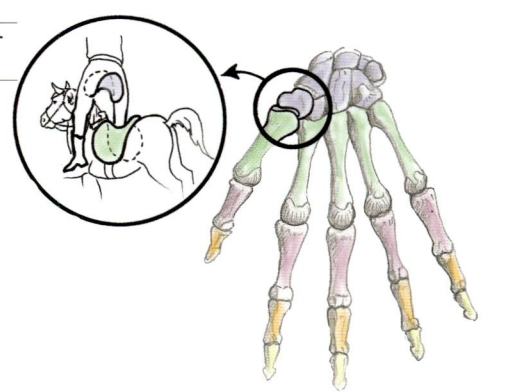

4. Condyloid joints

Permit limited circular movements

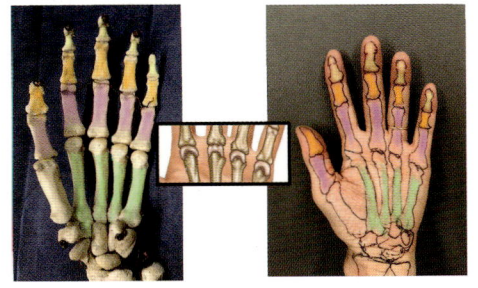

5. Ball-and-socket joints

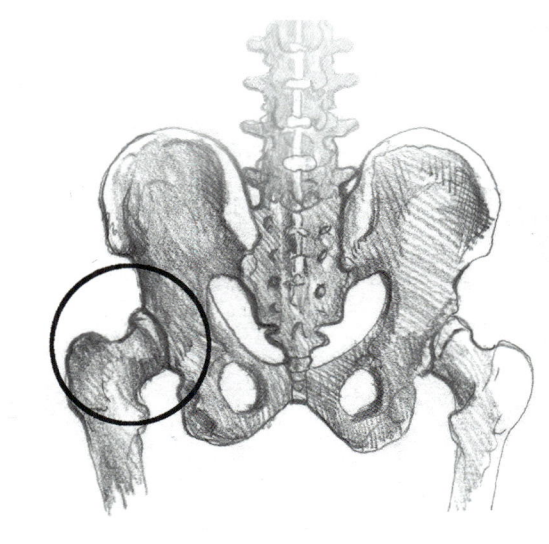

6. Ellipsoid joints

The ellipse-shaped ball and joint allows circular movement

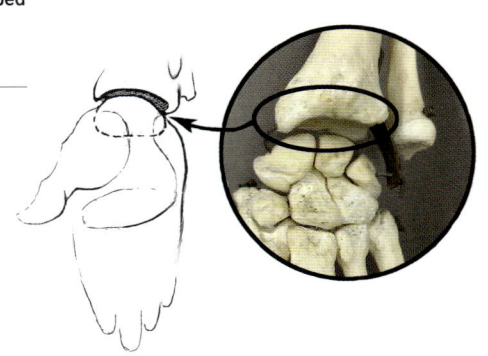

7. Pivot joints—atlas and axis

C-1 Atlas

C-2 Axis

C-7

T-1

First rib

Atlas and axis

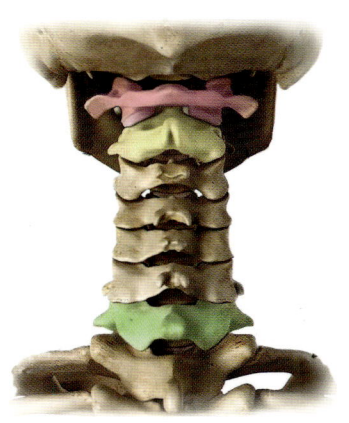

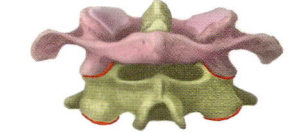

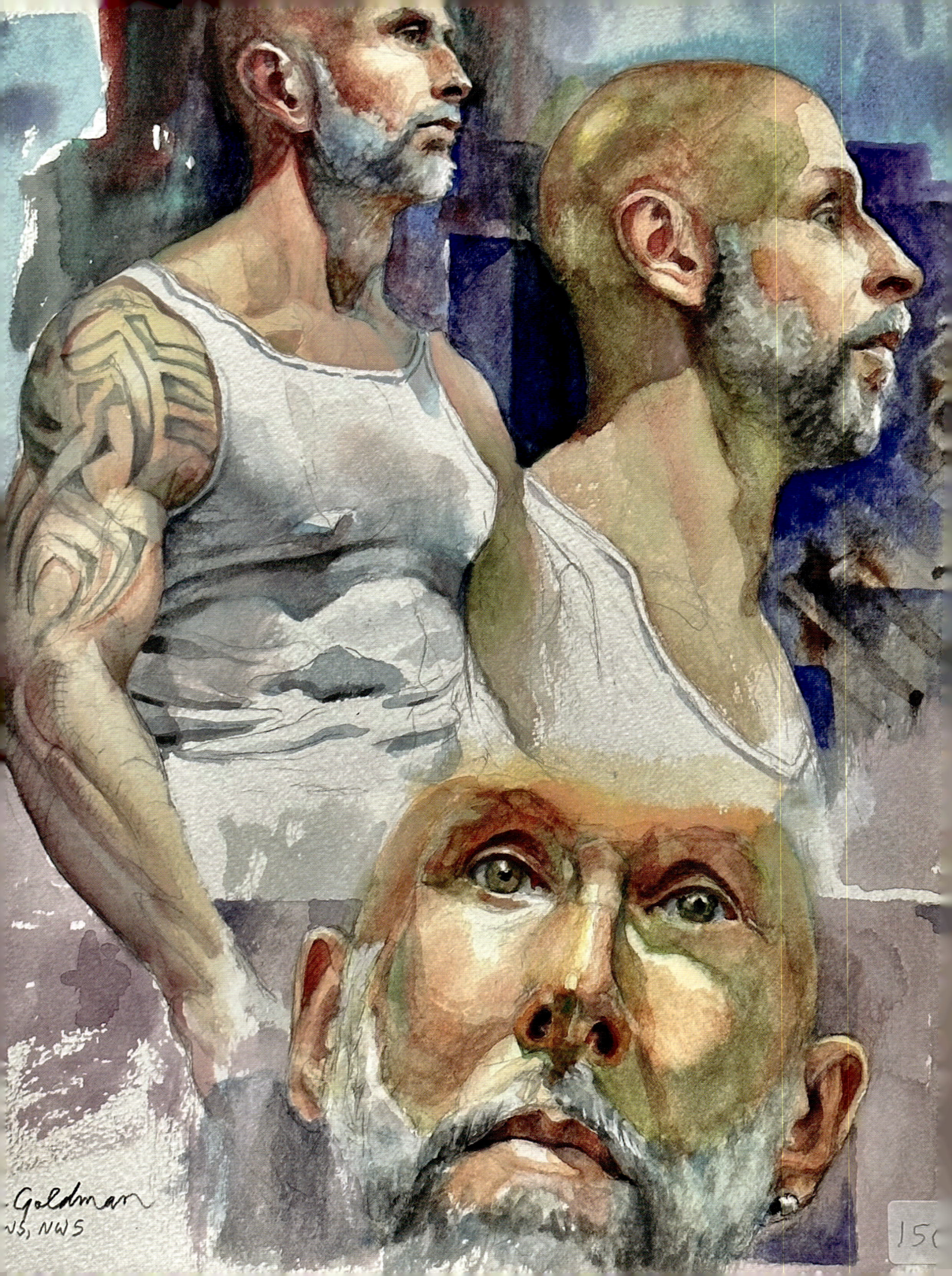

Goldman
NS, NWS

3

THE HEAD AND NECK

Here, you'll learn about the anatomy, planes, muscles, and proportions of the skull and neck. Also included are step-by-step drawings of the stages I think are most important to consider when constructing a portrait. Muscles of facial expression and mastication are also explored and illustrated, along with expressions of the six basic emotions: *happiness, sadness, surprise, fear, anger, and disgust.*

Ken Goldman, **Head Studies from Life,**
watercolor on paper, 12" × 9" (30 × 23 cm) (detail)
Painting from many foreshortened angles is a
rewarding challenge.

THE CERVICAL SPINE: COLOR CODED

The seven vertical vertebrae.

Back view of cervical spine.

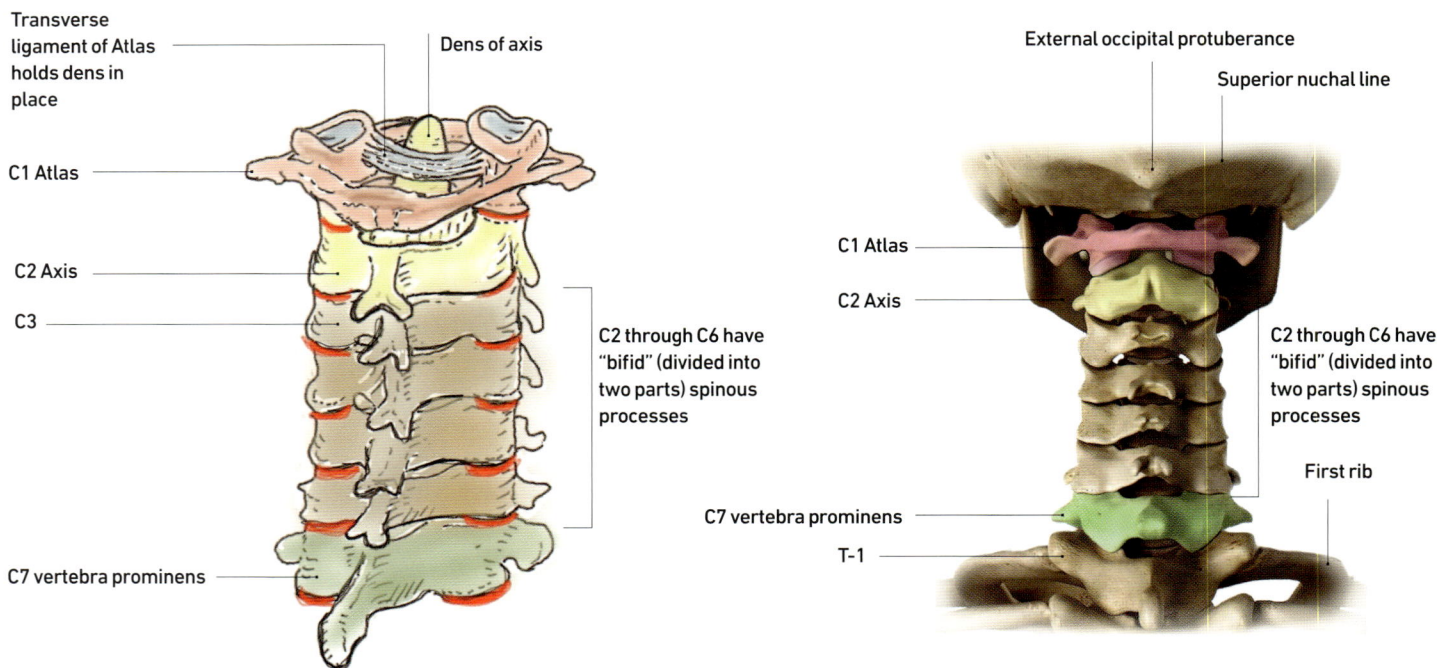

Transverse ligament of Atlas holds dens in place

Dens of axis

C1 Atlas

C2 Axis

C3

C2 through C6 have "bifid" (divided into two parts) spinous processes

C7 vertebra prominens

External occipital protuberance

Superior nuchal line

C1 Atlas

C2 Axis

C2 through C6 have "bifid" (divided into two parts) spinous processes

First rib

C7 vertebra prominens

T-1

The seven *cervical vertebrae* of the neck do not carry as much weight as the *thoracic and lumbar vertebrae*; therefore, they are the smallest in the entire *vertebral column* and also the most movable. The connecting joints that permit this movement are called *zygapophyseal* or *facet joints* and are classified as *plane joints* because they allow sliding and gliding movements. Each vertebra has a pair of these joints— one on the left and one on the right (red). These *facet joints* are encapsulated by connective tissues, coated with cartilage and lubricated with synovial fluid that enables smooth joint articulation.

The first two cervical vertebrae, *atlas C1* and *axis C2*, have unique shapes, while all the others, *C3 to C7*, are similar to one another in both shape and structure. The 7th cervical vertebra (green) is an important landmark for artists because its long spinous process is visible at the back of the neck, showing where the neck ends and the rib cage begins. For this reason, it is called *vertebra prominens*. One other distinguishing feature of vertebrae C2 to C6 is that they have *bifid spinous processes* not found on any other *vertebrae*.

VERTEBRAE C3 THROUGH C6 (TAN)

These vertebrae are all similar to one another in structure, including their *bifid* shaped spinous processes.

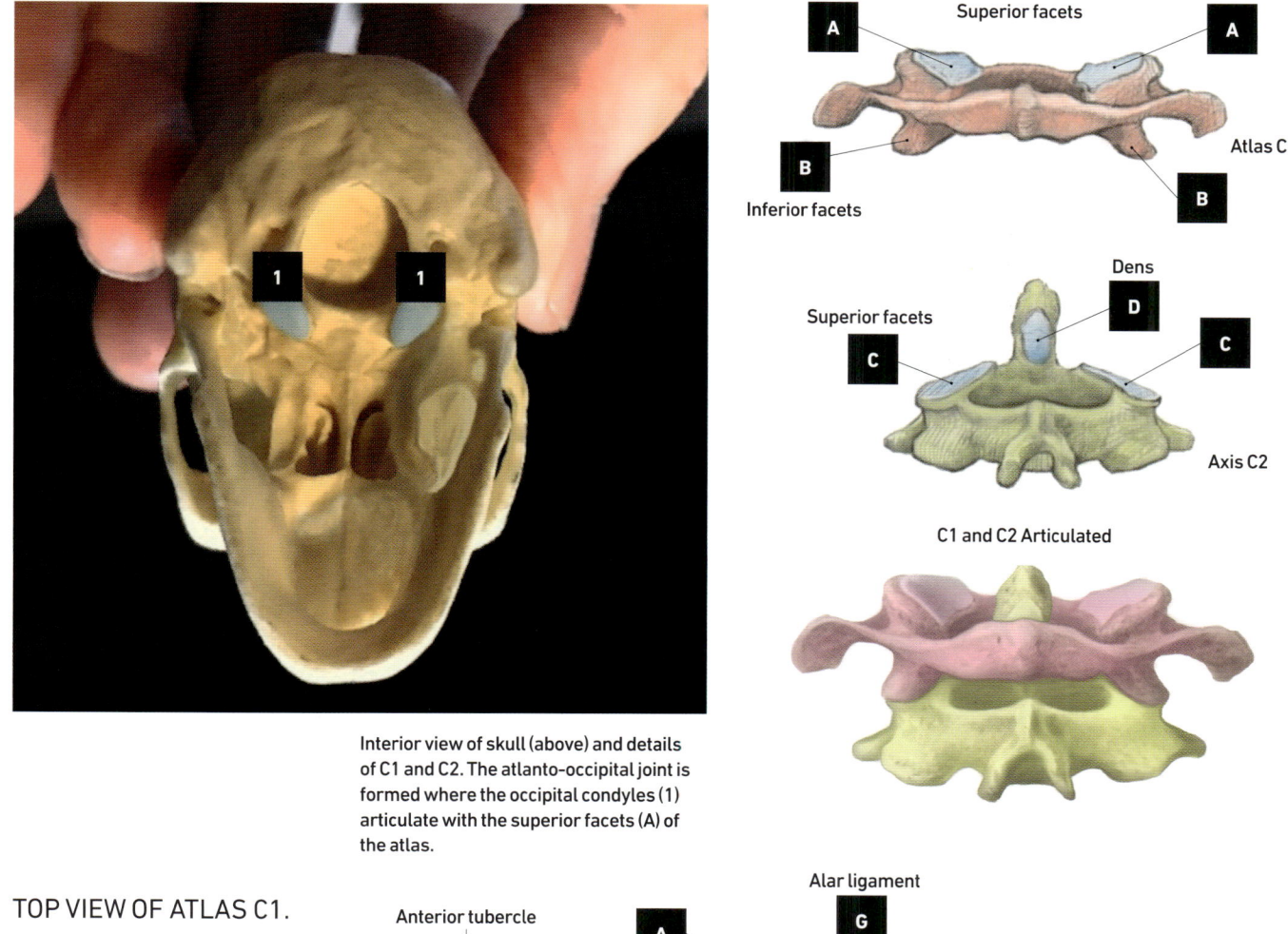

Interior view of skull (above) and details of C1 and C2. The atlanto-occipital joint is formed where the occipital condyles (1) articulate with the superior facets (A) of the atlas.

TOP VIEW OF ATLAS C1.

ATLAS C1 (PINK)

This first vertebra is unique because it lacks a body and a spinal process. It is named *atlas* because it holds up the weight of the entire *cranium*, like the Greek god Atlas who shouldered the entire world. Its two superior facets, which articulate with the skull's *occipital condyles* (blue) (**1 & A**), are called the *atlanto-occipital joints* (movable synovial ellipsoid joints). These joints permit the head to rock forward and backward (as when nodding "yes"). A slight degree of lateral tilting of the head is also permitted here. The foramen magnum (Latin for "big hole") transmits the spinal cord into the cranial cavity.

AXIS C2 (YELLOW)

The articulation between the *inferior facets of the atlas* (**B**) and the *superior facets of the axis* (**C**) are called *atlantoaxial joints* (gliding *synovial plane joints*). The *atlas* rotates on top of the *axis* by pivoting around the upward thrusting *dens* or *odontoid process* (**D**), which is stabilized by the *facet for dens of the atlas* (**E**) and its *transverse ligament* (**F**). This pivoting action around the *dens (synovial pivot joint)*, allows the head to turn from side to side as in saying "no." Excessive rotation is kept in check by the two *alar ligaments* attached to the front of the *dens* (**G**).

THE SKULL: BONY LANDMARKS

Skull, front view.

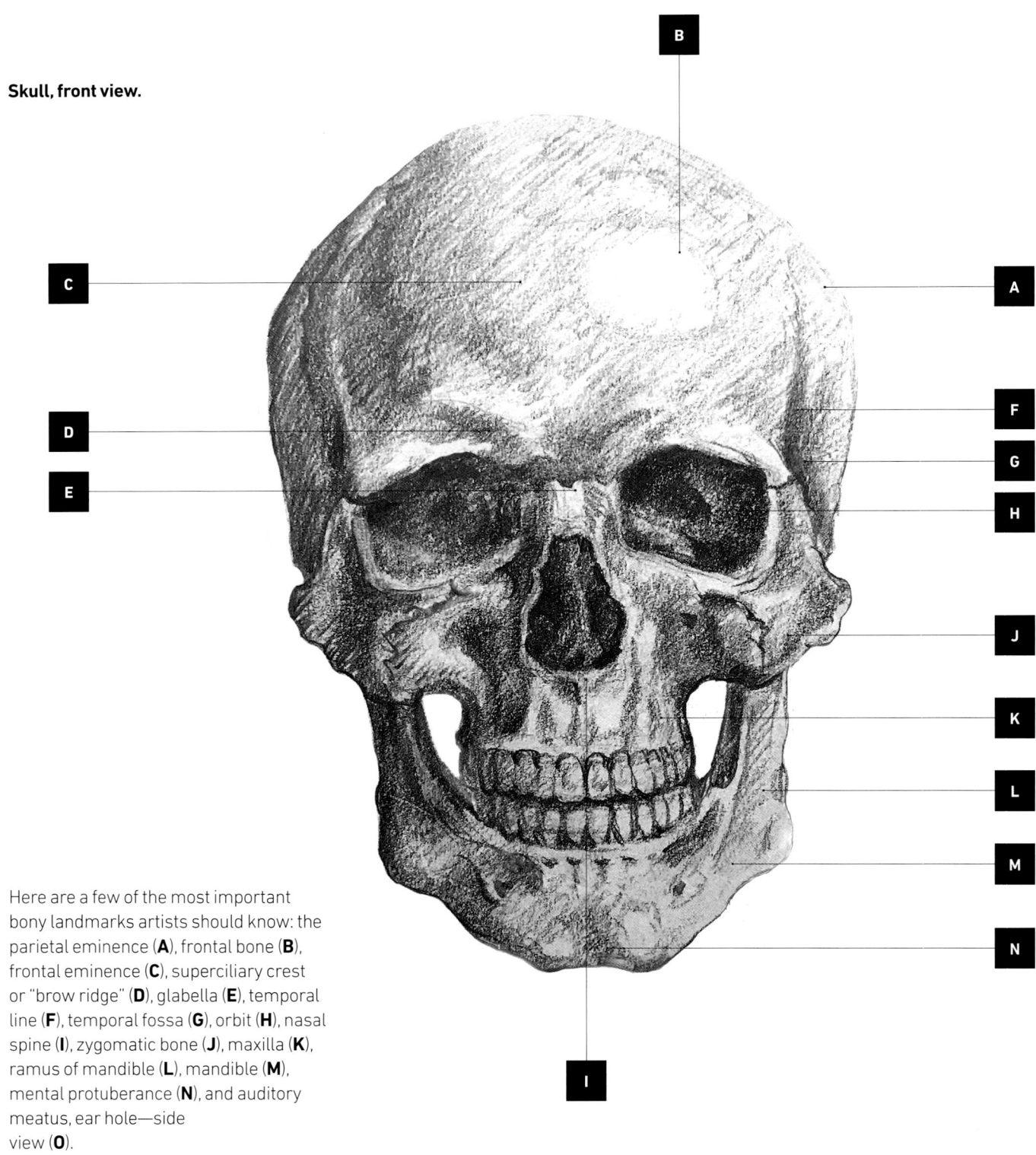

Here are a few of the most important bony landmarks artists should know: the parietal eminence (**A**), frontal bone (**B**), frontal eminence (**C**), superciliary crest or "brow ridge" (**D**), glabella (**E**), temporal line (**F**), temporal fossa (**G**), orbit (**H**), nasal spine (**I**), zygomatic bone (**J**), maxilla (**K**), ramus of mandible (**L**), mandible (**M**), mental protuberance (**N**), and auditory meatus, ear hole—side view (**O**).

Skull, side view.

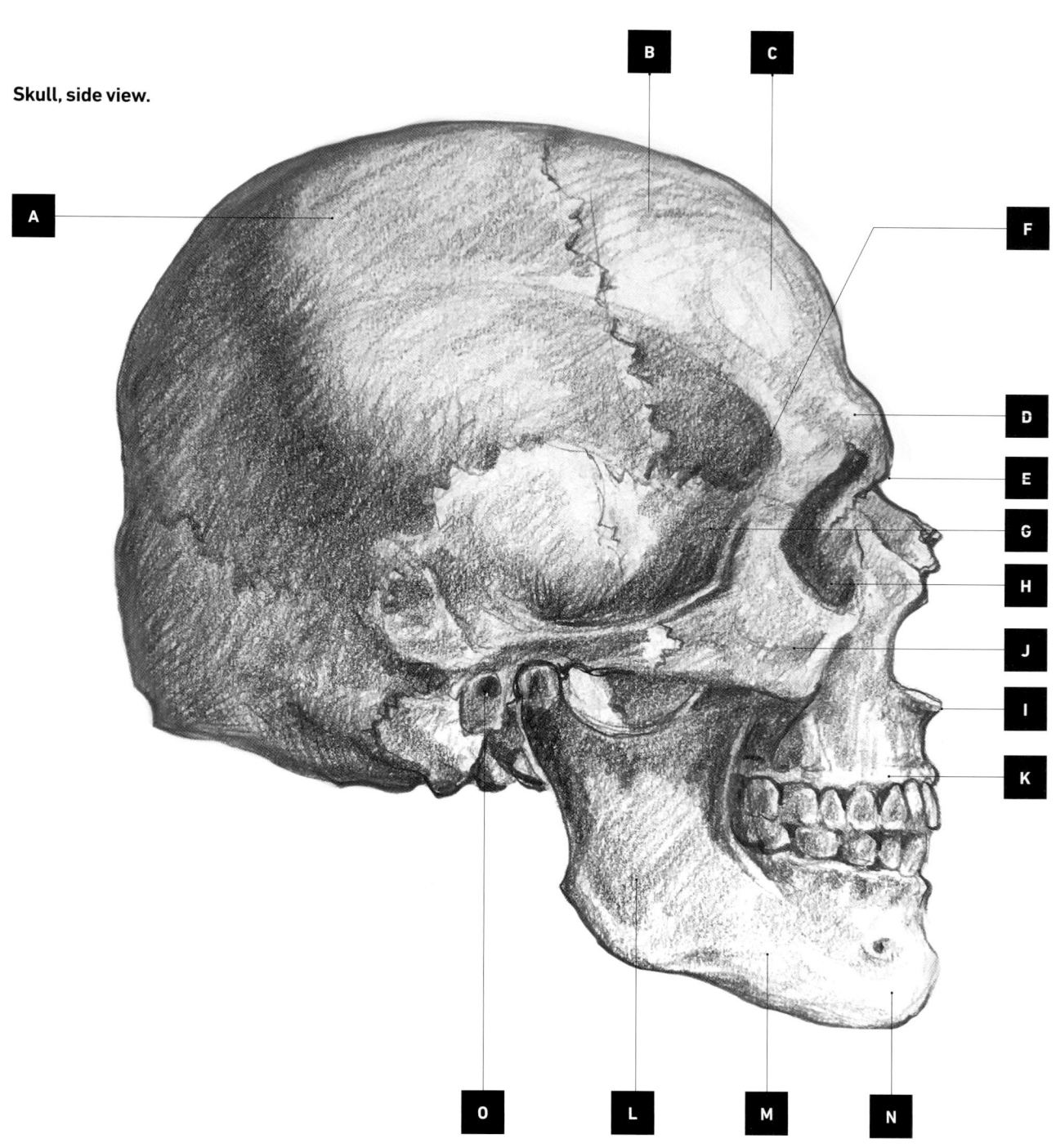

LESSON: SKETCHING FROM HANDHELD SKULLS

Becoming familiar with the head and skull is an excellent way to improve your portraiture skills. If you purchase a plastic skull (life-size, small, or both), you can practice drawing the skull from many different angles, as shown in these charcoal pencil studies.

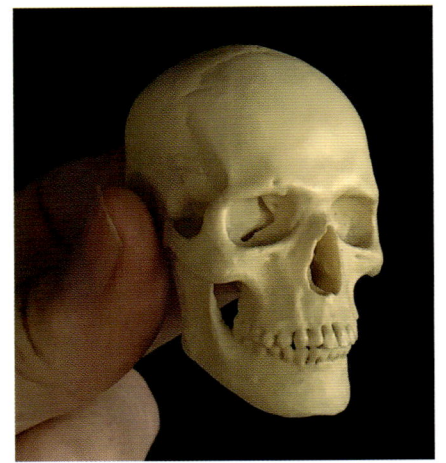

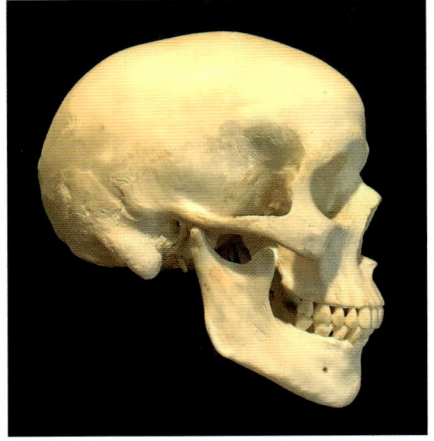

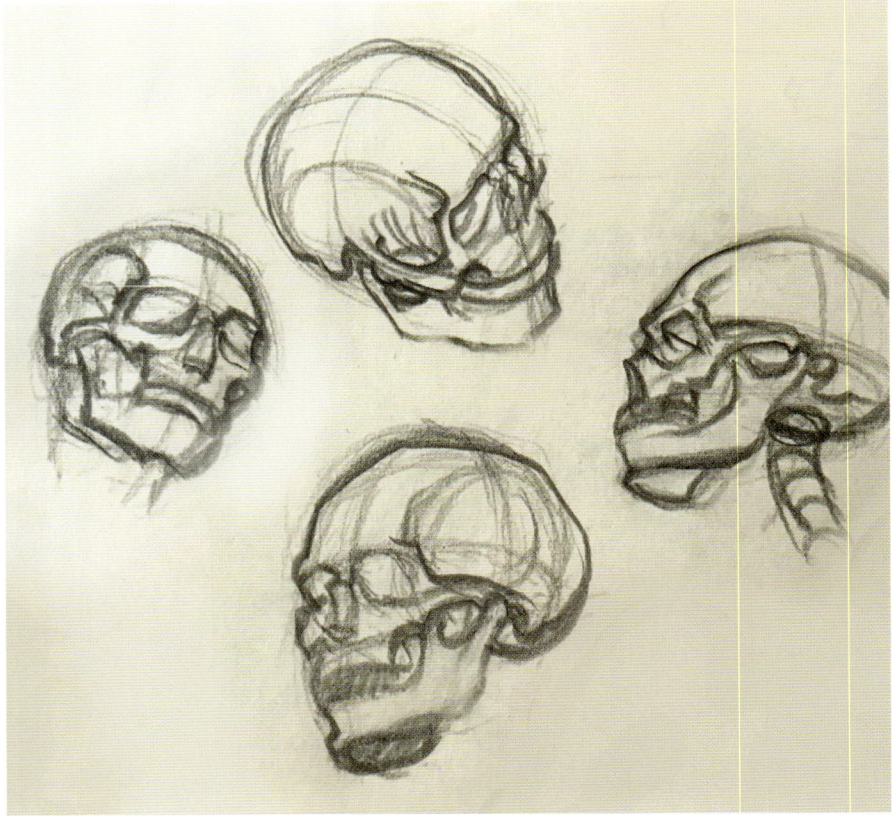

LESSON: VINE CHARCOAL "PICK-OUT"

Pick-out means to lift out light values from charcoal or graphite pencil with a kneaded eraser to create shapes on the light-facing planes.

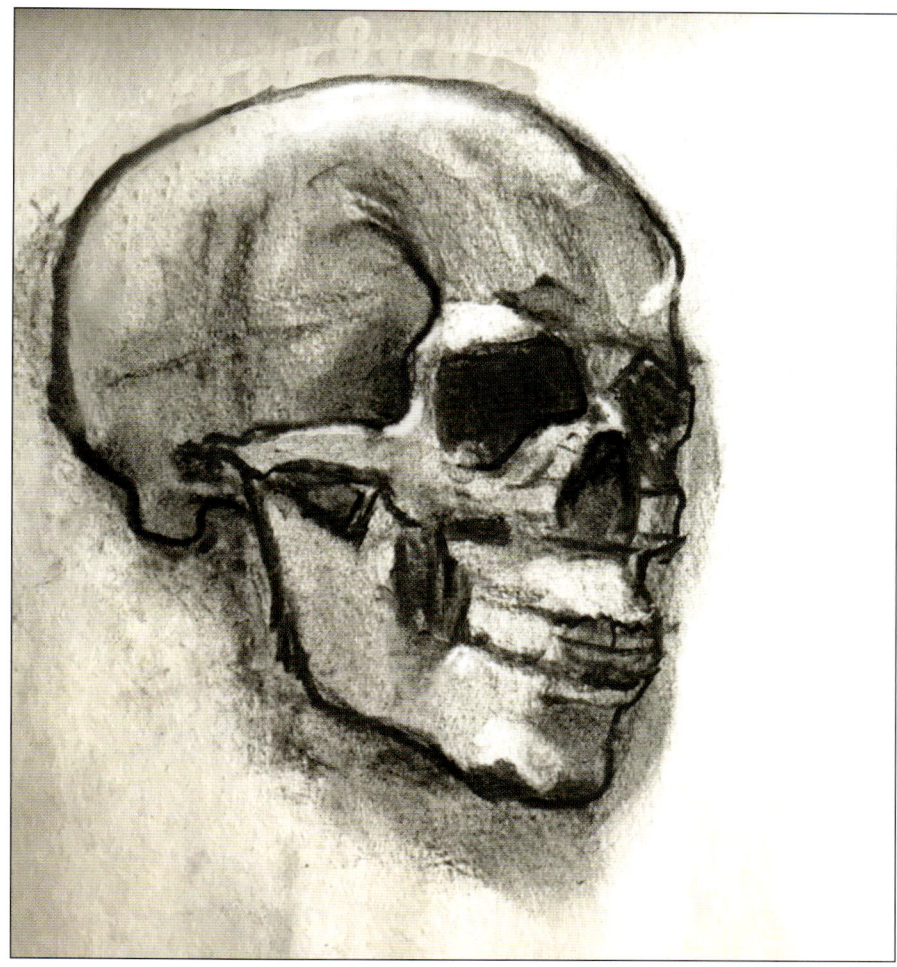

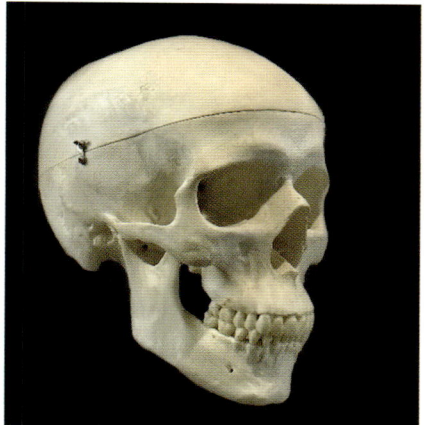

Start by laying down a vague gestural silhouette of the skull's overall shape. Vine charcoal is great for doing this because it is so erasable. The kneaded eraser is a drawing tool, not just an eraser. It should be used in the same way that opaque white paint is used in opaque oil or watercolor painting, i.e., to create forms and edges. This sketch looks rough because I only allowed myself five minutes to draw it. Doing quick sketches like this is a great way to be able to do lots of drawings and really get the feel of charcoal. Accuracy is secondary. For the darkest darks, use a charcoal pencil or a compressed charcoal. Set a timer.

Some other skull angles to practice.

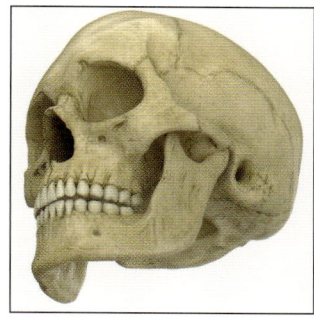
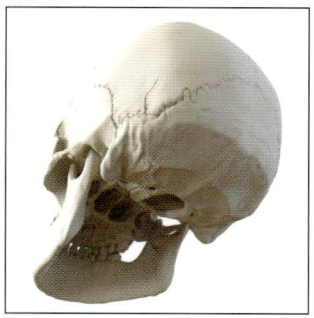
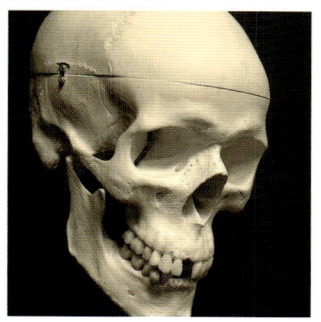
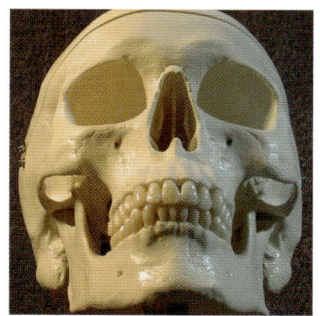

A SKULL IN A RECTANGLE, SKULL IN A SQUARE

A skull seen from the front fits into a rectangle; from the side, it fits into a square. On a side-view, the vertical centerline bisects the jawline next to the earhole. When constructing a head, this is a very convenient measurement to keep in mind. When I look for generalized proportions, I usually do not worry too much about where the hairline falls, but instead I concentrate on finding the brow-line to the base of the nose (nasal spine) measurement, and from there I add the same distance to locate the chin.

The thirds divisions below the base of the nose are:

One-third to the separation of the lips (over the front teeth)

One-third to the top of the chin area

The last third goes to the bottom of the chin

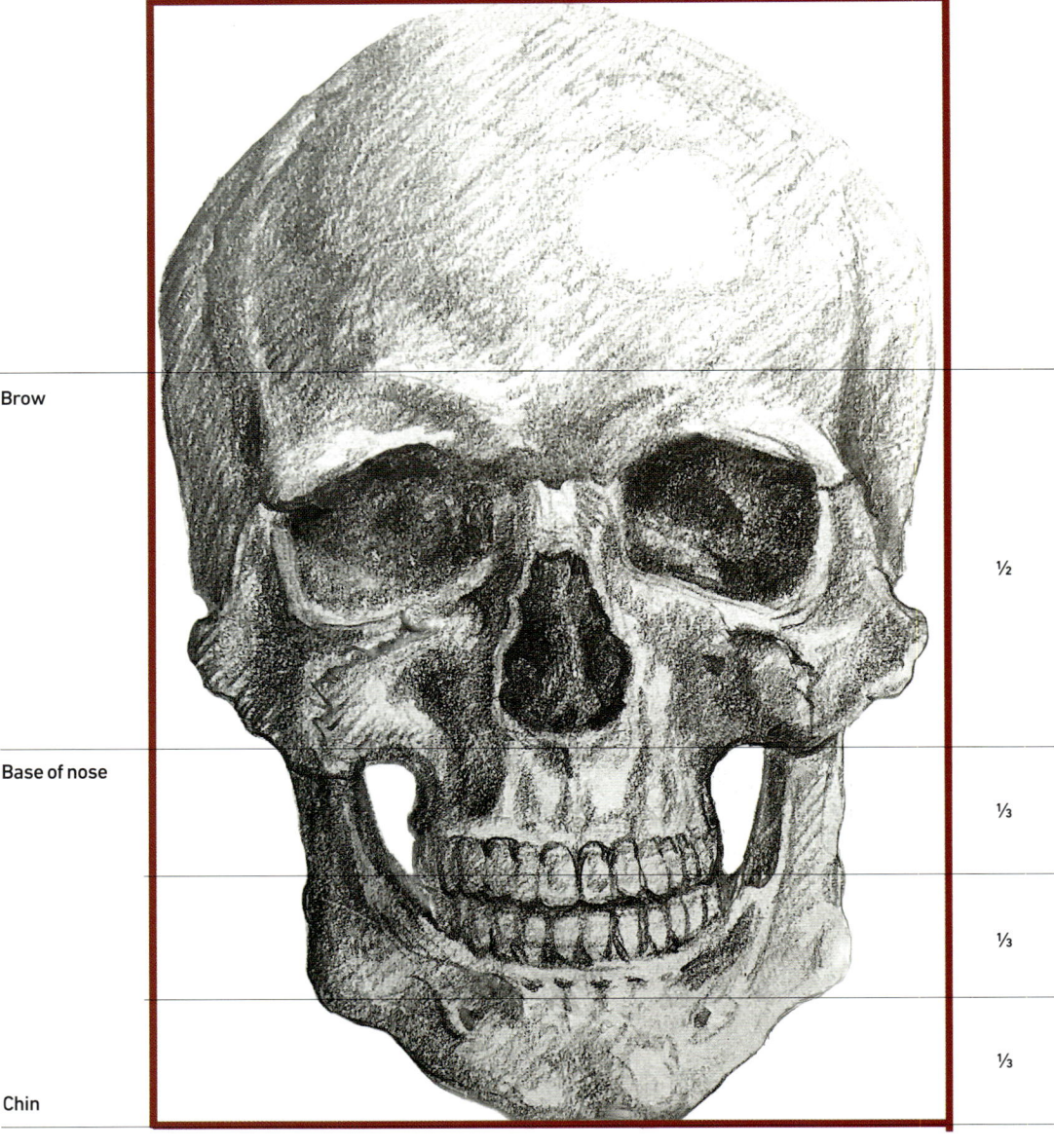

Brow

Base of nose

Chin

½

⅓

⅓

⅓

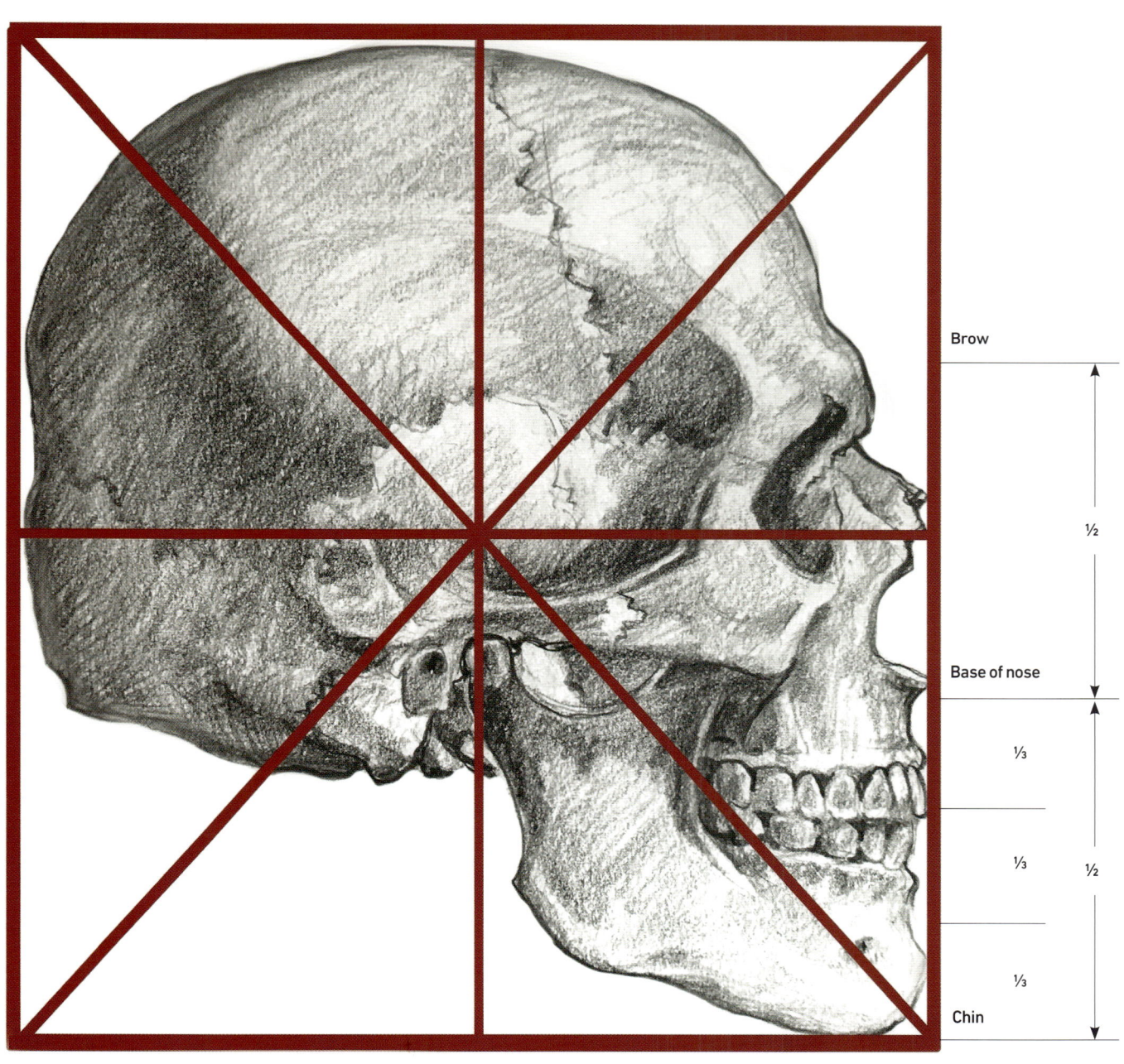

Brow

½

Base of nose

⅓

⅓

½

⅓

Chin

SKULL PROPORTIONS: THE BASICS

This method of finding proportions is based on identifying a few specific bony landmarks on the skull. There are many ways to start a drawing (such as sketching out a silhouette first), but I find this approach to be a very practical way to construct a head in almost any angle.

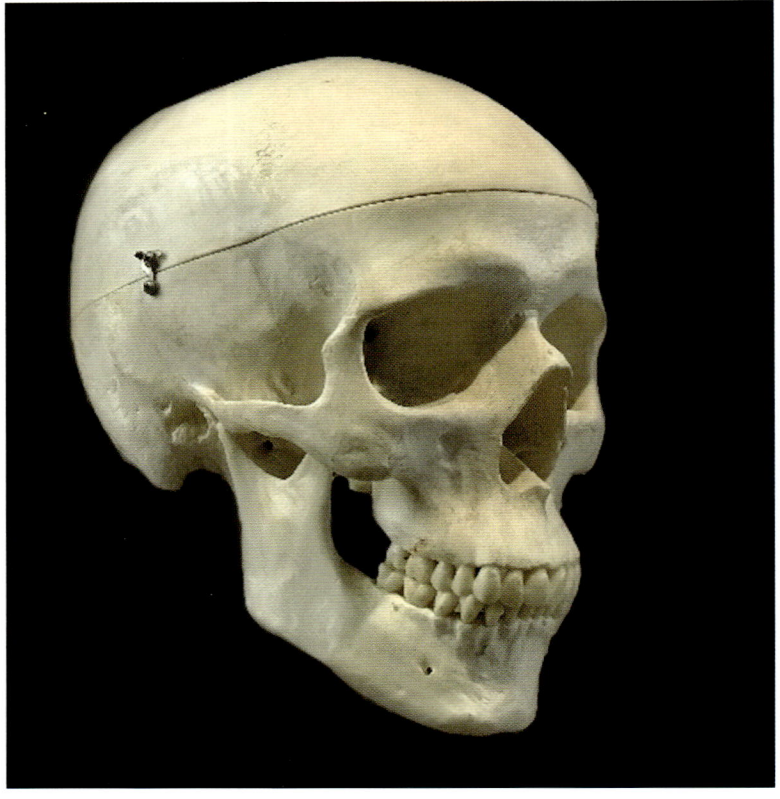

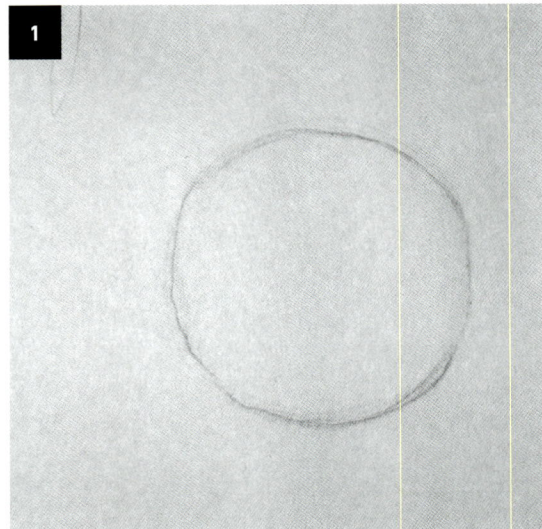

1. Begin with a circle.

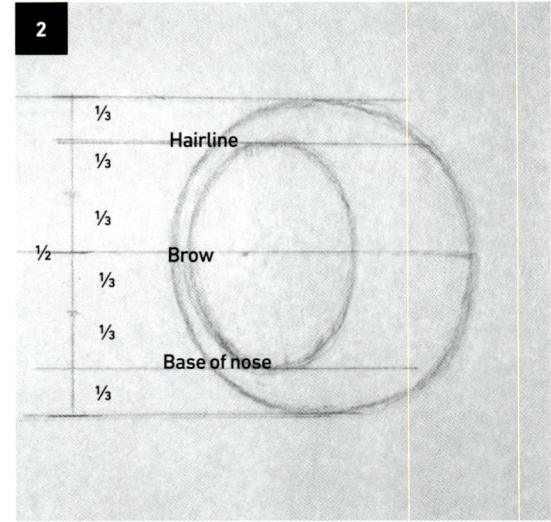

2. Then draw another circle that is two-thirds smaller (this becomes an oval in a three-quarter view) and divide it in half to find the level of the eyebrows. The outside of this circle will become the base of the nose and the hairline. This smaller circle also represents the temporal line of the skull and will remain evident in the final drawing.

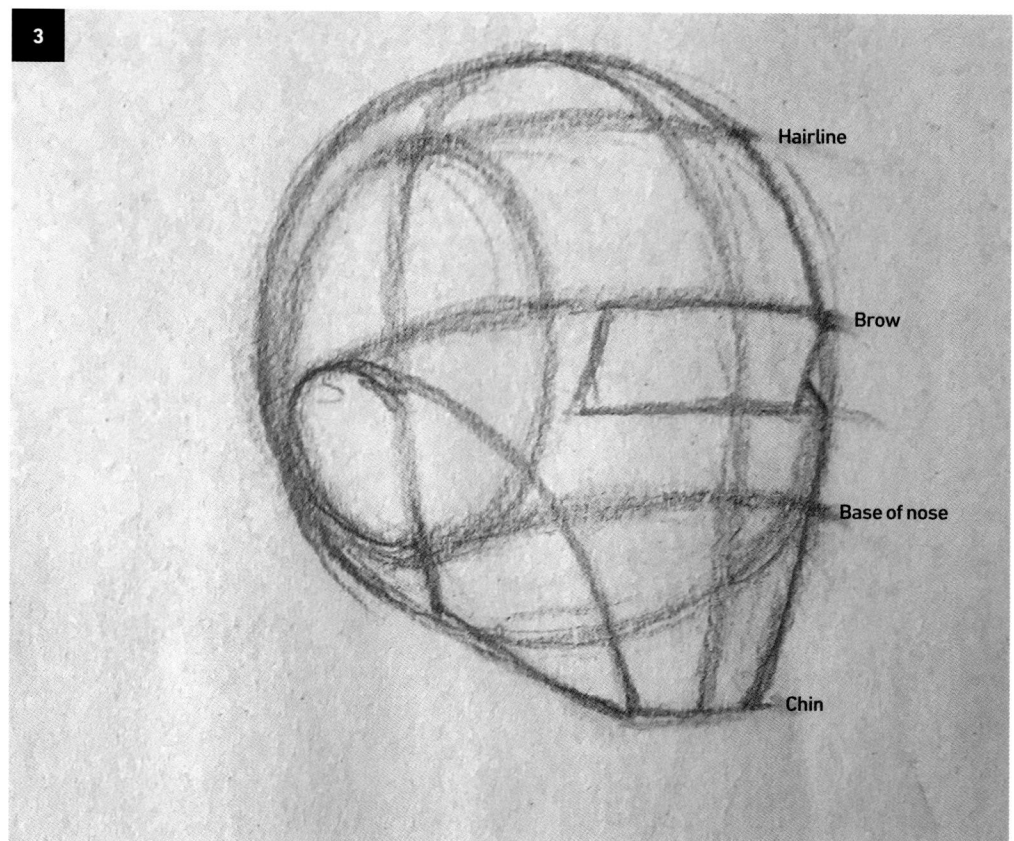

3

Hairline

Brow

Base of nose

Chin

3. Drop a centerline from the top of the head through the nose to the chin. This line, from nose base to chin, should be the same length as the brow to nose measurement. Also drop a vertical line through the center of the oval on the side of the head. This determines the placement of the ear.

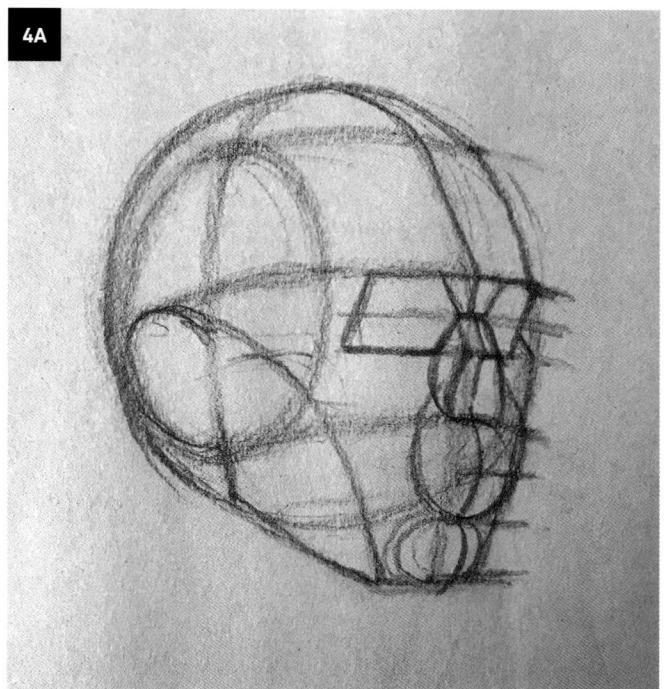

4A

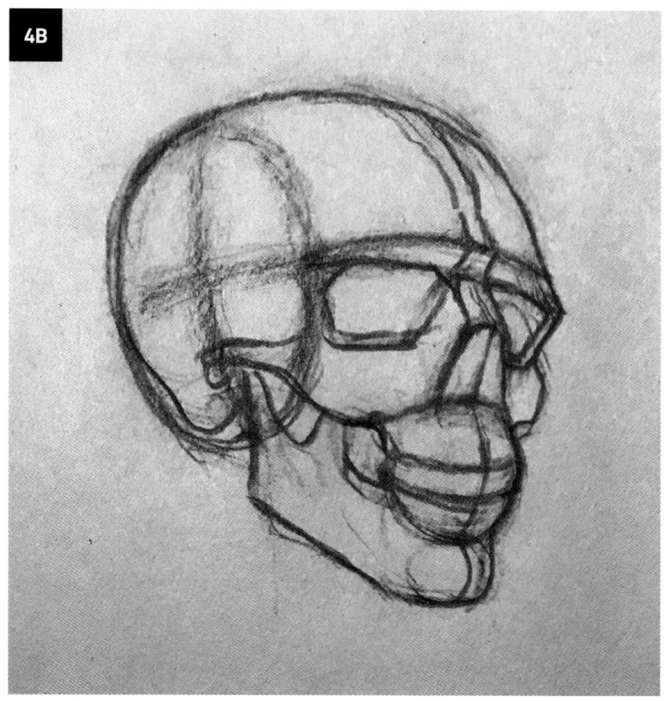

4B

4. Construct the downward-facing plane of the orbits, add a swoop from the top of the ears to the chin (this indicates the side of a head), and place the keystone shape between the eye sockets just above the nasal bone. Draw a rounded shape for the mouth (**4A, 4B**).

SKULL PROPORTIONS:
THE NEXT STAGE

Here are three demonstrations constructed quickly without using photo reference. The idea was to show how the proportions and landmarks of the skull relate to an actual head. Study each drawing carefully and you will recognize all of the proportions we've discussed so far.

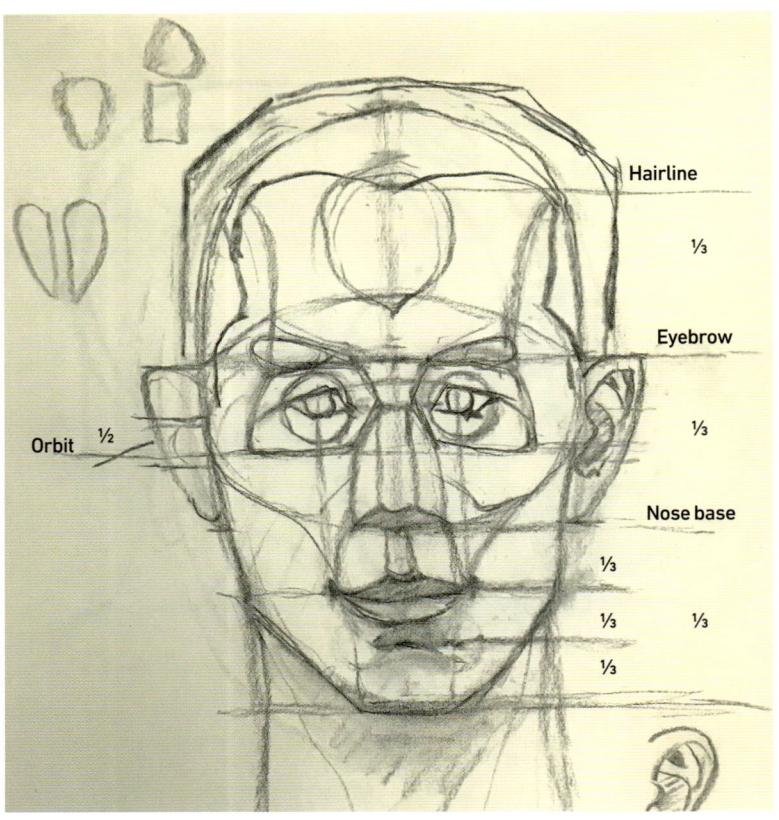

Front
The base of the orbit is halfway between the eyebrow and nose-base. Eyeballs sit in the middle of the orbits and the iris of each eye lines up with the corner of the lips. Notice how I am vaguely indicating the bony landmarks of the skull without being overly specific. Cheekbones line up with the base of the nose.

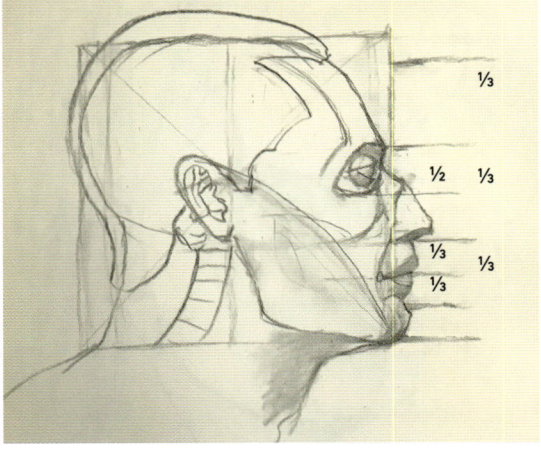

Side
Notice how the skull fits into a square, jawline is in the middle, the swoop from the top of the ear to the chin creates the side of the face. The cervical spine inserts into the bottom of the skull (foramen magnum) adjacent to the earhole and mastoid process. Notice how the zygomatic bone lines up with the base of the nose.

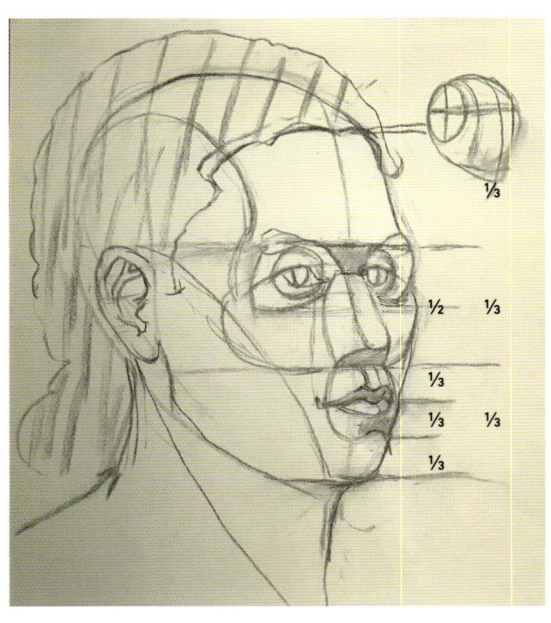

Three-Quarter View
Notice how the far eye is partially covered by the bridge of the nose (keystone—glabella). At this stage of a lay-in, the nose is kept very blocky with definite top, side, and bottom planes. A rhythmic gesture line connects the two upper eyelids. Because of the three-quarter perspective, the irises are drawn as ovals rather than circles.

SKULL PROPORTIONS: COLOR CODED

This sequence furthers the basic lay-in we've been discussing by introducing upward facing planes, downward facing planes, and side-planes, plus cylinders, blocks, and spheres. The side planes are depicted in blue, the downward facing planes in purple, and the upward facing planes are just the tone of the paper. The drawing on the left shows how this head looked at the beginning.

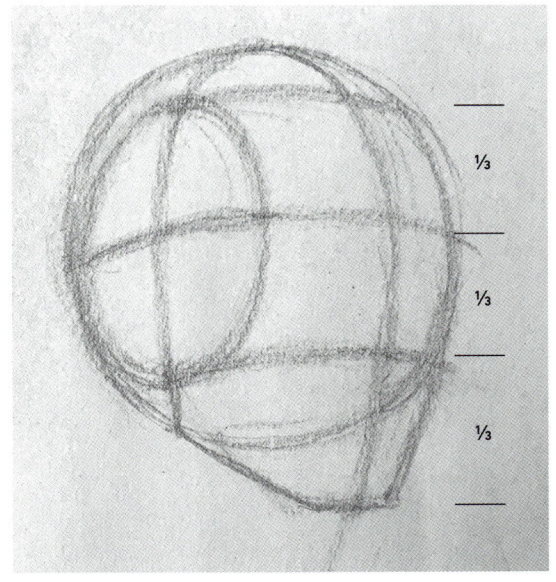

1/3

1/3

1/3

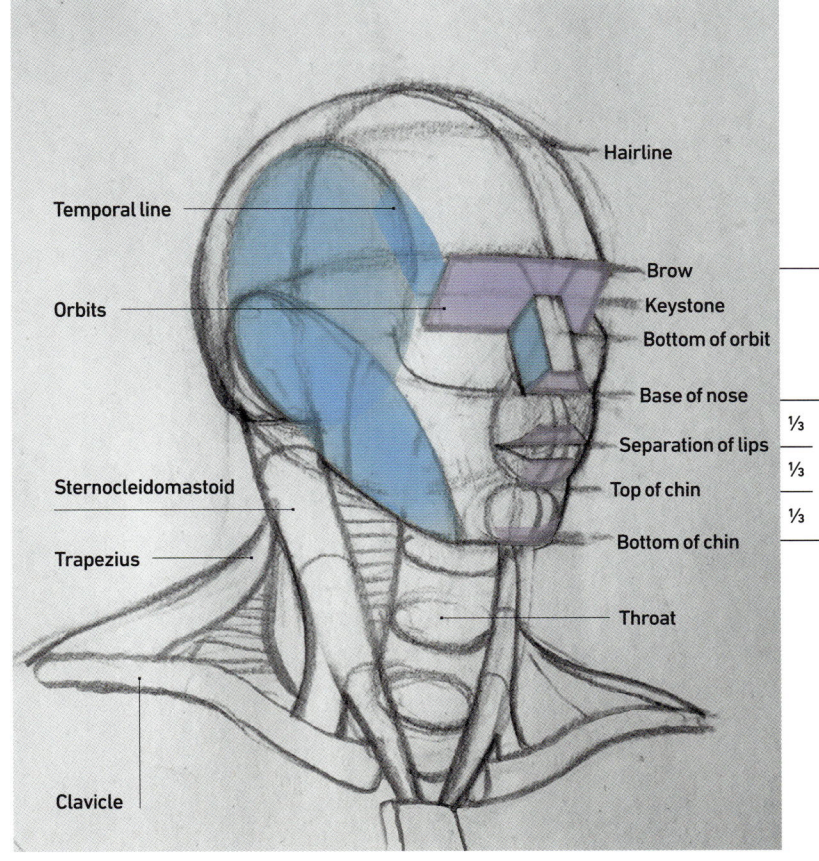

Hairline

Temporal line

Brow

Keystone

Orbits

Bottom of orbit — 1/2

Base of nose

1/3

Separation of lips

1/3   1/2

Sternocleidomastoid

Top of chin

1/3

Trapezius

Bottom of chin

Throat

Clavicle

Side planes

Down-facing planes

HEAD CONSTRUCTION SEQUENCES

THREE-QUARTER VIEW, ABOVE EYE LEVEL

When a model's head is higher than an artist's eye level, the model's head is seen in perspective, so accurate observation of angles becomes important. In this head, the angle from the ear to the *temporal line* slants upward and then, at the corner, slants back down through the eyebrow.

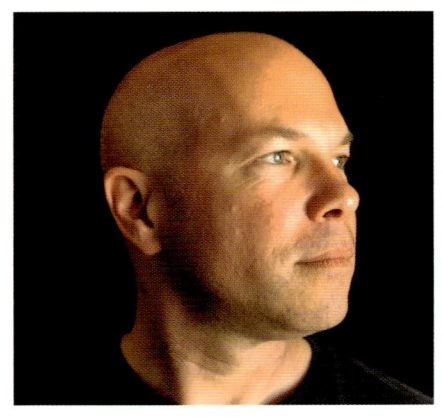

Midpoint at eye level

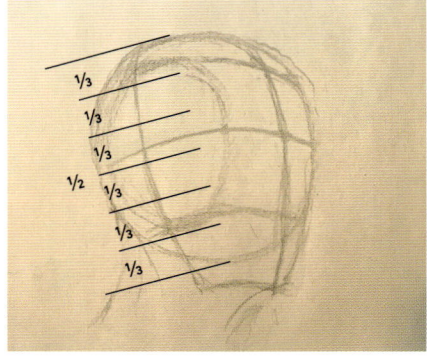

Midpoint in perspective

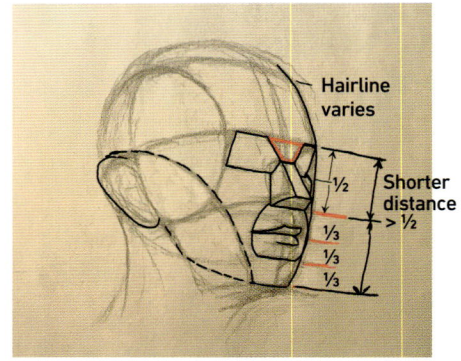

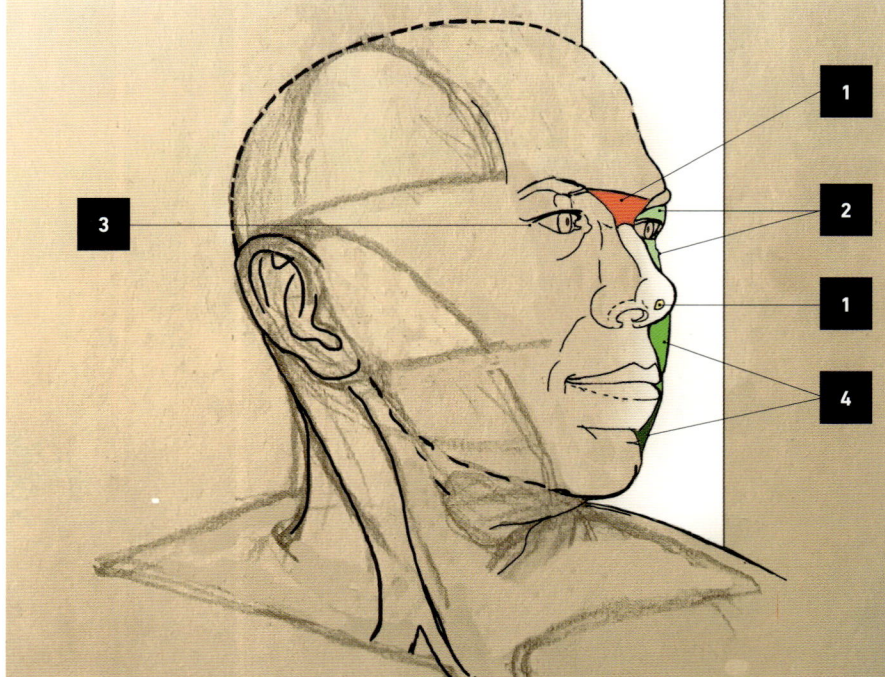

At this stage of a drawing, I like to tackle the far side first because I consider it to be the most critical part of a three-quarter-view portrait's likeness.

First draw in the keystone (red), and then look for the highlight (yellow dot) in relationship to the eye. This is a good way to make sure the nose doesn't get too long (a tendency when looking up at a model's foreshortened nose). The best way to evaluate placement correctly is to look at the negative shapes framing the edge of the head (white) and the inner negative shapes (green), defining the nose and mouth. Only after this part of the head is blocked in do I move on to the rest of the head.

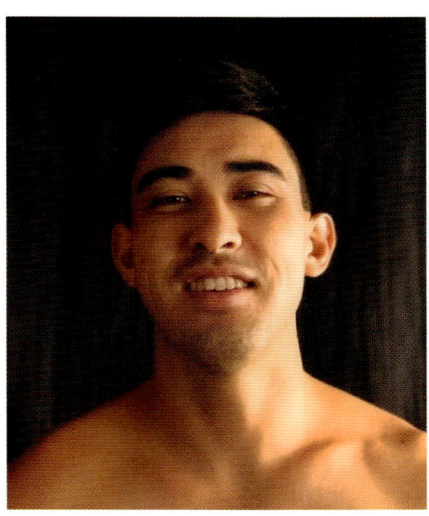

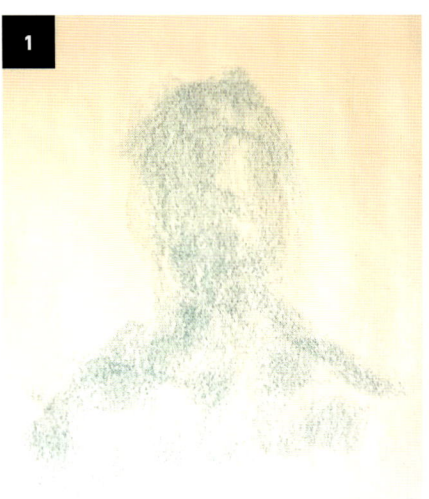

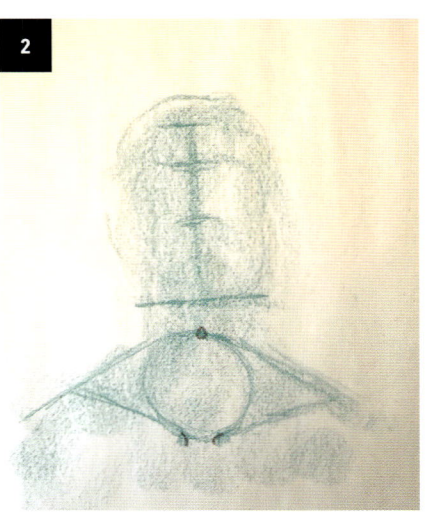

FRONT VIEW, BELOW EYE LEVEL

This model is being viewed from below eye-level, so standard one-third proportions go out the window. We know this because his ears are so far down below his eyes (at eye-level, brows normally line up with the tops of ears and the base of nose). In addition, the first third of this model's measurements, from chin to nose, is longer than the second measurement between his nose to eyebrows and also longer than the third measurement, brows to hairline. In fact, in this case, his brows are so large and so high above his eyes, this last dimension, brows to hairline, is the smallest proportion of all three. These are the types of proportional observations that should always be taken into consideration before even beginning to draw.

This anatomical construction demonstration uses a turquoise pastel stick and vine charcoal.

1. Start with a simple pastel silhouette of the head, neck, and sloping shoulders to get a sense of the head's placement.

2. Draw in a diamond shape to represent the trapezius and clavicles. Make two marks for the pit of the neck (proximal ends of clavicles), a point in the back representing the 7th cervical vertebra, and a circle for the cylindrical neck (for more about the anatomy of these landmarks, see "Muscles of the Head and Neck" on page 68). Find the "**T**" guidelines of the hairline, brow-line, nose-line, and chin-line (all slightly slanted but still at 90 degrees to the vertical centerline). This gives the head a proportional basis on which to add features.

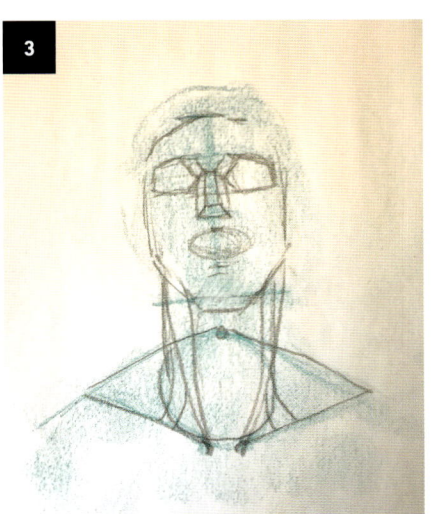

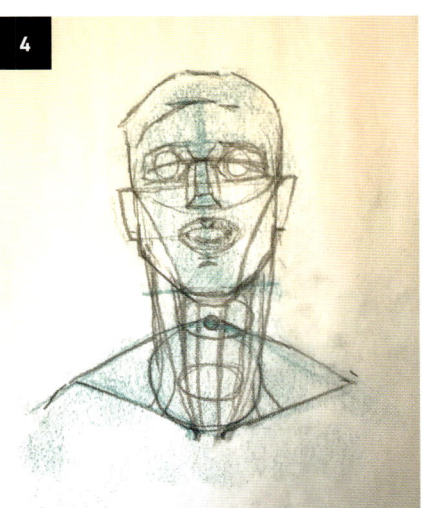

3. Draw the keystone (glabella), the blocky shape of the nose (top and side-planes with emphasis on the bottom plane, which is seen from below), the eye sockets (their base is halfway between the brows and base of the nose), the vague circular shape of the semi-opened mouth, and finally, the sternocleidomastoid muscles that give shape to the neck.

4. The windpipe (with Adam's apple is a small cylindrical shape within the larger cylinder of the neck. A gesturally curved line drawn through the base of the glabella and both eyes indicates the upper eyelids. Two swooping lines drawn down from the tops of the ears to the sides of the chin indicate the sides of the face, and finally, a curve drawn from one ear to the other going just below the nose is a guideline for placement of the cheekbones.

THREE-QUARTER VIEW, BELOW EYE LEVEL

This head is also being viewed from below. How do I know? Because when horizontal lines are drawn from the top and bottom of this model's left ear, they line up with the bottom of his right eye and the top of his lip, rather than lining up with his brows and nose-base. That's an instant giveaway.

As with the previous demonstration, this construction features turquoise pastel stick and vine charcoal.

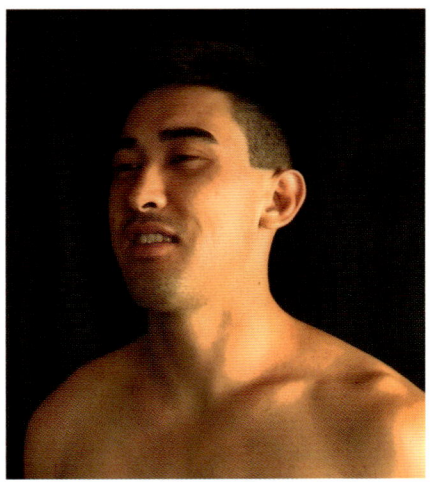

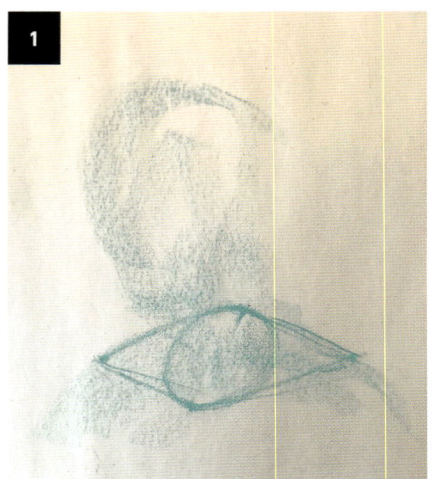

1. Start in a similar manner as the front view (see previous page) with a quick pastel silhouette for placement. Then draw in the diamond and an oval (rather than a circle) because of the three-quarter view's more oblique perspective.

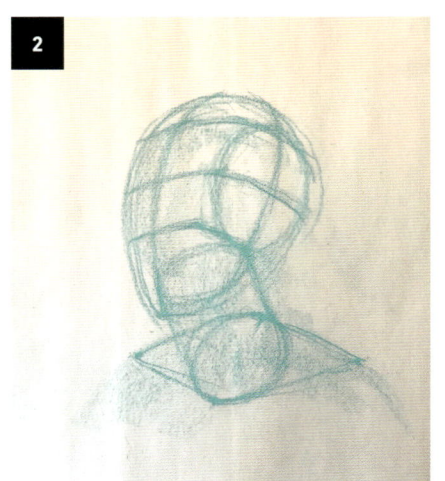

2. Extend the cylindrical neck from the oval and map out the proportions of the features with the same guidelines as the front view, but this time put them in perspective and draw in an oval for the side of the head at the temples with a centerline for the level of the brows. Be sure to keep the chin to nose measurement the longest, the nose to brow measurement second longest, and the brow to hairline the shortest.

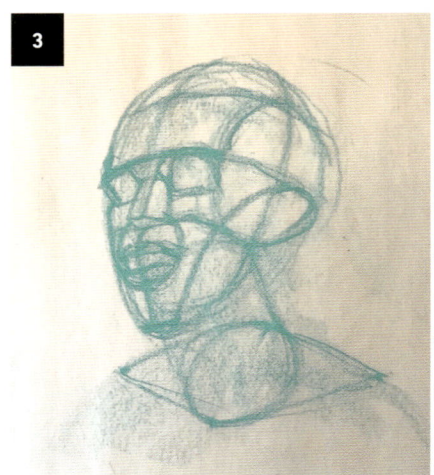

3. Sketch in the keystone (glabella), then the nose with its top, side, and bottom planes. Place the eye sockets (their base is halfway between the brows and base of the nose), draw the circular shape of the mouth, and lastly, add a swoop from the top of the ear to the side of the chin to delineate the side-plane of the face.

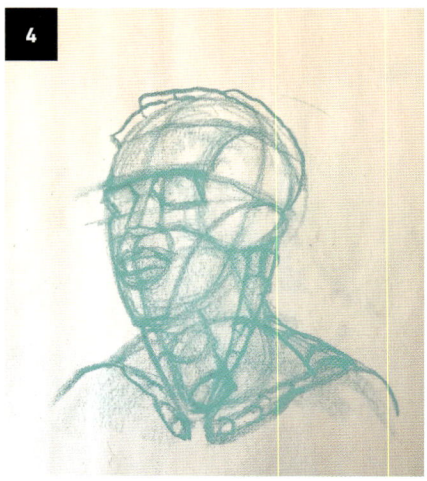

4. Again, the windpipe is a small cylindrical shape within the larger neck cylinder and is surrounded by the sternocleidomastoid muscles that connect to the clavicles. Cross-contours over the clavicle, trapezius, and windpipe show the three dimensionality of each form.

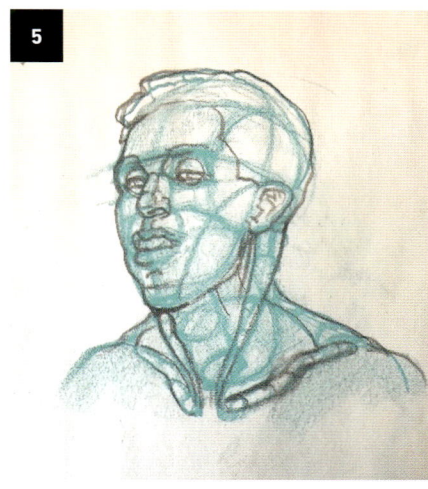

5. Finally, with a charcoal pencil, I am darkening some of the features as a way to show how they are only added on at the end.

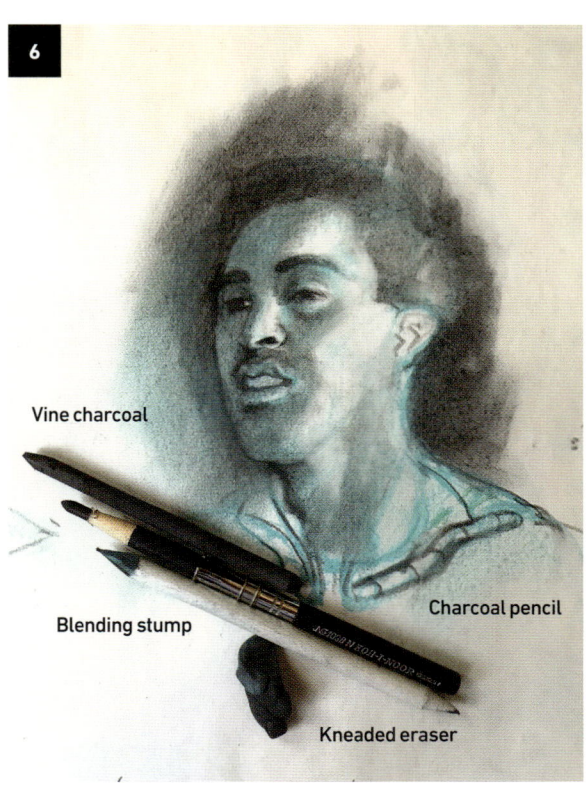

Vine charcoal

Blending stump

Charcoal pencil

Kneaded eraser

6. With the vine charcoal, charcoal pencil, blending stump, and a kneaded eraser, the drawing is softened up and refined a little. This drawing is far from complete because it is on newsprint (which doesn't allow for a lot of refinement), but it gives you the idea of the steps involved in getting to this stage of finish.

Digital Progression

A digital anatomical progression of the same steps as above. I found this to be an intriguing way to show the sequential stages of constructing the same head as above.

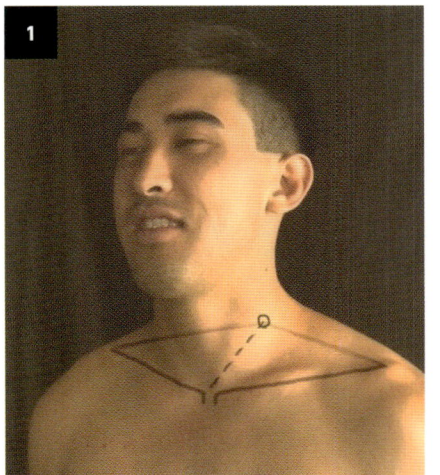

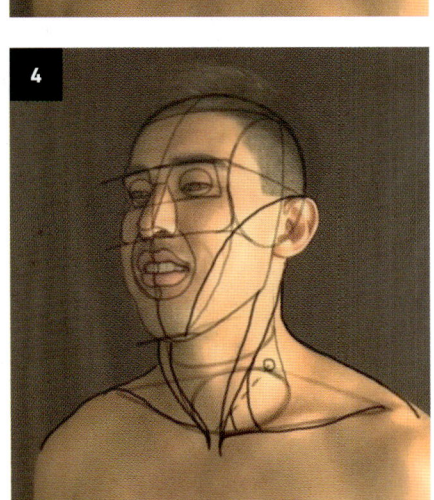

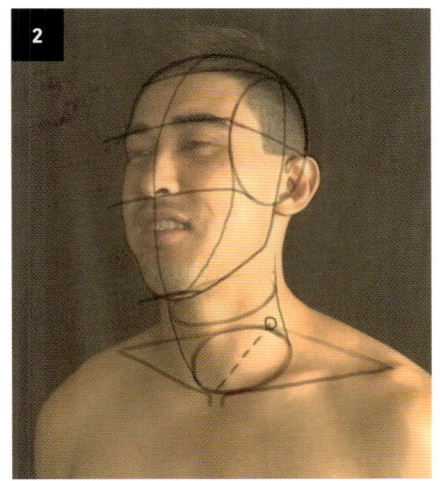

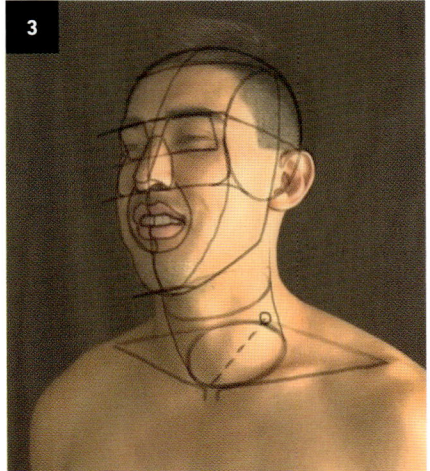

PLANES OF THE SKULL AND HEAD

So far, we've talked about planes that face up, down, or sideways. That is a good way to start a conversation about planes. But now we must also add the all-important *diagonal planes* that bridge the extremes of top and side planes in much the same way halftones in shading bridge the extremes of light and shadow in a drawing.

Another seldom mentioned topic is the teeth and their planar directions. The upper six teeth (from eye-tooth to eye-tooth, aka canines), are completely front facing (especially the two incisors). Then, the remaining upper teeth abruptly turn into a side plane. The lower six teeth also face directly forward, but the other lower teeth change their direction more slowly than those of the upper jaw. They begin with a small diagonal change and then, like the uppers, also abruptly become a side plane.

Here are breakdowns of the skull's important landmarks that affect the directions of the three major planes (with color-coding and identifying letters).

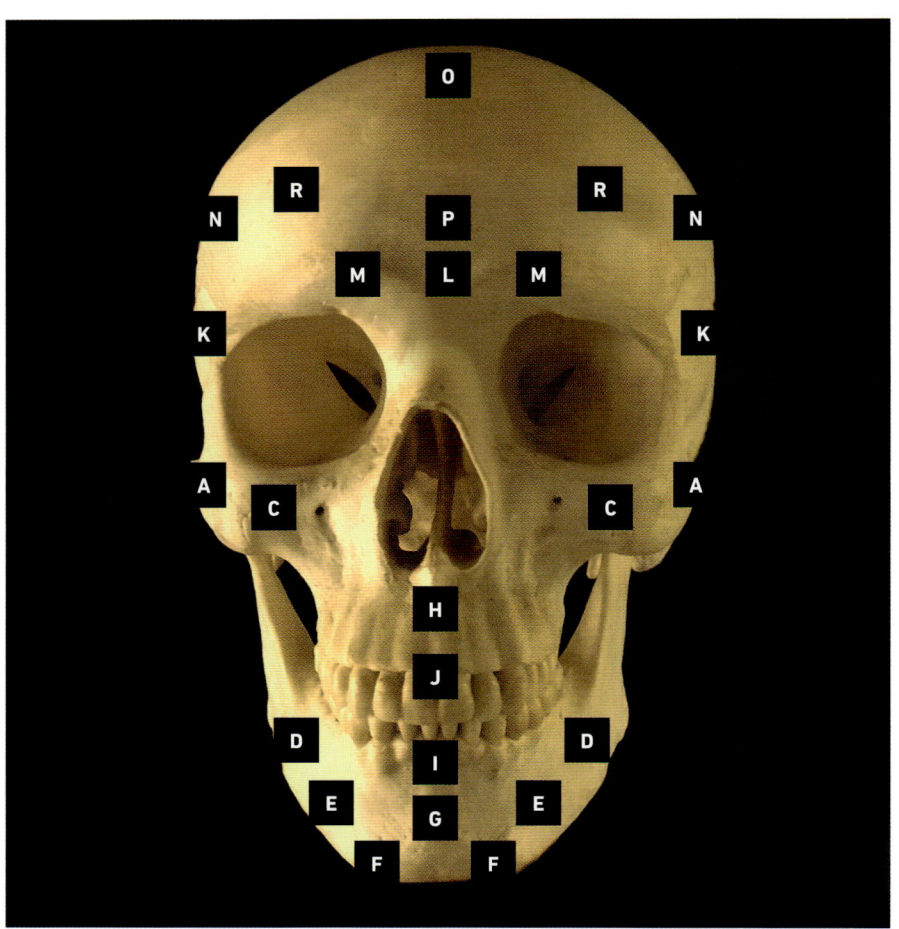

FRONT VIEW

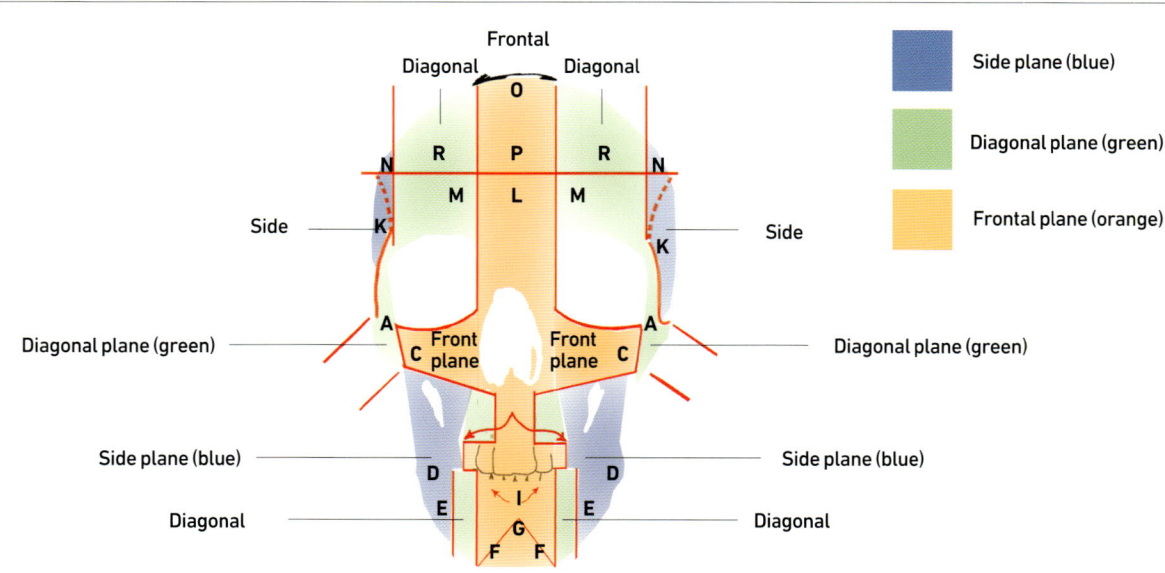

Key

A. Wide point of the *zygomatic arch* (widest part of face)

B. Back of eye socket

C. Front of *zygomatic arch*

D. Flat area where *masseter muscle* originates

E. Place on jaw where diagonal and side planes meet

F. Bottom points of chin

G. Top point of chin

H. Upper six teeth line

I. Lower six teeth line

J. Two front teeth (incisors)

K. Point on the temple where diagonal plane turns into side plane

L. Front plane of forehead

M. Point where diagonal and front plane meet

N. *Parietal eminence* (wide point of skull)

O. Peak of skull

P. Forehead crown line

Q. Diagonal planes of forehead

R. Inferior curve of *occipital part of skull*

S. Ear hole

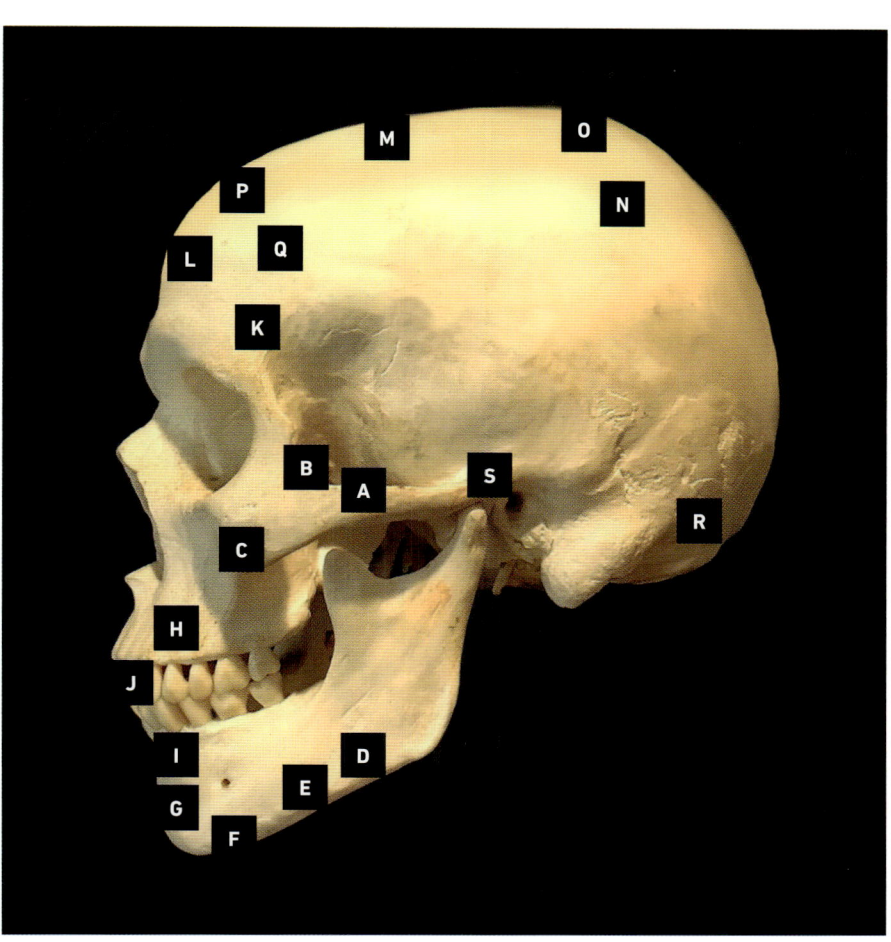

SIDE VIEW

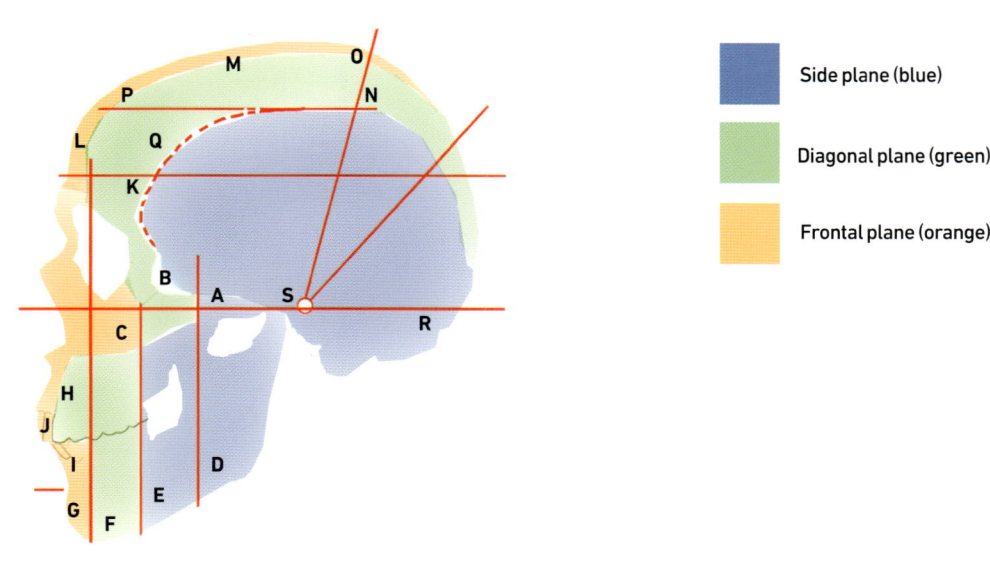

Side plane (blue)

Diagonal plane (green)

Frontal plane (orange)

THREE-QUARTER VIEW

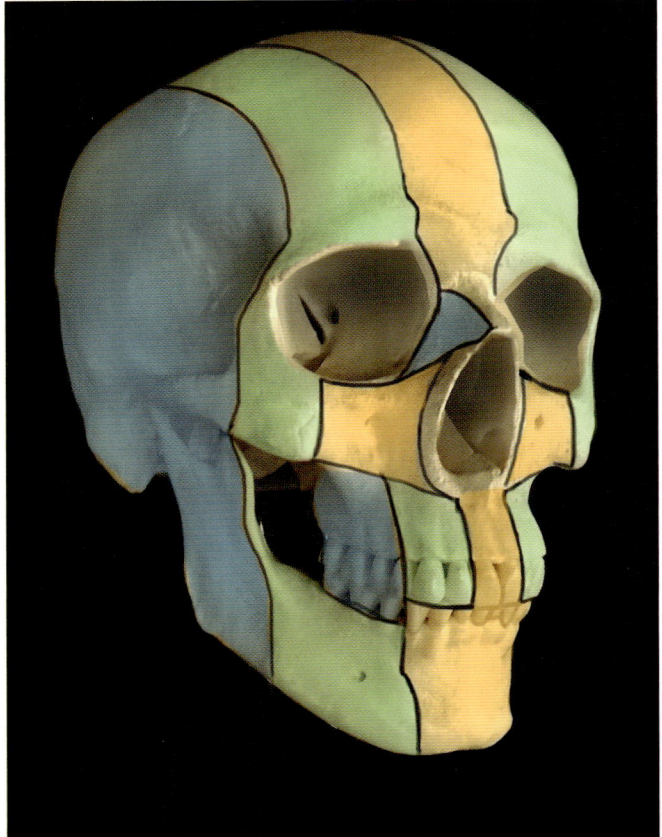

RECLINED VIEW

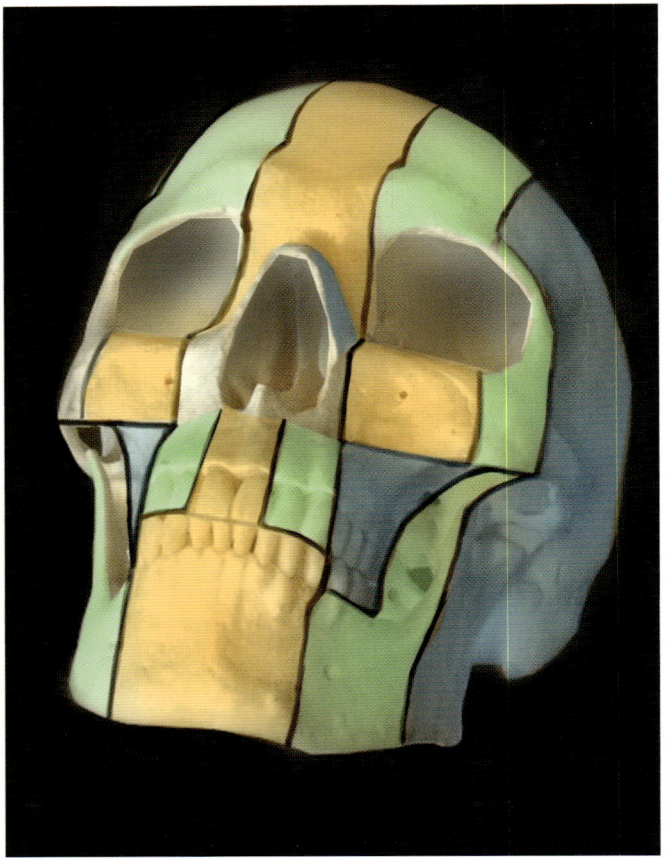

Frontal planes [orange]

Diagonal planes [green]

Side planes [blue]

PLANES IN RELATION TO A HEAD

These images show how the three planes of the skull affect the light and shadow on an actual head.

A diagram of the model with planes shown in color and a graphite drawing.

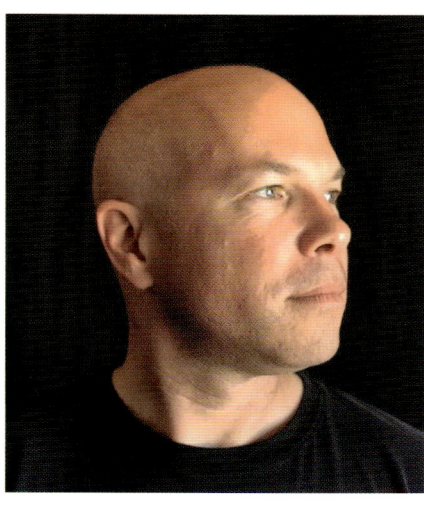

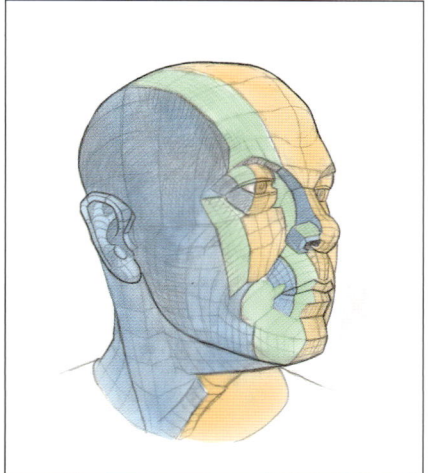

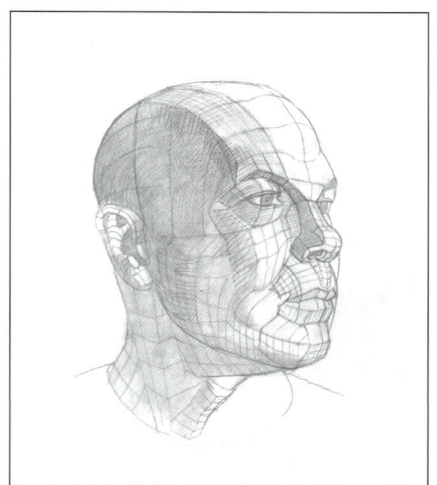

The Three Major Planes on Toned Paper

The lighting on this model's head is not very dramatic, but with squinted eyes (to see the subtleties of values differences) and knowing which planes to look for, all of the nuanced value changes can be seen and drawn. Toned paper is a great way to explore subtleties like this because the paper itself becomes the side-plane shadow, needing only a few well-placed darks (with paper showing through) to achieve a sense of roundness. Then, for the lighter diagonal and frontal facing planes, brightest and second brightest lights are added in with cross-hatching (still letting the paper tone show through) to give the head its final sense of illumination and dimension.

The model was drawn with graphite and pastel pencil on Strathmore Toned Gray paper. The pastel pencil was used for lights, a 0.5 HB mechanical pencil for dark details, and a Cretacolor Nero Black graphite pencil for darker soft tones. A stump was used for blending, and two erasers were used to darken lights, lighten shadows, and harden or soften edges.

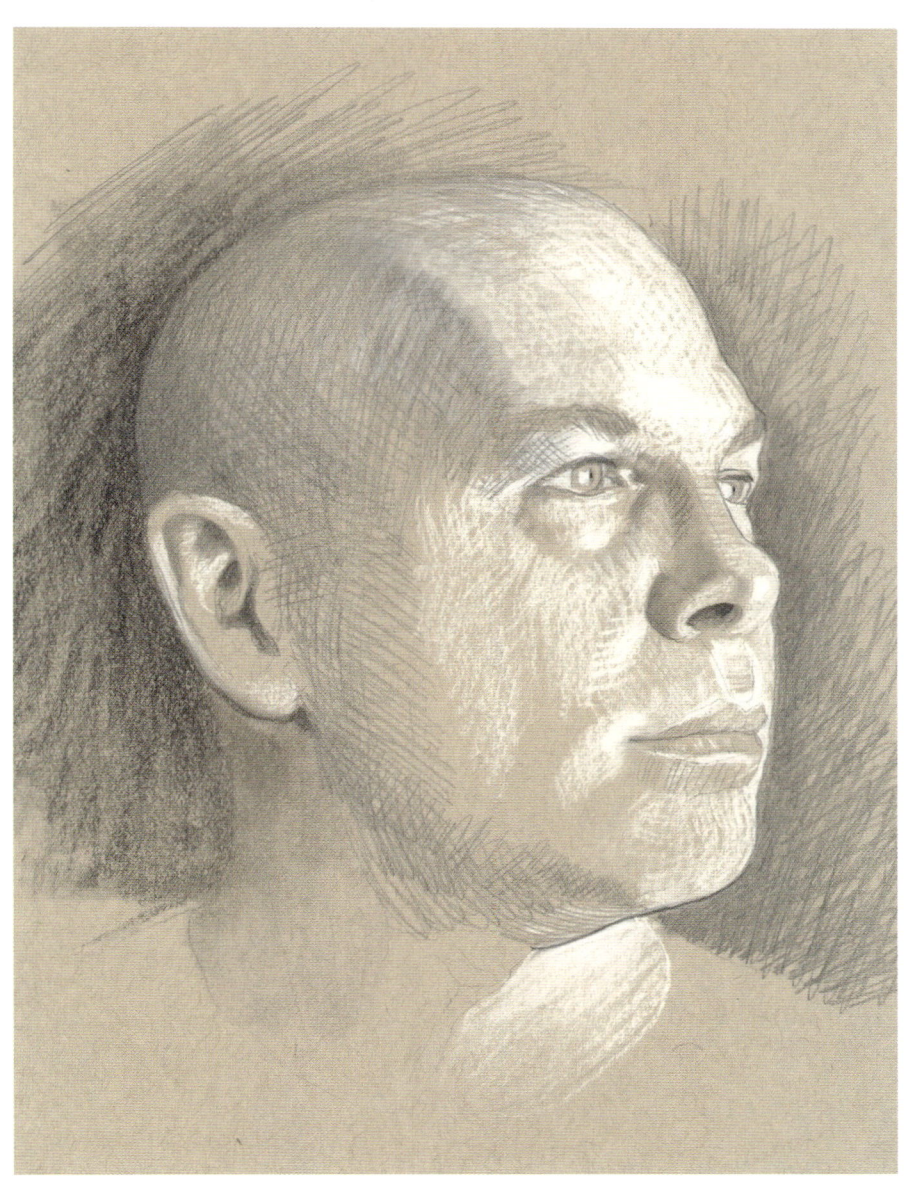

PUTTING PLANES OF THE HEAD INTO PRACTICE

JOHN ASARO'S ICONIC PLANES OF THE HEAD MANNEQUIN

Many academic instructors use plane head mannequins as models before going to live humans because it's much easier to accurately judge the values and color notes of each plane than it is to see the many variegated tones and curving forms of a real face.

One of the best tools for learning to draw and paint the human head and body was developed in 1976 by my fine artist friend, John Asaro. His company, Planes of the Head (www.planesofthehead.com), offers seven mannequin heads and two bodies designed specifically for artists to use as a precursor to live models. Below are a few examples of how I use the planes of the head in my own art.

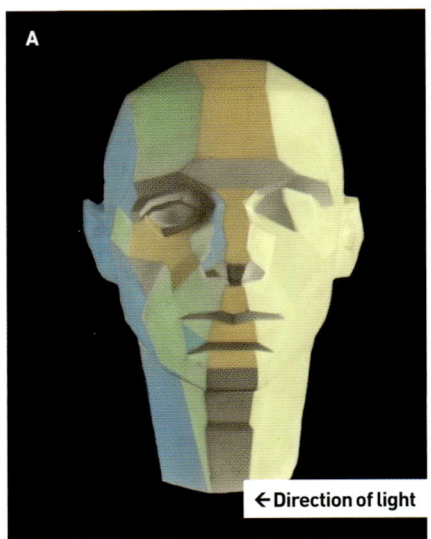

← Direction of light

(**A**) Light is coming from the mannequin's left side, so its entire right side is in shadow along with its color-coded front, diagonal, and side planes.

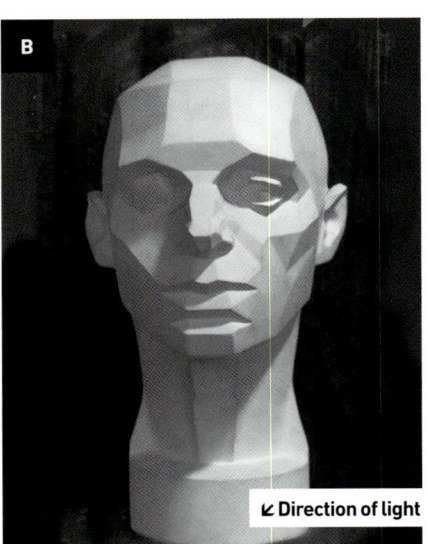

↙ Direction of light

(**B**) When light comes from the mannequin's upper left, the brightest parts of the head are the diagonal planes of the forehead, eyelids, and cheek planes.

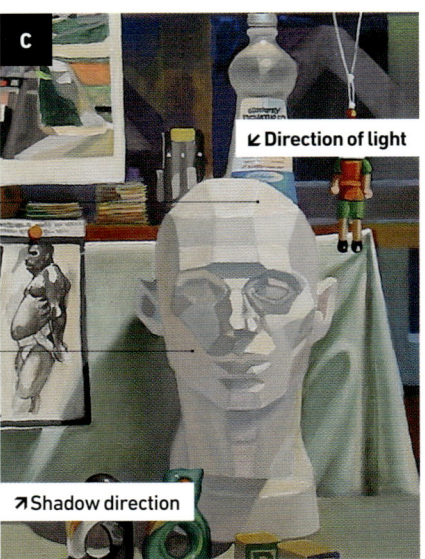

↙ Direction of light

Cool direct light from the head's upper left

Warm bounce reflected light

↗ Shadow direction

(**C**) This image is a crop from one of my still life paintings. The direct cool light first illuminates the top of the head, and then, after it has hit the ground on the opposite side, bounces back into the side plane of the mannequin as a warm reflected "bounce" light.

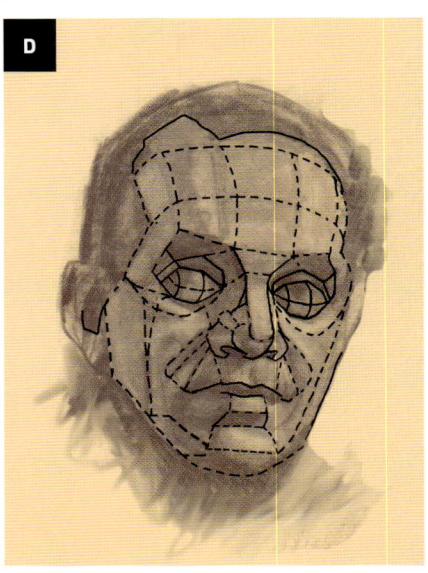

(**D**) This head shows the way I put the lessons learned from John Asaro's mannequin into practice. The dark lines indicate the way I visualize planes and contours when developing a head drawing.

LESSON: FINDING THE "FLOW LINES" OF FACIAL PLANES

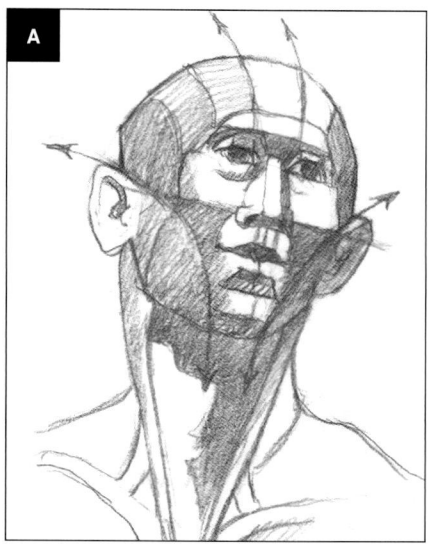

The face has certain predicable planes: frontal, three-quarter, and side portions (**A**).

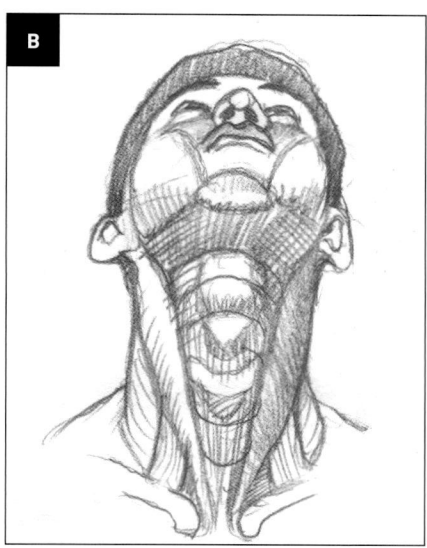

Side planes visually flow downward through the cylindrical-shaped throat and *sternocleidomastoid muscles* (**B**).

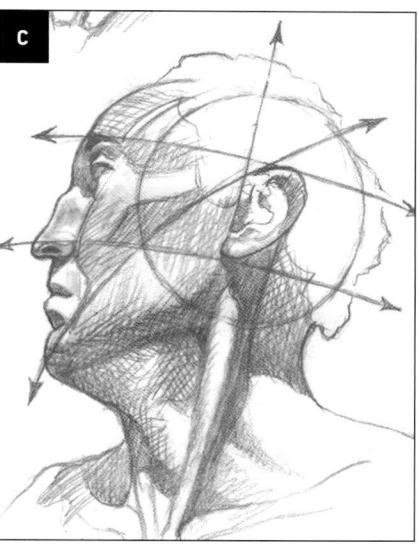

A circle drawn around the ear also becomes the *temporal line*. The *sternocleidomastoid muscle* bisects that circle at the jawline (**C**).

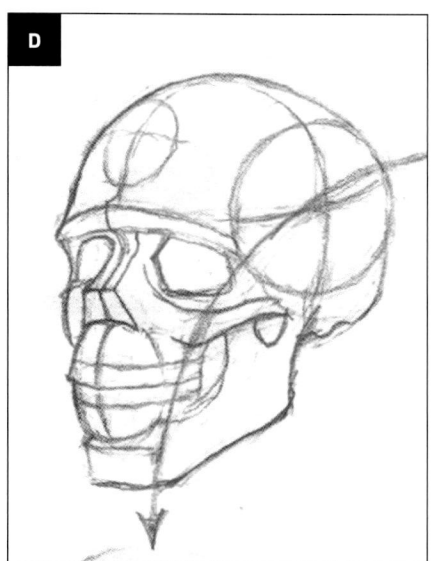

This drawing of a skull shows exactly how the circle is also the temporal-line (**D**).

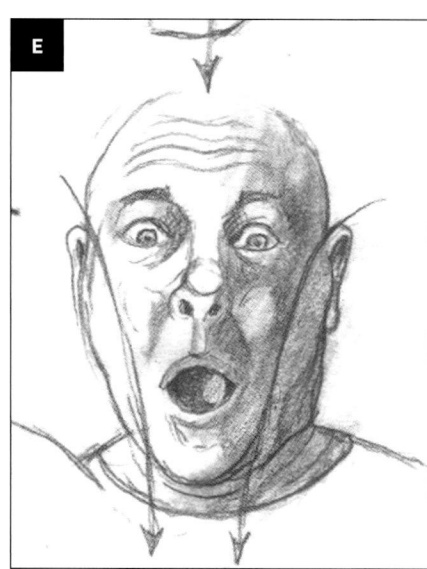

Open-mouthed surprise lengthens the entire face (**E**).

MUSCLES OF THE HEAD AND NECK

NECK MUSCLES

The neck can initially be visualized as a cylinder. The front of the neck (pit of the neck, the *manubrium*, between the *clavicles*) is lower than the back of the neck, which originates at the *spinous process* of the *seventh cervical vertebra*— C7.

Seen from the side, the back and front of the neck are not parallel; the neck is thicker at the top near the *skull* than it is at the bottom. The muscles of the neck consist of three main groups: *anterior*, *lateral*, and *posterior* muscles. Based on their positions in the neck, anatomists place neck muscles into several triangles for ease of study. In this book, since our only real concern is the visible muscles, we will not deal with the smaller anatomical sub-triangles but instead focus only on the *muscles and structures* that are always or sometimes visible within the two main triangles. The *muscles* in the *posterior triangle* are mostly responsible for extension, the *lateral muscles* for side-to-side movement, and the *anterior muscles* for pulling the head forward, swallowing, and other related functions.

The Neck: Side View
The anterior triangle of the neck

encompasses the area between the sternocleidomastoid muscle and the outline of the throat (green triangle). The following sequential images show the layering of the various neck muscles, from the deepest layers to the most superficial, with origins and insertions of each muscle colored with orange marks at attachments. For the limited purposes of this book, we will only identify the following six visible or sometimes visible structures and muscles of the *anterior triangle*.

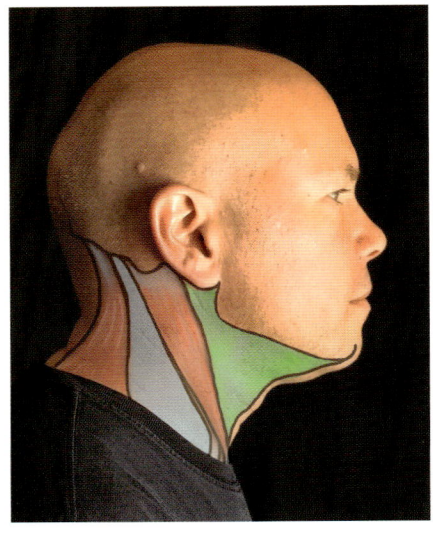

The *anterior triangle* is shown in green and the *posterior triangle* in gray.

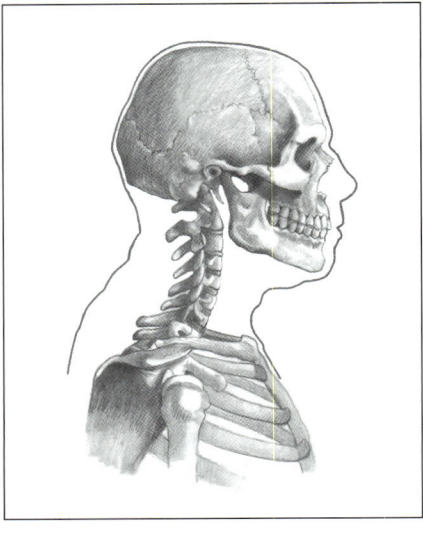

The *skull* and *vertebrae* are very well padded by the anatomical structures and muscles under the skin.

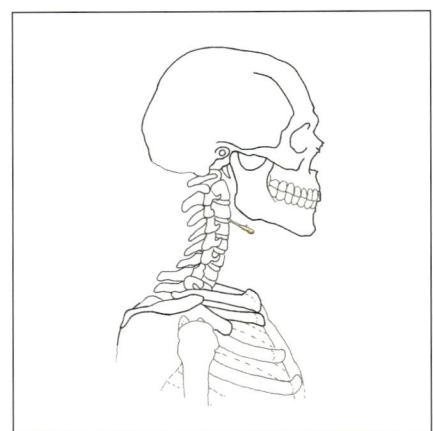

The skeleton with its hyoid bone.

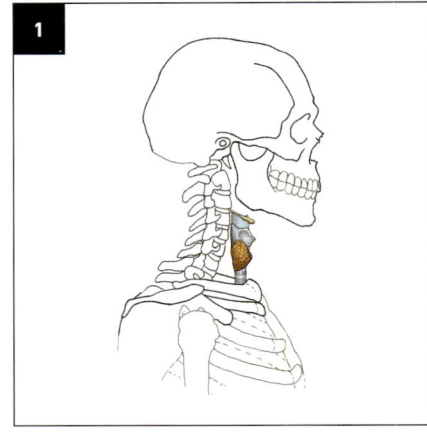

1. *Throat*

Larynx/trachea/thyroid, aka the windpipe, is a semirigid cylindrical structure connecting the mouth to the lungs. Its visible shape includes the triangular *Adam's apple*.

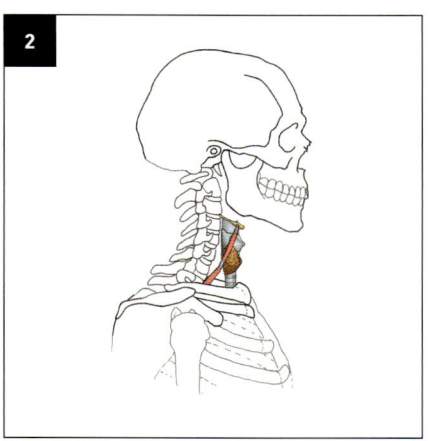

2. Omohyoid

Origin. *Superior border* of the scapula, adjacent to coracoid process.

Insertion. *Lateral sides* of the front of the *hyoid bone*.

Action. Pulls the *hyoid bone* down.

Observations. Two narrow flat bellies—a *superior* and *inferior belly*—connected end to end by a short *tendon* (occasionally seen when talking, swallowing, or turning the head).

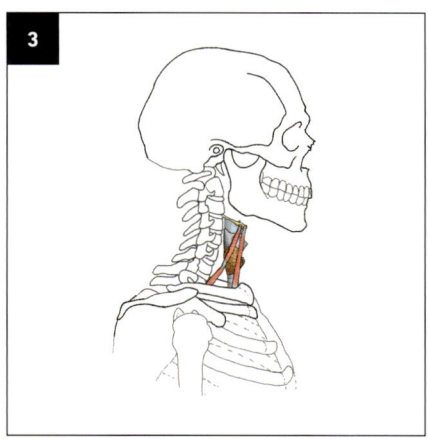

3. Sternohyoid

Origin. Lateral edge of the *manubrium*.

Insertion. *Medial part* of the hyoid bone toward the midline.

Action. Pulls the *hyoid bone* down, as in swallowing, assists in flexion of head and neck.

Observations. Two thin strap-like muscles separated by a short distance at the pit of the neck. Occasionally visible as two raised straps but more often confused with the anterior vertical ridges of the platysma (which form on the lateral side of the sternohyoid and are much firmer).

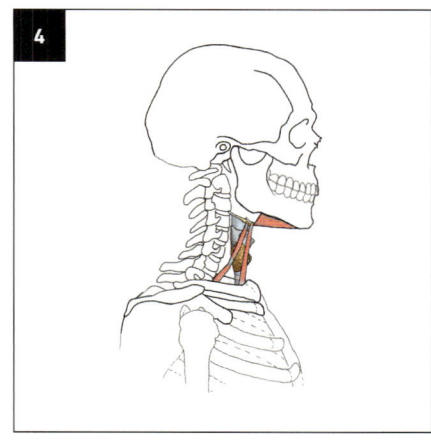

4. Mylohyoid

Origin. First three-quarters of the inner surface of the jawline.

Insertion. A tendinous medial line connected between the *hyoid bone* and inside of the jawline at the chin.

Action. Lifts the hyoid bone and the floor of the mouth when swallowing.

Observations. Flat triangular muscle that helps to create the soft form of the bottom plane of the jaw.

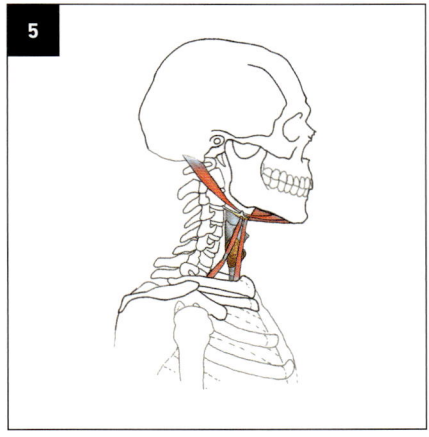

5. Digastric

Origin. *Mastoid notch* on the bottom of the *mastoid process* of the *skull*.

Insertion. Lower part of the chin near the center.

Action. Lifts the *hyoid bone* and helps to open the mouth by pulling the lower jaw down.

Observations. Has an *anterior and posterior belly* connected and tethered by a short centrally located *tendon*.

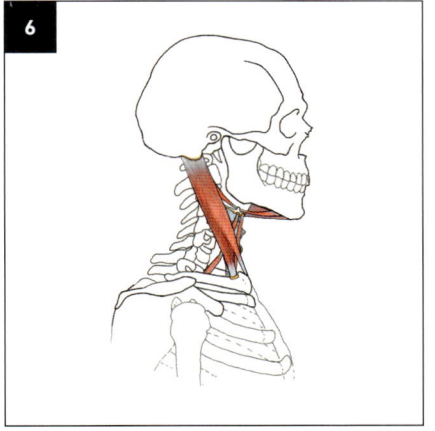

6. Sternocleidomastoid

Origin. Sternal head—upper part of manubrium. Clavicular head—upper part of the clavicles adjacent to the manubrium.

Insertion. Mastoid process and nuchal line of skull.

Action. Flexes the head and neck forward or side to side.

Observations. A wide strap-like muscle that is thickest at its center, spiraling alongside the cylindrical form of the neck.

The posterior triangle is formed between the *sternocleidomastoid muscle* and the *trapezius*. The seven muscles and tendons in this group are sometimes but not always visible.

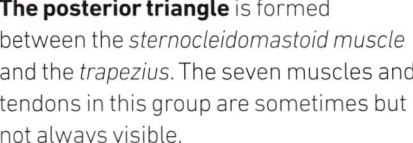

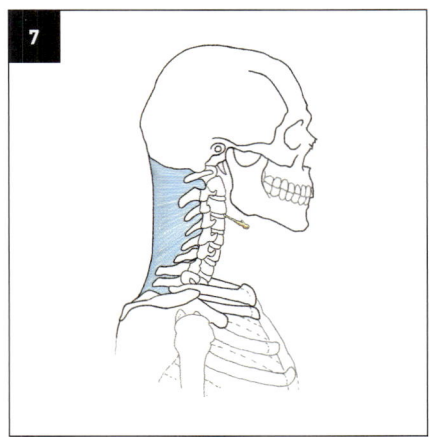

7. Nuchal Ligament

Origin. Extends from the *external occipital protuberance* to the *spinous process of C7*. It can be seen as a demarcation between the two cylinders of the upper trapezius muscle as it inserts into the neck.

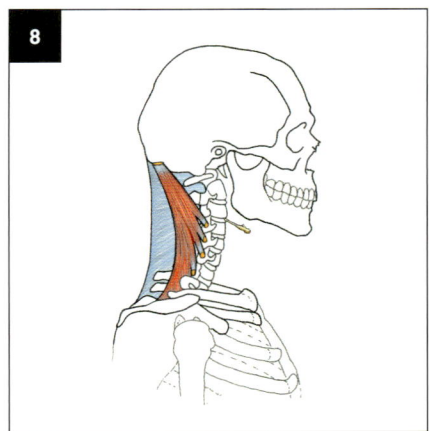

8. *Semispinalis Capitis*

Origin. Tips of *transverse processes* of the *vertebrae* from cervical C7 down to *Thoracic T6*.

Insertion. Base of the skull just *lateral* to the midline.

Action. Extends and rotates the head.

Observations. Rarely seen, usually covered by hair, it affects the shape of the *trapezius* cylinders where they attach to the skull.

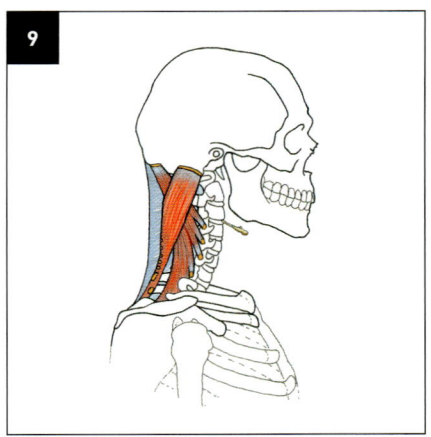

9. *Splenius Capitis*

Origin. *Posterior* edge of the *nuchal ligament* and the *spinal processes of C7 to T4*.

Insertion. Base of the skull at the *lateral* sides of the *mastoid processes*.

Action. *Extends* and *rotates* the head.

Observations. When seen at the upper part of the neck, its mass is directed toward the *mastoid process*.

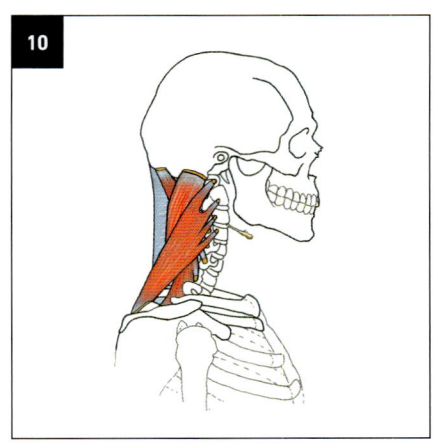

10. *Levator Scapulae*

Origin. *Transverse processes of C1 to C4*.

Insertion. Upper *vertebral margin of scapula*.

Action. Draws *scapula* up and inward.

Observations. When tensed, this is the most prominent of the neck muscles. Its mass points toward the earlobe.

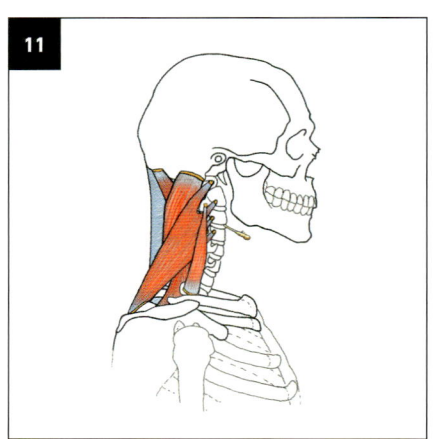

11. *Scalenus Medius*

Origin. *Transverse processes of C2 to C7*.

Insertion. Upper surface of the *first rib*.

Action. Bends the neck *laterally* and helps with *inhalation* by lifting the *first rib*.

Observations. Although there are two other *scalene muscles (posterior and anterior)*, this is the largest and most visible of the three. It is responsible for the diagonal flaring out of the base of the neck (front view).

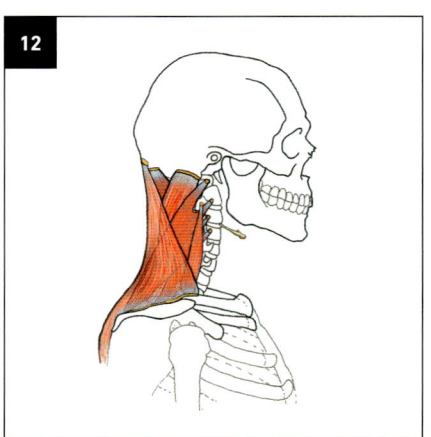

12. *Trapezius (upper descending part)*

Origin. *Occipital protuberance, nuchal ligament*, and *supraspinous ligament* down to T12.

Insertion. *Distal* end (last third) of *clavicle, acromion process*, and *spine of scapula*.

Action. *Extends* the neck.

Observations. *Upper fibers of trapezius* draw the scapula in and up; *lower fibers* draw it down. Usually, the *trapezius* is classified as a back muscle rather than a neck muscle, but it is included in this sequence because most artists consider it to be part of both.

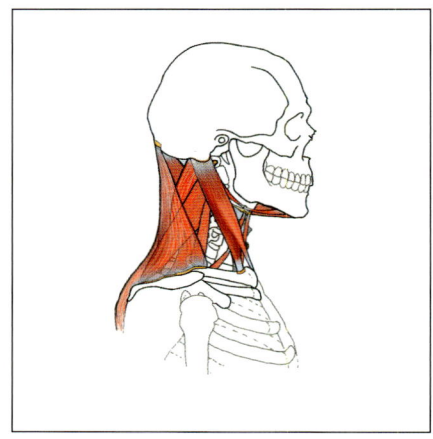

This image shows all muscles of the *anterior* and *posterior triangles* covered by the trapezius and sternocleidomastoid muscle.

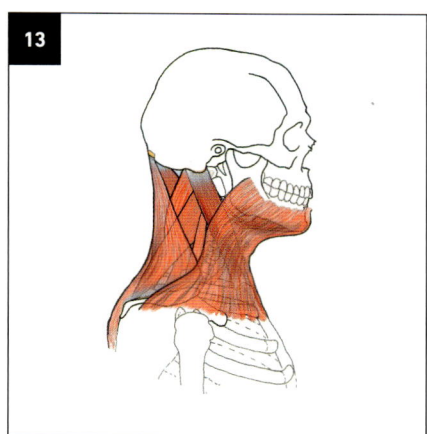

13. Platysma is the most *superficial* muscle of the neck, and once applied, covers up everything.

Origin. *Facia* and *skin* of shoulder and breast region.

Insertion. *Fascia* of face, overlying jaw and corner of the mouth.

Action. Draws the lower lip downward and outward; raises the skin of the neck from its underlying parts.

Observations. The platysma is a wide, thin muscular sheet covering most of the neck. When tensed, it pulls down the *corners of the mouth* and sometimes *parts* the lips. It is possible to activate only one side at a time or both sides together. Sometimes the *ribbed forms* of the *platysma* get confused with the *inferior belly* of the *omohyoid muscles* on the sides of the neck and the strap-like *sternohyoid* in the front of the neck.

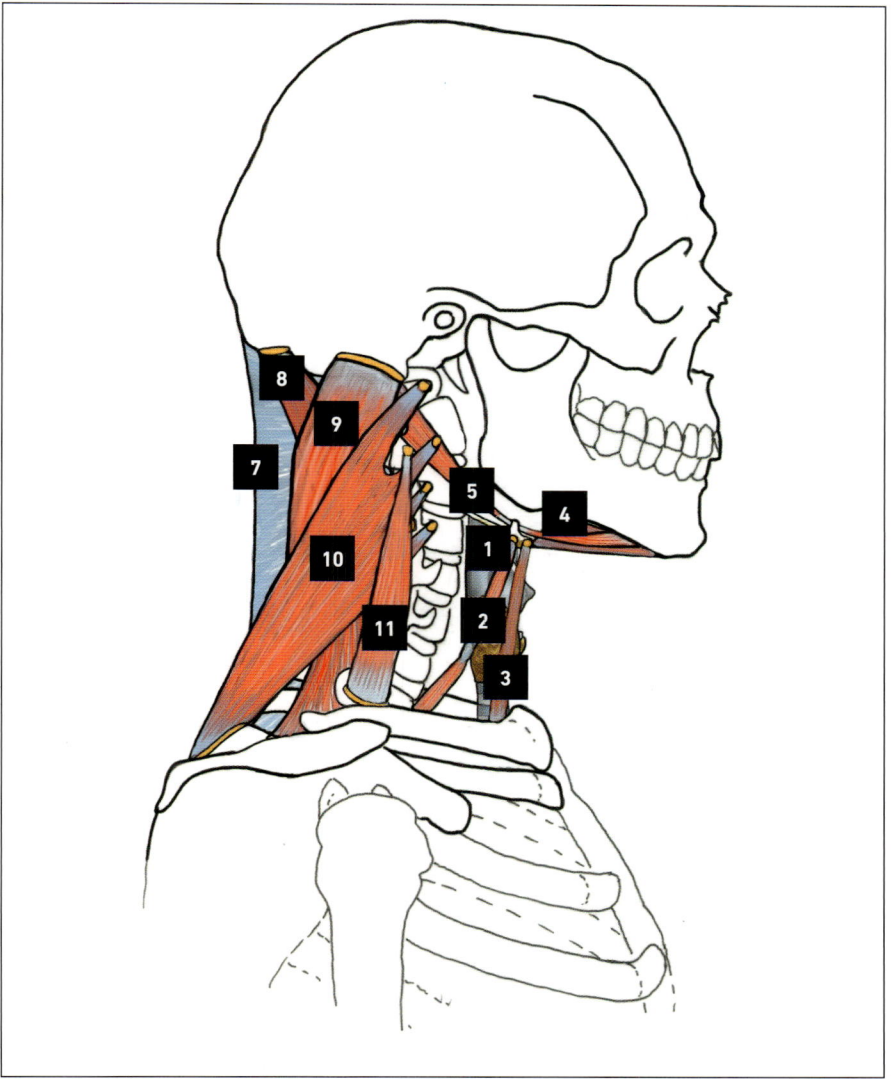

NECK MUSCLES WITH IDENTIFYING NUMBERS

THE NECK: FRONT VIEW

Frontally, the sides of the neck are parallel until they reach the base, where they flare out along with the diagonal mass of the scalene muscles. The names, origins, and actions of these muscles are the same as those already described in the side-view. The orange marks at the end of the muscles represent origins or insertion points. There are fewer neck muscles to describe in a front view than there are on the side view.

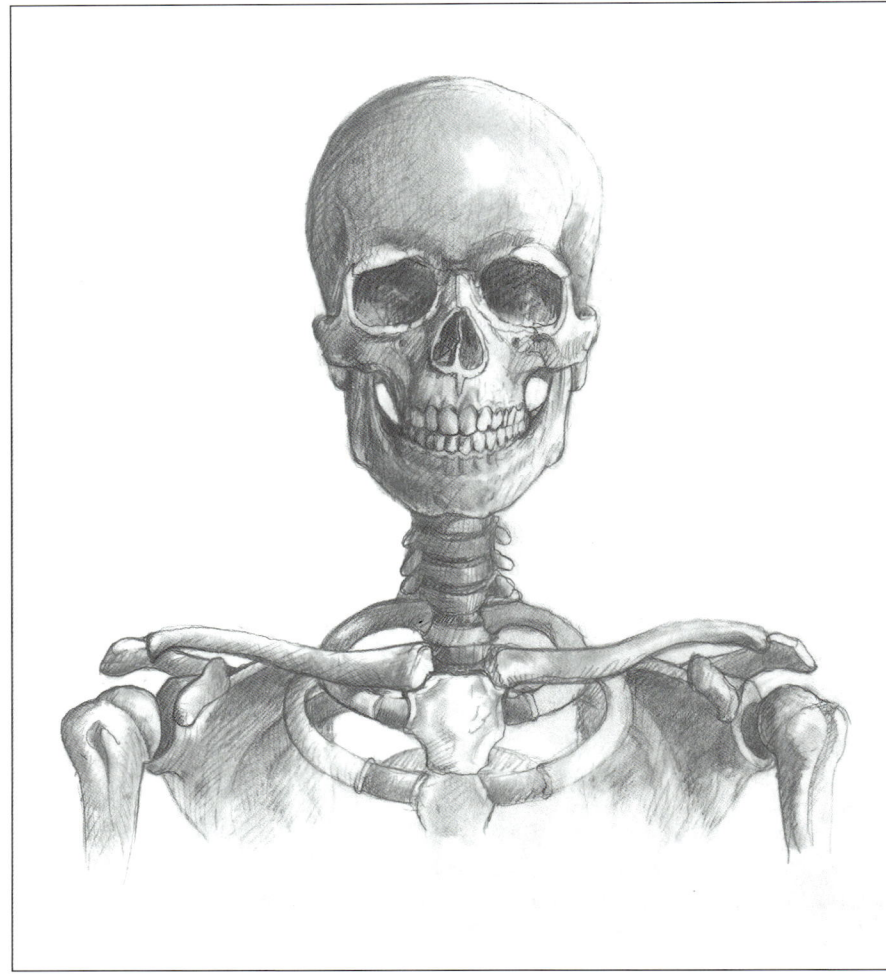

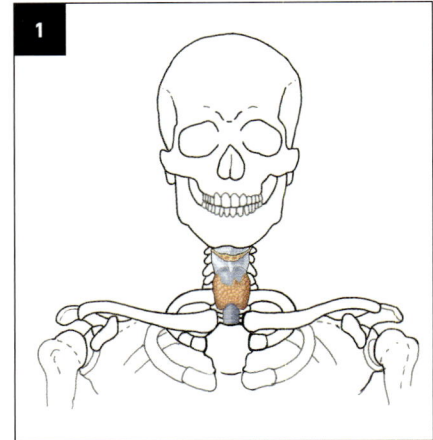

1. Skeleton with *hyoid bone* (in beige) and windpipe (*larynx, trachea*, and *Adam's apple*).

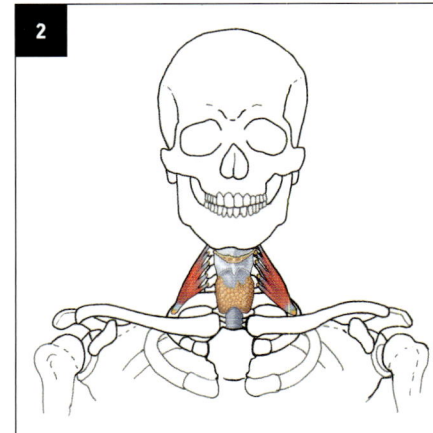

2. *Scalenus medius* (not showing *anterior* and *posterior scalenes*).

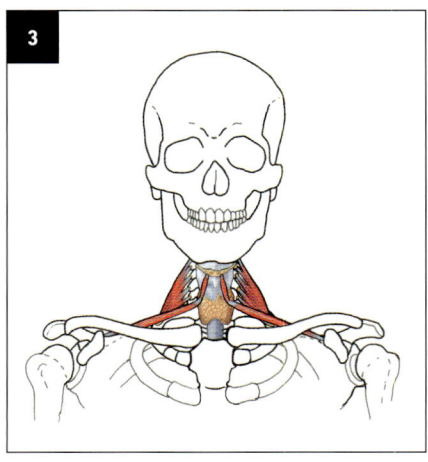

3. *Omohyoid.*

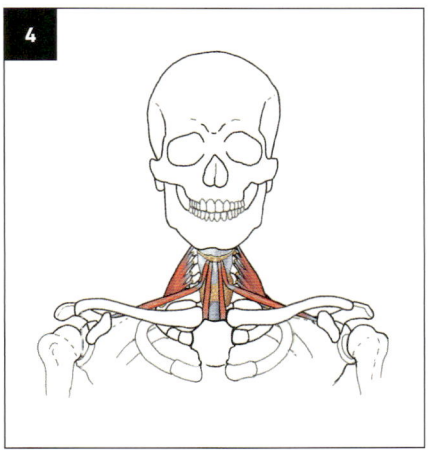

4. *Sternohyoid.*

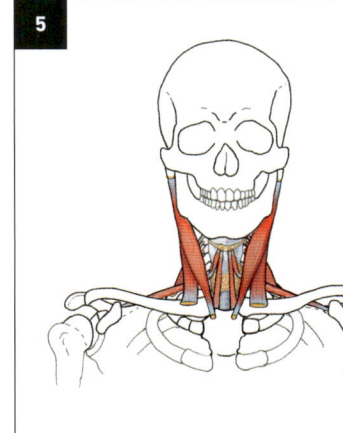

5. *Sternocleidomastoid.*

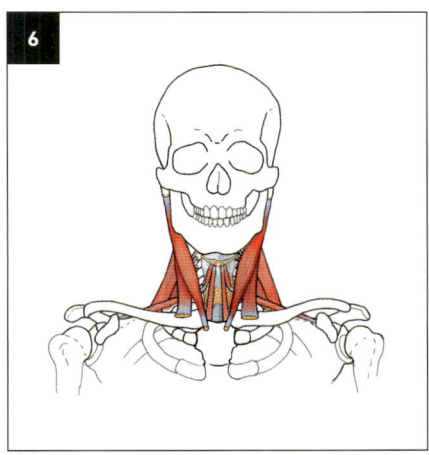

6. *Levator scapulae.*

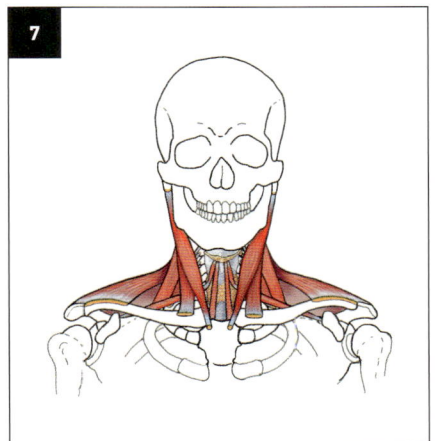

7. *Trapezius.*

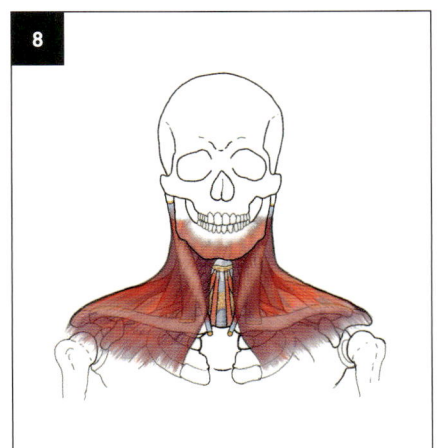

8. *Platysma.*

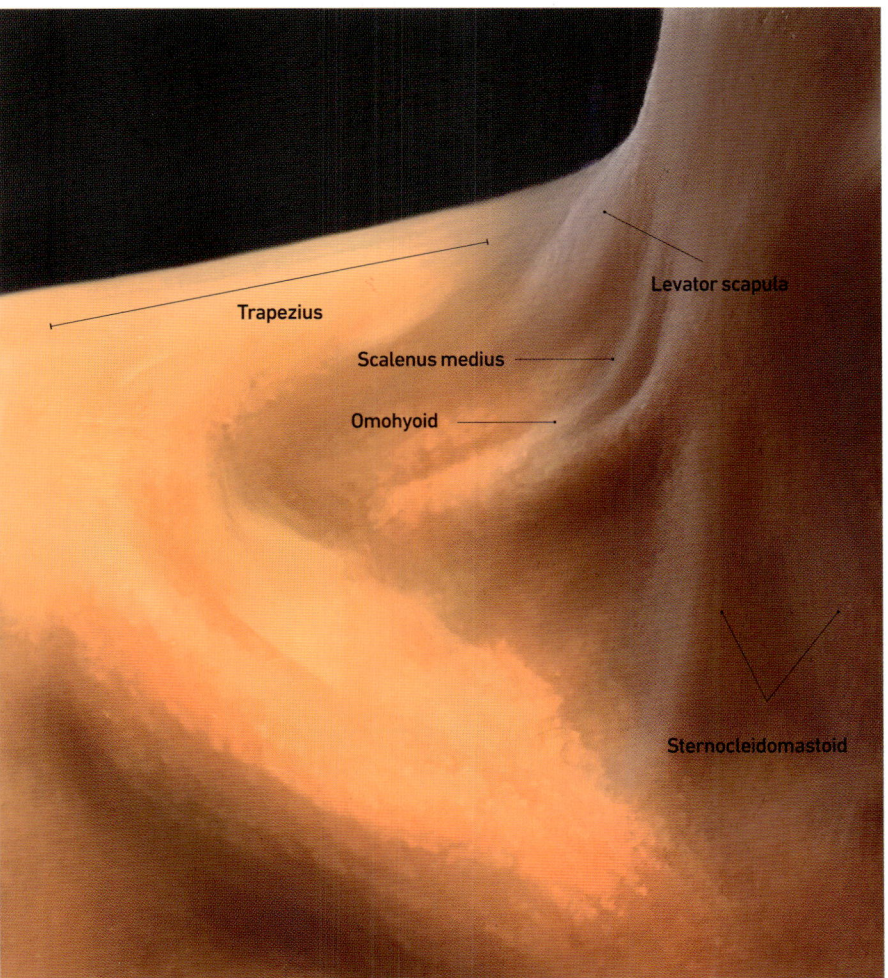

Trapezius

Levator scapula

Scalenus medius

Omohyoid

Sternocleidomastoid

A few of the neck muscles can be seen on this model.

THE NECK: BACK VIEW

From this view, it's the broad upper trapezius and sternocleidomastoid's attachments at the base of the skull and mastoid processes that are most obvious. But it is still good to know about three deeper muscles that also influence the forms and movements of the neck. The orange marks at the ends of each muscle are the same origins and insertions as those in the side view.

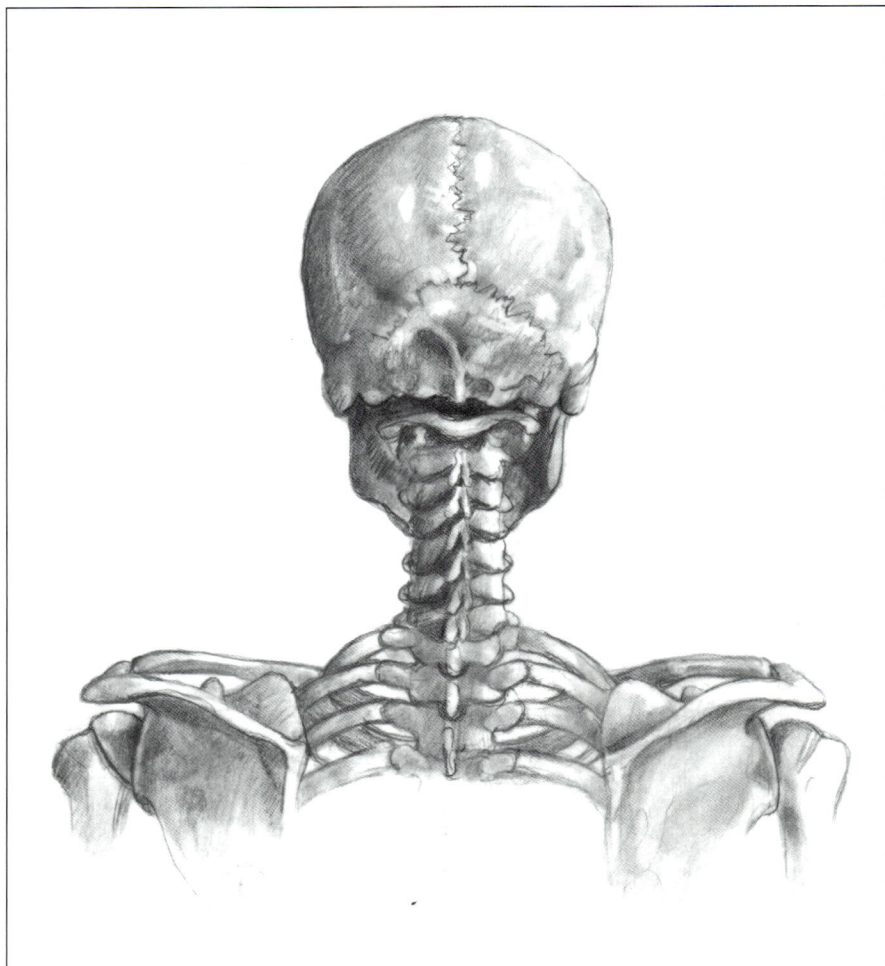

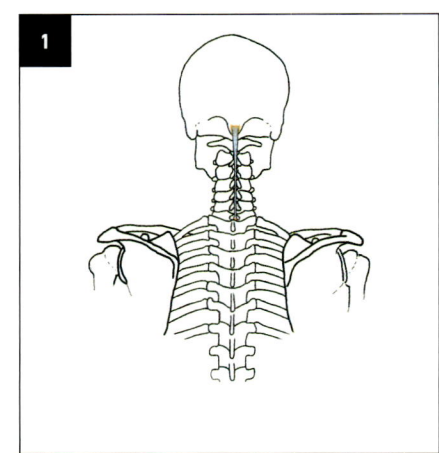

1. Nuchal ligament.

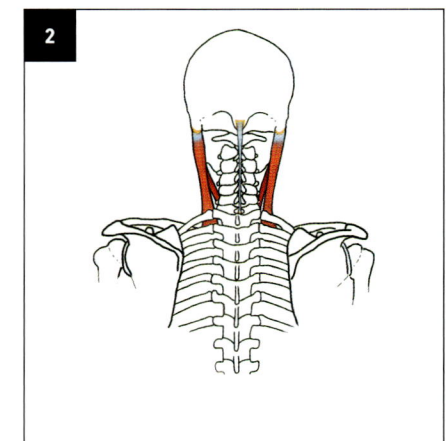

2. Sternocleidomastoid.

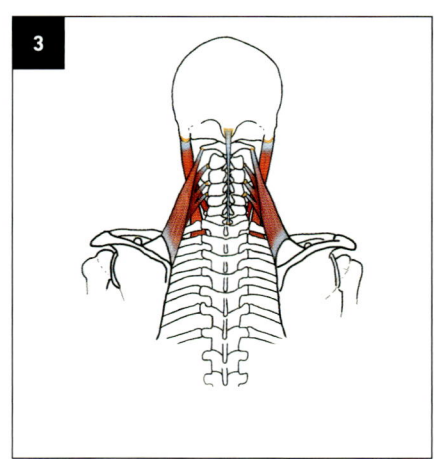

3. Levator scapulae.

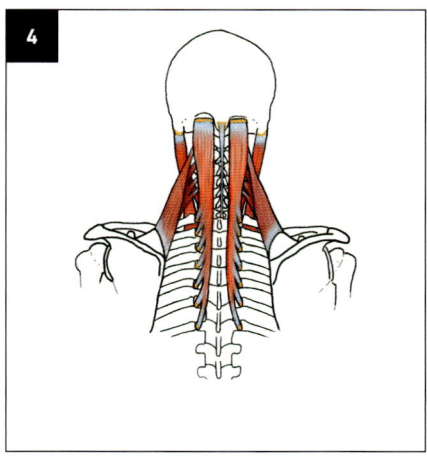

4. Semispinalis capitis.

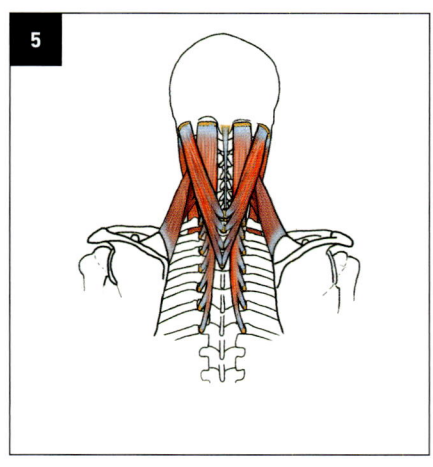

5. Splenius capitis, (directly under trapezius).

STRUCTURES AND MUSCLES OF THE THROAT

STRUCTURES OF THE THROAT

The *larynx* (voice box) consists, in part, of the *thyroid cartilage*, vocal cords, and *cricoid cartilage*. The *thyroid cartilage* is the largest cartilage of the throat and is suspended from the *hyoid bone* by a *membrane*. The *Adam's apple* is at its point. Under the *Adam's apple* is the smaller *cricoid cartilage*, visible on males as a slightly smaller bump. In females, the cricoid cartilage is often partially hidden by the roundish shape of the *thyroid* gland, which lies roughly on the same level. The *trachea* begins just below the *cricoid cartilage*.

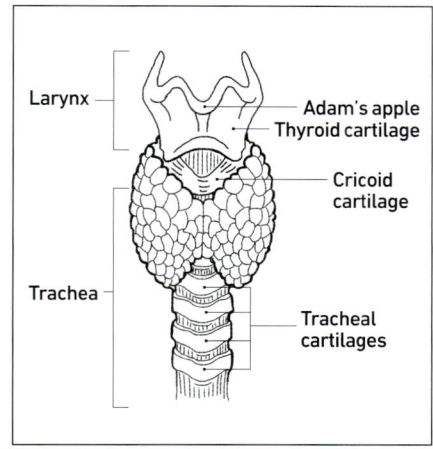

The throat consists of a *larynx, trachea, thyroid gland*, and *Adam's apple*.

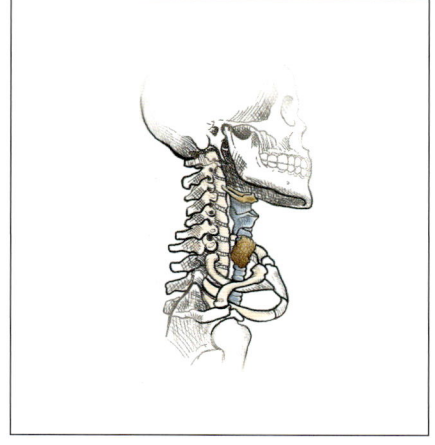

Side view of the *larynx, trachea, thyroid gland*, and *Adam's apple*.

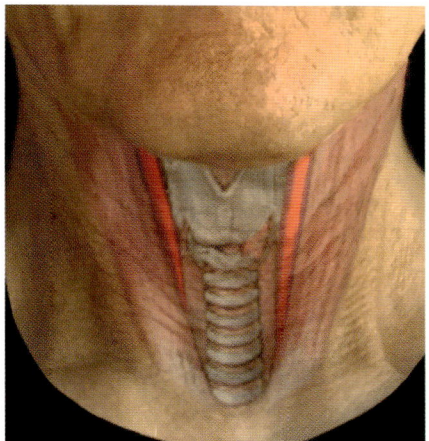

The *carotid arteries* run along either side of the windpipe and the *carotid pulse* can be felt right next to the *hyoid bone*.

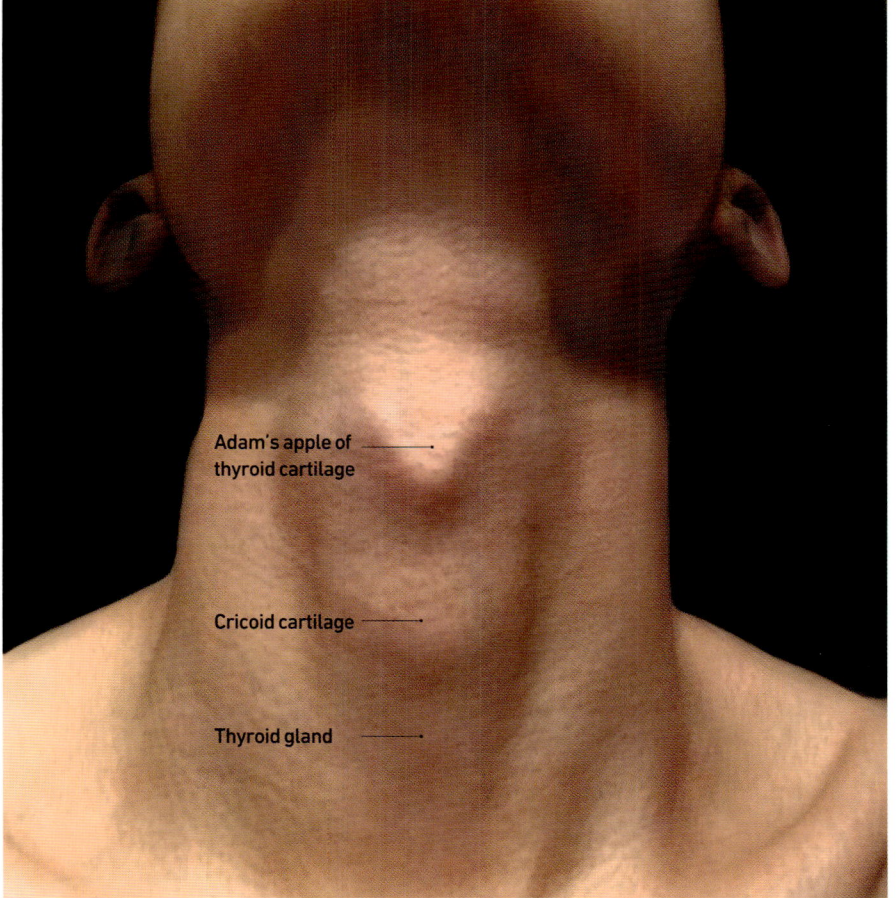

The *Adam's apple, cricoid cartilage*, and *thyroid gland* are most evident during extension.

MUSCLES OF THE THROAT

The *upper front edge of the throat cylinder* is formed by the U-shaped *hyoid bone*, which lies at the junction between the bottom plane of the jaw and the front of the neck cylinder. The cylinder is relatively wide, almost half the width of the neck, and lies between the two bellies of the *sternocleidomastoid muscles.* Also contributing to its rounded form are the strap-like *sternohyoid* and *omohyoid muscles* adjacent to the trachea.

See page 59 for a demonstration of how to construct the cylindrical neck.

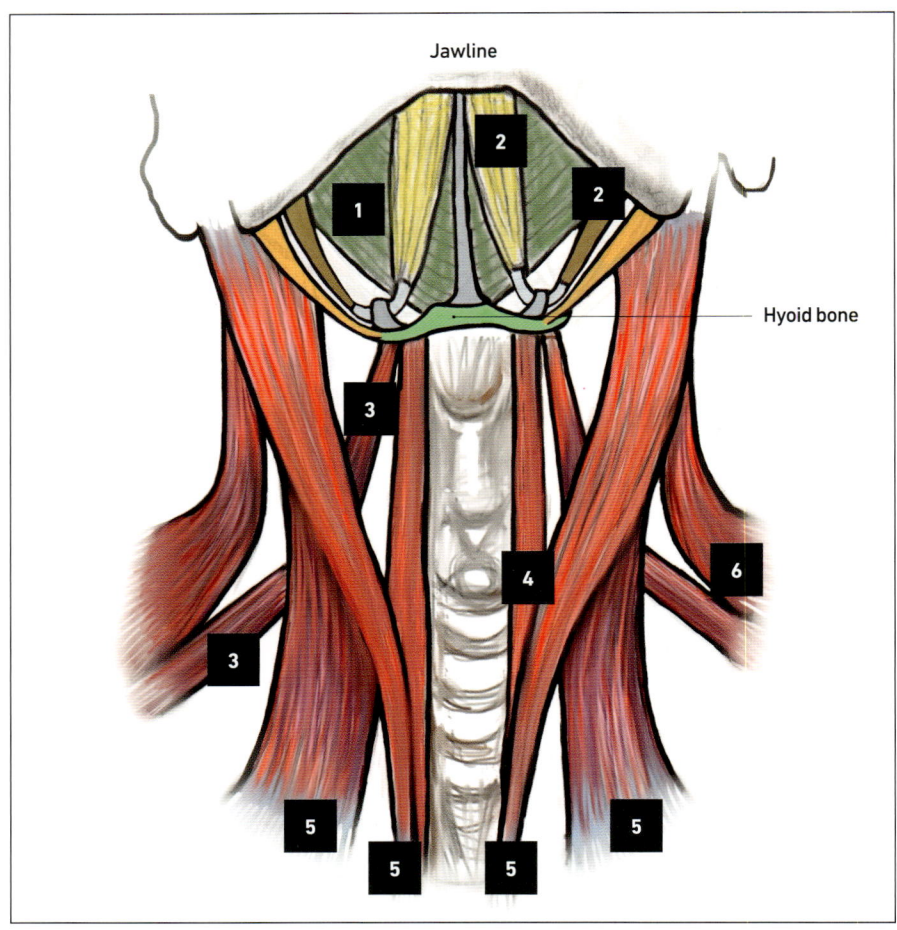

Jawline

Hyoid bone

Placement of neck muscles.

1. Mylohyoid. Lifts the floor of the mouth and the *hyoid bone* when swallowing.

2. Digastric. Lifts the *hyoid bone* and opens the mouth by pulling the front of the lower jaw down.

3. Omohyoid. Pulls the *hyoid bone* down.

4. Sternohyoid. Assists in flexion of head and neck; pulls the *hyoid* down when swallowing.

5. Sternocleidomastoid. Both acting together flex the neck forward; each creates side-to-side movement when acting alone.

6. Trapezius. Draws the head backward and rotates it.

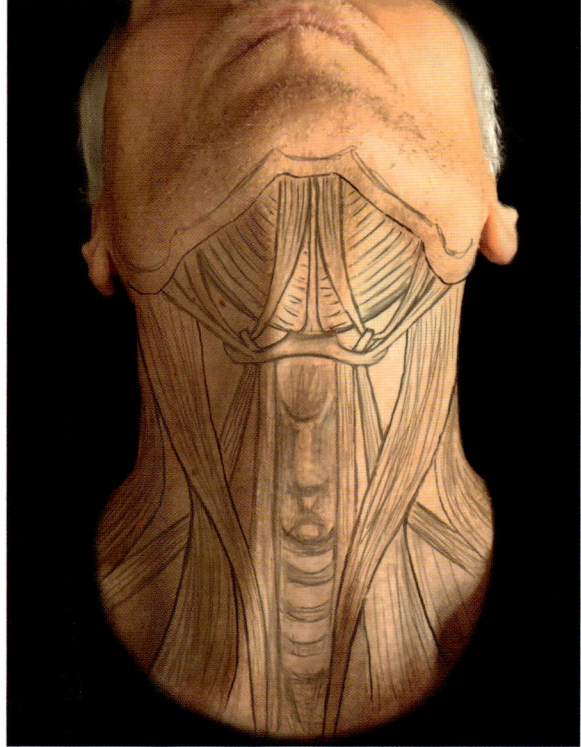

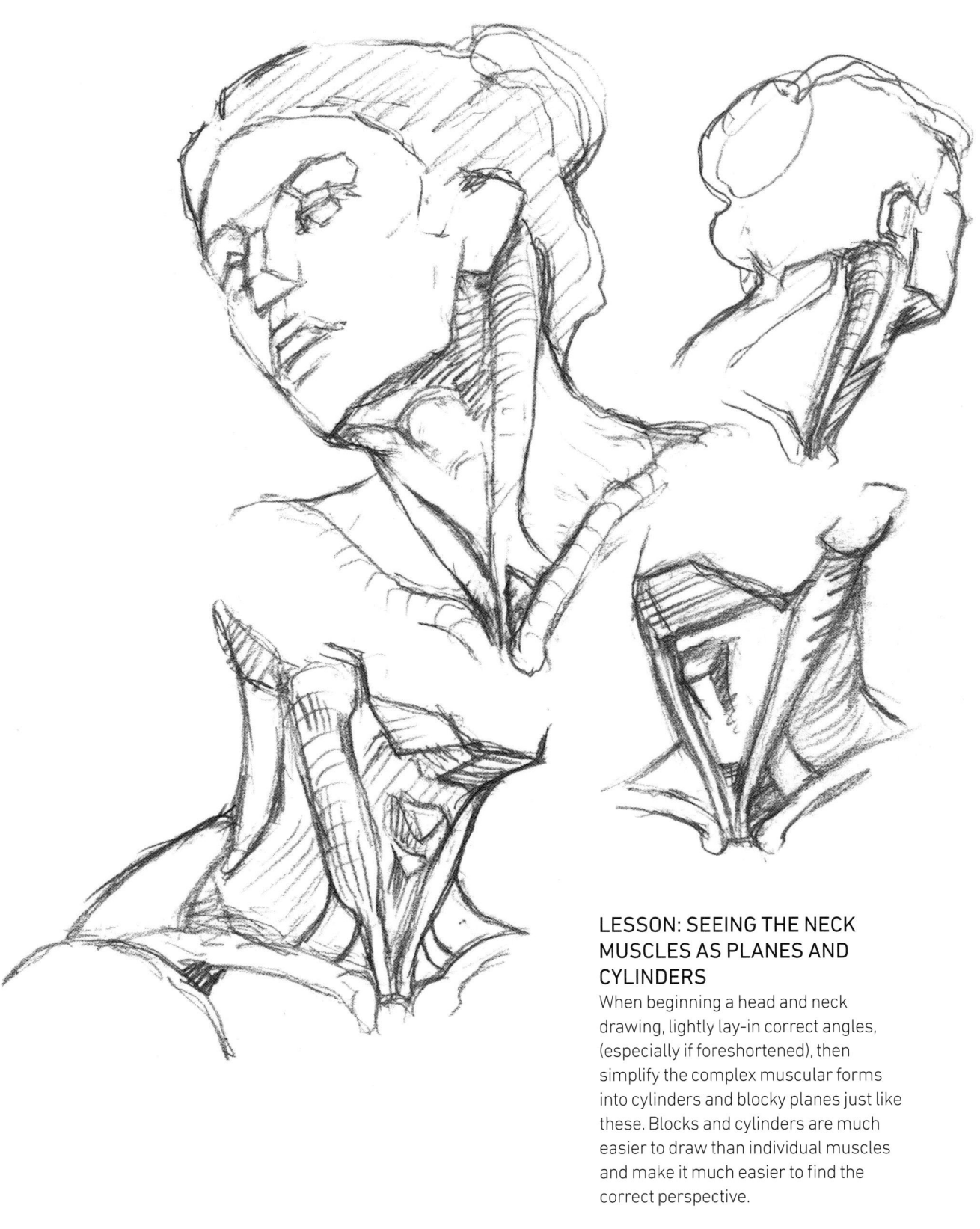

LESSON: SEEING THE NECK MUSCLES AS PLANES AND CYLINDERS

When beginning a head and neck drawing, lightly lay-in correct angles, (especially if foreshortened), then simplify the complex muscular forms into cylinders and blocky planes just like these. Blocks and cylinders are much easier to draw than individual muscles and make it much easier to find the correct perspective.

MUSCLES OF FACIAL EXPRESSION

Muscles of facial expression are not like other muscles, so it is difficult to define them in simple terms of *origin and insertion*. They do tend to arise from *bony landmarks* of the facial bones and even adjacent muscles, but then they go on to insert themselves into either another facial muscle or into fascial connective tissues beneath the skin. As for function, these muscles contract and relax to control the expressions of your face, revealing whether you are happy, sad, angry, frightened, disgusted, or surprised. This is why they are called the muscles of facial expression. We won't be covering all twenty muscles of facial expression in this section; however, the muscles we will be looking at can be divided into three groups: *the oral muscles, the nasal muscles*, and the *orbital muscles*.

THE ORAL GROUP

This is the largest group.

1. Orbicularis oris
A large muscle surrounding the mouth that purses or protrudes the lips, closes the mouth, and allows us to whistle and kiss.

2. Buccinator
The two buccinators form the muscular basis of our cheeks. When they contract, the cheeks press against our teeth preventing a buildup of food. This muscle also aids in the forceful expulsion of air from the cheeks. In Latin, *buccinator* means "trumpeter."

3. Levator labii superioris alaeque nasi.
Located on either side of the nose, assists in flaring out the nostrils.

4. Levator labii superioris
As the name suggests, this muscle elevates our upper lip, sometimes into a smirk.

5. Zygomaticus minor
One of four smiling muscles, pulls the corners of the mouth upwards and outwards.

6. Zygomaticus major
Smiling muscle number two also draws the corners of the mouth up and outward.

7. Levator anguli oris
Lifts the corners of the mouth from a slight angle, which again creates a smile.

8. Risorius. Draws the corners of the mouth upwards and outwards. In Latin, *risus* means "laughter."

9. Depressor anguli oris
This muscle opposes the levator anguli oris, pulling the corners of the mouth downwards creating a sad face.

10. Depressor labii inferioris
This muscle pulls the lower lip downwards and outwards into a pout.

11. Mentalis
Lifts and protrudes the lower lip, which wrinkles the skin of the chin into teeny dimples.

THE NASAL GROUP

12. Nasalis
This muscle is composed of a transverse and alar part. The larger transverse part (compressor nasalis) compresses the nostrils while the alar part (dilator nasalis) causes the nostrils to flare.

13. Procerus
This muscle pulls the eyebrows downward, causing wrinkles on the bridge of the nose. It is activated when there is an unpleasant odor.

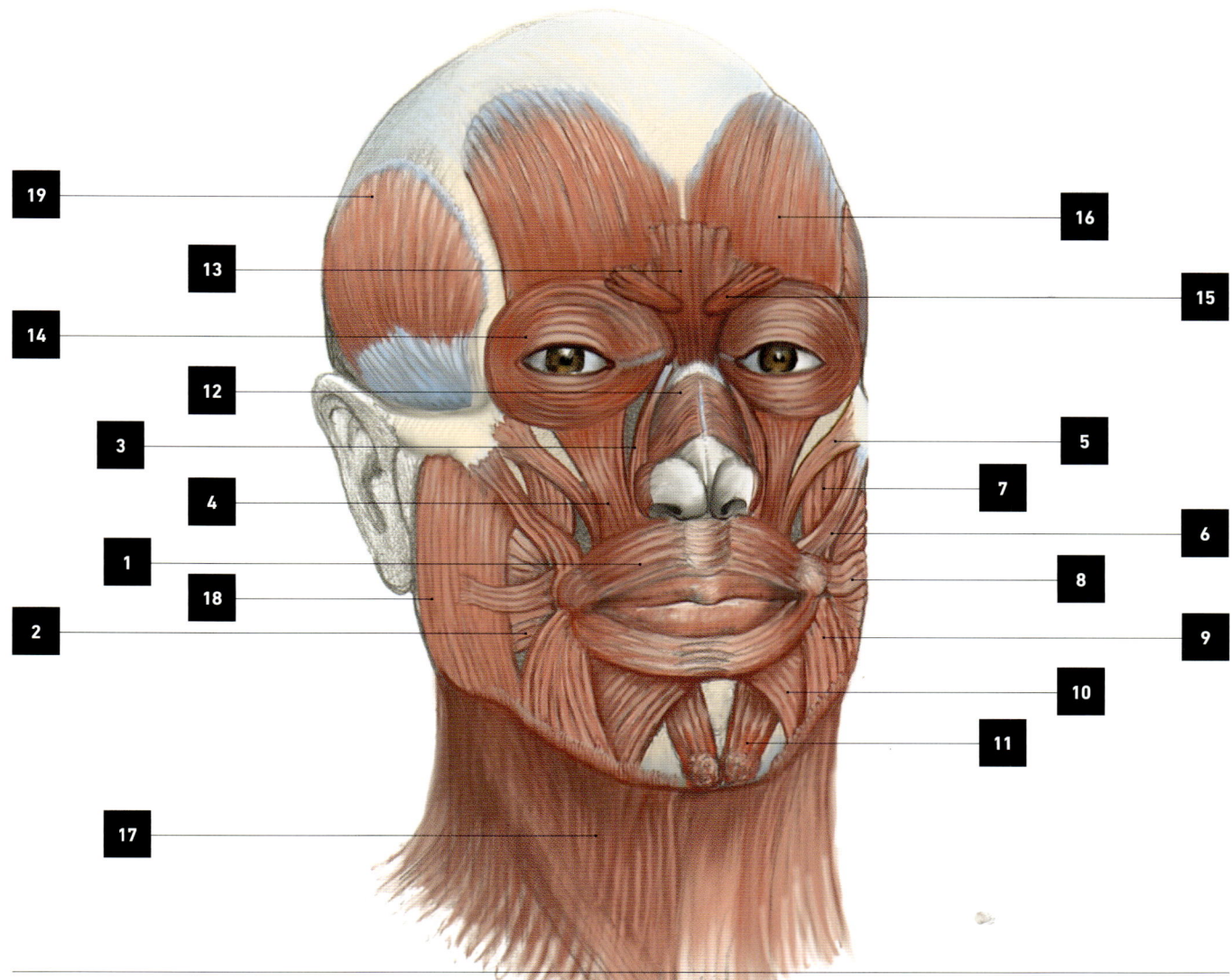

THE ORBITAL GROUP

14. Orbicularis oculi

This muscle, which surrounds the eye, consists of three parts: an orbital part, a palpebral part, and a lacrimal part. When the outer orbital part contracts, it closes the eyes, forcefully producing wrinkling of the forehead. It is also used when you wink. The palpebral part, found within the region of the eyelids, closes the eyes more gently, such as when we blink. Lastly, the lacrimal part, near the side of the nasal bone, compresses the lacrimal sac, which aids in the flow of tears.

15. Corrugator supercilii

This muscle lies deep under the eyebrows. When it contracts, it pulls the eyebrows inward and downward into a frown.

THE FOREHEAD AND OCCIPITAL REGION

16. Frontalis

From a front view, this muscle acts alone, elevating the eyebrows and wrinkling the forehead horizontally (especially when one is surprised).

16A. Occipitofrontalis

From a side view, it can be seen that the *frontalis muscle* is connected to the *occipitalis muscle* on the back of the skull via an epicranial aponeurosis; hence, these two muscle bellies have a combined name—*occipitofrontalis*. As for function, the *frontalis* elevates the eyebrows and wrinkles the forehead, while the *occipitalis* pulls the scalp backwards.

THE NECK

17. Platysma

This muscle lies in the *superficial fascia* of the neck. When it contracts, it tenses the skin of the neck. It also depresses the lower lip and draws the corners of the mouth downwards.

MUSCLES OF MASTICATION

Chewing is something we do every day without much thought. Here are two of the four *muscles of mastication*.

18. Masseter. This is the strongest muscle of mastication and is roughly rectangular in shape. It elevates the mandible so you can close your mouth to crush up food.

19. Temporalis. Arising from the temporal fossa, the temporalis descends through the gap of the zygomatic arch, forming a thick tendon. When this muscle contracts, it elevates the mandible, resulting in contact between the teeth, and it can also pull the mandible backwards in retraction.

Here is a side-view sequence that shows the two muscles of mastication better than the front view.

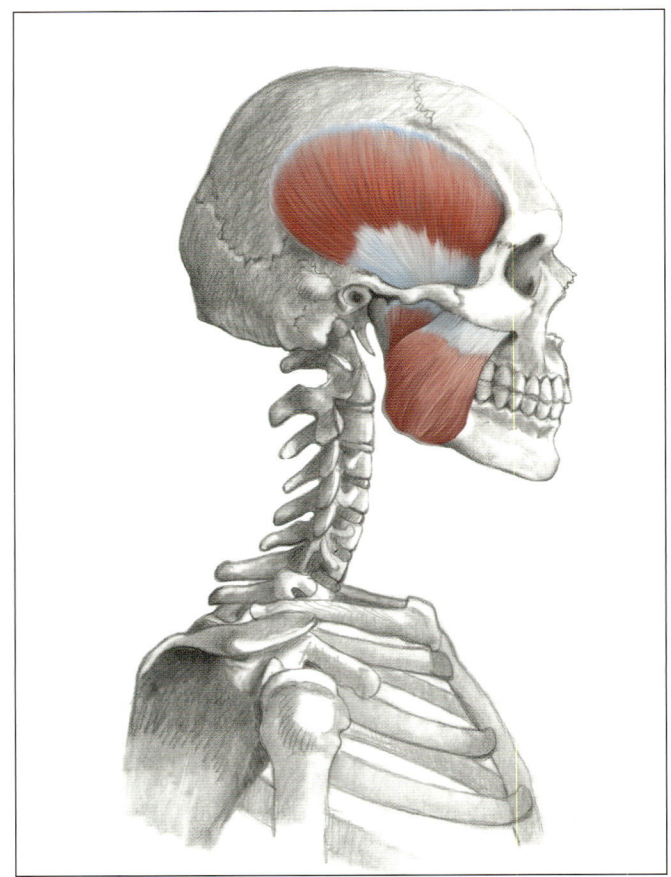

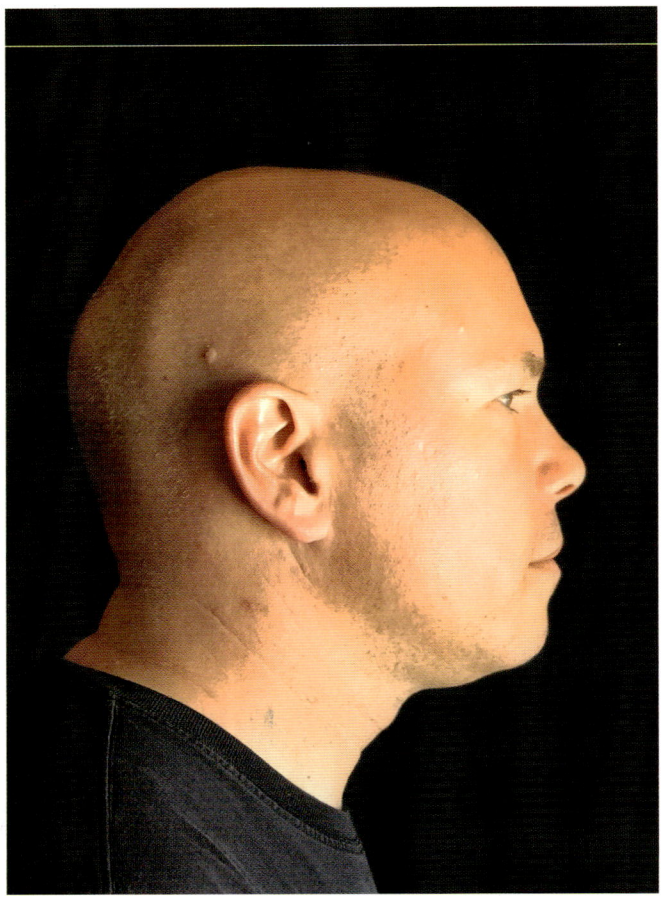

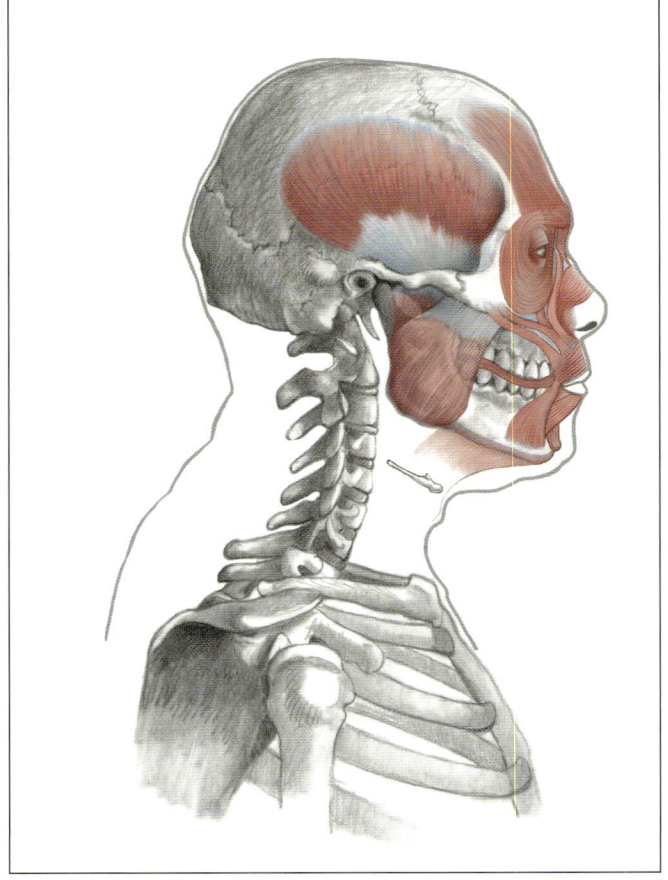

EXPRESSIONS OF EMOTION

Expressions of emotion are produced by contraction of the facial muscles. Each basic expression can have different versions, such as open or closed mouth, and each version can vary in expressive intensity. A neutral face has no muscle contraction other than normal muscle tone.

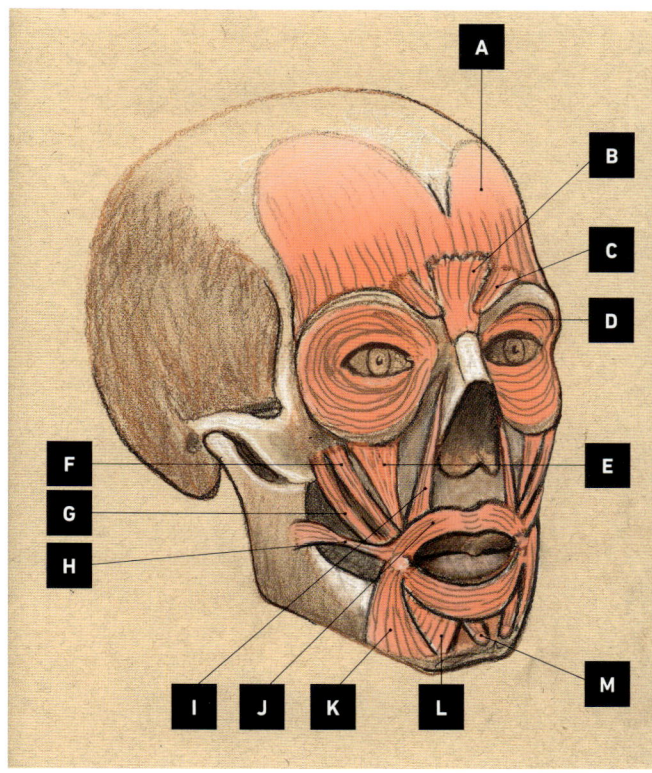

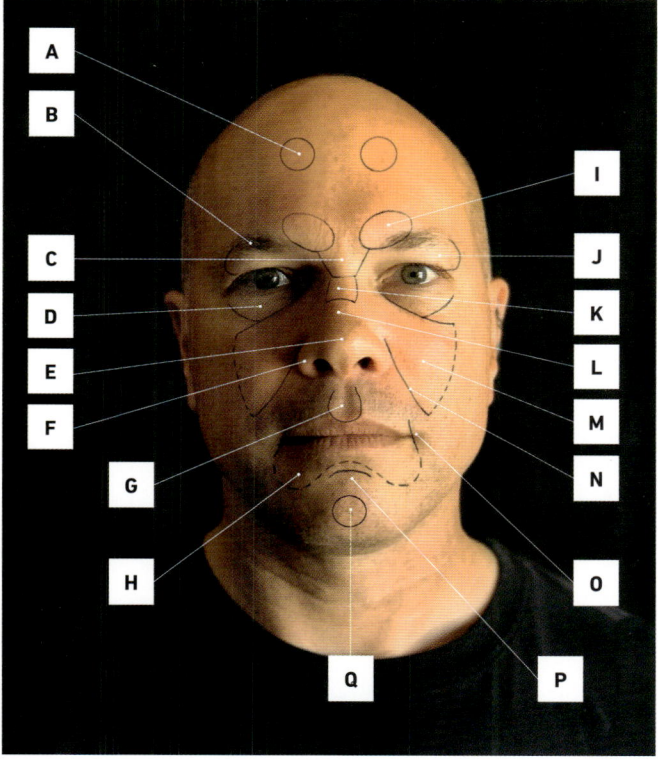

KEY: MUSCLES MOST ACTIVE IN FACIAL EXPRESSION

A. Frontalis
B. Procerus
C. Corrugator supercilii
D. Orbicularis oculi
E. Levator labii superioris
F. Zygomaticus minor
G. Zygomaticus major
H. Risorius

I. Levator labii superioris alaeque nasi
J. Orbicularis oris
K. Depressor anguli oris
L. Depressor labii inferioris
M. Mentalis

KEY: SUPERFICIAL FACIAL LANDMARKS

A. Frontal eminence
B. Eyebrow
C. Glabella
D. Tear bag
E. Alar cartilage
F. Nose wing
G. Philtrum
H. Pillars of mouth
I. Brow ridge
J. Eye cover fold

K. Nasal bone
L. Septal cartilage (bridge of the nose)
M. Infraorbital triangle
N. Nasolabial furrow
O. Mouth angle furrow
P. Mentolabial furrow
Q. Mentolabial protuberance

FACIAL EXPRESSIONS

The six basic emotions are *happiness, sadness, surprise, fear, anger*, and *disgust*.

Many more muscles than those shown here work together to create facial expressions, but for simplicity's sake, only the most important actors are described below.

The drawings and photos highlight which main muscles form *expressions of emotion*. In the drawings, the **bold letters** identify the names of the muscles; the **bold numbers** describe how each muscle affects the appearance of facial features and facial skin.

HAPPINESS

Happiness ranges from a slight smile to a broad open mouth grin or laughter. The forehead remains relaxed during an expression of happiness (**1**). No frontalis activity takes place.

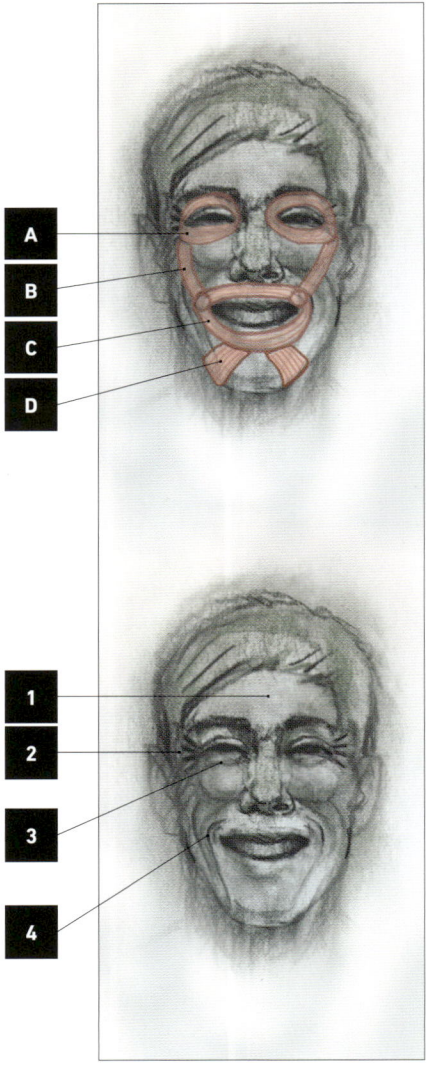

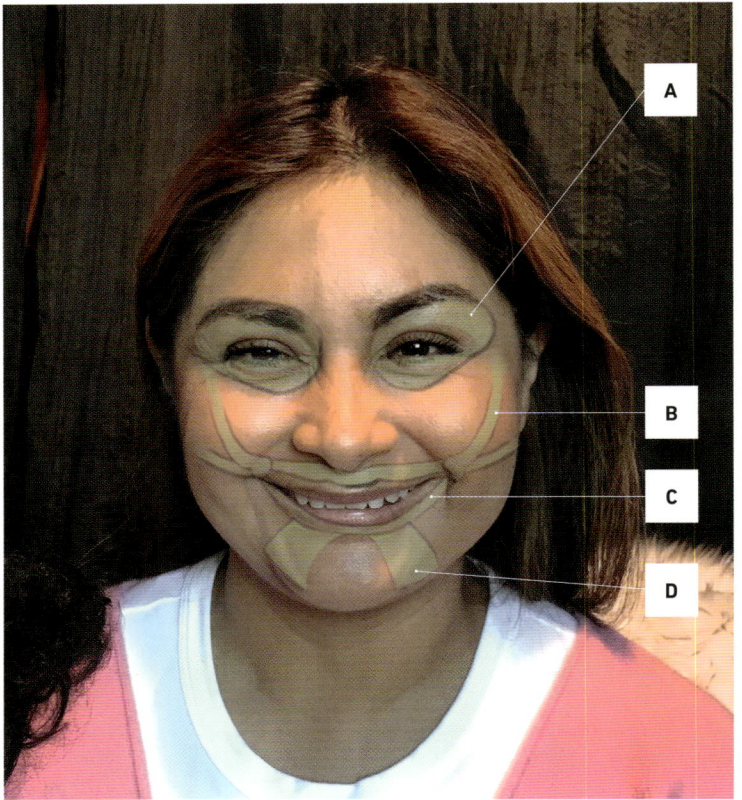

(**A**) *Orbicularis oculi – orbital portion.* When contracted, "crow's feet" radiate from the corner of the eye, and cheeks push upwards to create "laughing eyes" (**2 & 3**).

(**B**) *Zygomaticus major.* The angle of the mouth is pulled outward, upward, and backward. This movement deepens the crease of the *nasolabial furrow* (**4**).

(**C**) *Orbicularis oris. Lips* remain relaxed while being pulled from above and below.

(**D**) *Depressor labii inferioris.* Depresses (pulls down) the lower lip from below.

SADNESS

Despair, depression, dejection, grief, sorrow, hopelessness, low spirits, sulkiness, loss, disappointment.

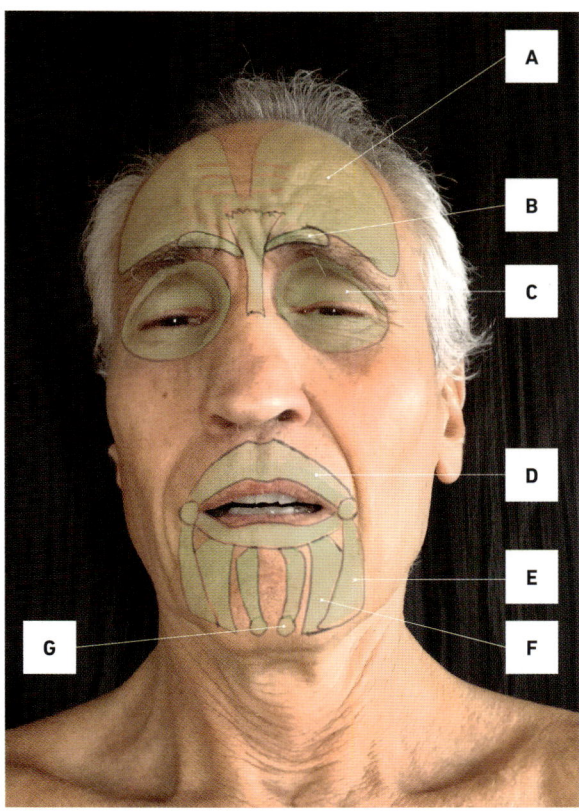

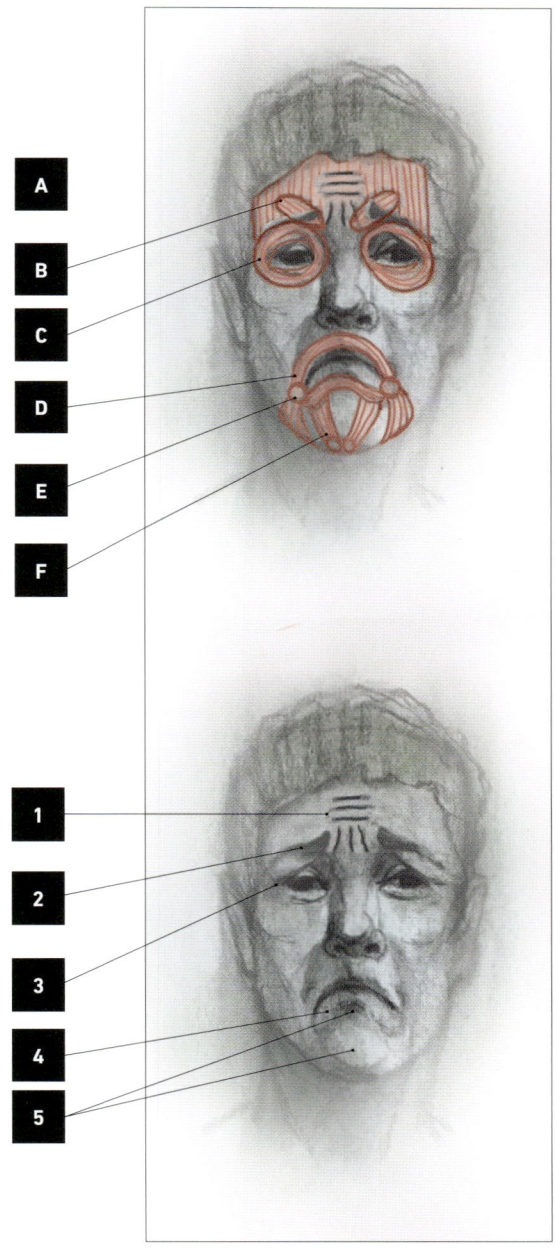

(A) *Frontalis*. Creates short slightly curved wrinkles on the forehead (**1**).

(B) *Corrugator supercilii*. Elevates inner corner of eyebrows and creates vertical wrinkles over glabella.

(C) *Orbicularis oculi*. Lateral parts of eyebrow and eye cover folds are slanted downward (**2** & **3**).

(D) *Orbicularis oris*. Compresses and protrudes the lips.

(E) *Depressor anguli oris*. Pulls the corners of the mouth down (**4**).

(F) *Mentalis*. Elevates and protrudes the lower lip into a pout while crinkling the skin of the chin (**5**).

SURPRISE

Varies from startled surprise to questioning surprise. Long horizontal wrinkles appear on the forehead (**1**). The brows are raised up and arched (**2**).

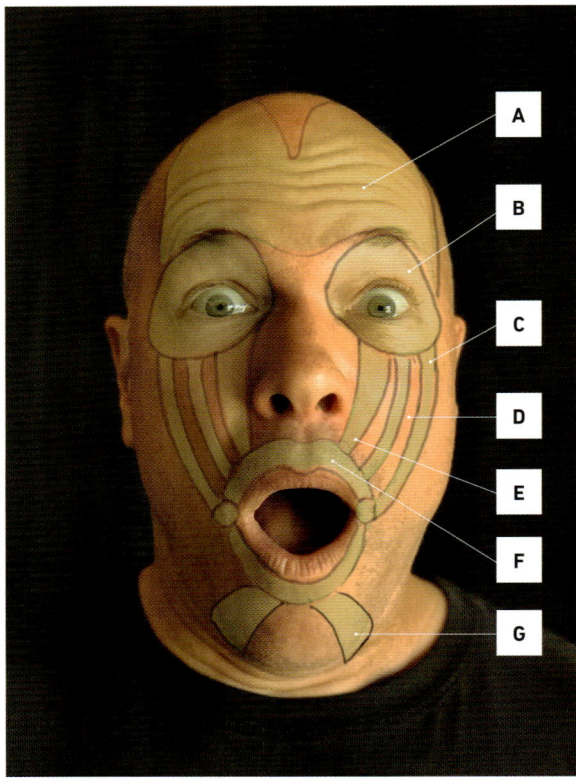

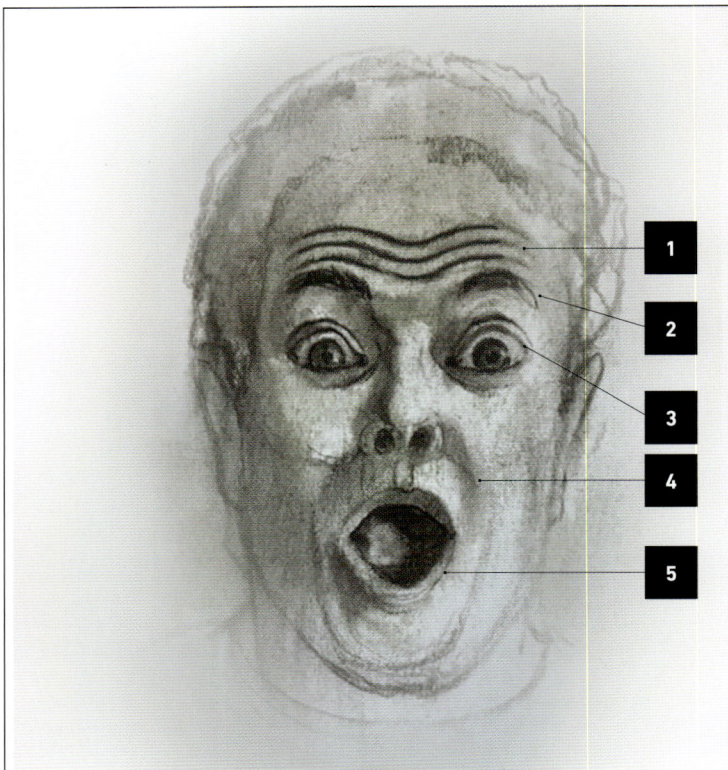

(A) *Frontalis.* Elevates eyebrows; wrinkles skin of forehead.

(B) *Orbicularis oculi.* The upper eyelids are raised showing white above the iris (**3**).

(C) *Zygomaticus minor.* Elevates the lateral part of the upper lip.

(D) *Zygomaticus major.* The medial part of the mouth is pulled upward.

(E) *Levator labii superioris.* Elevates the part of the upper lip that is nearly under the nose.

(F) *Orbicularis oris.* The lips and mouth are relaxed, the mouth opens as an oval, the nasolabial furrows are deepened (**4**).

(G) *Depressor labii inferioris.* Depresses the lower lip from below (**5**).

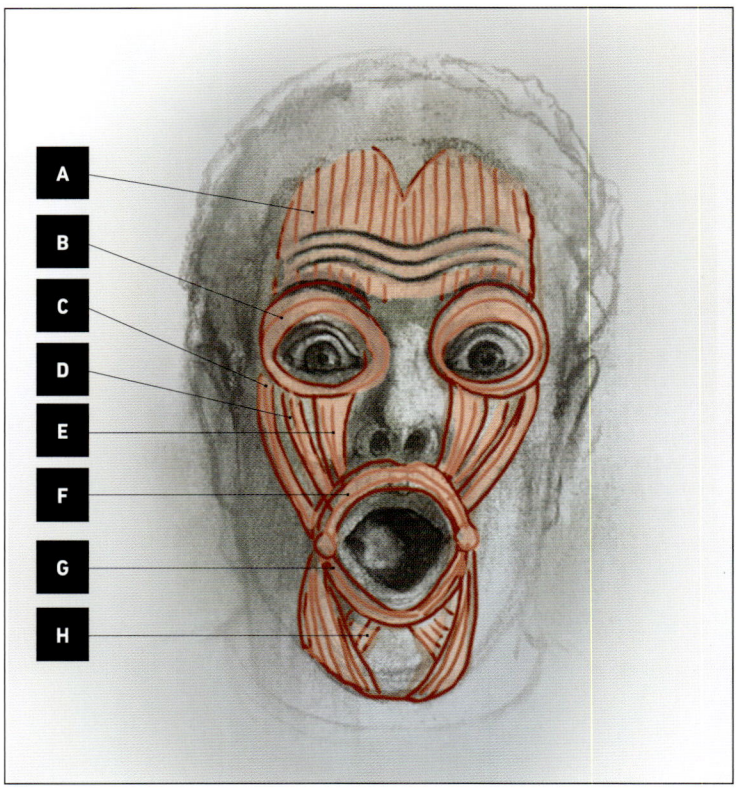

FEAR

Ranges from horror, shock, and terror, to worry and apprehension.

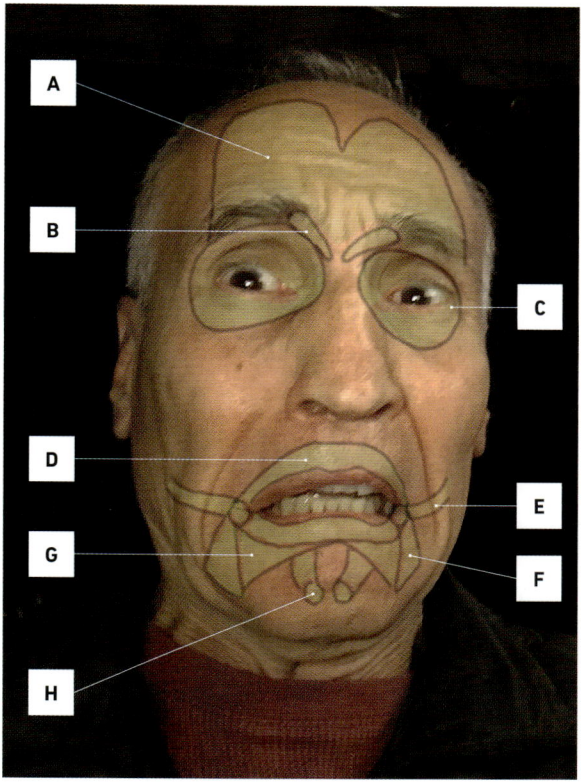

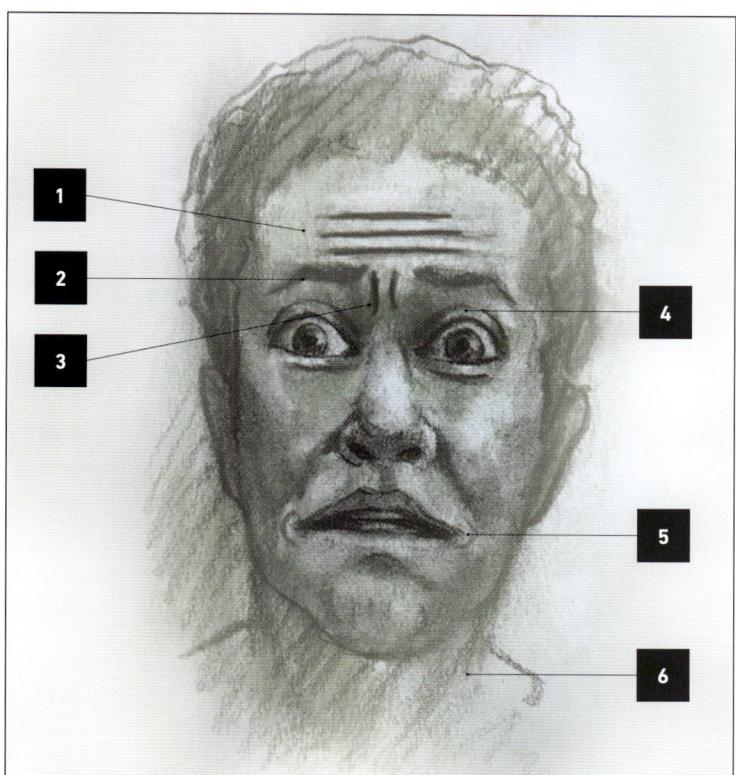

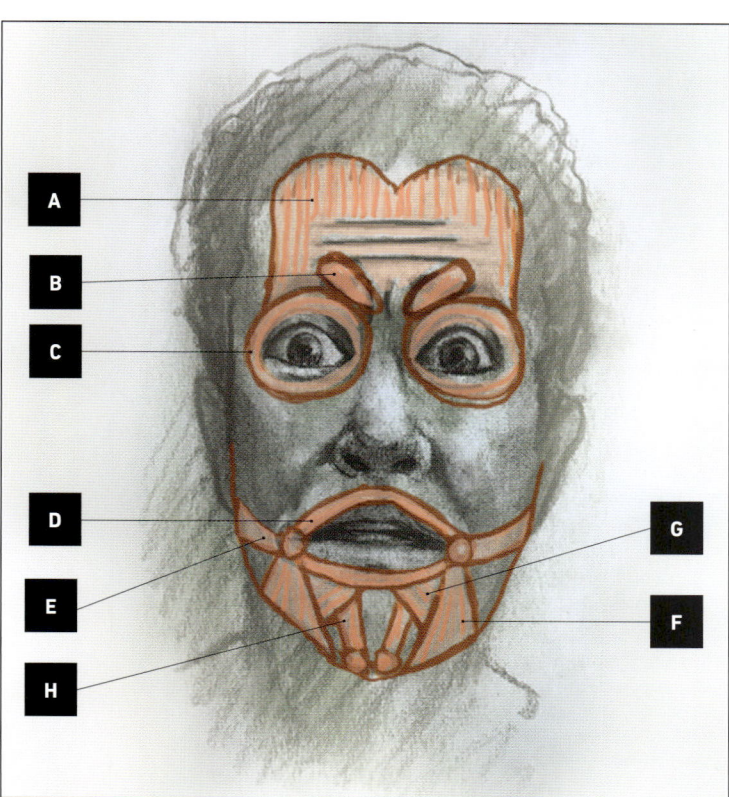

(A) *Frontalis*. Horizontal wrinkles appear across the entire forehead (1). The brows are raised and drawn together, remaining straight, not arched. Often there is a kink in the medial portion of the eyebrow because of the upward pull of the *medial* part of *frontalis* (2).

(B) *Corrugator supercilii*. Vertical wrinkles appear between the eyebrows (3).

(C) *Orbicularis oculi*. The lower eyelids are tensed upward, and the upper eyelids are raised, showing the whites of the eye (4).

(D) *Orbicularis oris*. Jaw drops, the mouth is usually open, and the lips are strongly parted in preparation for a scream. Nasolabial furrows deepen (5).

(E) *Risorius*. This muscle aids in strongly parting the lips.

(F) *Depressor anguli oris*. Tautly stretches the corners of the lips (5). This contraction may also cause the entire *platysma* of the neck to contract, producing stringy ridges on the neck (6).

(G) *Depressor labii inferioris*. Slightly depresses the lower lip while keeping it in a horizontal position.

(H) *Mentalis*. Tenses the chin box.

ANGER

Ranges from fury and rage to slight irritation and annoyance.

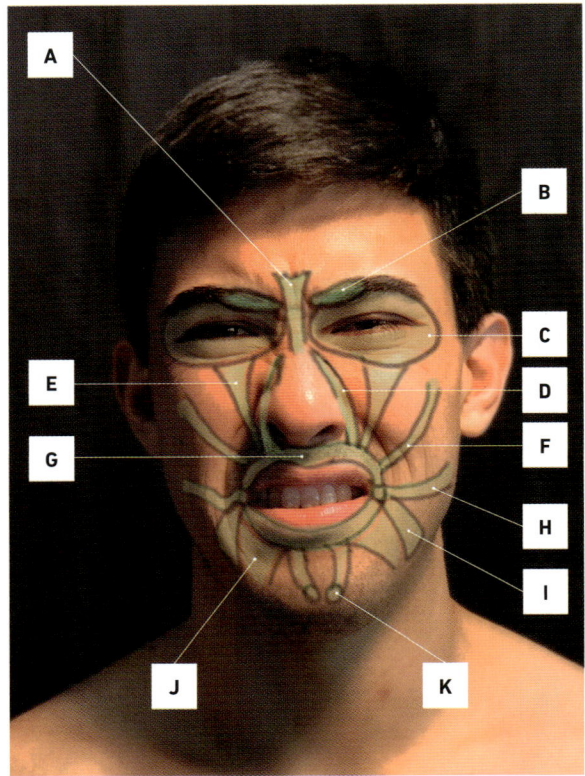

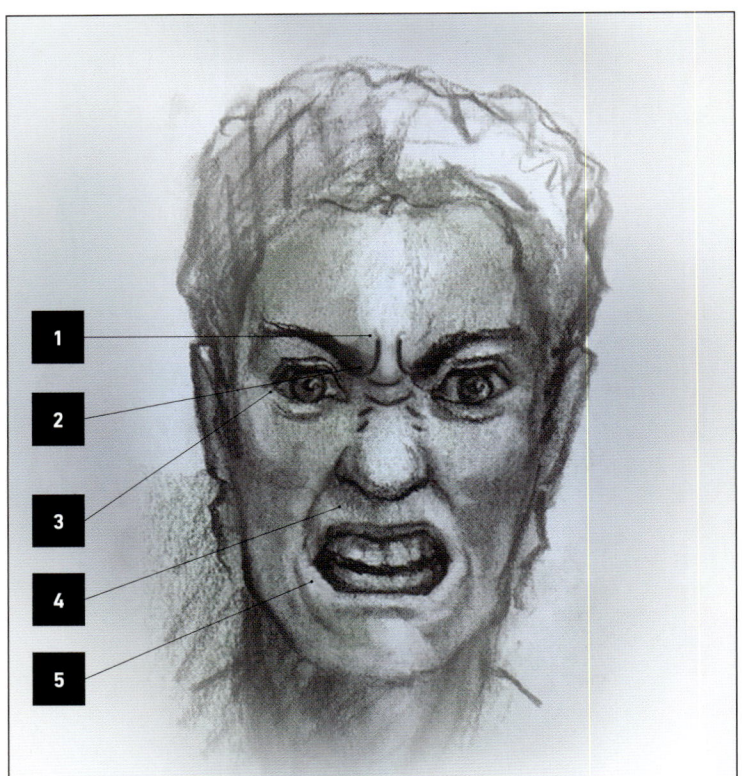

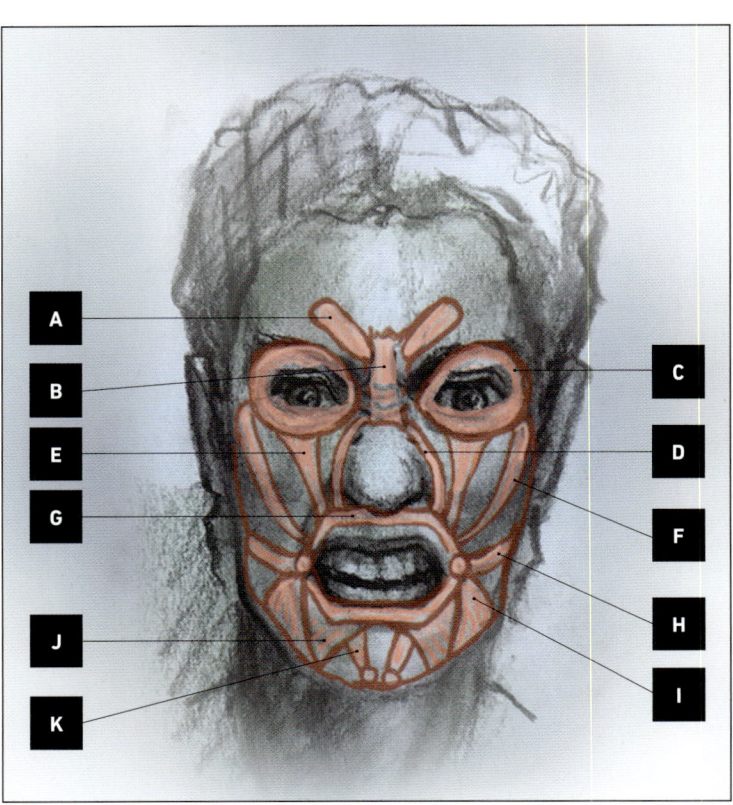

(A) *Corrugator supercilii.* Vertical wrinkles appear between the eyebrows (**1**). The forehead is wrinkle-free.

(B) *Procerus.* Pulls down the medial ends of the eyebrows and wrinkles the skin of the glabella (**2**).

(C) *Orbicularis oculi.* The upper eyelids and eye covers are pushed downward. Upper eyelids are raised and will often disappear under the eye cover folds. Eyes bulge and look intense (**3**).

(D) *Levator labii superioris alaeque nasi.* Wrinkles the bridge of the nose and raises the upper lip into a double-sided sneer (**4**).

(E) *Levator labii superioris.* Elevates the upper lip into a snarl to expose the teeth.

(F) *Zygomaticus major.* The angle of the mouth is pulled outward, upward, and backward. This movement deepens the crease of the *nasolabial furrow* (**4**).

(G) *Orbicularis oris.* The mouth is opened and squared off with teeth and gums showing. *Nasolabial furrow* deepens and connects to a crease around the outer part of the lips.

(H) *Risorius.* Widens the mouth to further expose the teeth. Muscular contraction during *anger* may also cause the *platysma* to contract, producing stringy ridges on the neck. Neck vein often bulges out too.

(I) *Depressor anguli oris.* Draws the lower lip downward and outward into a grimace.

(J) *Depressor labii inferioris.* Pulls down on two parts of the lower lip causing a tight angular appearance (**5**).

(K) *Mentalis.* Tenses the chin box.

DISGUST

Repulsion, nausea, aversion, dislike.

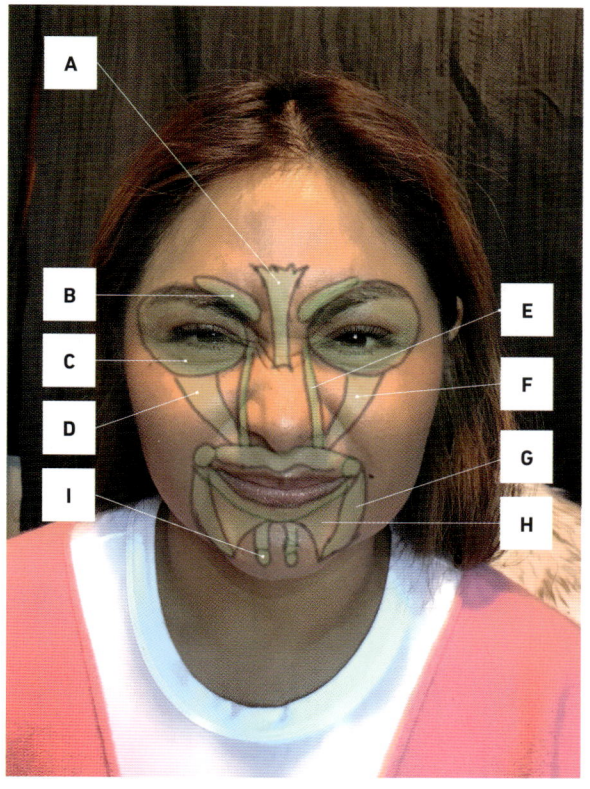

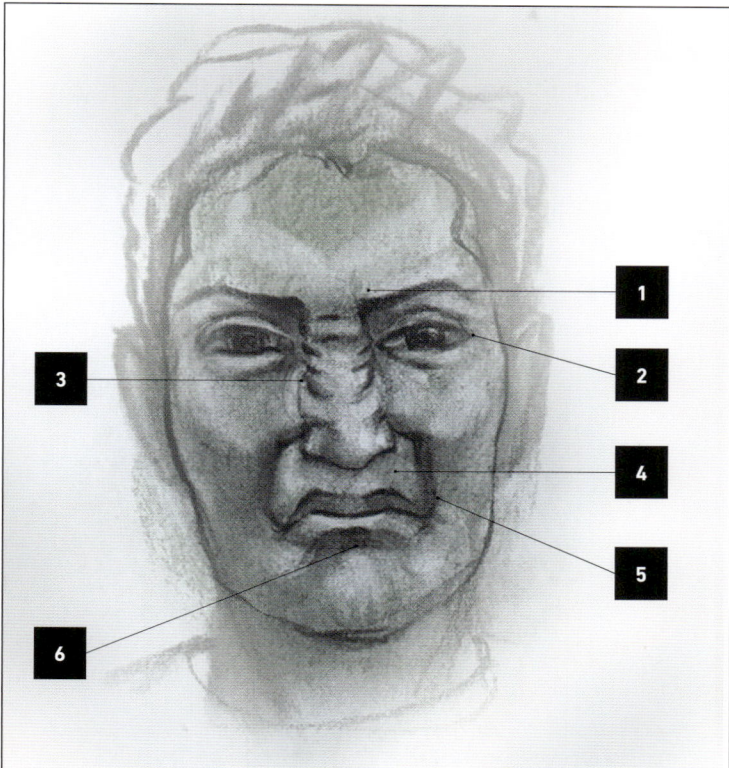

(**A**) *Procerus.* Pulls down the medial ends of the eyebrows and wrinkles the skin of the glabella (**1**).

(**B**) *Corrugator supercilii.* Remains relaxed, which allows horizontal wrinkles to form from contraction of *procerus.*

(**C**) *Orbicularis oculi.* The upper eyelids are pushed downward over the *iris* causing a squinted look (**2**).

(**D**) *Levator labii superioris.* Elevates the upper lip into a snarl.

(**E**) *Levator labii superioris alaeque nasi.* This muscle wrinkles the bridge of the nose (**3**) and raises the upper lip into an "M" shape (**4**).

(**F**) *Orbicularis oris.* The mouth is pursed, which deepens the *nasolabial furrow* (**5**).

(**G**) *Depressor anguli oris.* Tautly stretches the corners of the mouth downward.

(**H**) *Depressor labii inferioris.* Pulls two parts of the lower lip downward.

(**I**) *Mentalis.* Tenses the chin box and pouts the lower lip.

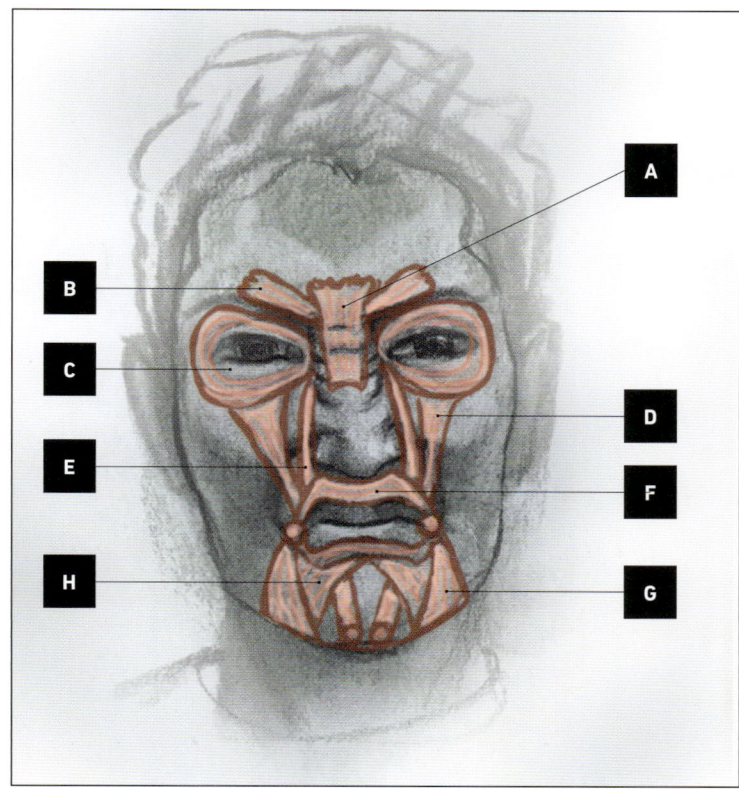

FACIAL FEATURES

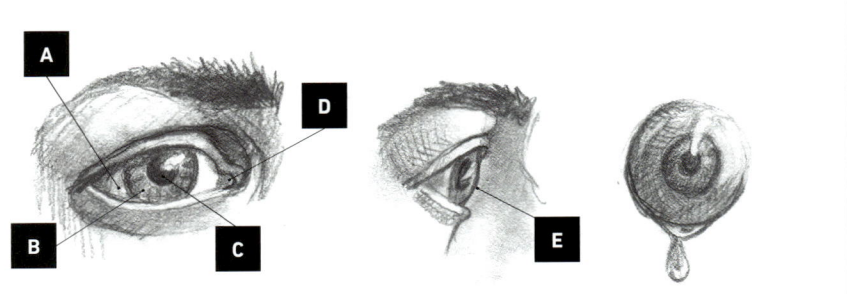

The Eye. The eyeball is a moist sphere. Because its surface is glossy, the cornea (**E**) often features a highlight.

DRAWING TIPS

The sclera (**A**) is the white of the eye. The iris (**B**) is a colored disc that controls the amount of light entering the round opening of the pupil (**C**). The domelike, transparent cornea (**E**) sits over the iris. The inner canthus (**D**) at the corner of the eye is an important feature of the shape of the eye.

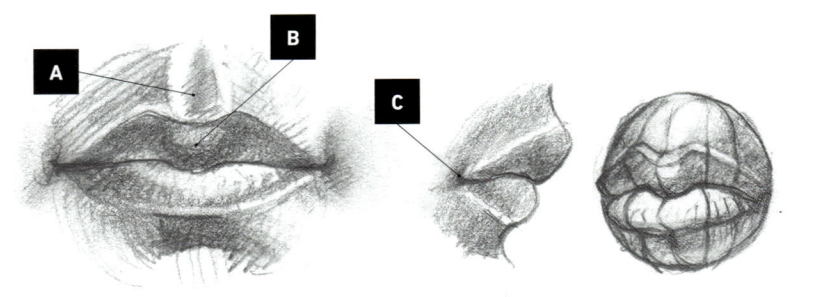

The Lips. Because the lips curve around the cylinder of the teeth, it's helpful to draw and shade the mouth as if it were a sphere.

DRAWING TIPS

The vertical furrow between the nose and upper lip is the philtrum (**A**). The tubercle (**B**) of the upper lip is a small, rounded form surrounded by two elongated forms; it fits into the middle of the two elongated forms of the lower lip. The node (**C**) is an oval muscular form on the outer edge of the mouth.

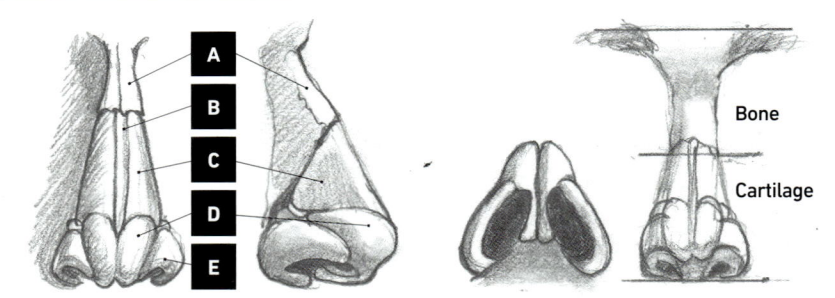

The Nose. The nose is made up of bone, cartilage, and fatty tissue. Halfway down from the eyebrows, cartilage replaces the bone.

DRAWING TIPS

The bridge of the nose is formed by two nasal bones (**A**). The middle section of the nose is made of a rigid septal cartilage (**B**) surrounded by two lateral cartilages (**C**). The bulb of the nose is formed by two greater alar cartilages (**D**). Two wings (**E**) create the nostrils.

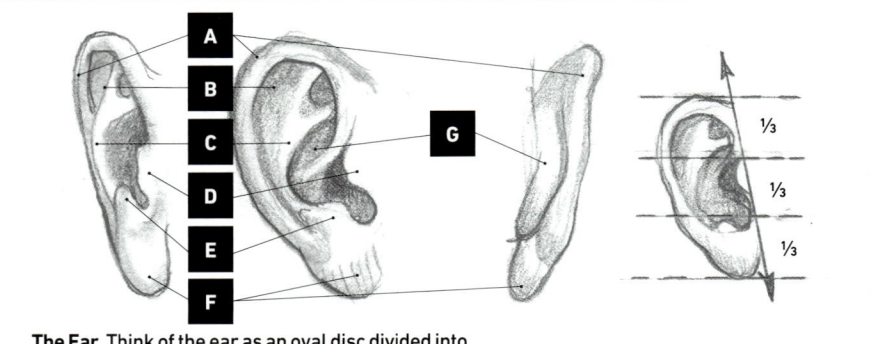

The Ear. Think of the ear as an oval disc divided into three sections and placed on a diagonal angle.

DRAWING TIPS

The cartilaginous helix (**A**) forms the outer rim of the ear. The antihelix (**C**) lies just inside the helix, running roughly parallel to it; the two are divided by the scapha (**B**). The tragus (**D**) is a cartilaginous projection located over the bowl (the concha, **G**). The antitragus (**E**) is located opposite the tragus and just above the fatty lobe (**F**).

LESSON: BREAKING DOWN FEATURES

This is one of my typical practice pages of noses, eyes, and lips. As with the overall face, individual features are also broken down into top, three-quarter, side, and bottom planes.

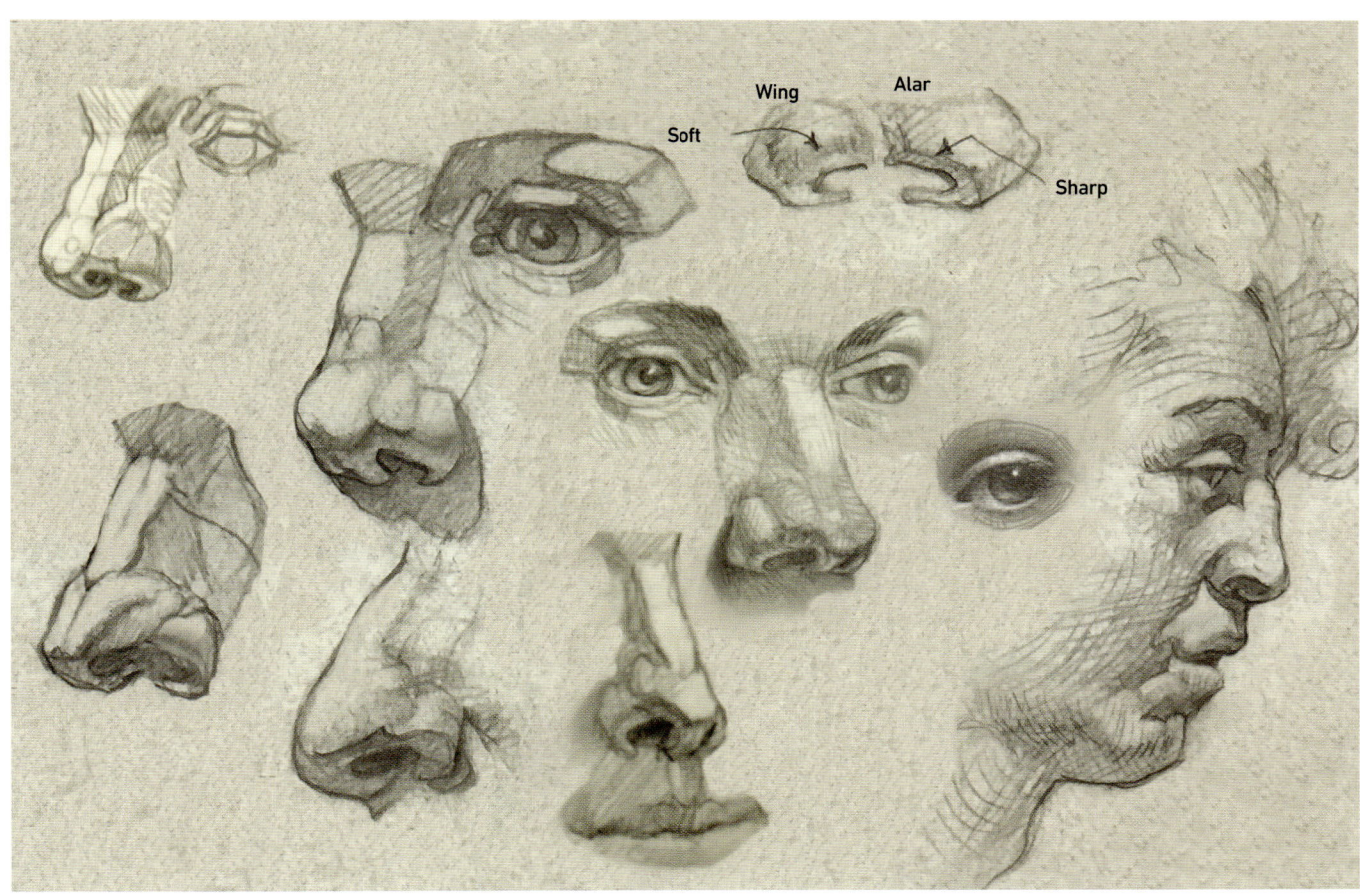

On the nose, notice how the wing of the nose has a soft edge, while the alar cartilage in the front has a harder edge.

With eyes, notice how the iris gets a little lighter opposite the highlight because reflected light is bouncing back out from the retina.

On a profile, always be sure the lids sit well outside of the eyeballs so they can believably be envisioned closing over the eyeballs when shut.

ANATOMY IN PRACTICE: THE HEAD AND NECK

CHARCOAL PENCIL WITH WHITE HIGHLIGHTS ON GRAY TONED PAPER (RIGHT)

This portrait was begun with vine charcoal, and then I switched to charcoal pencil to achieve greater detail. The paper's color serves as a halftone. Notice how paper is left untouched between areas where the lighting is neither very dark nor very light. Let the paper's halftone play a major part when adding dark shadows and light accents.

WORKING WITH WATER-SOLUBLE BRUSH PENS (BELOW)

If you decide to use water with a brush, you will see how quick and easy it is to guide bleeding ink into a shadow area. The hatched strokes are used to delineate planes (or edges) and are a part of the finished look, with water softening their edginess. I did not use a pencil at first on these sketches, but it's fine to use them if you lightly pre-draw and then remove the marks with a kneaded eraser before wetting the paper.

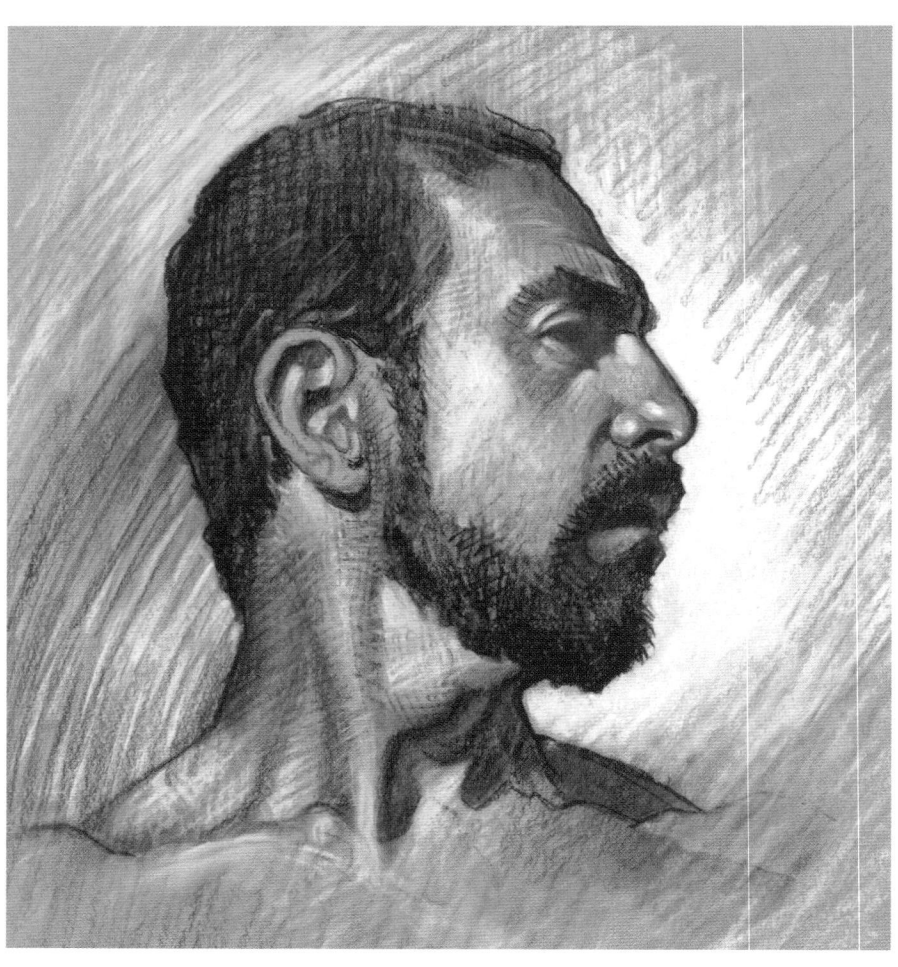

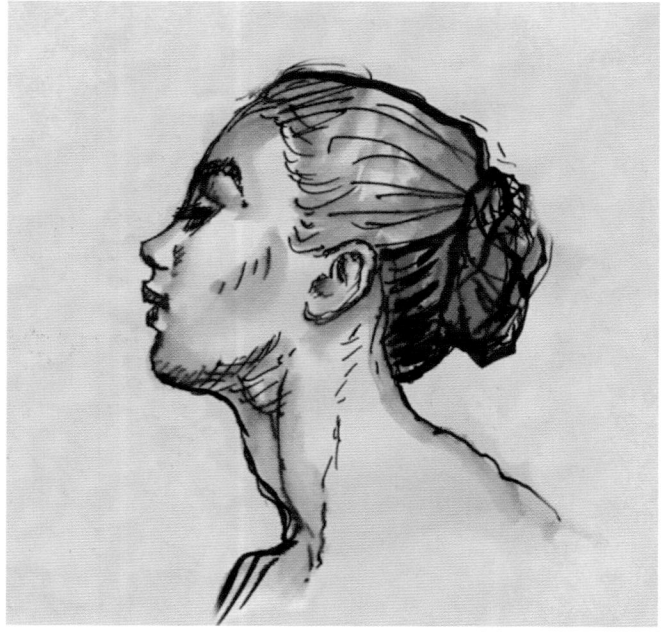

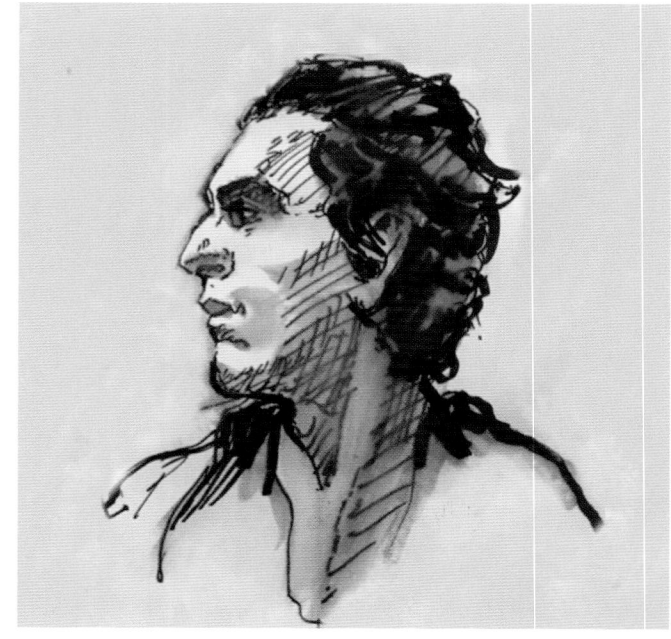

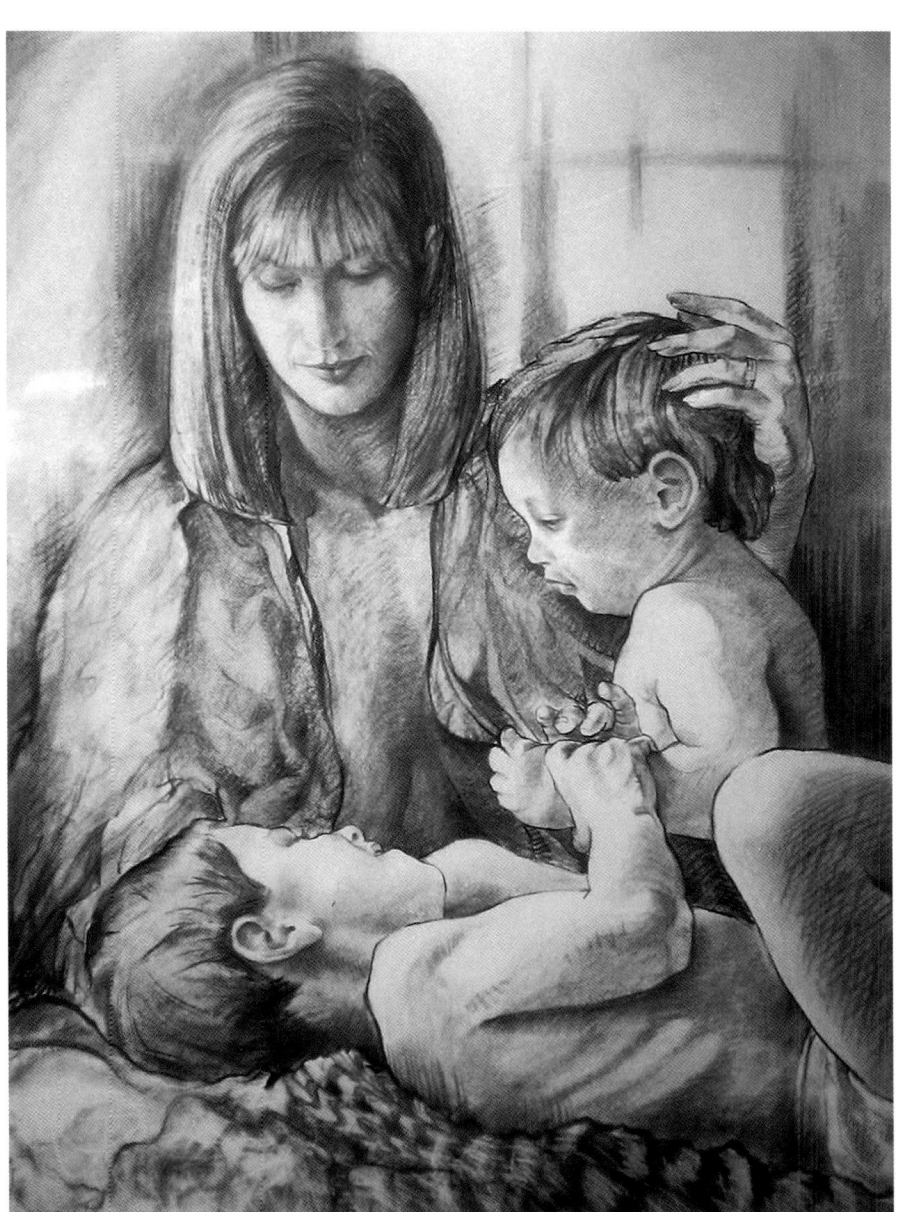

Vine charcoal on Stonehenge paper,
50" × 36" (127 × 91.5 cm)

HOW MATURATION CHANGES ANATOMY AND PROPORTIONS

Young children have enormous heads in relation to the size of their bodies, and their eyes are just as large at birth as they will ever be. Heads are large because they hold big brains; brains and eyes are large because there is much to see and learn quickly. As a child gets older, the limbs and trunk grow steadily, but the head does not get much bigger. Proportion-wise, a newborn baby's head is more than one-fourth of its total length. By adulthood, there are nearly eight heads to a body's length. Children's foreheads are large and round. Jaws with baby teeth are small and undeveloped. Because of baby fat, bony landmarks are often dimples rather than prominences, but by age 10 a child's proportions have changed dramatically, with baby fat melting away and features and muscles becoming much more prominent. Study this drawing of an 18-month-old and 3½-year-old to see what I mean.

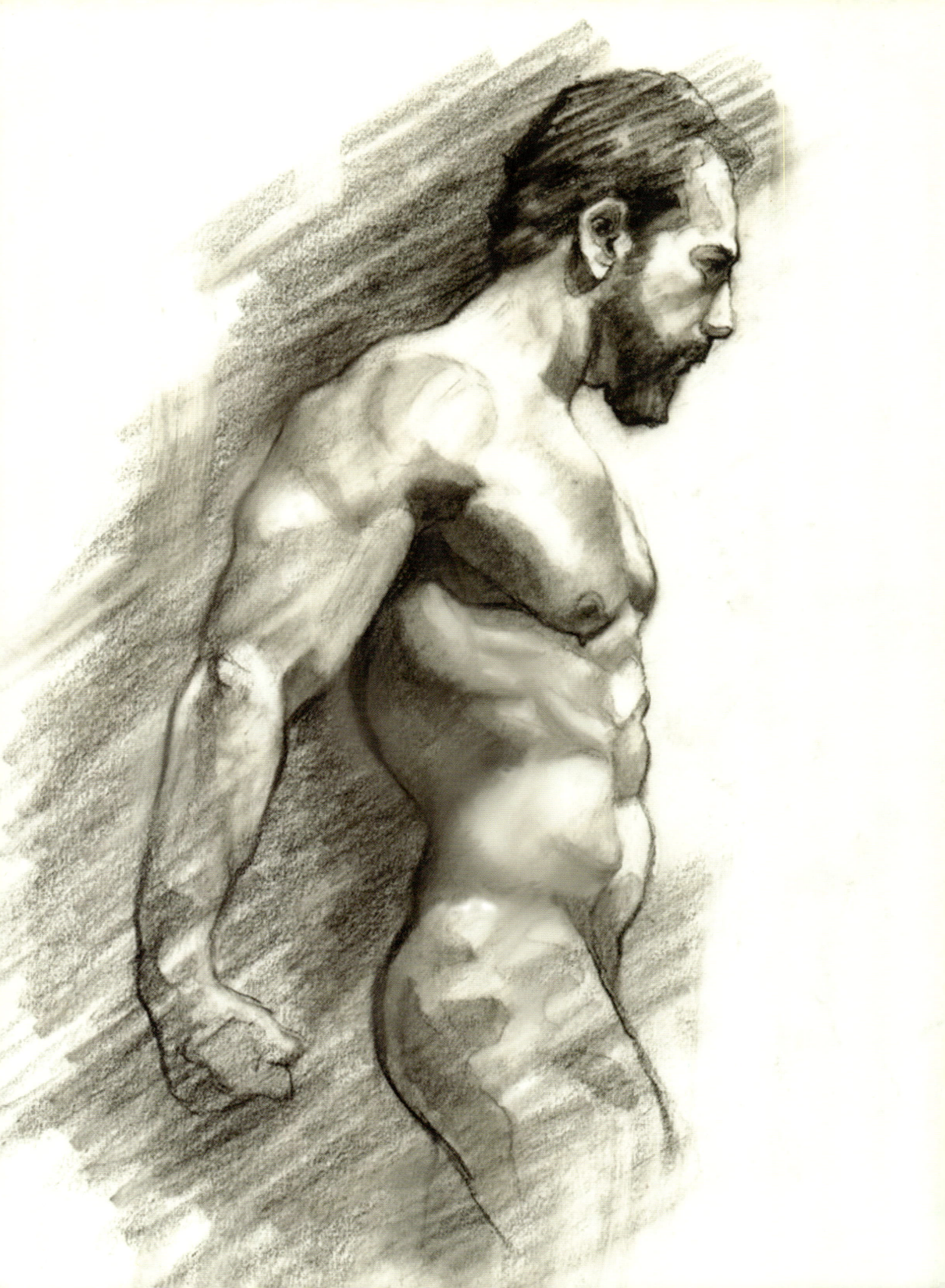

4

THE TORSO AND PELVIS

The region from the shoulders to the pelvis is called the torso. Most of the muscles described in this section lie on the torso itself, although some cross over from the shoulders to the neck. The shape of the torso is largely determined by the shape of the rib cage upon which the shoulders and their muscles sit. The rib cage, with its 12 thoracic vertebrae, is separated from the pelvic girdle by the five semi-flexible lumbar vertebrae that allow, and also limit, the movements possible between the rib cage and the pelvis.

Ken Goldman, *Profile*, charcoal on paper, 12" × 7" (30 × 18 cm)
When it comes to rendering nuances of form, vine charcoal and charcoal pencils yield endless possibilities.

THE TORSO, FRONT VIEW

SKELETON

Some parts of the *torso's skeletal system* are important to the artist because they are prominent and so serve as visual landmarks. Several bones of the *torso's frontal skeleton* are obvious even beneath the skin, including the *clavicles, acromion processes, sternum, thoracic arch, tenth rib, anterior superior iliac spines (ASIS),* and *great trochanters.* To restate what has been covered in Chapter 2, the *spinal column* is comprised of *twenty-four vertebrae*, divided into three sections: *the cervical region has seven vertebrae* (light pink), the *thoracic region* has twelve (beige), and the *lumbar region* has five (dark pink). Attached to the *thoracic vertebrae* are the twelve ribs of the rib cage (beige). Riding on top of the rib cage is the *scapula* (green). Under the *lumbar vertebrae* is the *pelvic girdle* (purple).

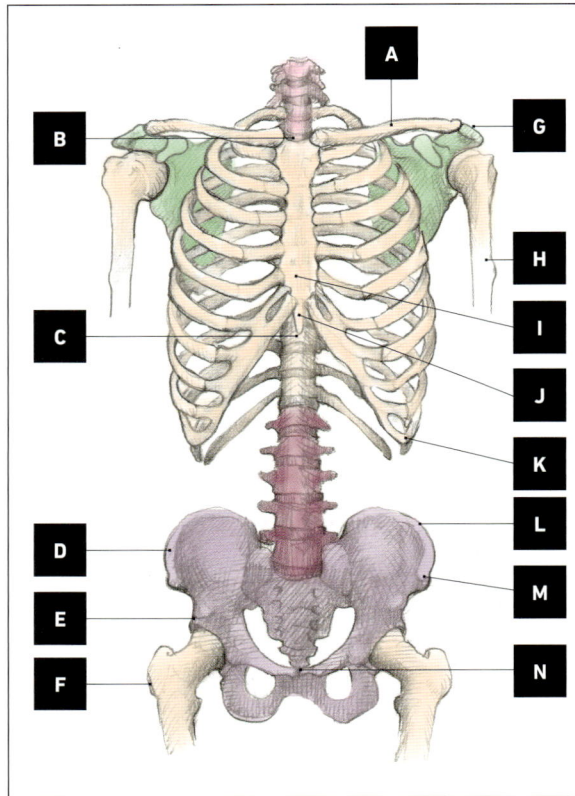

A. Clavicle
B. Jugular notch
C. Thoracic arch
D. Pelvic girdle
E. Anterior inferior iliac spine
F. Great trochanter
G. Acromion process
H. Humerus
I. Sternum
J. Xiphoid process
K. 10th rib
L. Iliac crest
M. ASIS—anterior superior iliac spine
N. Symphysis pubis

Cervical region
Thoracic region
Lumbar region
Scapula
Pelvic girdle

MUSCLES

The torso's movement is dependent on, and restricted by, the *spine*—both the chest and the *pelvis* twist and turn on this fixed, yet flexible, column. And the relationship between the rib cage, the shoulders, and the pelvis creates the shape of the torso's muscles. The *pectoral* (breast) muscles are divided by the *sternum*, the *rectus abdominis* is divided by the *linea alba*, and the *external obliques*—which are interwoven with the *serratus anterior*—bind the eight lowest ribs to the *pelvic girdle*.

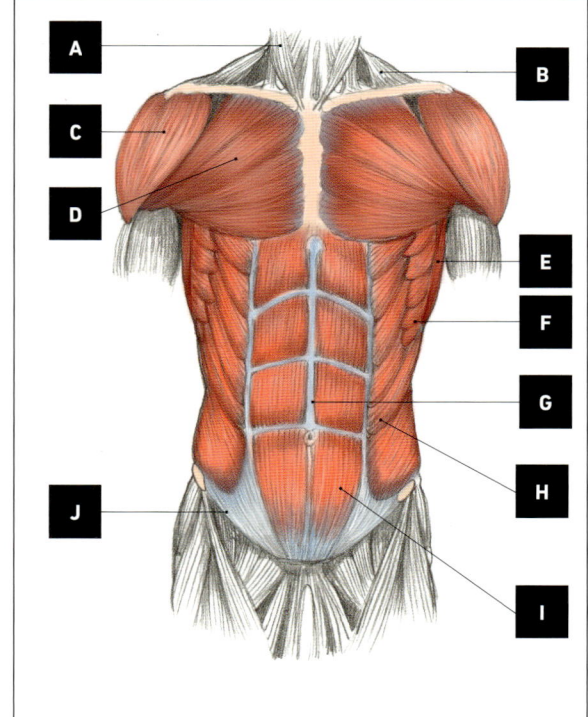

A. Sternocleidomastoid
B. Trapezius
C. Deltoid
D. Pectoralis major
E. Latissimus dorsi
F. Serratus anterior
G. Linea alba
H. External oblique
I. Rectus abdominis
J. Inguinal ligament

DIAGRAM OF LANDMARKS

The observable muscles and bony landmarks labeled on this illustration are the most important for artists who want to draw the torso's surface anatomy from the front view.

Focus on accurately portraying these anatomical features to achieve a lifelike drawing, such as the example below.

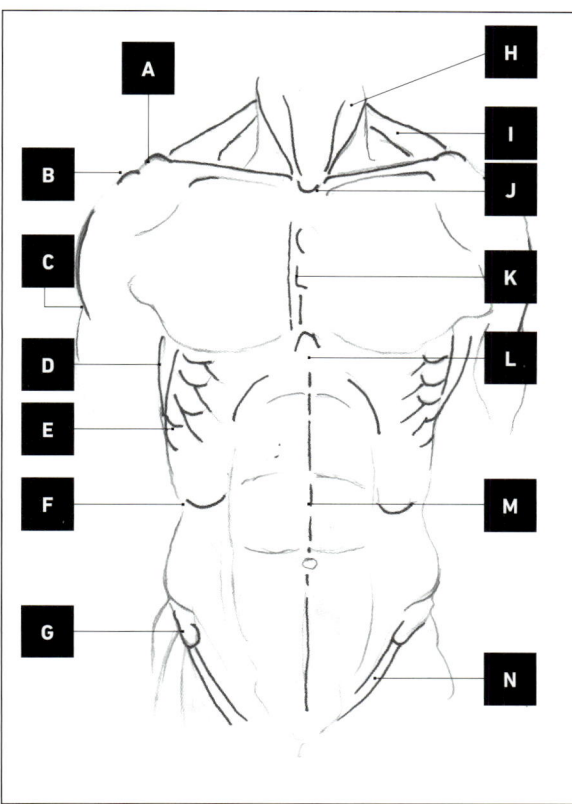

A. Clavicle
B. Acromion process
C. Deltoid
D. Latissimus dorsi
E. Serratus anterior
F. 10th rib
G. Anterior superior iliac spine
H. Sternocleidomastoid
I. Trapezius
J. Jugular notch
K. Sternum
L. Xiphoid process
M. Linea alba
N. Inguinal ligament

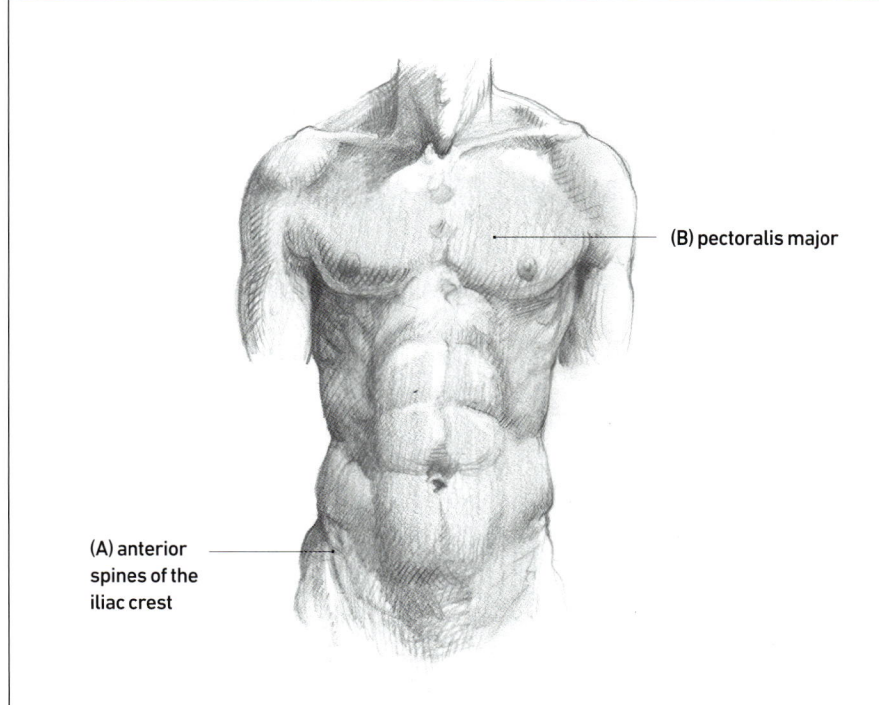

(B) pectoralis major

(A) anterior spines of the iliac crest

DRAWING TIPS

Use the bony skeletal landmarks, which are apparent despite the layers of muscles, to guide the placement of the features. For example, the nipples align vertically with the *anterior superior iliac spine of the pelvis (ASIS)*. Note also that the *pectoralis major* sweeps across the chest and over to the arm, ending nearly horizontal to the nipples.

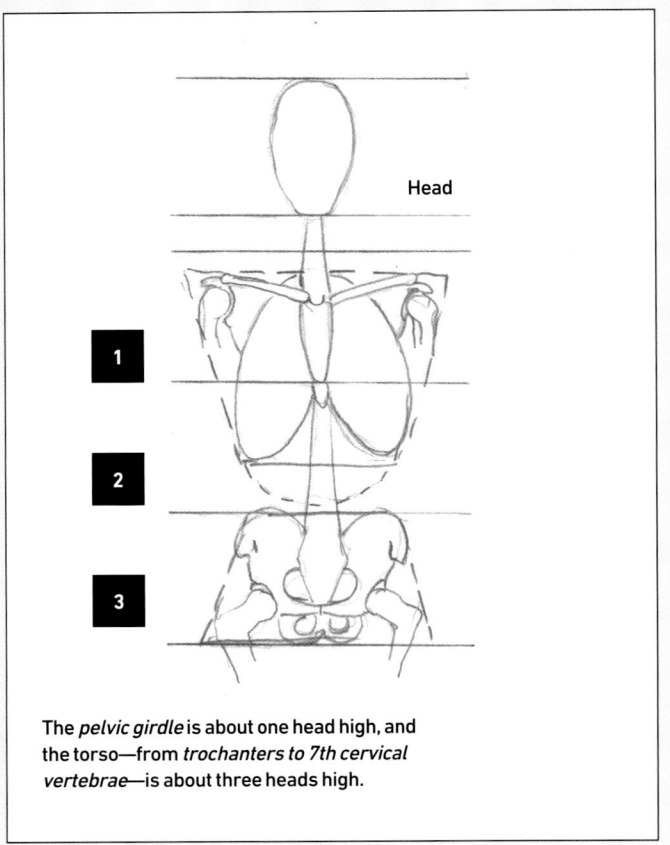

Head

1

2

3

The *pelvic girdle* is about one head high, and the torso—from *trochanters to 7th cervical vertebrae*—is about three heads high.

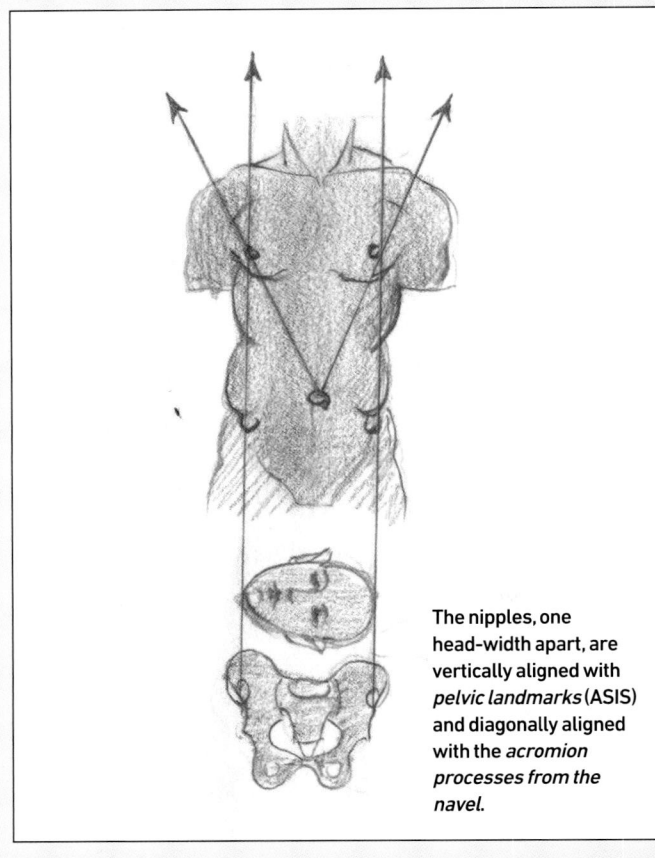

The nipples, one head-width apart, are vertically aligned with *pelvic landmarks* (ASIS) and diagonally aligned with the *acromion processes from the navel.*

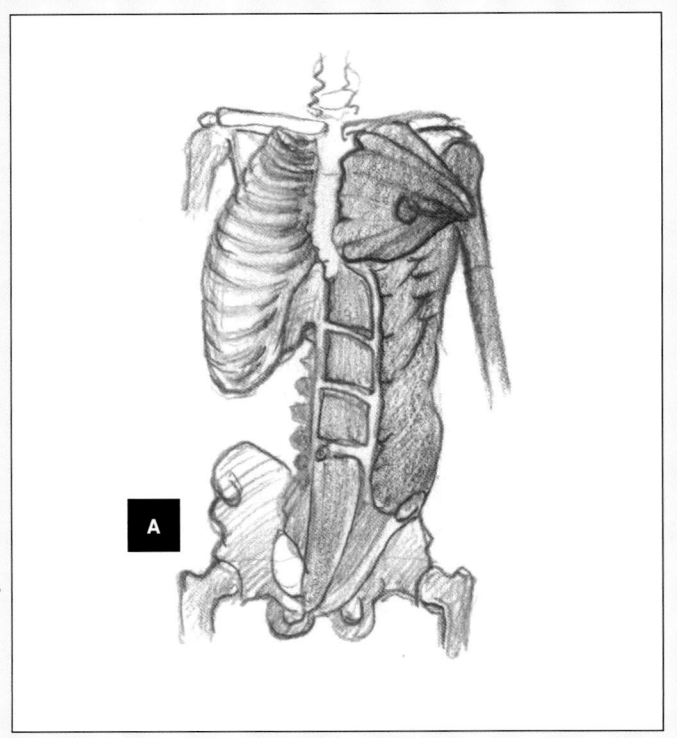

A

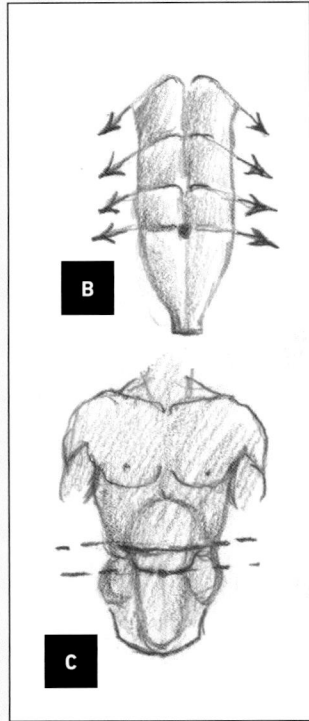

B

C

Note the relationship between the skeletal and muscular structures (**A**). The *linea alba* (interrupting tendons) of the *rectus abdominis* create a "six pack" appearance as they arch progressively higher toward the *sternum* (**B**). Two of the interrupting tendons line up with the 10th rib and the navel (**C**).

MUSCLES OF THE FRONT TORSO

This section provides an overview of the origins, insertions, and actions (shown in orange) of each muscle of the front torso.

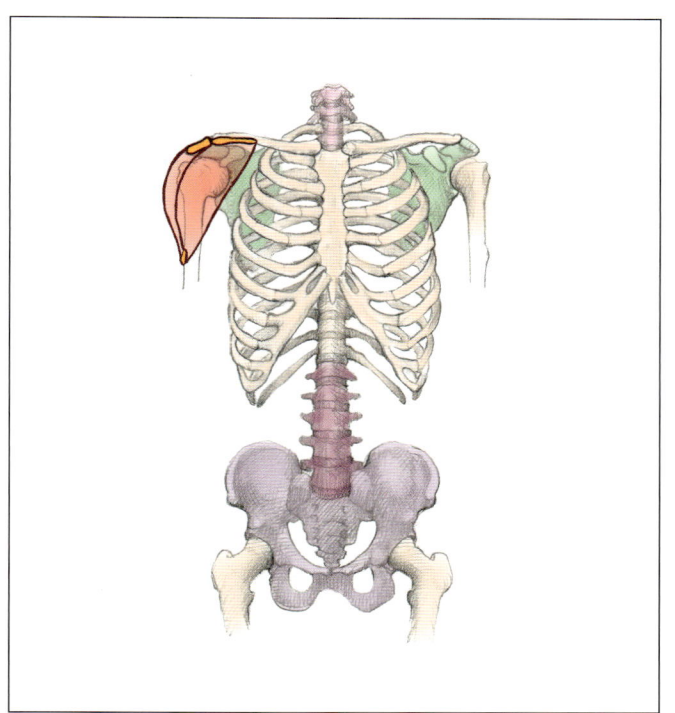

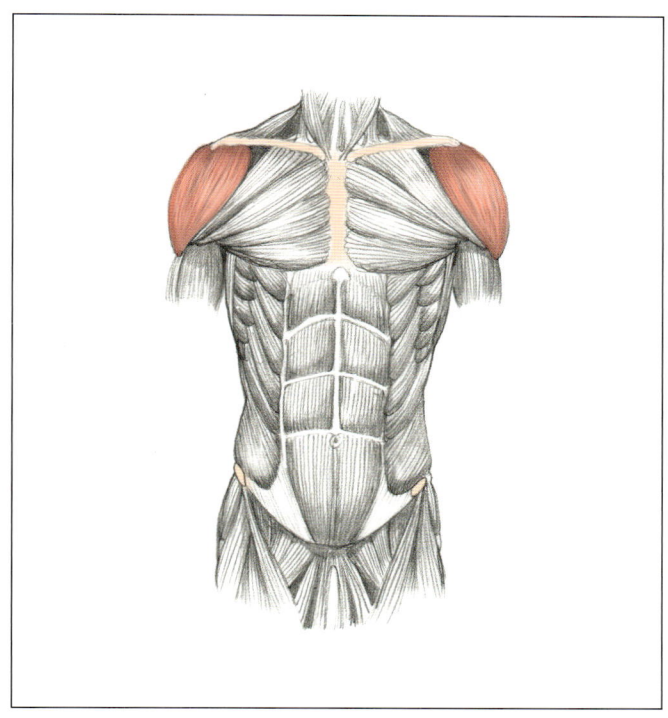

DELTOID

Origin. There are three:
Posterior: *spine* of the *scapula*.
Middle: *acromion process*.
Anterior: *lateral* third of the *clavicle*.

Insertion. *Deltoid tuberosity* on the *lateral* side of the *humerus*.

Action. Raises the arm; anterior part draws the arm forward and rotates it inward; posterior part draws the arm backwards and rotates it outward.

OBSERVATIONS

It is easiest to see the continuous line of the three origins of the three parts of the deltoid muscle from above. Muscle origins are shown in orange.
(**A**) The *spine of the scapula*: back *(posterior section)*.
(**B**) The *acromial part*: middle *(lateral section)*.
(**C**) The *clavicular part*: front *(anterior section)*.

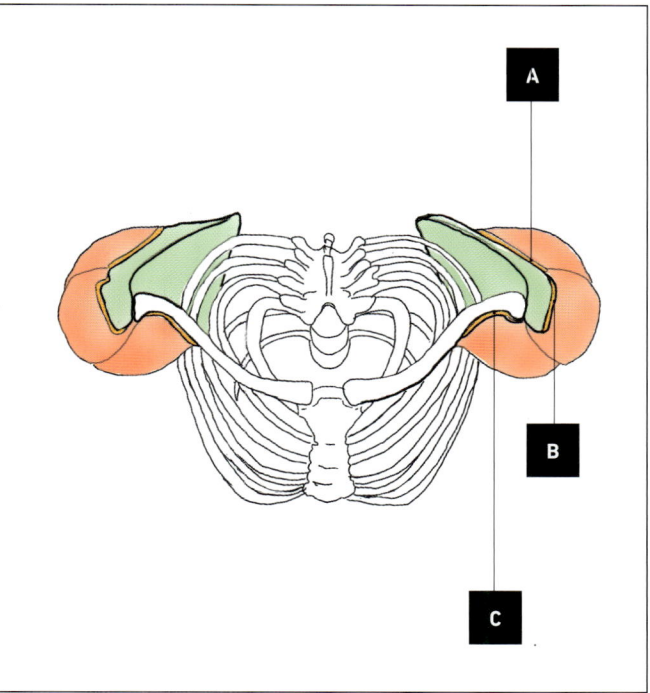

PLANES OF THE TORSO

When drawing a torso, first try to see the musculature as simplified box-like forms with top, front, and side-facing planes, as in the white outlines over this figure. Also, initially think of the neck and arms as simple cylinders. Details of anatomy come later, after the proportions and masses are drawn correctly in a simplified way.

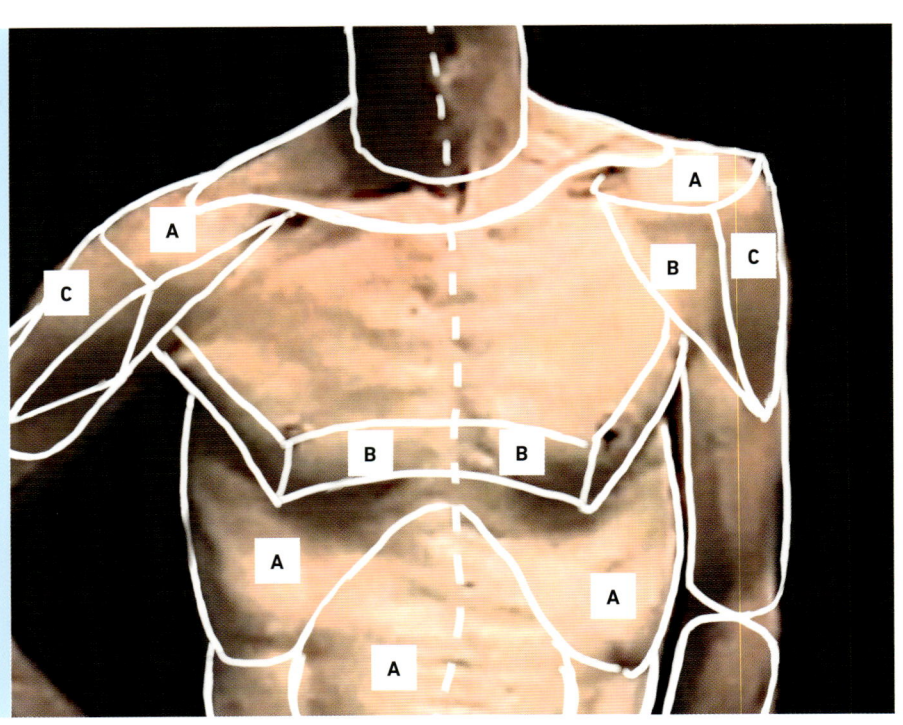

A. Top-facing planes

B. Front-facing planes

C. Side-facing planes

PECTORALIS MAJOR

Origin. *Clavicular* portion: Medial one-half of the *clavicle*; *sternal* portion: entire anterior lateral edge of sternum (not including xiphoid process) and *costal* cartilages of ribs 1 through 6; *abdominal* portion: upper end of the *abdominal sheath* (orange/black dash lines).

Insertion. Ridge of the *bicipital groove* on the upper part of the *humerus*.

Action. *Clavicular* portion raises the arm; *sternal portion* pulls (adducts) the arm across the chest and rotates it medially; *abdominal* portion pulls the arm down.

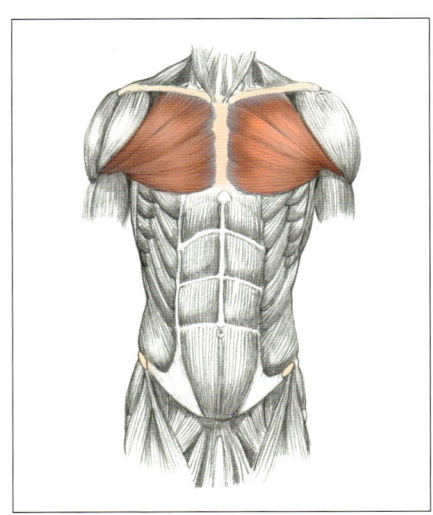

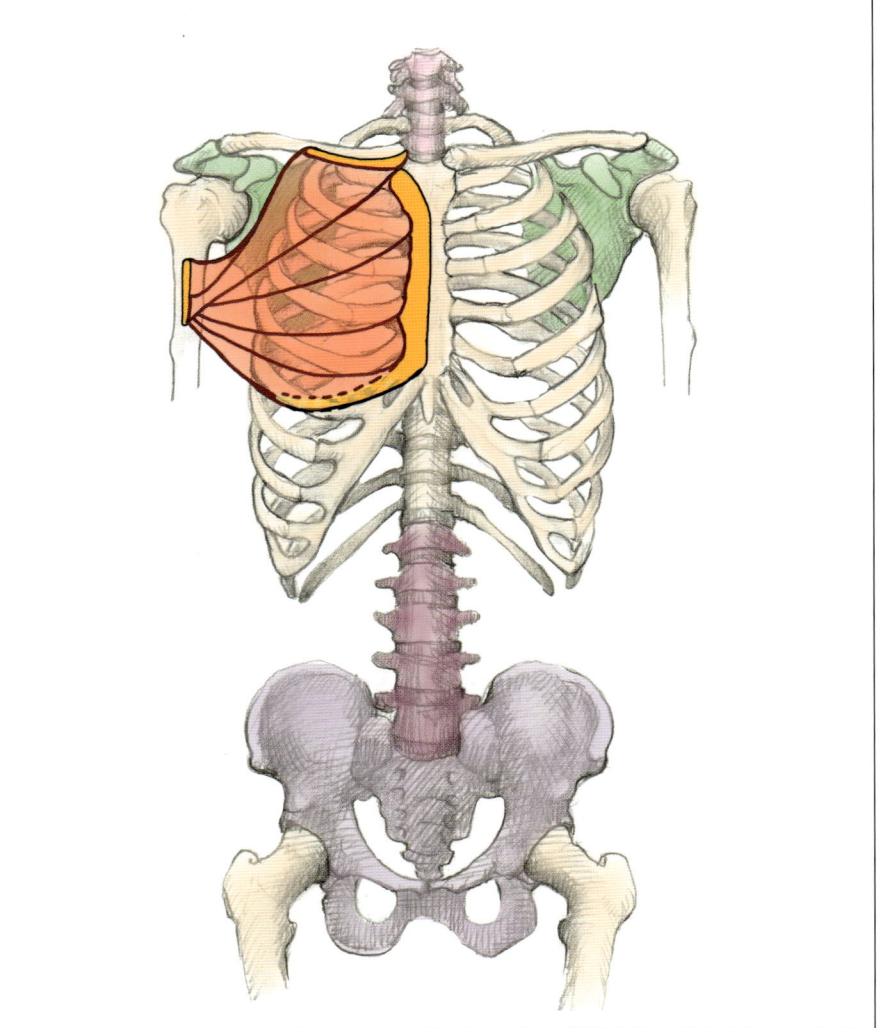

EXTERNAL OBLIQUE

Origin. Eight ribs, numbers 5 through 12. First four *ribs*, 5 through 8 interdigitate with slips of *serratus anterior*, the lower three interweave with *latissimus dorsi*.

Insertion. Anterior two-thirds of the *iliac crest* and the *abdominal aponeurosis tendon*, which ultimately inserts into the *linea alba* between the *xiphoid process* and *symphysis pubis*. The lowest fibers of the *external oblique* form the flank pad.

Action. Bends the torso laterally and rotates it side to side. When both sides work together, it bends the spine forward and elevates the pelvis.

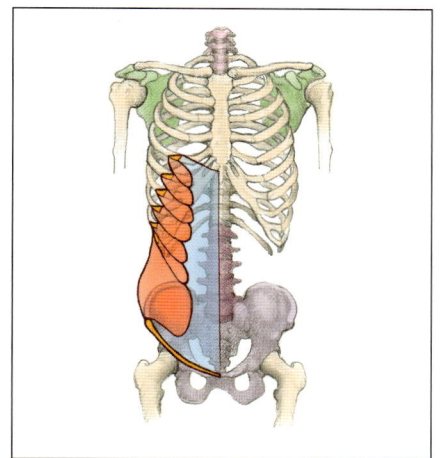
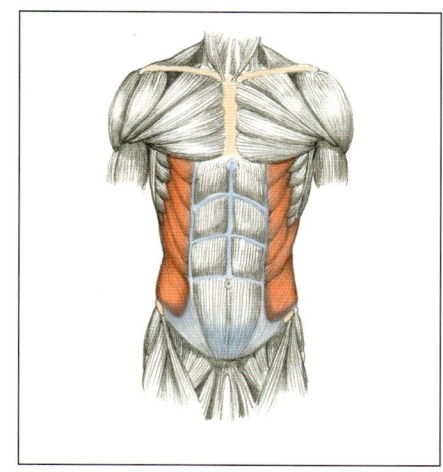

RECTUS ABDOMINIS

Origin. Anterior surface of the *symphysis pubis* at the crest of the *pubic bone*.

Insertion. *Costal cartilages* of ribs 5 through 7 and the *xiphoid process* of the *sternum*.

Action. Flexes the *torso* at the *lumbar vertebrae* and elevates the *pelvis*.

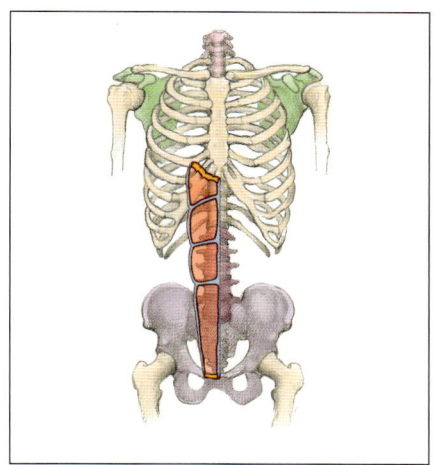
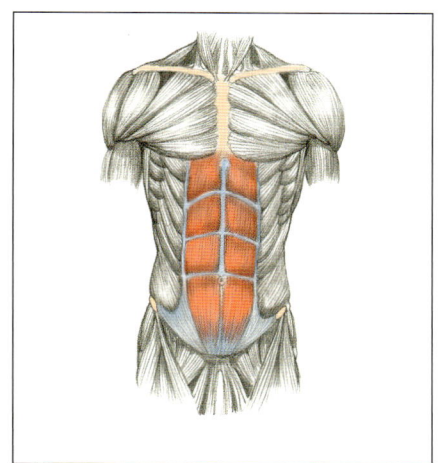

LATISSIMUS DORSI AND SERRATUS ANTERIOR

Because these muscles barely show up in a front view, they are covered more fully in "The Torso, Back View" (page 100) and "The Torso, Side View" (page 110). Here they are as they appear from the front.

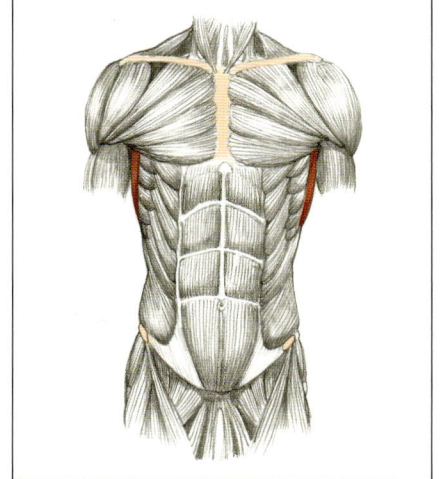
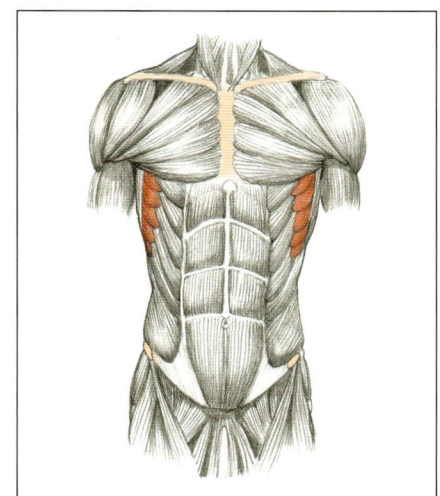

Latissimus dorsi

Serratus anterior

THE TORSO, BACK VIEW

SKELETON

The back is one of the most challenging parts of the body to draw because of its skeletal and muscular complexity. From the artist's point of view, the most important bones visible from the rear skeletal view are the 7th cervical vertebrae, the posterior superior iliac spines (PSIS—dimples on the *pelvic girdle*), and the *sacrum*, which together form the *sacral triangle*—a major anatomical landmark at the base of the spine.

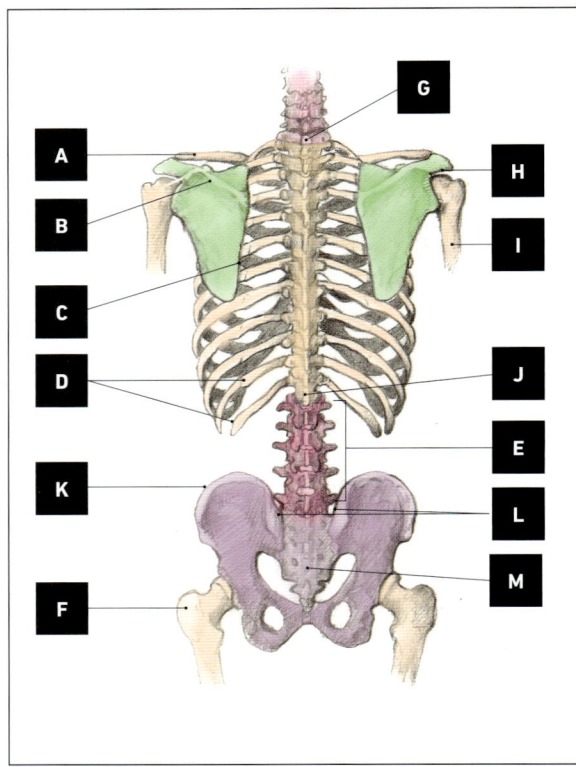

A. Clavicle

B. Spine of scapula

C. Inner margin of scapula

D. 11th and 12th ribs

E. Lumbar region

F. Great trochanter

G. 7th cervical vertebrae

H. Acromion process

I. Humerus

J. 12th thoracic vertebrae

K. Iliac crest

L. Posterior superior iliac spine (PSIS)

M. Sacrum

MUSCLES

The back has many overlapping muscles; our focus will be on the superficial (upper) layers, which are more immediately apparent to the eye. The *trapezius* muscle connects the *skull to the scapula* (shoulder blade). The *deltoid, infraspinatus, teres minor, and teres major* are visible scapular muscles that connect the shoulder to the arm. The *latissimus dorsi* attaches under the arm, extending down to the *pelvis*, and the *gluteus medius* bulges at the hip before meeting with the *gluteus maximus*.

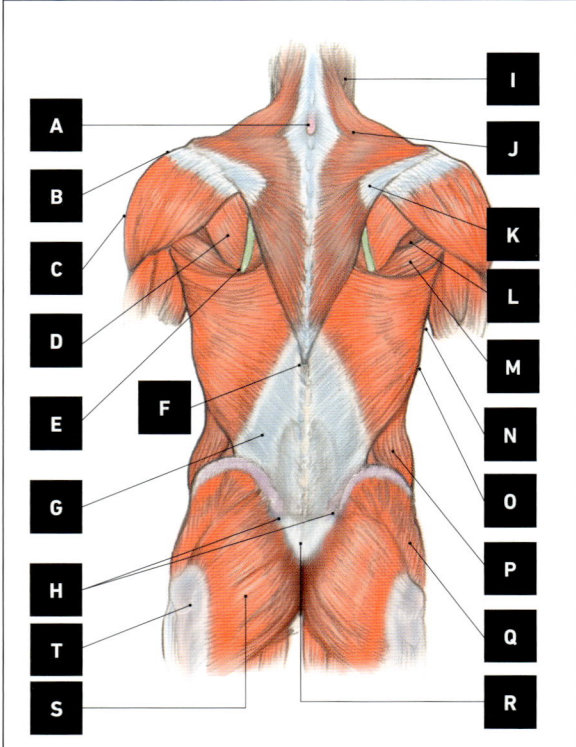

A. 7th cervical vertebrae

B. Acromion process

C. Deltoid

D. Infraspinatus

E. Inner margin of scapula

F. 12th thoracic vertebrae

G. Sacrospinalis

H. Posterior superior iliac spine (PSIS)

I. Sternocleidomastoid

J. Trapezius

K. Spine of scapula

L. Teres minor

M. Teres major

N. Serratus anterior

O. Latissimus dorsi

P. External oblique

Q. Gluteus medius

R. Sacrum

S. Gluteus maximus

T. Great trochanter

DIAGRAM OF LANDMARKS

The observable muscles and bony landmarks labeled on this illustration are the most important for artists who want to draw the torso's surface anatomy from the rear view. Focus on accurately rendering these anatomical markers to achieve a lifelike drawing, such as the example below.

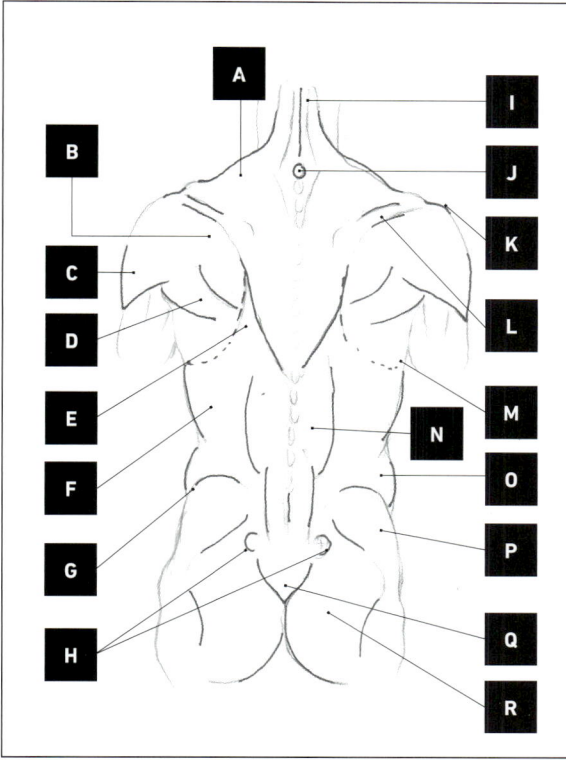

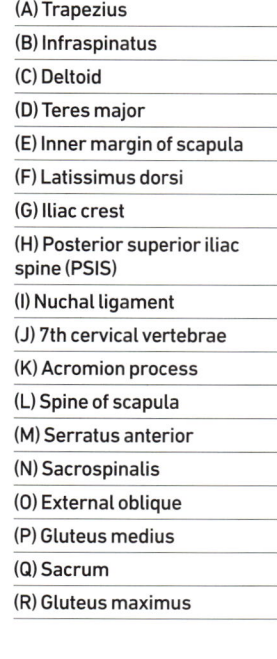

(A) Trapezius

(B) Infraspinatus

(C) Deltoid

(D) Teres major

(E) Inner margin of scapula

(F) Latissimus dorsi

(G) Iliac crest

(H) Posterior superior iliac spine (PSIS)

(I) Nuchal ligament

(J) 7th cervical vertebrae

(K) Acromion process

(L) Spine of scapula

(M) Serratus anterior

(N) Sacrospinalis

(O) External oblique

(P) Gluteus medius

(Q) Sacrum

(R) Gluteus maximus

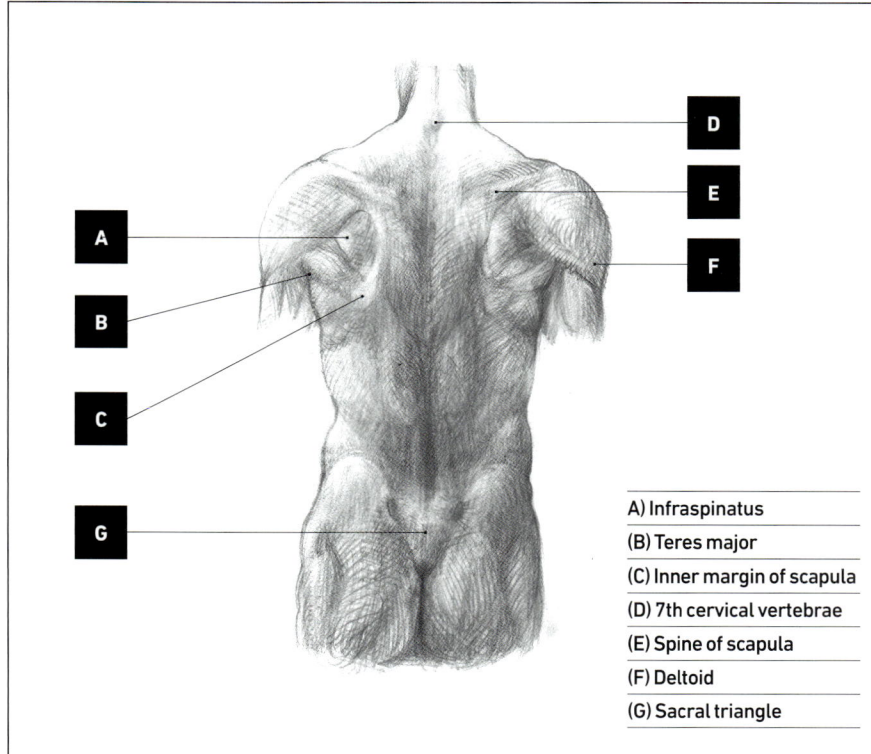

A) Infraspinatus

(B) Teres major

(C) Inner margin of scapula

(D) 7th cervical vertebrae

(E) Spine of scapula

(F) Deltoid

(G) Sacral triangle

DRAWING TIPS

Under the skin, back muscles are not easy to discern. However, the *trapezius, 7th cervical vertebrae, spine of scapula, inner margin of scapula, deltoid, infraspinatus,* and *teres major* are all fairly evident. To depict the *nuchal ligament, 7th cervical vertebrae, spinal column,* and *sacral triangle,* draw a long line and an upside-down triangle.

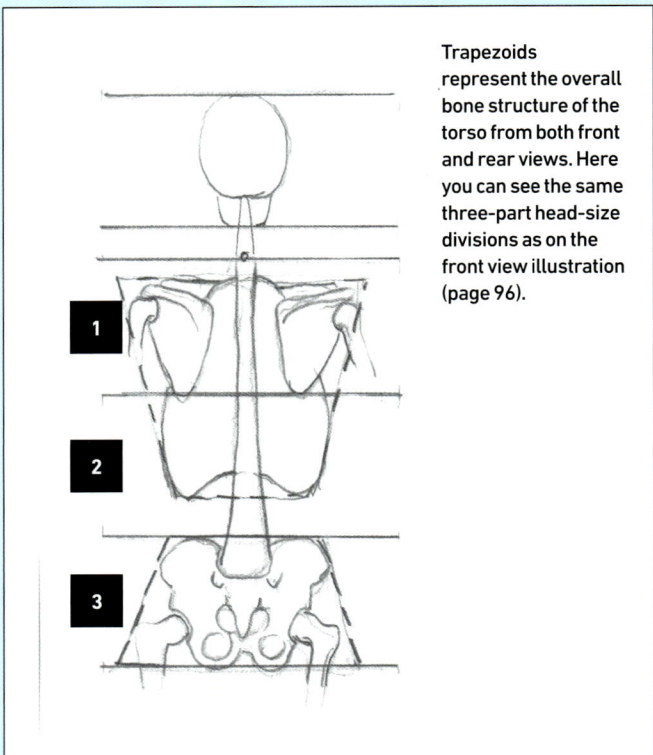

Trapezoids represent the overall bone structure of the torso from both front and rear views. Here you can see the same three-part head-size divisions as on the front view illustration (page 96).

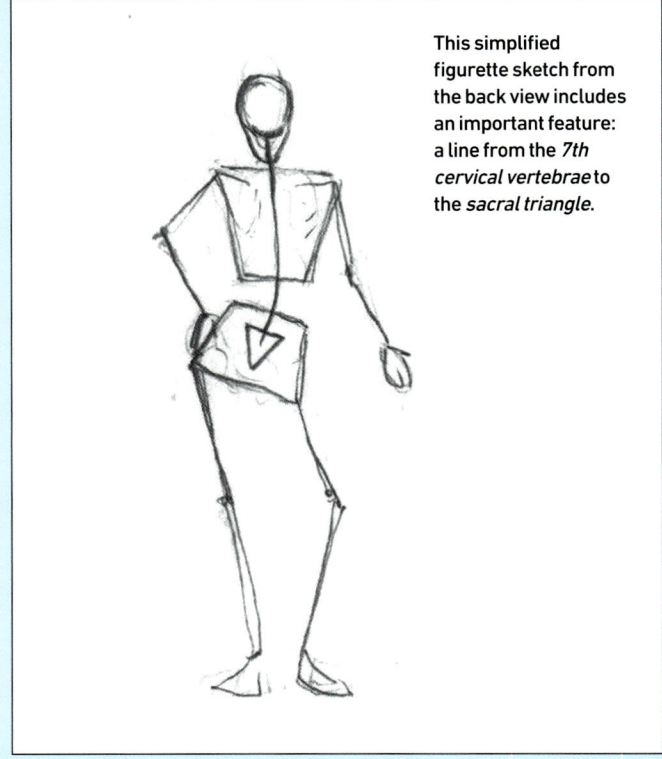

This simplified figurette sketch from the back view includes an important feature: a line from the *7th cervical vertebrae* to the *sacral triangle*.

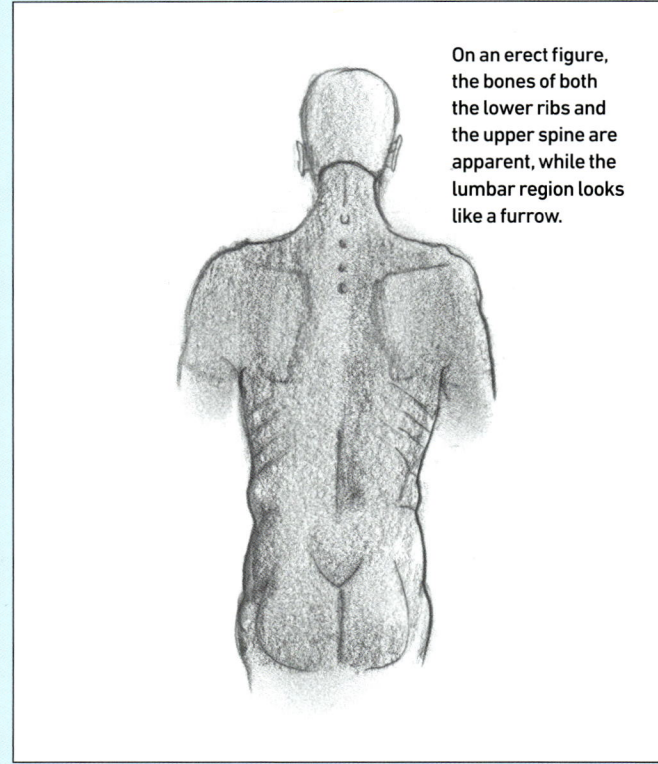

On an erect figure, the bones of both the lower ribs and the upper spine are apparent, while the lumbar region looks like a furrow.

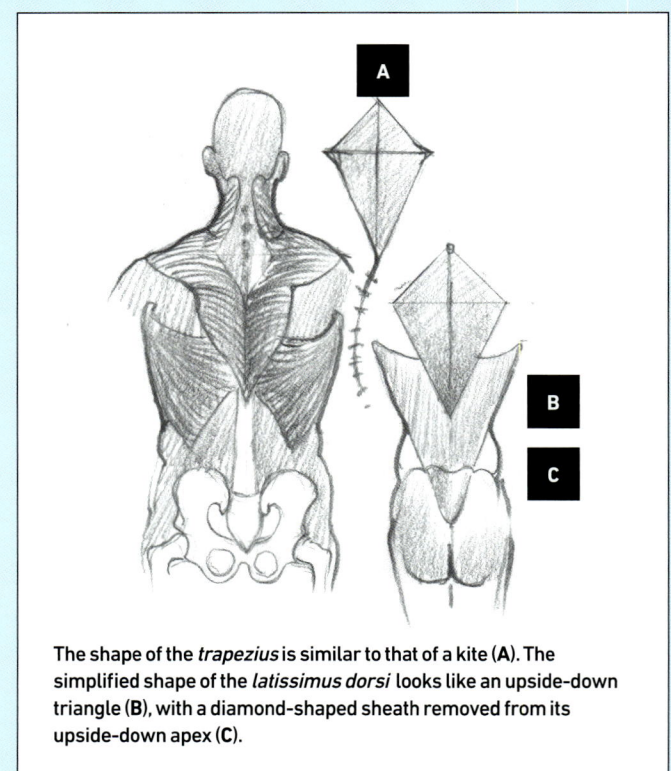

The shape of the *trapezius* is similar to that of a kite (**A**). The simplified shape of the *latissimus dorsi* looks like an upside-down triangle (**B**), with a diamond-shaped sheath removed from its upside-down apex (**C**).

MUSCLES OF THE BACK TORSO

This section provides an overview of the origins, insertions, and actions of each muscle of the back torso.

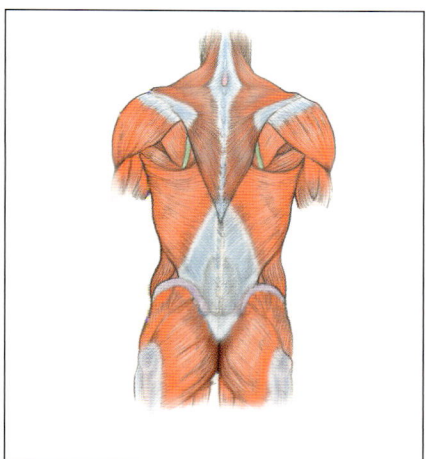

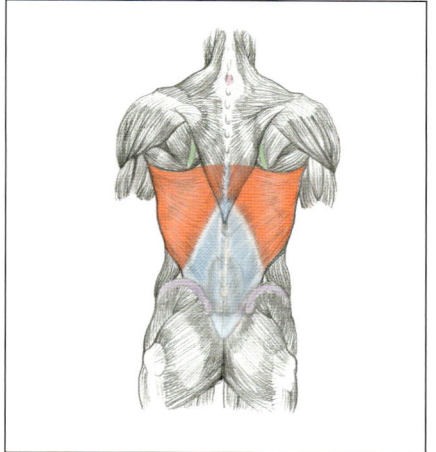

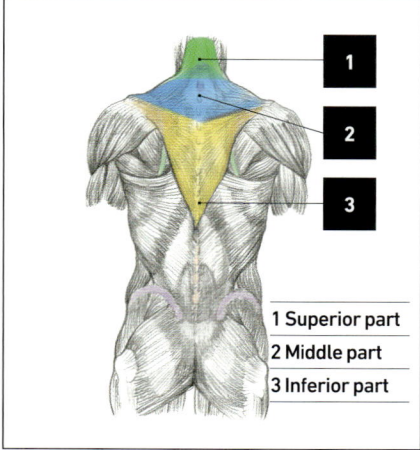

1 Superior part
2 Middle part
3 Inferior part

The muscles of the back are divided into two major groups. The *superficial back muscles* (the layer we can see on the backs of others), and beneath that layer, a group of muscles known as the *deep intrinsic muscles*. This drawing is focused mainly on the *superficial muscles*, which an artist can easily see. Only one deeper muscle, the *erector spinae (sacrospinalis)* will be discussed later because it influences the surface form of the *latissimus dorsi* to such a high degree.

LATISSIMUS DORSI
The *latissimus dorsi* is the widest muscle of the body and overlies many muscles, though not the *trapezius*.

Action. Lowers the arm and helps to rotate it mediately. Surfers use this muscle when they paddle. Rock climbers use it when they pull themselves up.

Origin. The broadness of this muscle means that it has a lot of *origin sites* with four defined parts. First, a *vertebral part* originates from the *spinous processes of T-7 to T-12*. Second, the "diamond shaped" *fascia of the lower latissimus* is part of another origin called the *iliac part*. This second part originates from the *posterior third of the iliac crest*. Third, the *costal part* originates from *ribs 9 through 12*, and fourth, the *scapular part* has a small origin on the *inferior angles of the scapula*.

TRAPEZIUS
The trapezius is a triangular, flat muscle that can be divided into three parts. The *superior part* is also called the *descending part* because its fibers descend downward along the neck. The *middle part* is called the *transverse part* because its fibers travel horizontally across the upper back. Finally, the *inferior part* is called the *ascending part* because its fibers ascend back up toward the *scapula*.

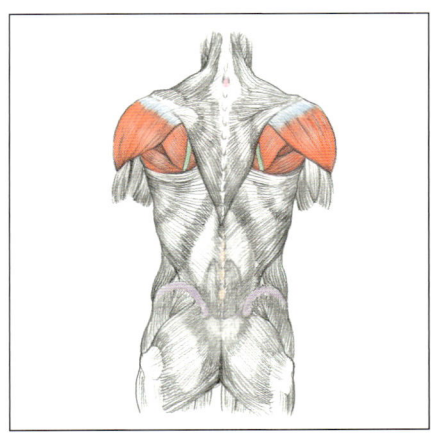

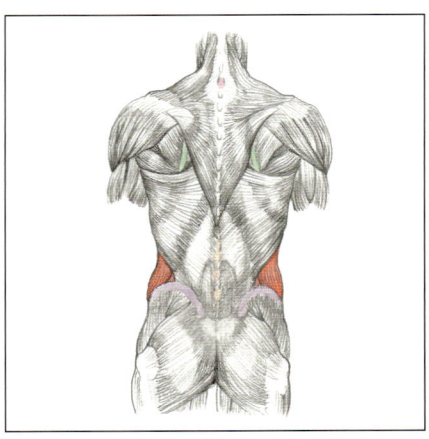

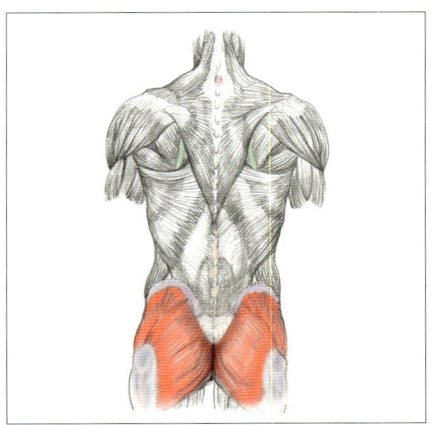

SHOULDER

A third prominent set of muscles are those of the shoulders, where a ball-and-socket joint is formed between the rounded head of the *humerus* and the cup-shaped *glenoid cavity of the scapula*. The muscles connecting the *humerus with the scapula* (green, *medial border of scapula*) are the *infraspinatus, teres minor, and teres major* underneath the rounded *deltoid*. A little bit of the rhomboid can also be seen as it attaches to the *medial border of the scapula*. These muscles will be covered more fully when we discuss the *rotator cuff muscles and teres major*.

EXTERNAL OBLIQUE

Already covered in the front view, the gently rounded *external oblique muscles* are the most important muscles an artist can use to convey the graceful connection between the *thoracic and the pelvic areas*.

GLUTEUS MEDIUS AND MAXIMUS

These two muscles grouped together are what an artist drawing a back view calls the hip region. In terms of function, the *gluteal muscles* facilitate *abduction and extension* of the thighs and are also important for a variety of other activities, including walking up stairs or even just standing on one leg.

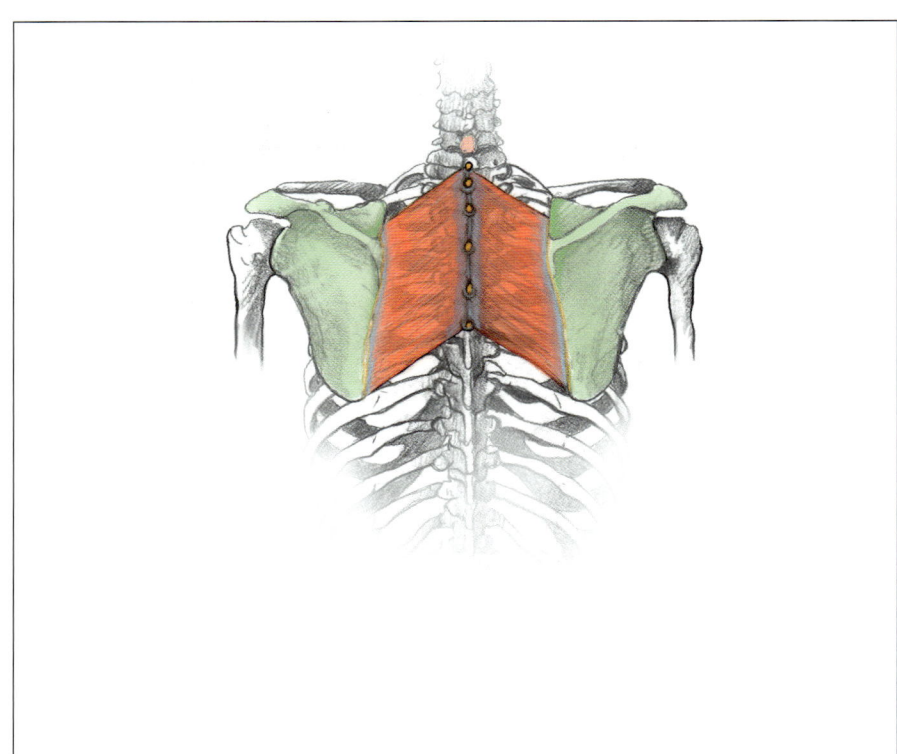

RHOMBOIDS

The *rhomboids*, although seldom seen, are an important muscle to know about because they do occasionally appear as an oval bulge near the medial edge of the *scapula*.

Origin. *Spinal processes of thoracic vertebrae 1 through 5* (orange dots on spines).

Insertion. The very edge of the entire vertebral border of the scapula (long orange line).

Action. Rotates *scapula* medially and upward.

INTERMEDIATE MUSCLES

The two related drawings on page 101 (see "Diagram of Landmarks" and "Drawing Tips") are meant to help a reader recognize the *superficial muscles and bony landmarks of the torso*. However, there is one other group of *intermediate* (deeper but not deepest) *intrinsic muscles*, the *erector spinae or sacrospinalis*, that also needs mentioning here, because they influence the back's muscular forms to such a high degree.

Erector Spinae Muscle (Sacrospinalis)

The *erector spinae* consists of three combined thick elongated muscles that run alongside the *spinal column from the sacrum* to the *base of the skull*. They are roundest in the *lateral lumbar region* and are divided into three paired groups, from *medial to lateral*. The *medial form, spinalis* (**1**) is most evident just above the *sacral triangle* (this includes the even deeper cylinder-like *multifidus muscle* that underlies it). This portion of the *sacrospinalis group* is often called the strong cords (**A**). The *longissimus* (**2**) and *iliocostalis* (**3**) together comprise the *lateral form* of this group (**B**) and are wider and rounder than the strong cords.

Origin. *Pelvis (crest of the sacrum and the posterior third of the iliac crest),* all five *lumbar vertebrae,* and the two lowest *thoracic vertebrae.*

Note. *Origins* are shown in orange from the sacrum and PSIS to the bottom of the thoracic area; *insertions* are shown in orange from 12th vertebrae up to the skull.

Insertion. Into the backs of all 12 ribs, the *spinous and/or transverse processes of the thoracic and cervical vertebrae*, and finally, into the *mastoid processes of the skull.*

Action. Bilateral contraction of these muscles extends the spine, while unilateral contraction causes lateral flexion. This muscle also helps to maintain upright posture by steadying the spine during walking or standing.

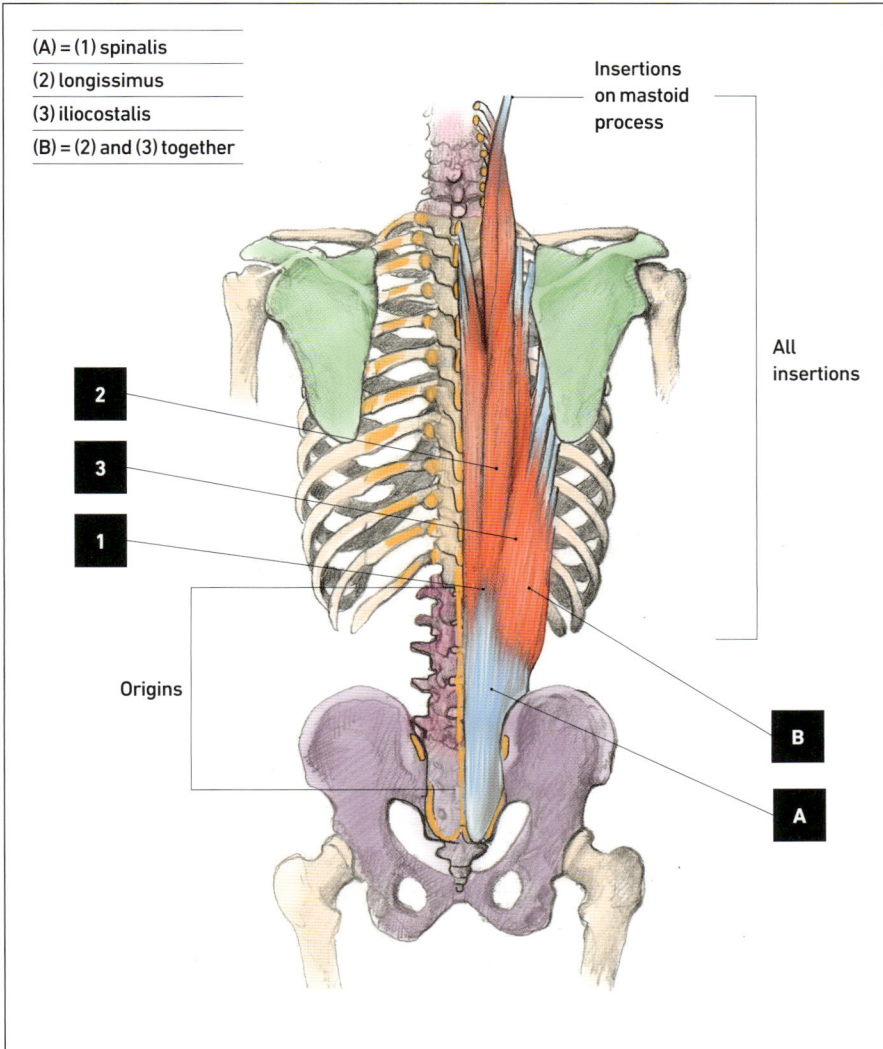

(A) = (1) spinalis
(2) longissimus
(3) iliocostalis
(B) = (2) and (3) together

Insertions on mastoid process

All insertions

Origins

B

A

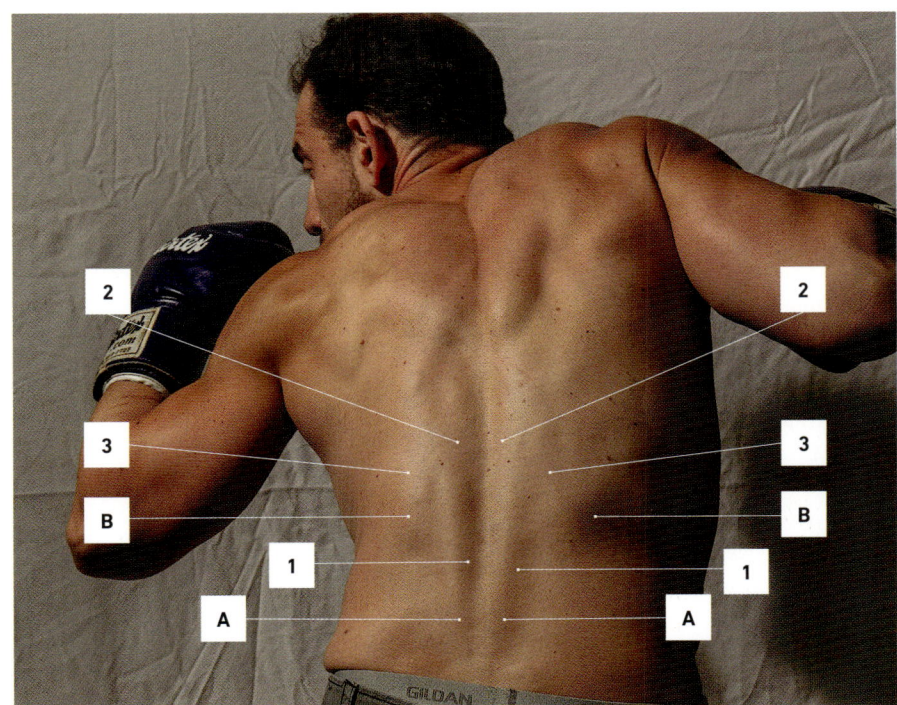

A photo of a muscular back with numbers and letters that identify the paired *erector spinae* forms.

The *erector spinae* has two distinct masses on each side of the spine. The paired thin columns nearest to the *sacrum* are the *medial forms* (**A**). The wider, softer forms above it are the *lateral forms* (**B**).

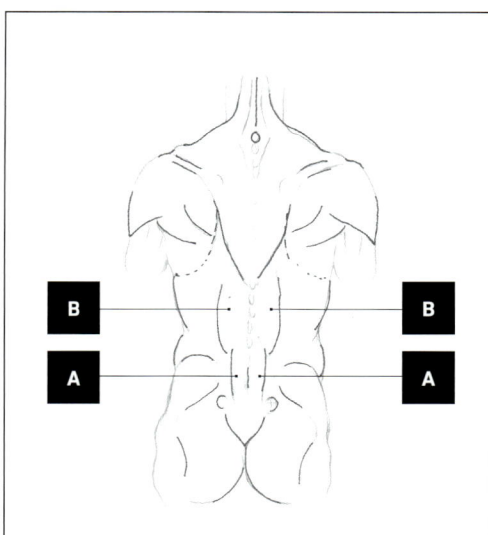

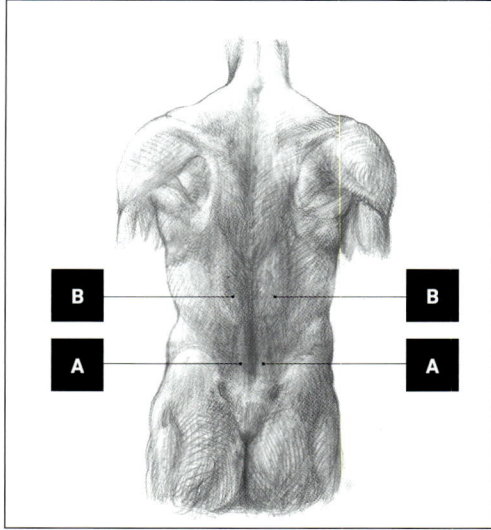

This image shows the correlation of **A** and **B** on a drawing.

MOVEMENT: RAISED ARM
Back view observations:
A generalized colored map of the entire back, with a raised right arm subtly affecting everything on the model's right side.

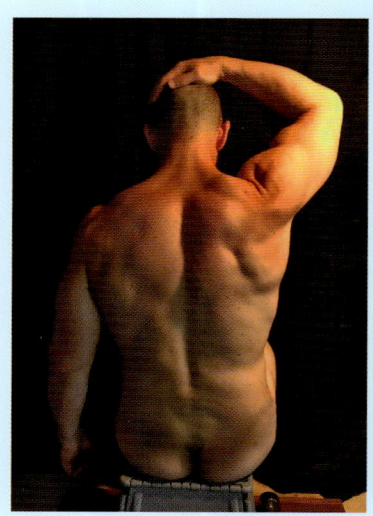

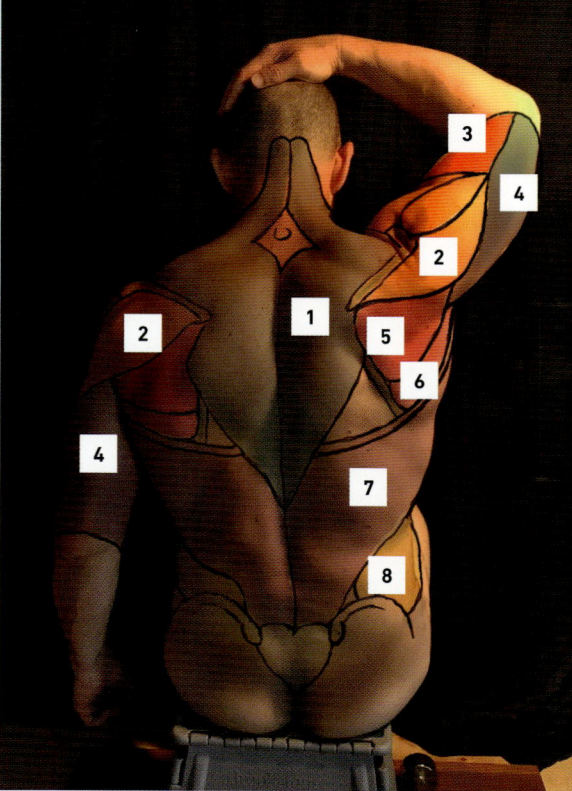

1. Blue, *Trapezius*—Pulled taught by its attachment to the vertebral (medial) border of the raised scapula.

2. Orange. *Deltoids—posterior portion* is stretched and the *lateral portion* is pinched at the *acromion process*.

3. Flexor part of upper arm. *Biceps and brachialis muscles* are relaxed because the *deltoid* is contracting.

4. Extensor part of upper arm. *Triceps* are also relaxed while the *deltoid* contracts.

5. Infraspinatus. Rides over the *triceps* toward its insertion point.

6. Teres major. Weaves under the *triceps* toward its insertion point.

7. Latissimus dorsi. Also weaves under the *triceps* on its way to its insertion point.

8. External oblique. Right side is stretched higher than the left because of the raised arm.

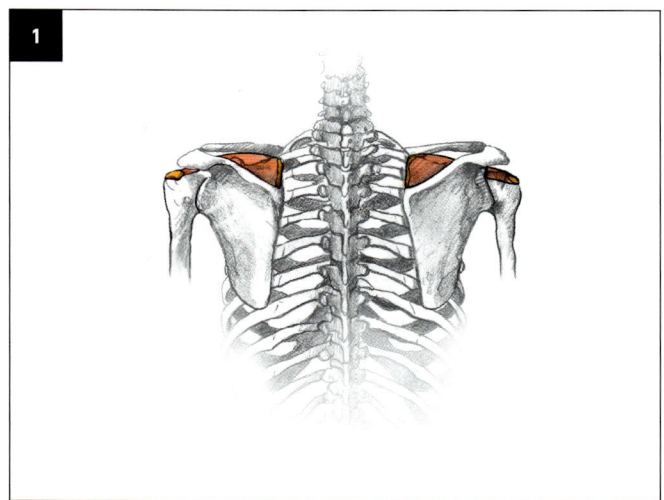

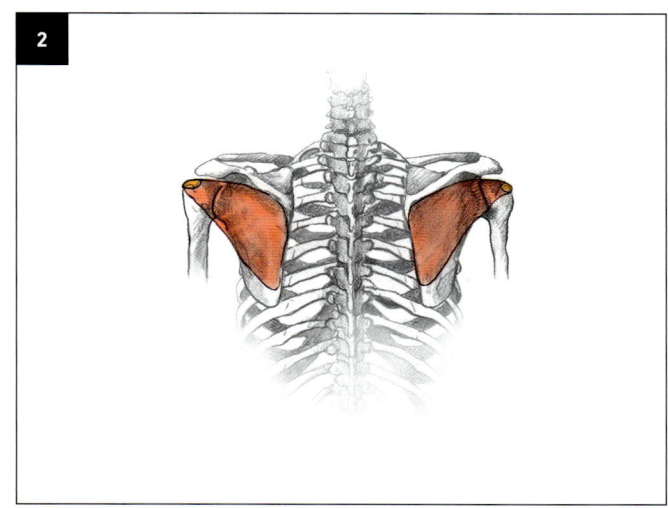

THE ROTATOR CUFF MUSCLES

The four muscles of the *rotator cuff*, just below the *deltoid*, originate from the *scapula* and insert into the *greater tubercle of the humerus*. These muscles work together to stabilize the shoulder joint and also play a major role in rotation of the arm.

(1) Supraspinatus muscle. This muscle, originating atop the scapula in the *supraspinous fossa* above the scapula's spine, inserts into the *greater tubercle of the humerus*. This muscle initiates *abduction of the arm at the shoulder joint, then the deltoid takes over*.

(2) Infraspinatus muscle. *Inferior to the spine of the scapula* is the *infraspinatus muscle*, which originates in the *infraspinous fossa* of the scapula. Like the *supraspinatus*, it, too, inserts into the *greater tubercle of the humerus*. When contracted, it causes lateral rotation of the arm at the shoulder joint.

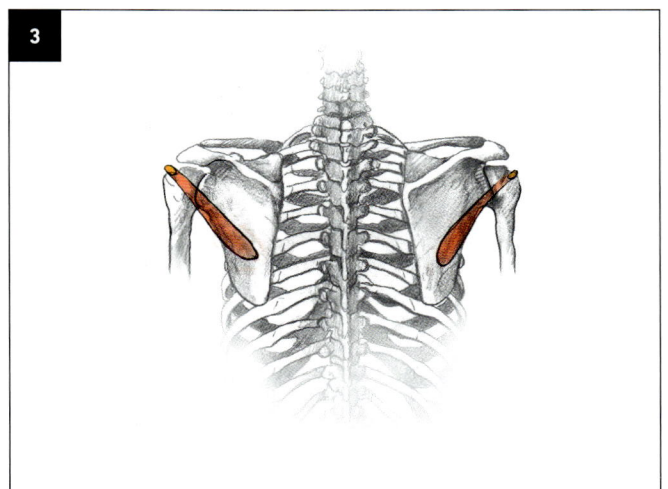

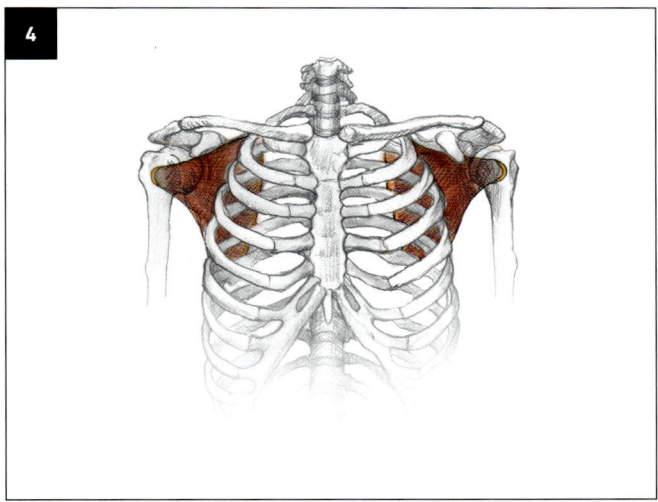

(3) Teres minor muscle. *The teres minor* originates in the *infraspinous fossa of the scapula* and inserts into the *greater tubercle of the humerus*. Like the *infraspinatus*, this muscle is also responsible for *lateral rotation* of the arm at the shoulder joint.

(4) Subscapularis muscle. The last muscle of the *rotator cuff* originates under the *scapula*, thus it can only be viewed from a frontal view. It originates from the *subscapular fossa* but, unlike the other *rotator cuff muscles*, inserts into the *lesser tubercle on the anterior side of the humerus*. Contraction of the *subscapularis* results in medial rotation of the arm at the shoulder joint (i.e., arm wrestling).

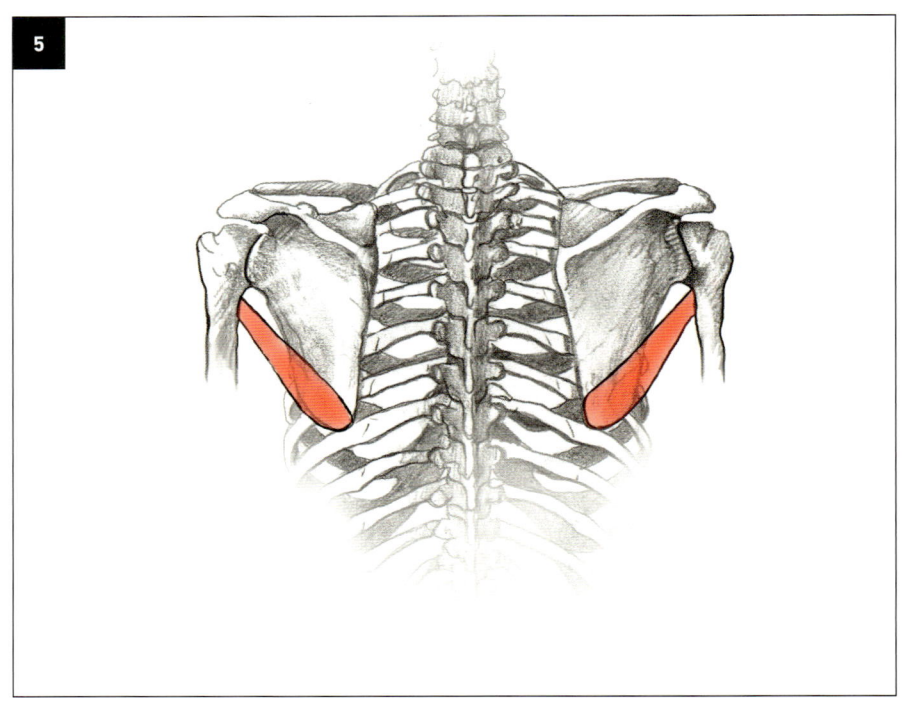

ONE MORE IMPORTANT SHOULDER MUSCLE

(5) Teres major muscle. *The teres major* originates on the *inferior angle of the scapula* underneath the *teres minor* but is **not** a part of the *rotator cuff muscles*. This muscle is responsible for *medial rotation and extension* of the arm at the shoulder joint and is much more noticeable than the *teres minor*. Instead of attaching to the *greater tubercle of the humerus,* as the rotator cuff muscles do, the *teres major* wraps underneath the *greater tubercle* and attaches to the front of the *humerus* into the *crest of the lesser tubercle* just below the insertion point of the *subscapularis*.

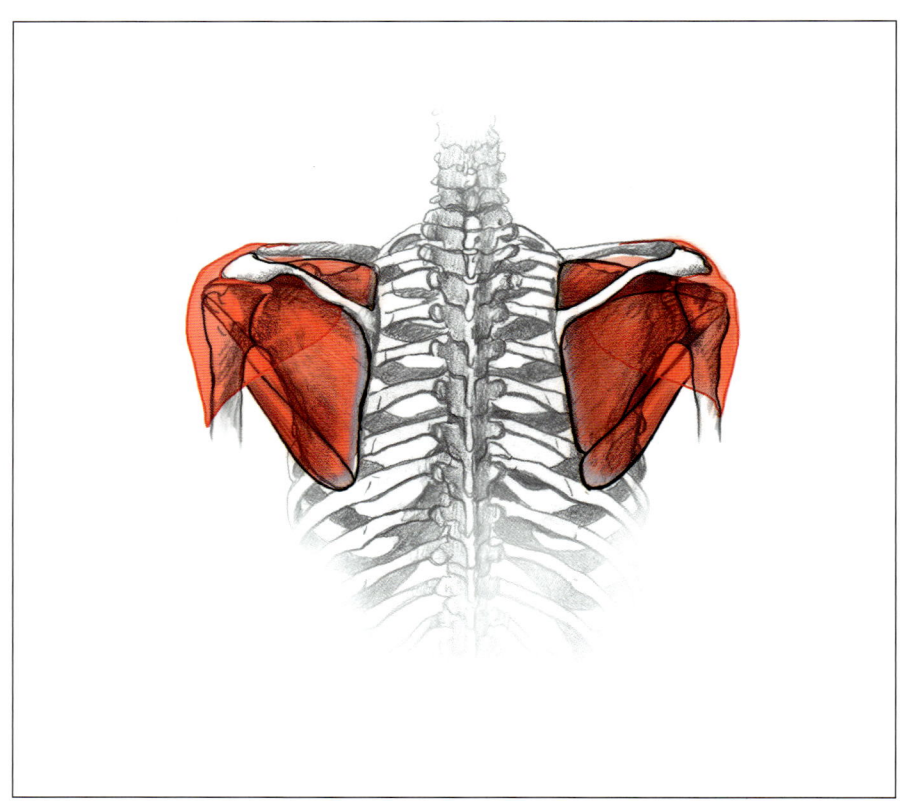

SHOULDER MUSCLES

Include a transparent deltoid that usually hides the *supraspinatus*. This is a back view diagram of three of the *rotator cuff muscles* and *teres major*. Because the *subscapularis* originates on the underside of the *scapula*, it is not visible here.

LESSON: IMPORTANT MUSCLES OF THE BACK VIEW

As you look at each individual muscle listed here, also take note of the stroke directions used to visually describe their shapes. (See page 121, "Stroke Direction: Defining Torso Anatomy.")

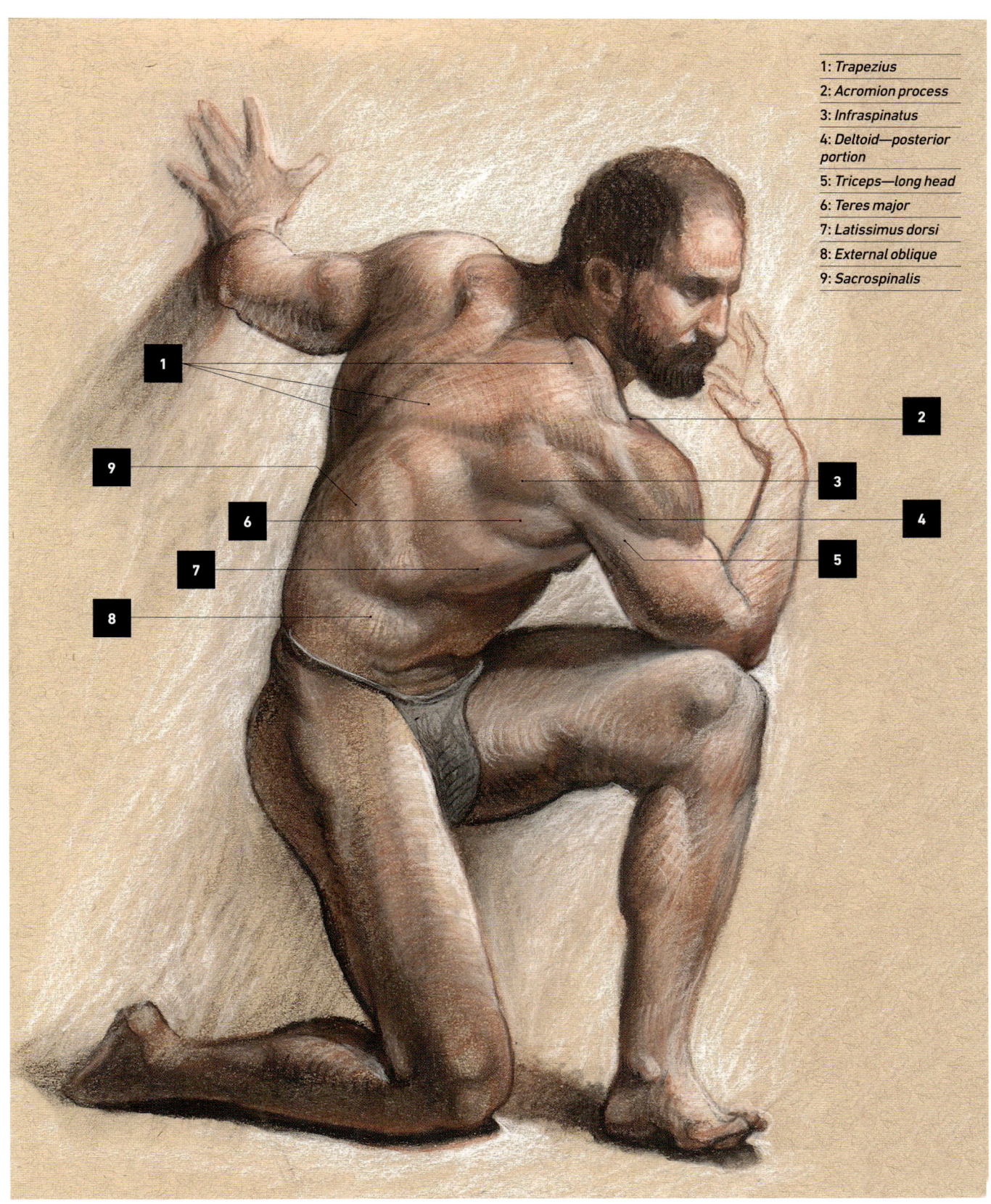

1: *Trapezius*
2: *Acromion process*
3: *Infraspinatus*
4: *Deltoid—posterior portion*
5: *Triceps—long head*
6: *Teres major*
7: *Latissimus dorsi*
8: *External oblique*
9: *Sacrospinalis*

THE TORSO, SIDE VIEW

SKELETON

The visual landmarks of the skeleton in profile are the *7th cervical vertebrae, acromion process, inner margin of scapula,* and *vertebral column. The vertebral column's four curves—cervical (forward), thoracic (backward), lumbar (forward), and sacral (backward)*—arrange the head, chest, and pelvic girdle over the legs for balance.

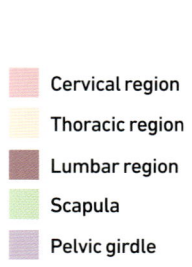

- Cervical region
- Thoracic region
- Lumbar region
- Scapula
- Pelvic girdle

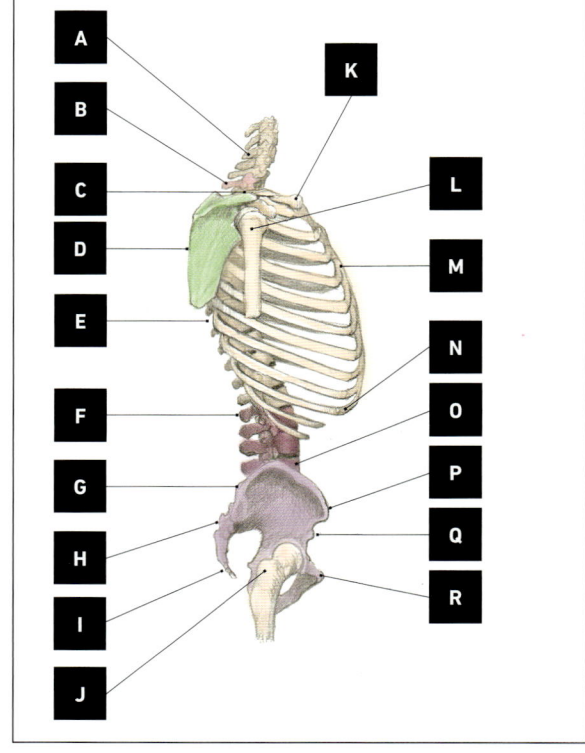

(A) Cervical curve
(B) 7th cervical vertebrae
(C) Acromion process
(D) Inner margin of scapula
(E) Thoracic curve
(F) Lumbar curve
(G) Sacrum
(H) Sacral curve
(I) Coccyx
(J) Great trochanter
(K) Clavicle
(L) Humerus
(M) Sternal angle
(N) 10th rib
(O) Iliac crest
(P) Anterior superior iliac spine (ASIS)
(Q) Anterior inferior iliac spine
(R) Pubic bone

MUSCLES

The upper torso muscles—as well as the *scapula*, which is anchored by muscle to the spine, ribs, and arms—follow and influence all arm movement. Mid-torso muscles, such as the *external oblique, rectus abdominis,* and *latissimus dorsi,* bend, twist, and stabilize the rib cage and pelvis. Muscles below the *pelvic girdle* activate the legs.

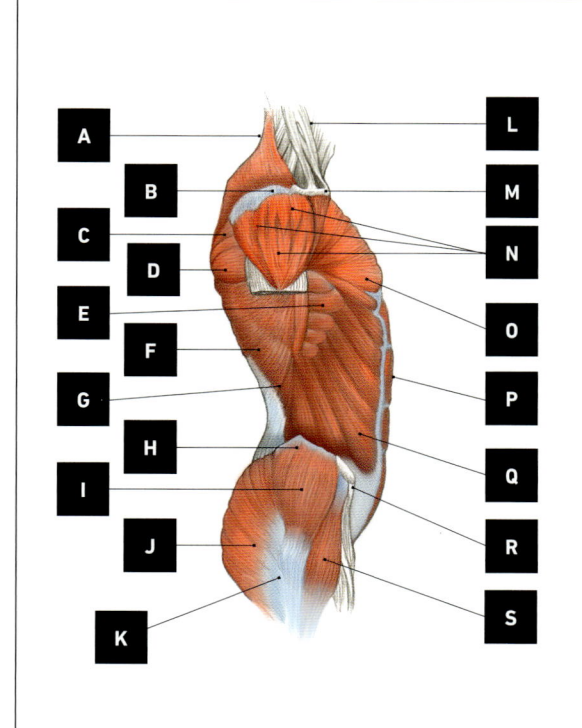

(A) Trapezius
(B) Acromion process
(C) Infraspinatus
(D) Teres major
(E) Serratus anterior
(F) Latissimus dorsi
(G) Sacrospinalis
(H) Iliac crest
(I) Gluteus medius
(J) Gluteus maximus
(K) Great trochanter
(L) Sternocleidomastoid
(M) Clavicle
(N) Deltoid
(O) Pectoralis major
(P) Rectus abdominus
(Q) External oblique
(R) Anterior superior iliac spine (ASIS)
(S) Tensor fascia lata

DIAGRAM OF LANDMARKS

It is lack of fat in addition to degree of muscularity that determines surface definition *in both males and females.* To render an average female form, it's important to become familiar with fat deposit areas that differ slightly from those of males, which include the flank (iliac crest), buttocks (gluteus), and stomach (*abdomen*), especially below the navel. Mammary fat accounts for the smoothness of the breast.

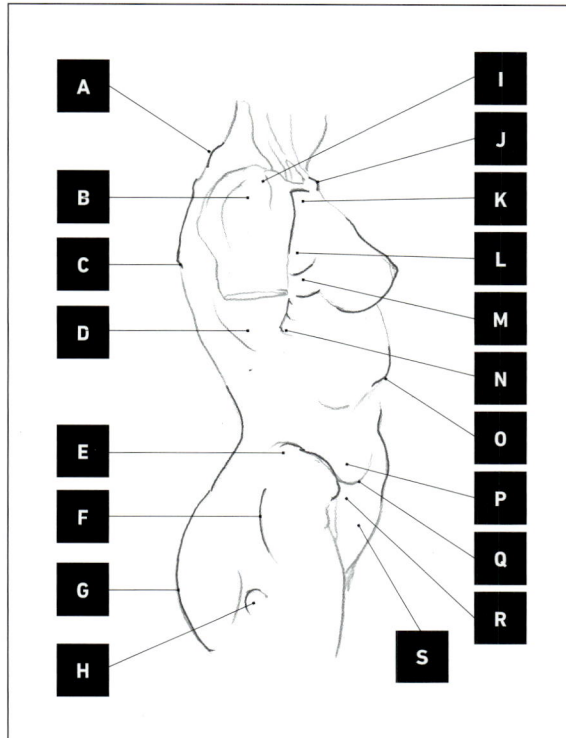

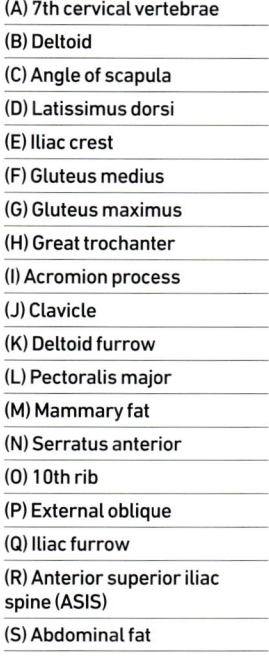

(A) 7th cervical vertebrae
(B) Deltoid
(C) Angle of scapula
(D) Latissimus dorsi
(E) Iliac crest
(F) Gluteus medius
(G) Gluteus maximus
(H) Great trochanter
(I) Acromion process
(J) Clavicle
(K) Deltoid furrow
(L) Pectoralis major
(M) Mammary fat
(N) Serratus anterior
(O) 10th rib
(P) External oblique
(Q) Iliac furrow
(R) Anterior superior iliac spine (ASIS)
(S) Abdominal fat

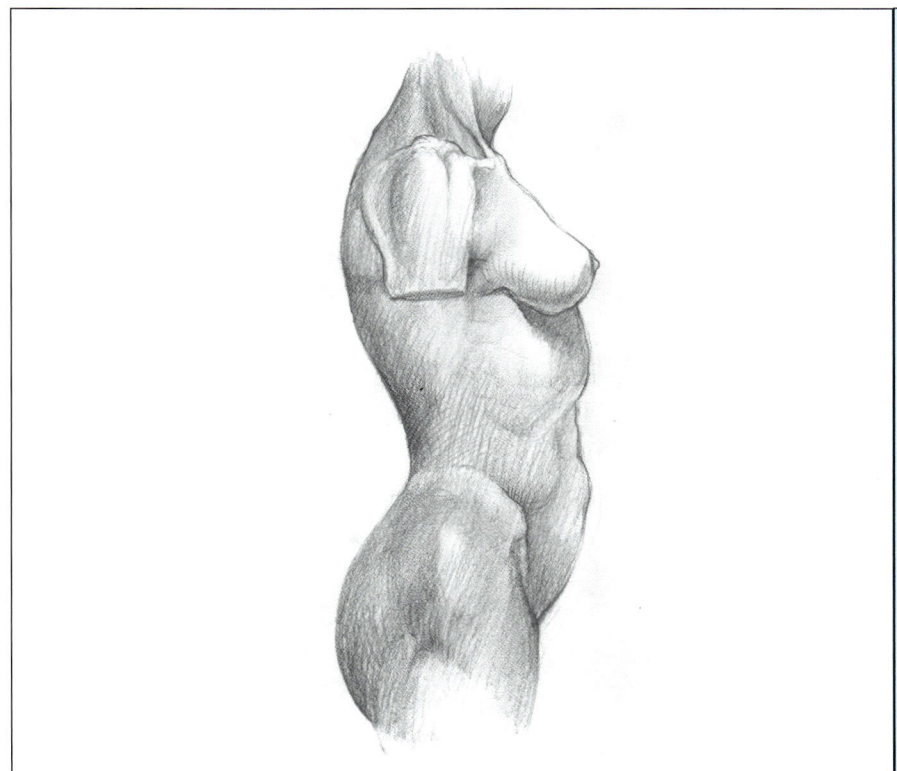

DRAWING TIPS

Female figures display a more fluid contour than do male figures, largely because of the female's extra fatty layer, which serves a reproductive purpose but also obscures muscular form. Muscular structure is basically the same for both sexes, but the width and angle of the pelvis makes the skeleton more recognizably male or female.

PROPORTIONS: SIDE VIEW

The simplified torso from the side view has a bean-shaped appearance, but the same three proportional head-size divisions of the torso apply.

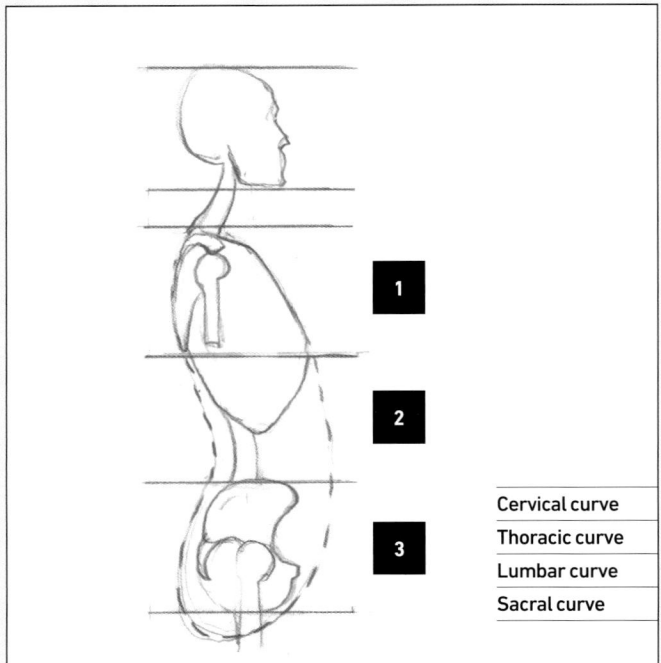

1

2

3

Cervical curve
Thoracic curve
Lumbar curve
Sacral curve

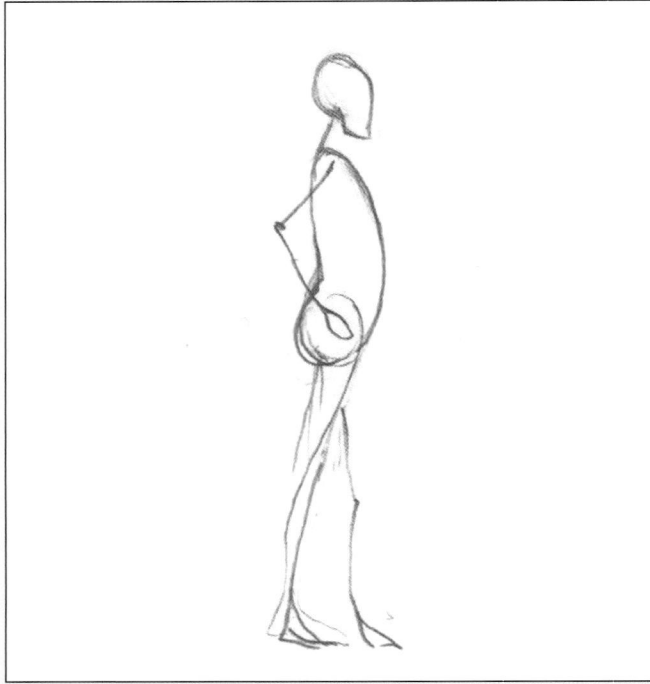

The simplified figurette in profile makes use of the bean and oval shapes that appear in the proportional drawing at left.

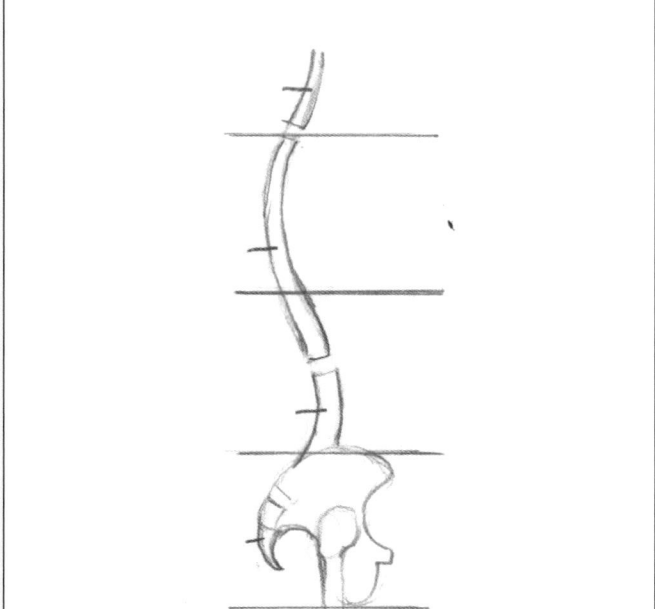

Each spinal segment curves more as the column descends toward the *sacrum*. The *thoracic region* has the longest curve.

MUSCLES OF THE TORSO, SIDE VIEW

This section provides an overview of the origins, insertions, and actions of each muscle of the torso as seen from the side.

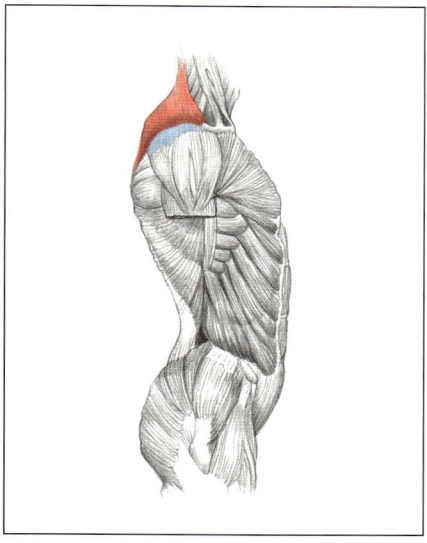

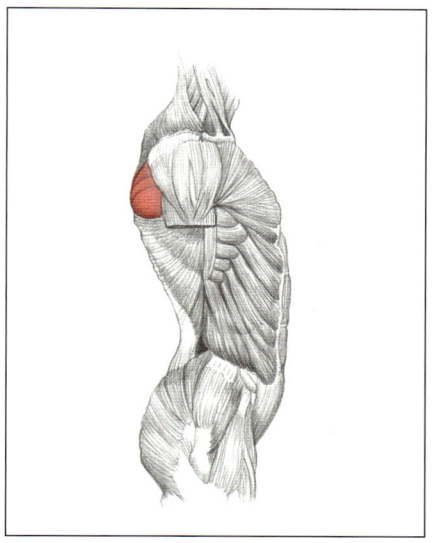

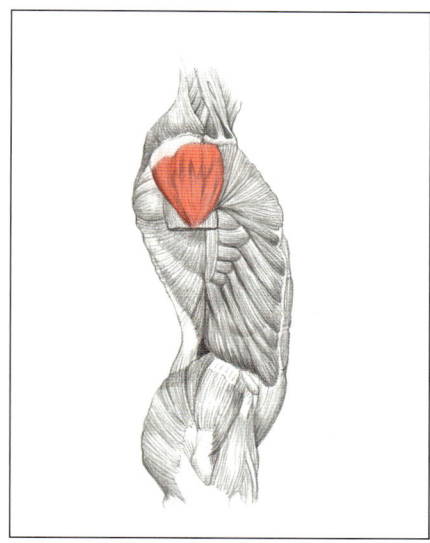

TRAPEZIUS

See "The Torso, Back View" (page 100) for specifics about origins and insertions. For artists viewing traps from the side, this is the muscle they consider most useful in showing the neck's graceful transition from shoulders to the bottom of the skull.

SCAPULAR MUSCLES

See the "The Torso, Back View" (page 100) for specifics about origins and insertions. Starting just below the *seventh cervical vertebrae*, this group of muscles forms a slightly roundish bulge that ends at the *inferior edge of the scapula* where the horizontal muscle belly of the *teres major* and the upper edge of *latissimus dorsi* meet.

DELTOID MUSCLES

Origin. Because the *deltoid muscle* has three distinct parts, an *anterior, middle (lateral),* and *posterior*, it also has three origins: Anterior—the *clavicular part* originates from the *lateral third of the clavicle.* The *acromial* (middle) part, originates from the *acromion process of the scapula*, and the *posterior part* originates on the *spine of the scapula.*

Insertion. All three sections of the *deltoid muscle* converge to insert into the *deltoid tuberosity* on the *lateral surface* of the upper part of the *humerus.*

Action. The *anterior part* raises the arm in front of the body and rotates it inward. The middle *acromial part abducts* the arm powerfully to the side, and the *posterior spinal part* extends the arm backwards.

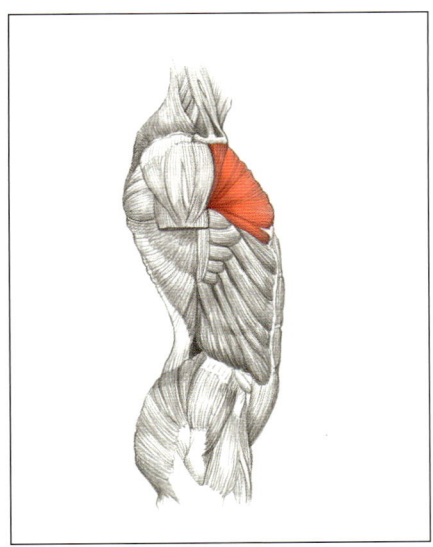

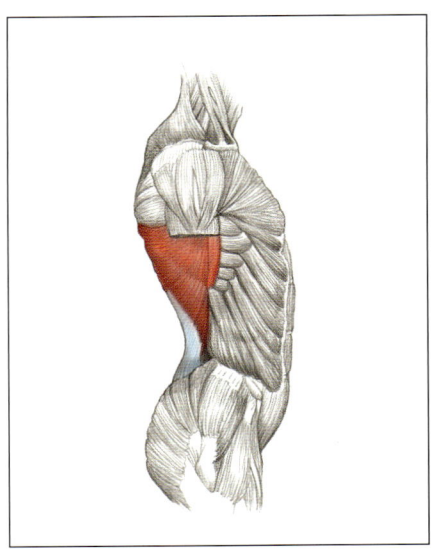

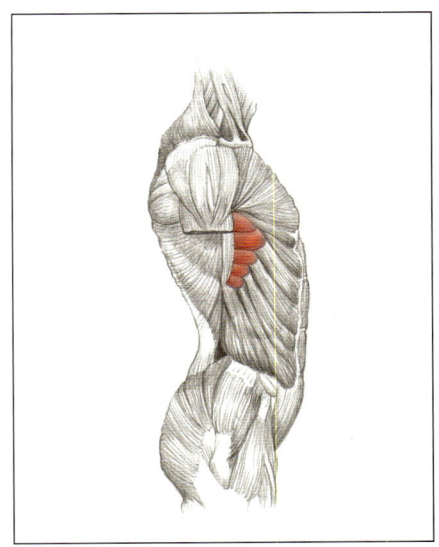

PECTORALIS MAJOR

See "The Torso, Front View" (page 96) for specifics about origins and insertions. From a side view, the horizontal upper edge of the *latissimus dorsi* lines up with the lowest part of the *pectoralis major* at the top of *rectus abdominis*.

LATISSIMUS DORSI

See "The Torso, Back View" (page 100) for specifics about origins and insertions. The *latissimus* is so thin that deeper muscles, such as the *sacrospinalis* and the *serratus anterior*, can be easily seen on a lean muscular individual.

SERRATUS ANTERIOR

One of the most important muscles of the mid-torso side view is the *serratus anterior*.

Origin. A line of small *triangular-shaped attachments* on the *outside of the first eight or nine ribs*.

Insertion. The *vertebral margin* of the underside of the *scapula* (between the ribs and scapula).

Action. Slides the *scapula forward* (as in punching), and *laterally*, as in elevating the shoulder.

SERRATUS ANTERIOR: DETAILS

The form of the *serratus anterior* embraces the rounded shape of the *rib cage*.

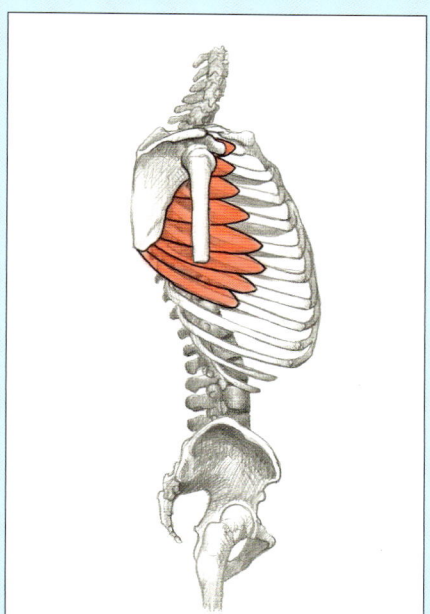

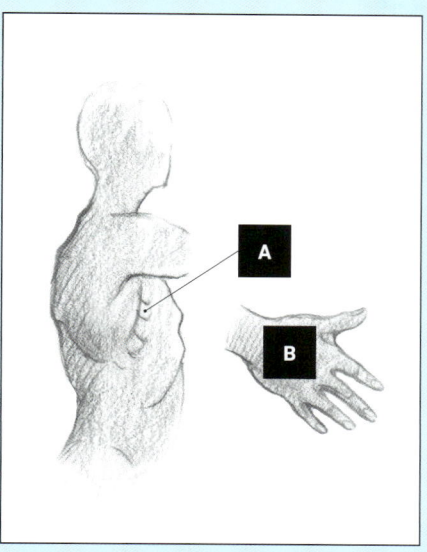

The main mass of the *serratus anterior* appears as a bulge underneath the *latissimus dorsi* (**A**). At the muscle's origin (on the ribs), it looks a little like the fingers of a hand (**B**).

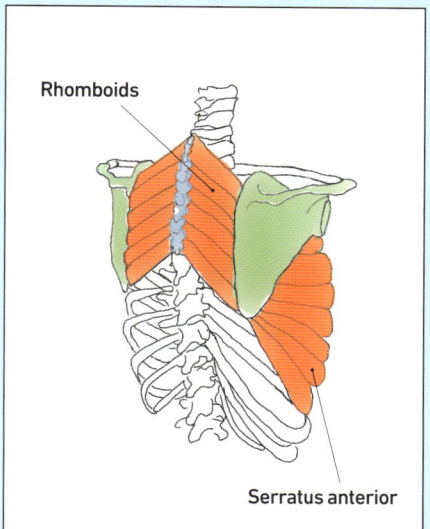

The *serratus anterior and rhomboid muscles* pull the *scapula* diagonally against one another. Actually, the "freewheeling" *scapula* can be pulled in almost any direction, like a raft on the water with ropes attached to all of its sides. The names of these "ropes," with their differing insertion points on the *scapula*, are the *trapezius*, *rhomboids*, and *serratus anterior* muscles.

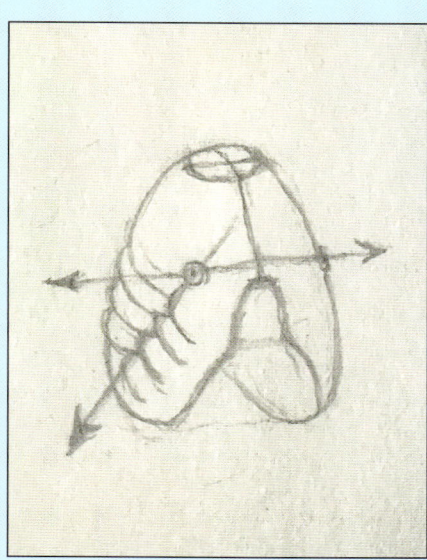

When drawing a male torso, remember that the line of *inter-digitation* between the *serratus anterior* and the *external oblique muscles* always lines up diagonally with the nipples. Knowing this is a great help.

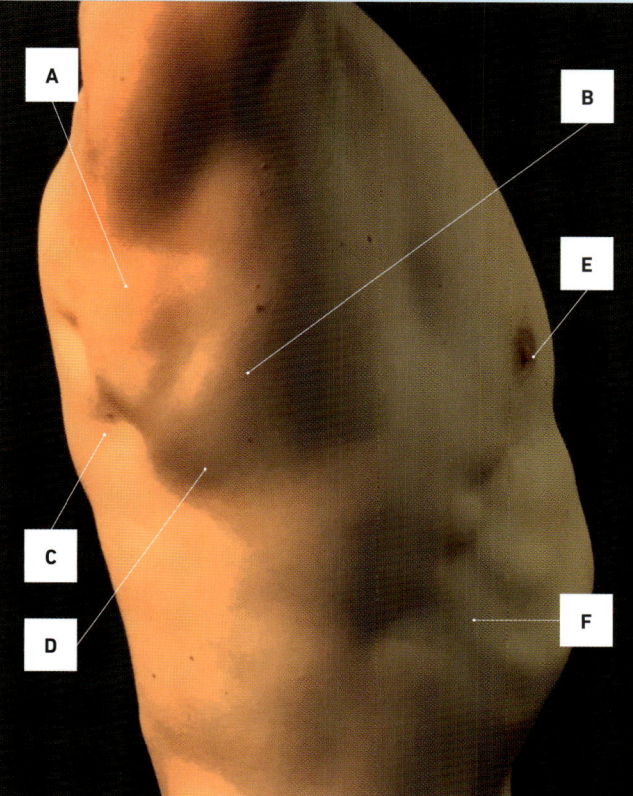

Observations on the model:

(**A**) infraspinatus

(**B**) teres major

(**C**) vertebral border of scapula

(**D**) inferior angle (bottom) of *scapula*

(**E**) diagonal angle of the *serratus anterior's digitations* always point toward nipple

(**F**) Where the *serratus anterior* and *external oblique muscles* meet, the fingerlike forms of the *serratus muscles over the ribs* are rounded, whereas the thinner *oblique strap-like forms* of *external oblique* are flat.

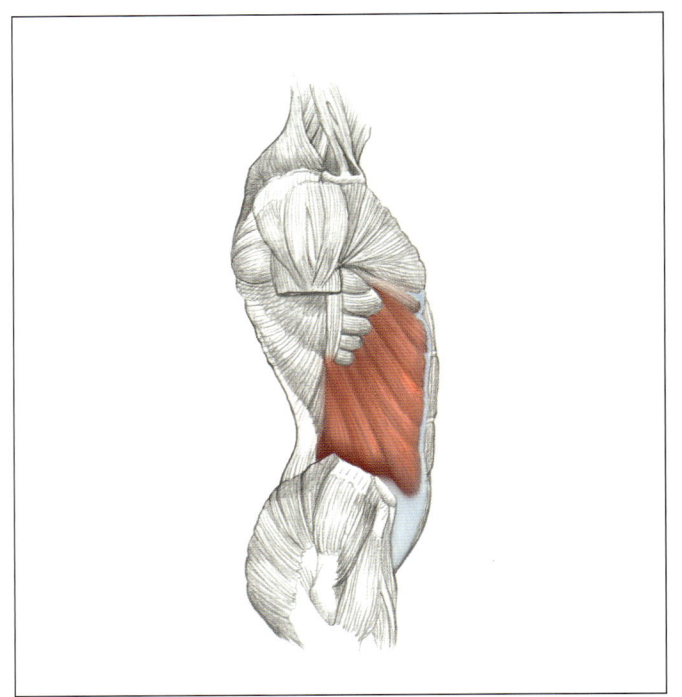

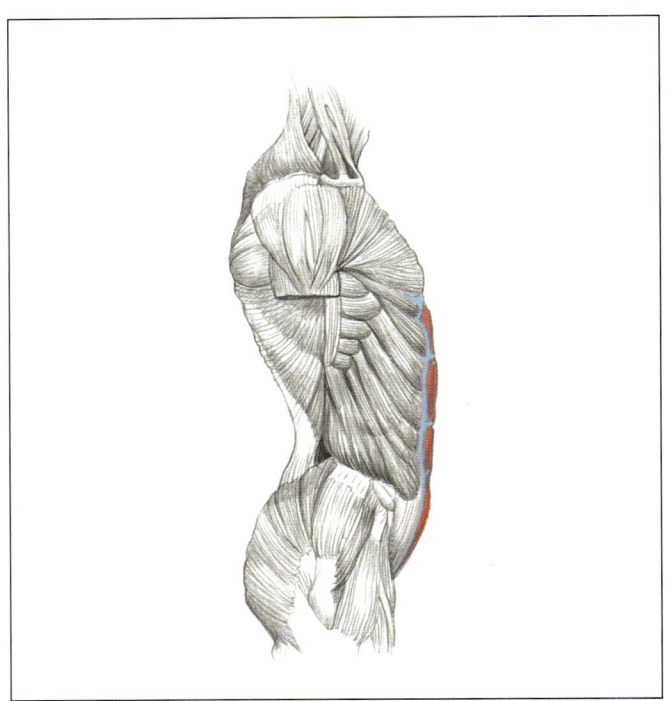

EXTERNAL OBLIQUE

Origins and insertions are covered in "The Torso, Front View" (see page 96). The *external oblique* consists of a large, thin muscular sheet on the side of the torso with a large *aponeurosis* that stretches over the entire *abdomen on top of the rectus abdominis* (see front view). The muscular portion of this muscle is divided into two parts: an *upper thoracic portion and a lower flank portion.*

RECTUS ABDOMINIS

See "The Torso, Front View" (page 96) for origins and insertions.

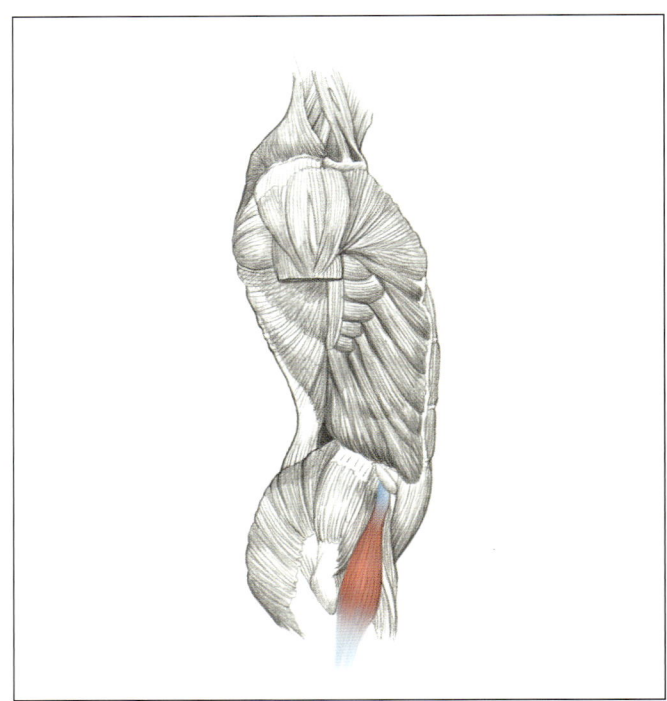

TENSOR FASCIA LATA, GLUTEUS MEDIUS, AND GLUTEUS MAXIMUS

These three muscles, grouped together with the *pelvis*, collectively comprise the outer *hip region*. While the front plane of this area is formed by the lower portion of the abdomen *(rectus abdominis)*, the sides are formed by the *gluteus maximus, gluteus medius*, and *tensor fascia lata*. The *greater trochanter* is central to all three as an insertion point.

Tensor Fascia Lata

Origin. Anterior superior iliac spine—ASIS.

Insertion. Upper portion of the *iliotibial band (IT band)*.

Action. Flexes, abducts, and medially rotates the thigh. Provides tension for the *iliotibial band and stabilizes the knee joint.*

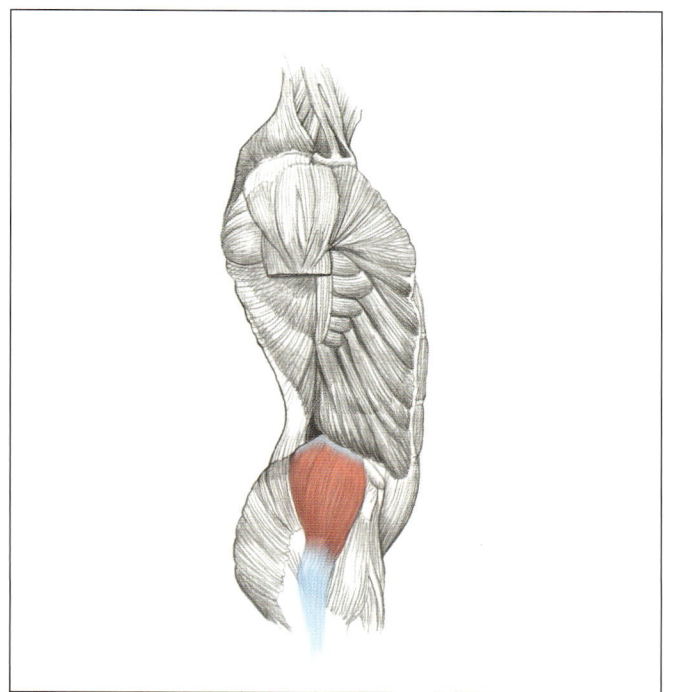

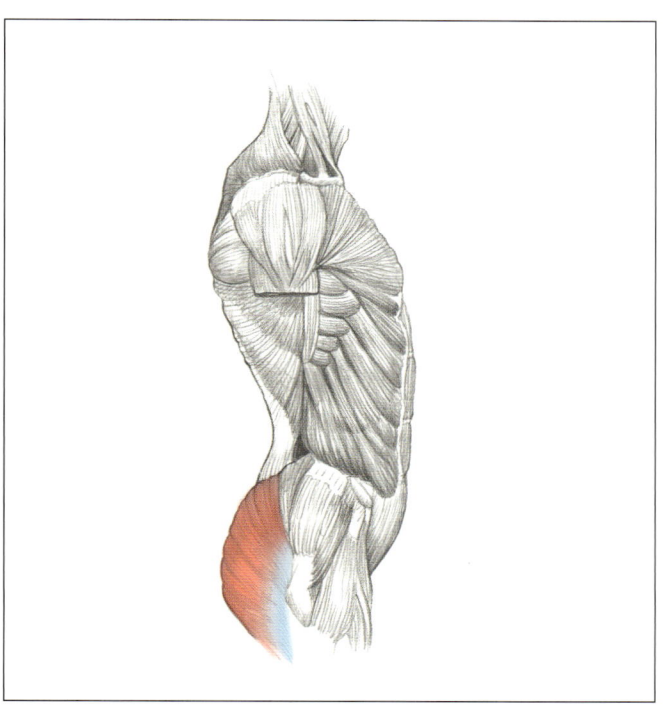

Gluteus Medius

Origin. Outer surface of a portion of the *ilium (pelvis), up to the iliac crest.*

Insertion. *Greater trochanter of the femur.*

Action. Abducts the thigh, rotates the thigh *medially and laterally.*

Gluteus Maximus

Origin. *Lateral surface of ilium* including the *posterior superior iliac spine (PSIS)* and a small part of the *ilium.*

Insertion. Upper portion of the *iliotibial band. Posterior shaft of the femur just below trochanters.*

Action. Facilitate *abduction and extension* of the thigh backwards, *rotates it outward and provides tension for the iliotibial band.*

LESSON: LOOKING UNDER THE SKIN

The entire purpose of this book is to enable artists to not only be able to see well-lit surface forms but to also understand which bones and muscles cause those forms. Look carefully at this drawing and see if you can identify the following muscles:

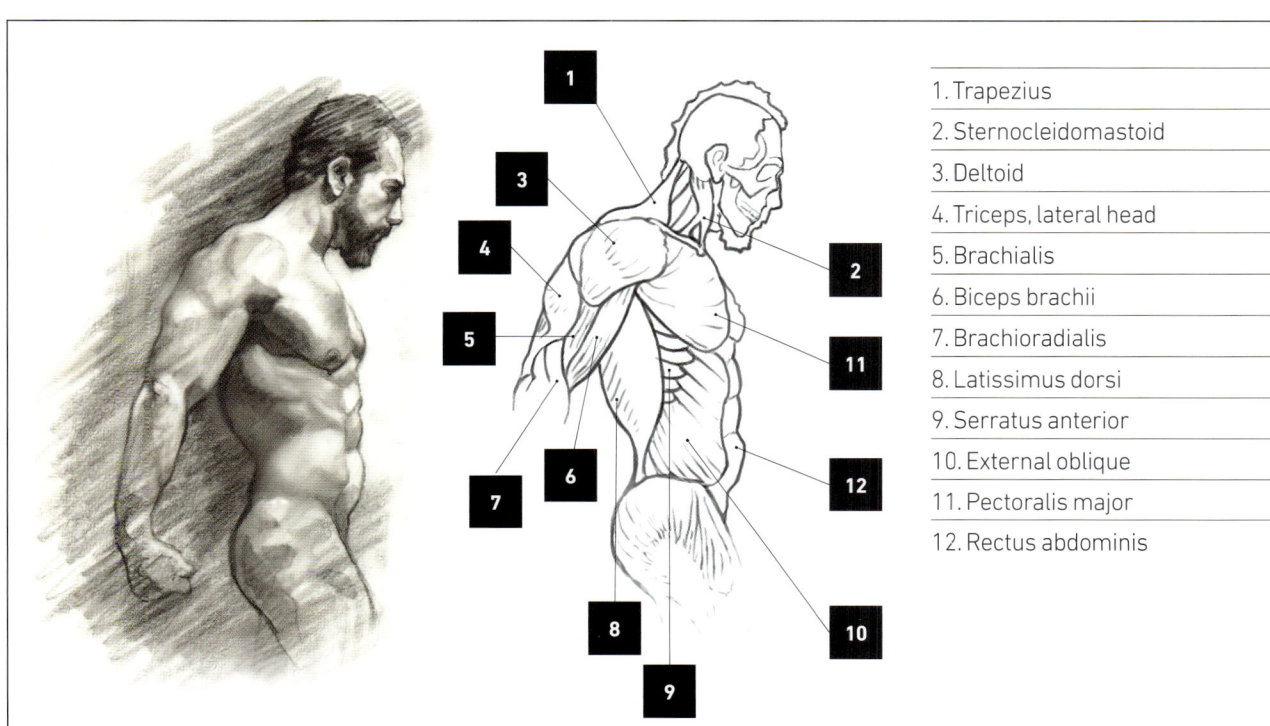

1. Trapezius
2. Sternocleidomastoid
3. Deltoid
4. Triceps, lateral head
5. Brachialis
6. Biceps brachii
7. Brachioradialis
8. Latissimus dorsi
9. Serratus anterior
10. External oblique
11. Pectoralis major
12. Rectus abdominis

ANATOMY IN PRACTICE: THE TORSO

SIMPLIFYING SHADOW SHAPES

Because the human form is so complex, artists throughout time have come up with effective, simple methods to start drawings in a way that each sequential stage of the process is a firm foundation for the next. Drawing 1 shows the best way to begin: Simplify the main shadow into a single large shape with definite accurate angles. Then place the lighter halftones next to it as a transition between the shadow and the highlights. The refinement seen in Drawing 2 is accomplished by simply softening and rounding out the angled edges with a blending stump and a kneaded eraser.

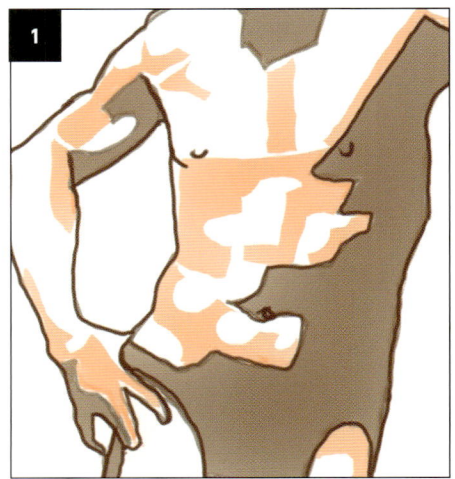

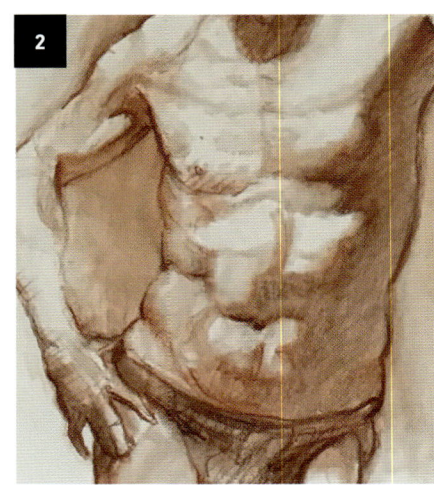

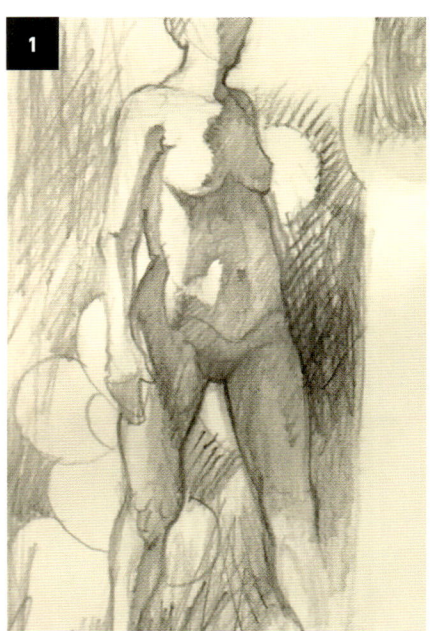

This simple 20-minute graphite sketch shows how basic shapes of light and dark are very effective, even without details. Invented arbitrary shapes make the negative space around this figure more interesting.

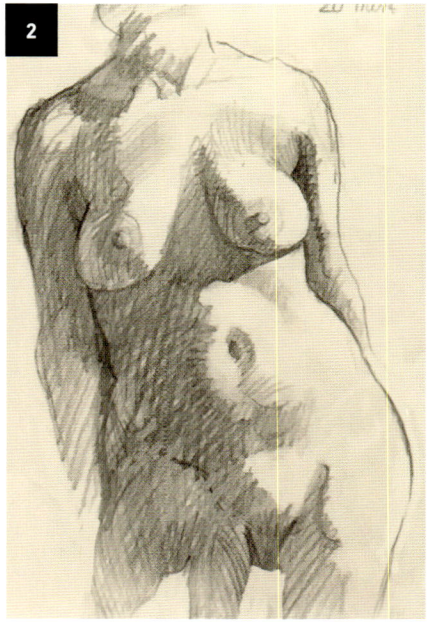

An artist should always focus on the part of the figure they find most interesting. In this 20-minute crosshatched sketch of a torso, I was intrigued mostly by the overall lighting and how the cast shadow came off the model's left breast and blended into the form shadow on her roundish belly.

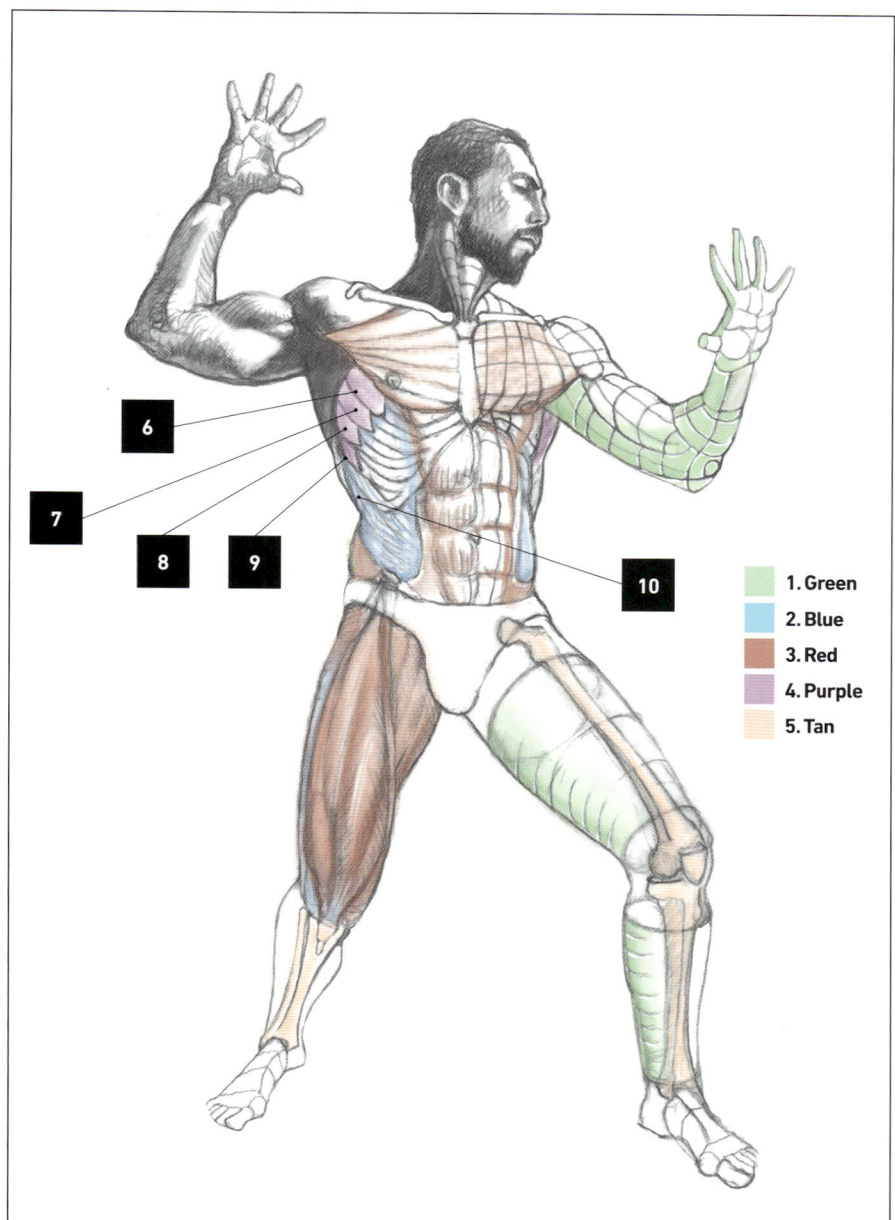

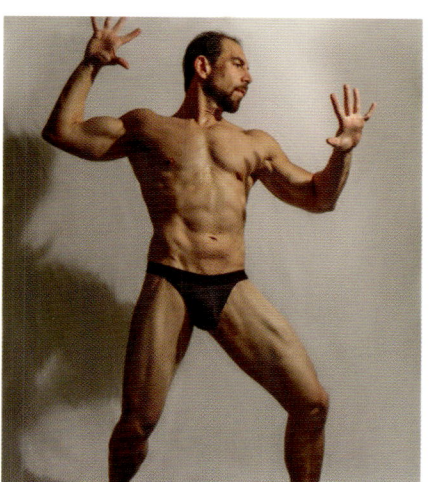

1. Green
2. Blue
3. Red
4. Purple
5. Tan

The serratus anterior originates on ribs 1 through 9; however, it only becomes visible on ribs 6 through 9 (shown here). The tenth rib is a separate but important landmark that indicates where the bottom of the rib cage is.

This drawing is a potpourri of several anatomy and drawing lessons:

1. **Green.**

Left leg: A figure's limbs are first conceived as cylinders.

Left arm: The wrist is a block that becomes a cylinder with cross-contours on the forearm. Study the directional lines of these cross-contours; they have the same stroke directions as the actual shading on this model's fully rendered right hand, arm, and head.

2. **Blue.** The *external oblique* is a visually important muscle to know about when constructing a torso.

3. **Red.** The right side of this model shows the anatomy of the *pectoralis major and the rectus abdominis*, and on the right leg, the *quads, iliotibial band, sartorius*, and *adductors*.

The left side of the torso shows how cross-contours follow the undulating planes of the breast and belly, and how following their directions creates a sense of volume.

4. **Purple.** *Ribs 6 through 9* reveal the visible part of the *serratus anterior muscle*.

5. **Tan**

Left leg: Shows the placements of the *femur, patella*, and *tibia*.

Right leg: The *tibia* and *fibula*.

Study these lessons in relation to the anatomy we've covered thus far, and consider these ideas the next time you draw a standing figure.

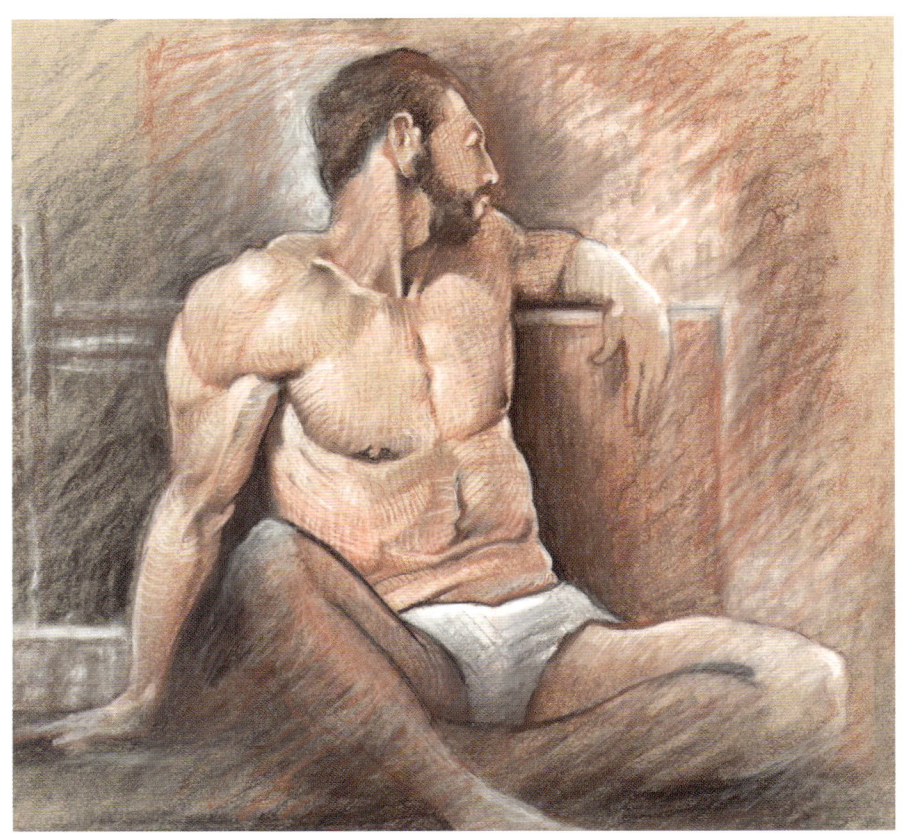

IMPORTANT LANDMARKS ON THE TORSO AND UPPER ARM

This is a relaxed pose; however, there is still quite a bit of supportive weight on the model's right arm.

1. This rounded bulge, caused by the arm's upward pressure, is the *head of the humerus and acromion process* being pushed up.

2. The *deltoid*, because of the upward pressure, is slightly flexed too.

3. The *triceps lateral head* is also slightly flexed.

4. The *brachialis* can be barely seen (like a small piece of meat sandwiched between *triceps and biceps*).

5. *Biceps* are, of course, always very visible.

6. The *serratus anterior* is relaxed so it is barely visible.

7. The *external obliques* are also very relaxed and difficult to see.

8. The *pectoralis major* weaves over the *biceps* and under the *deltoid* where it attaches to the *humerus*.

9. This dark indentation just below the *clavicle* is the *infraclavicular fossa*, a small area of separation between the *pectoralis major* and *deltoid muscles*.

10. The *sternum* is an important landmark as it is always parallel to the sides of the rib cage, no matter what the other muscles are doing. Artists rely on the sternum's direction when deciding how to angle the rib cage.

11. The anatomical centerline, *linea alba*, is as important as the sternum because it connects the pit of the neck (via the *sternum*) to the *symphysis pubis* of the pelvic girdle, which helps to add dimension to a torso.

STROKE DIRECTION: DEFINING TORSO ANATOMY

I am a big fan of making each stroke direction on the flat 2D papers we draw on count toward creating a convincing illusion of 3D forms. The best way to learn how to do this is to practice drawing lots of cross-contours (as shown in the previous lesson).

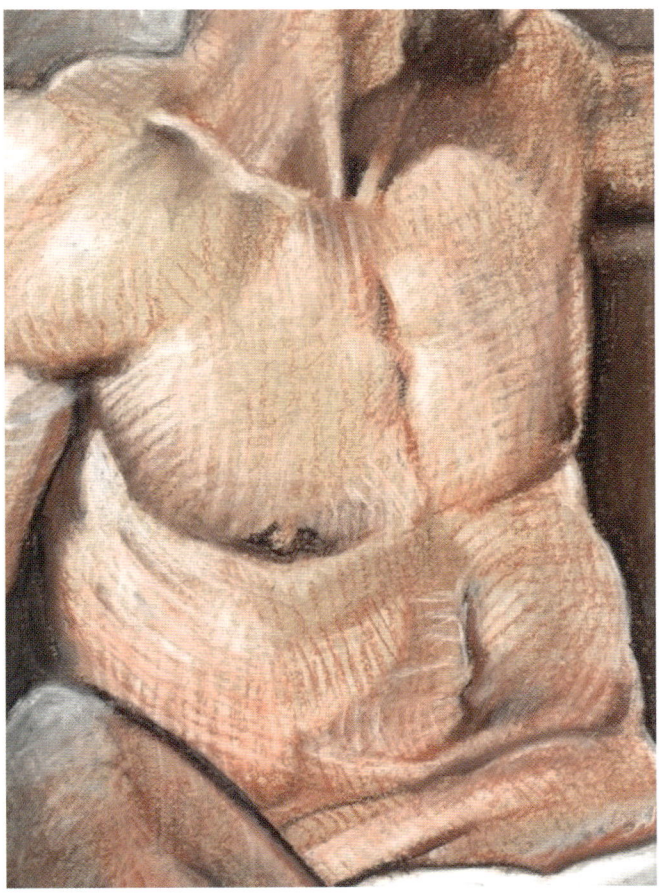

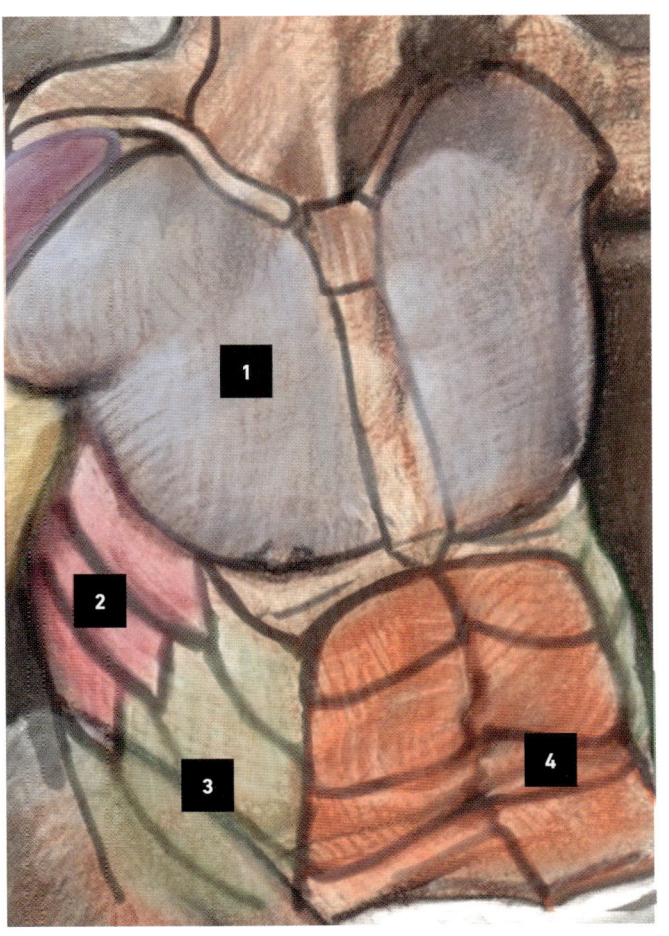

1. Where the *pectoralis major* muscle meets a flat rib cage on the bottom and side planes, the cross-hatched strokes are curved. They then travel vertically and horizontally when the front plane becomes flat.

2. Because the *serratus anterior* and **3**. *external oblique* muscles both travel in an oblique direction, the strokes used here are also oblique because *flat side-lighting* does not bring out any particular forms to define.

4. Notice how the direction of the strokes changes when a crease at the navel redirects the *rectus abdominis muscle* from a *front-facing plane* into an *up-facing plane*. This clarifies the new planar direction to a viewer.

IMPORTANT PALPABLE BONY LANDMARKS

In anatomy, any prominent bone that can be seen and felt is considered to be palpable. Of course, there are many more palpable bones than the ones listed here, but the ones below are all important landmarks. Try feeling each one on your own body to become more familiar with what you will see on a model.

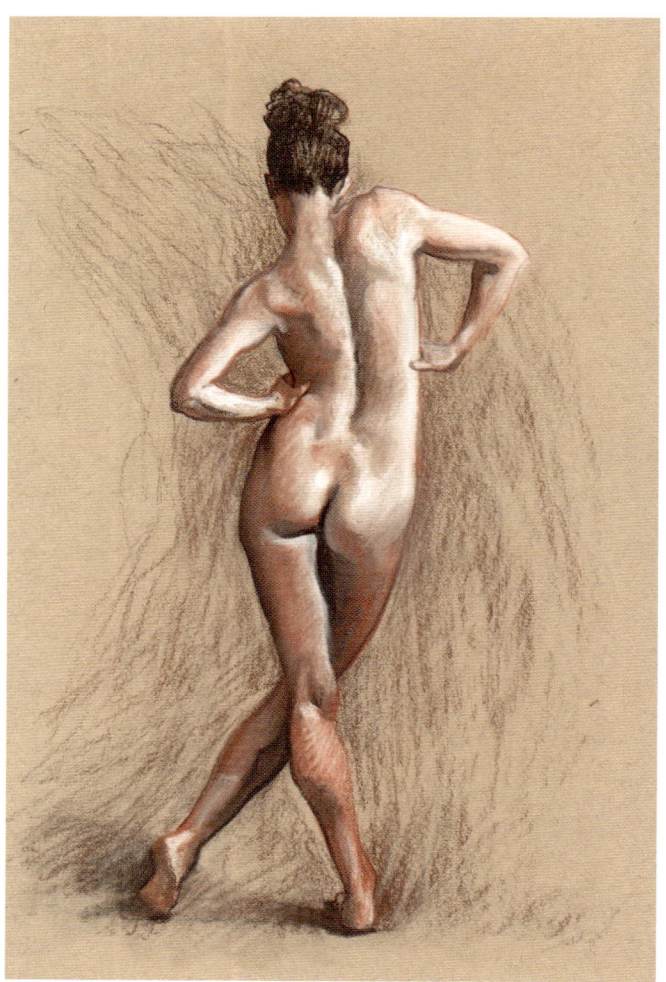

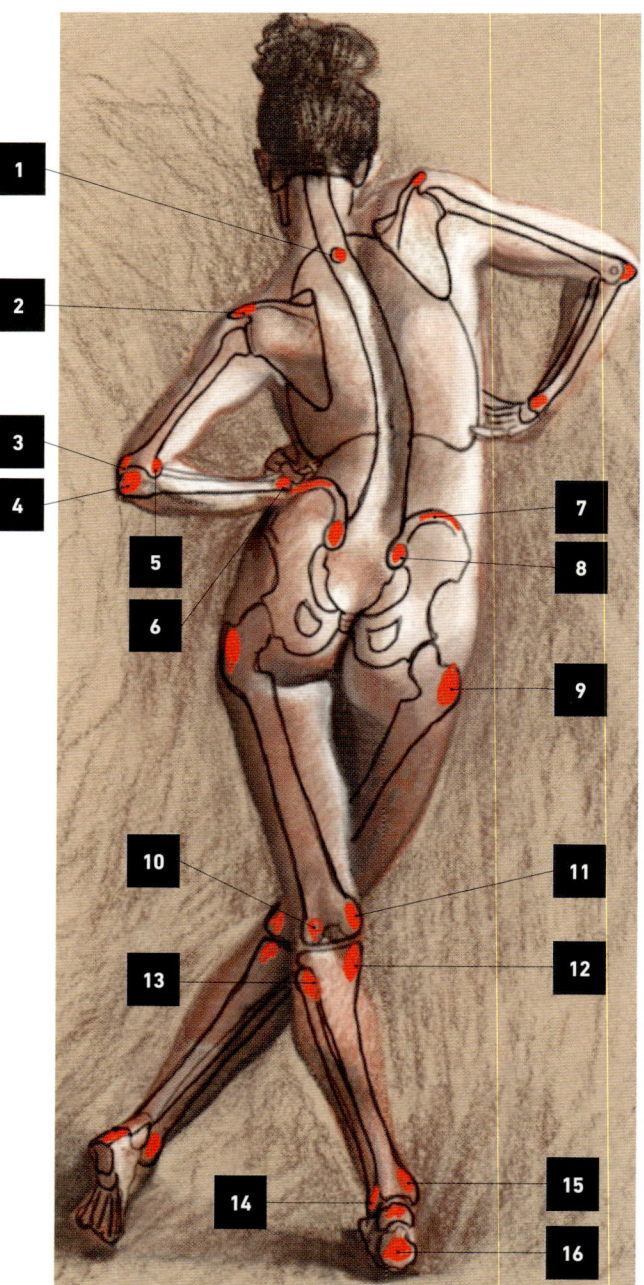

1. *Seventh cervical vertebra*

2. *Acromion process* (end of the *spine of the scapula*)

3. *Lateral epicondyle*

4. *Olecranon (elbow)*

5. *Medial epicondyle*— the funny bone *(ulnar nerve)* is also palpable if you accidentally bump it.

6. *Styloid process of radius*

7. *Iliac crest*

8. *Posterior superior iliac spine (PSI)*

9. *Greater trochanter*

10. *Lateral condyle of the femur*

11. *Medial condyle of the femur*

12. *Medial condyle of the tibia*

13. *Head of the fibula*

14. *Lateral malleolus*

15. *Medial malleolus*

16. *Calcaneus*

UNDERSTANDING PROPORTIONS

Proportions are an important aspect of figure drawing. Proportion is the correct size of one form in relation to another form, such as the size of the head in comparison to the chest. And establishing the correct proportions of a figure before you start developing your drawing is essential for creating realistic renderings. Basic artistic anatomy will provide you with guidelines to the general proportions that apply to all human figures, but it's also important to note the subtle differences among individual subjects.

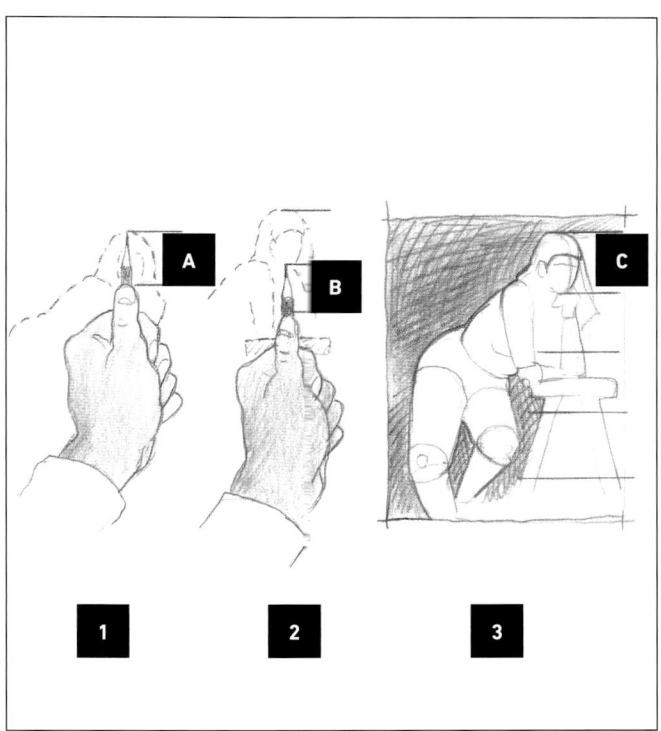

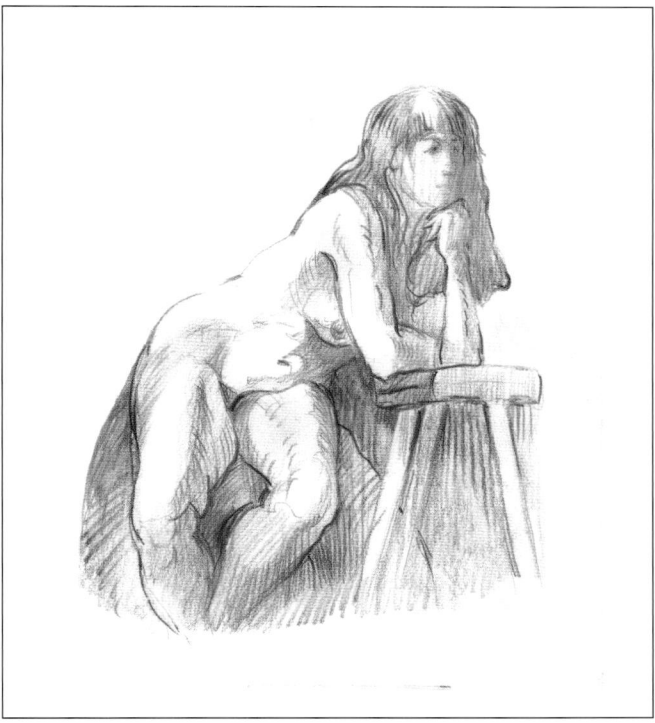

Measuring Proportions. To establish general proportions, stretch your arm out straight, visually align your pencil tip with the top of the model's head, and align your thumbnail with the chin (**1**). This establishes your unit of measurement, one head length (**A**)

Now lower your arm until the tip of the pencil is aligned with the chin (**2**). The point where your thumbnail rests is the end of the second head length (**B**). Continue this procedure until you establish the total number of head lengths that make up the figure.

Use the proportions you've established as a guide (**C**) as you sketch (**3**). To further develop your drawing, simplify complex anatomy by thinking in terms of basic lines and shapes, such as curved lines and cylinders. And fill in the negative space (the area surrounding the object) to define the edges of the positive space (the model).

Creating Depth. Separating the dark values of the shadows from the light areas of the drawing helps produce a sense of depth and volume. Only a few lines are necessary to show where the edges meet and blend.

DIVIDING SPACE INTO QUARTERS AND HALVES TO FIND PROPORTIONS

Sometimes, rather than using a specific measurement (such as a head) as a standard, it's easier to just look for simpler measurements such as halves and quarters and see what parts of the pose they might line up with. Here are two examples.

On this particular pose, it turned out that a *head to shoulder measurement* happened to *fit into this model's entire length four times*. The second fourth measurement *landed on her waist*, the third fourth *on the bottom of the bench*, and the fourth fourth *at her toes*. This was a good way to find starting proportions.

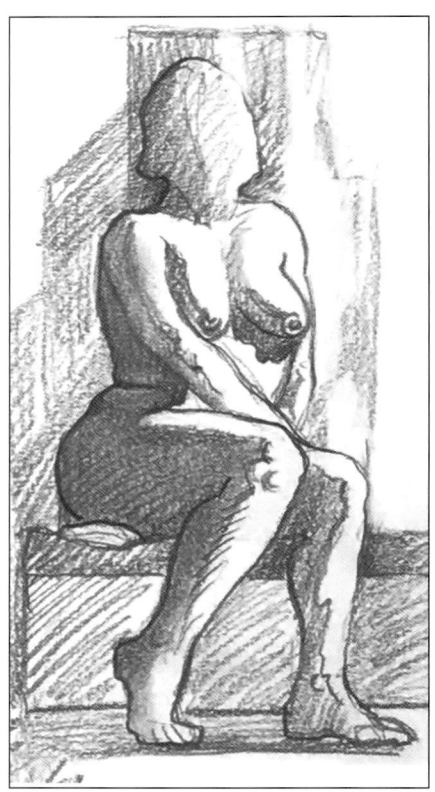

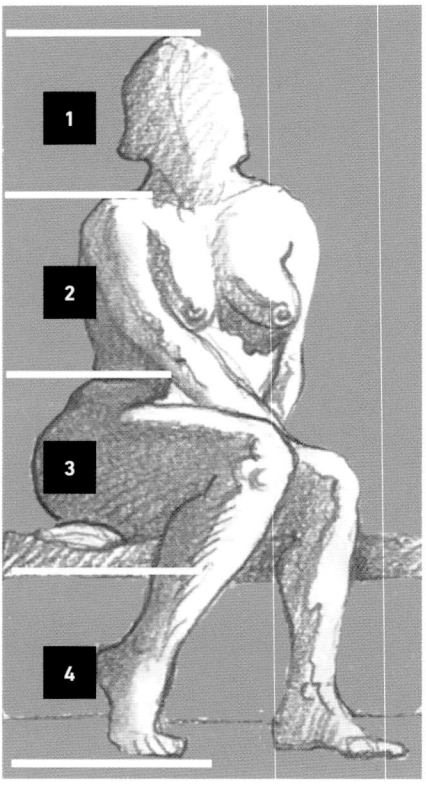

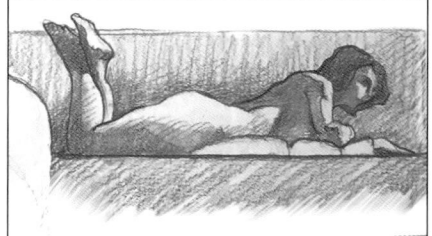

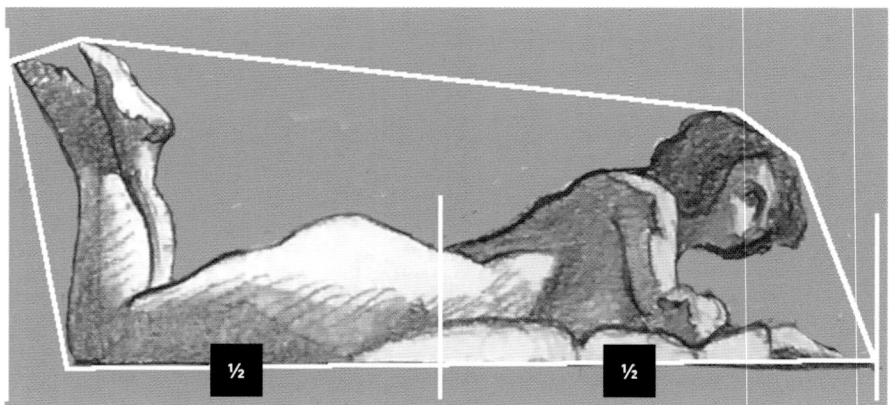

Placing a linear envelope (white line) around this reclining pose's extremities helped to gauge *how much higher the feet were than the head*. I was also very fortunate to find a measurement *at the transition from her butt to lower back* that just happened to be *exactly one-half of the entire pose*.

Since both of these poses needed to be finished in 20 minutes, I simplified the faces (which would have taken too long) and instead just focused on only the most essential parts, the grace of the poses and the dramatic lighting.

TWO STAGES OF A 20-MINUTE LIFE DRAWING

The drawings in this demonstration were done with vine charcoal and green pastel.

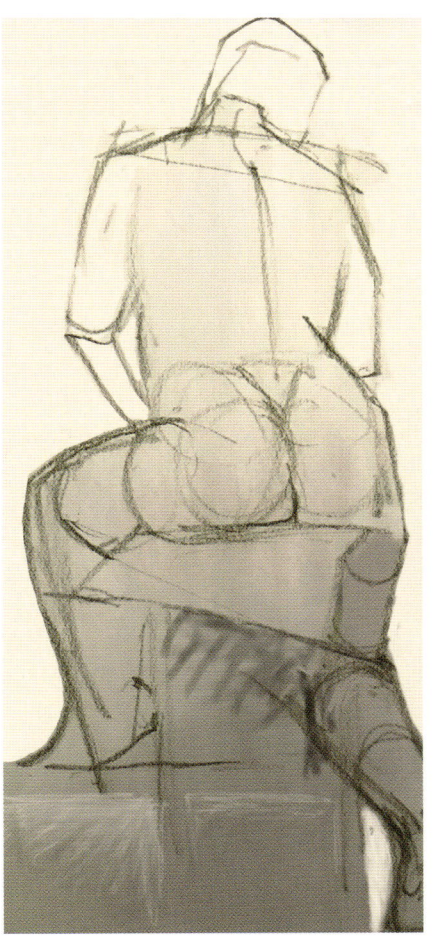 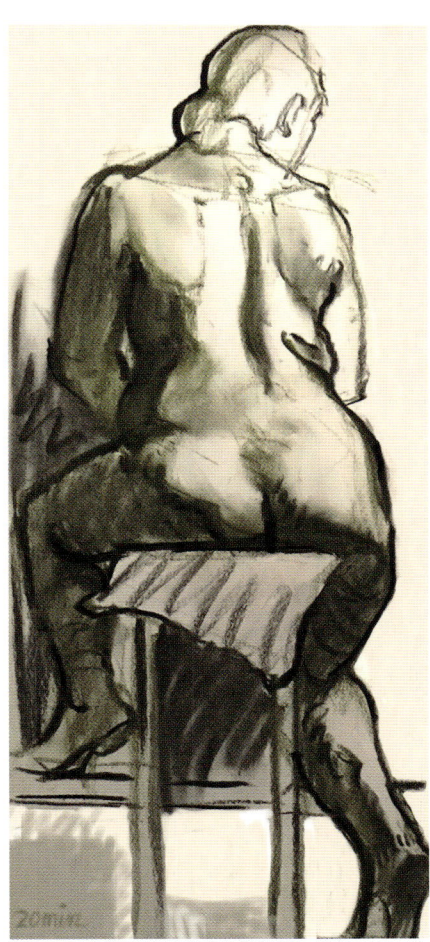

Stage 1

1. In this pose, I found that *a measurement from the top of the head to the right slanted shoulder* (where it meets the chin) *went into the entire length of the figure seven times* (see the two previous sections on how to measure).

2. The next step (pictured here) was to lightly sketch in the outer shapes with correct angles while paying special attention to the surrounding negative spaces. Cylinders were added wherever there was foreshortening, and faint guidelines determined important anatomical placements, such as the spine, sacral triangle, C7 vertebra, and the two scapulas.

Stage 2

3. Using a combination of green pastel and vine charcoal, the shadow shape was massed in first, then the half-tones, and finally edges between shadow and light were blended together with a finger. For final touches, accented dark lines and a slight indication of features were added just before the timer went off.

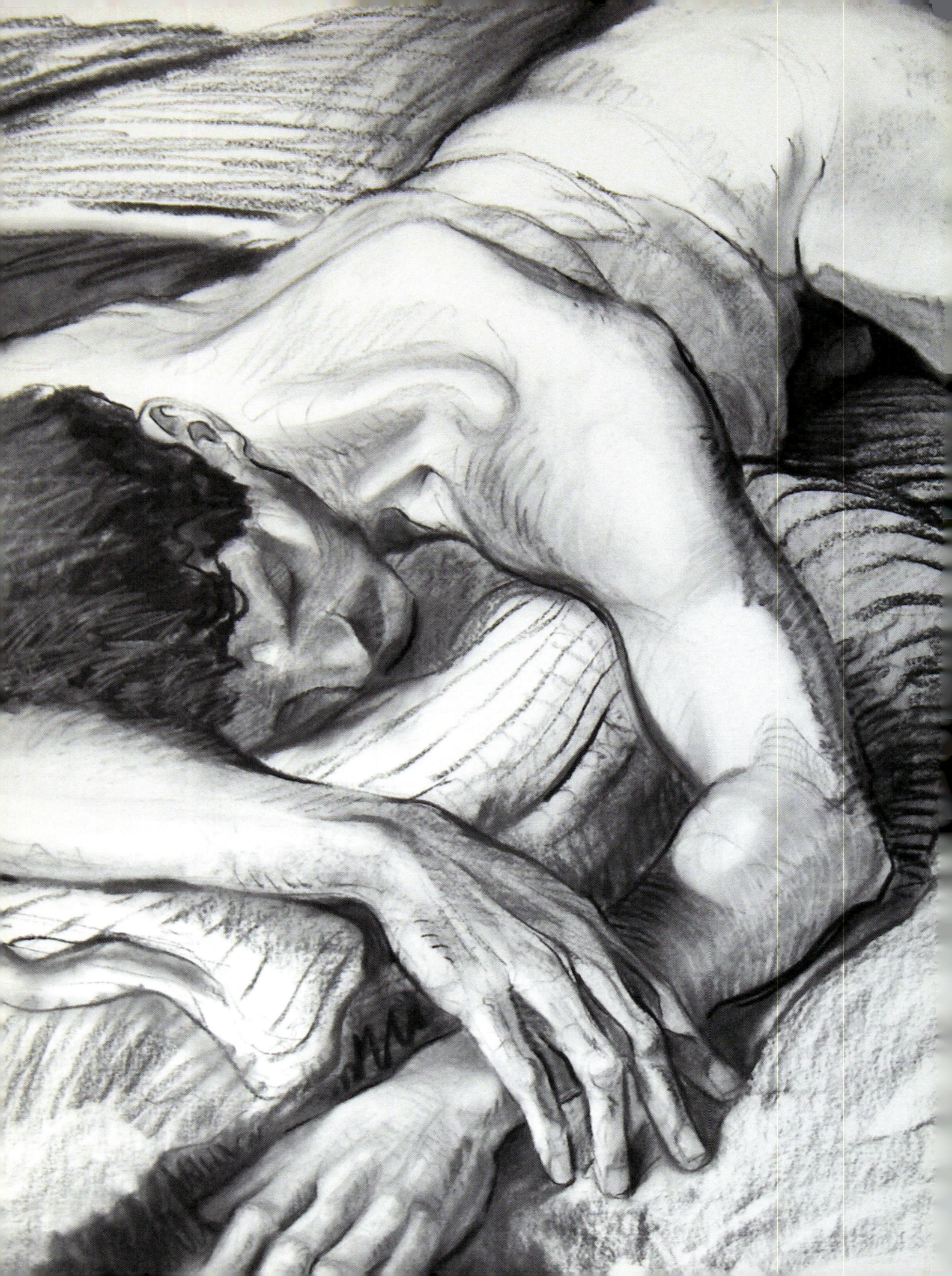

CHAPTER 5

THE UPPER AND LOWER LIMBS

This chapter explores the proportions and anatomy of bones, muscles, and joints of the arms, legs, hands, and feet from the standpoint of each individual muscle with its origins, insertions, and actions. Their appearance in their entirety is also shown from front, back, and side views.

Ken Goldman, *Reclining Male*, vine charcoal on stonehenge paper, 32" × 50" (81 × 127 cm) (detail)
"First we draw what we see; then we draw what we know; finally, we see what we know . . ."
—Robert Beverly Hale

UPPER ARMS

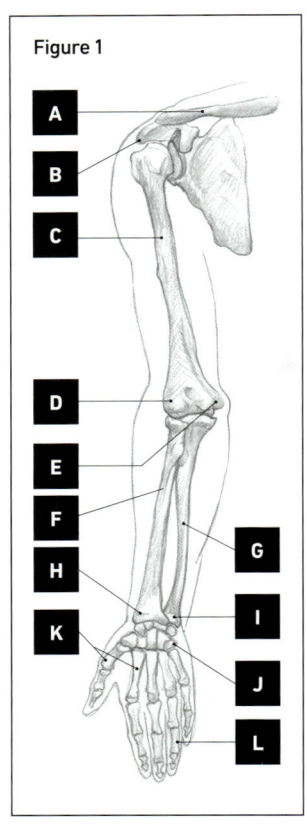

Figure 1

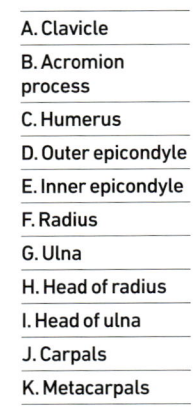

A. Clavicle
B. Acromion process
C. Humerus
D. Outer epicondyle
E. Inner epicondyle
F. Radius
G. Ulna
H. Head of radius
I. Head of ulna
J. Carpals
K. Metacarpals
L. Phalanges

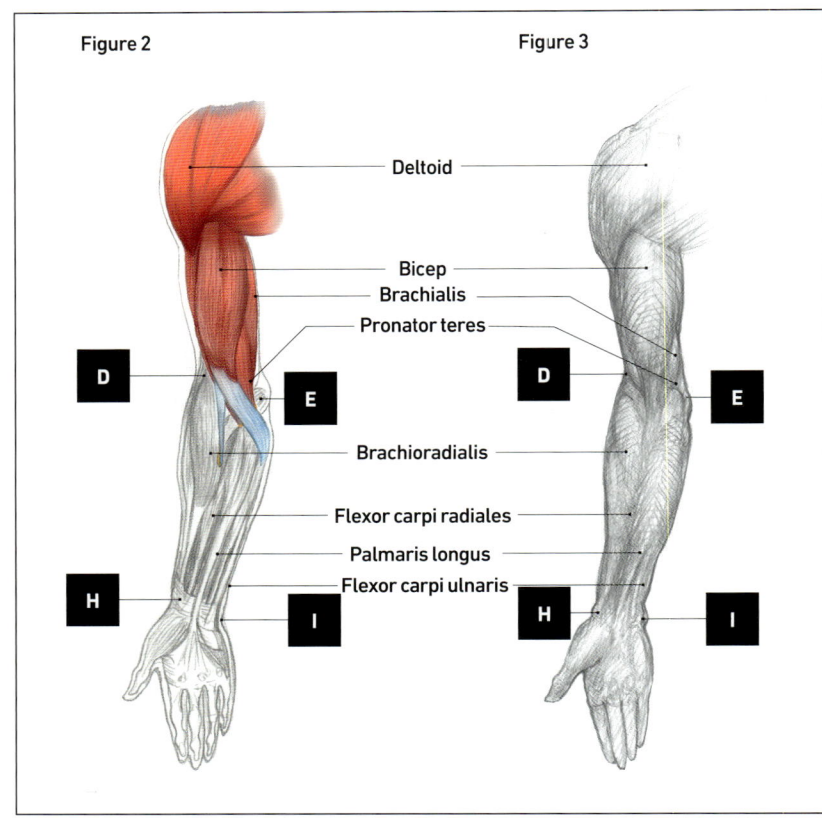

Figure 2   Figure 3

Deltoid
Bicep
Brachialis
Pronator teres
Brachioradialis
Flexor carpi radiales
Palmaris longus
Flexor carpi ulnaris

BONES OF THE ARM: FRONT VIEW

The underlying skeletal structure determines much of the overall shape of the arm (Figure 1).

However, for the upper arm in particular, the inner epicondyle (**E**) acts as a main visual landmark that is identifiable even under layers of muscle (Figure 2) and skin (Figure 3).

MUSCLES OF THE ARM: FRONT VIEW

The upper and lower portions of the arm each consist of three major muscle masses. The bicep and brachialis of the upper arm bend the lower arm, the tricep straightens it, and the deltoid raises the entire arm. In the lower arm (forearm), which is covered in the next section, the flexors bend the palm and clench the fingers; the extensors on the back of the arm straighten the palm and open the fingers; and the supinators rotate the hand outward. A fourth, smaller muscle, the *pronator teres*, rotates the palm inward. Finally, there is a longish sheet-like tendon called the *bicipital aponeurosis* attached to the distal end of the bicep muscle. This tendon wraps diagonally around the forearm flexors just below the medial epicondyle and helps to hold the flexors in place.

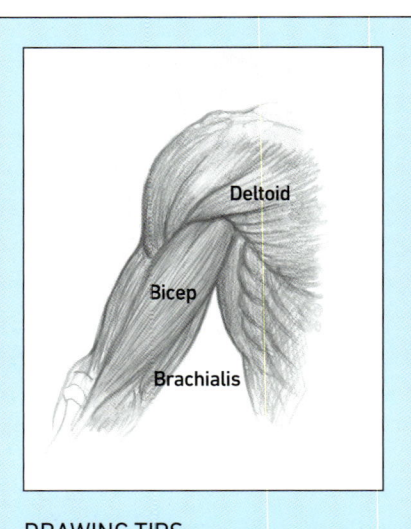

Deltoid
Bicep
Brachialis

DRAWING TIPS

The bicep does not extend across the full width of the upper arm. The deltoid inserts in between the brachialis and the bicep.

UPPER ARM MUSCLES: FRONT VIEW

The upper arm, or *brachium*, is located between the shoulder joint and elbow joint. There are four muscles in the upper arm: three flexor muscles in the front—*coracobrachialis, brachialis, biceps brachii*—and one extensor muscle in the back—*triceps brachii*. The *deltoid muscles* were discussed in the "The Torso, Side View" on page 113, but since they also relate to the upper arm muscles by helping to lift and rotate the arm, they are included here again, but only for visual context (see Figure 2).

INDIVIDUAL UPPER ARM MUSCLES SEEN FROM THE FRONT (ANTERIOR FLEXORS)

This section provides an overview of the origins, insertions, and actions of each muscle of the upper arm.

A good way to remember the three anterior upper arm muscles is BBC (*biceps, brachialis, coracobrachialis*). In describing the individual upper arm muscles, I'll begin with the deepest, least visible muscle—the *coracobrachialis*.

VISIBILITY OF THE CORACOBRACHIALIS

The *coracobrachialis* is seen best when the arm is raised and slightly flexed.

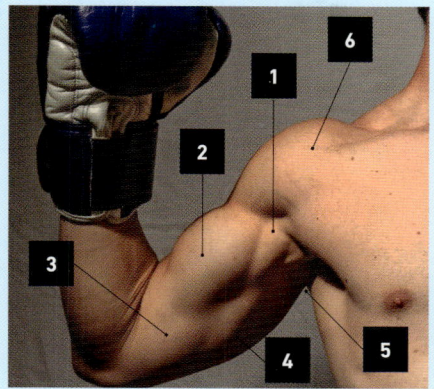

1. *Coracobrachialis*
2. Flexed *bicep*
3. A slightly bulging *brachialis* muscle
4. *Tricep—long head*
5. The thinnest upper part of the *triceps— long head* (see back view)
6. *Deltoid*

CORACOBRACHIALIS

Origin. Originates from the tip of the *coracoid process of the scapula*.

Insertion. A short vertical line on the *medial side of the humeral shaft*, half way down at the same level (but on the opposite side) of the *deltoid tubercle*.

Action. Flexion of the arm at the shoulder, and weak adduction.

BRACHIALIS

Origin. Lower half of the *medial and lateral surfaces of the humeral shaft*.

Insertion. Anterior surface of the ulnar tuberosity (coronoid process), just below the elbow joint.

Action. Flexes the forearm.

BICEPS BRACHII

The *biceps brachii* is a two-headed muscle. Although the majority of the muscle mass is located over the *humerus*, it has *no attachment to the humerus itself*. Its two origins attach to the *scapula* and then insert into the *radius*.

Origin. Long head: Originates from the supraglenoid tubercle on top of the glenoid fossa (socket of the scapula). Short head: Originates from the coracoid process of the scapula (*in common with the coracobrachialis*).

Insertion. Both heads insert into the radial tuberosity.

Action. Supination of the forearm. It also flexes the arm at the elbow and at the shoulder.

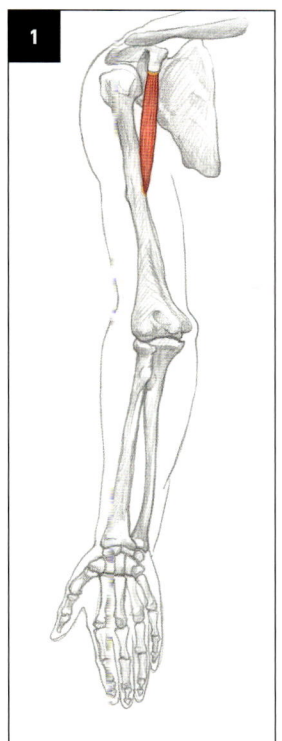

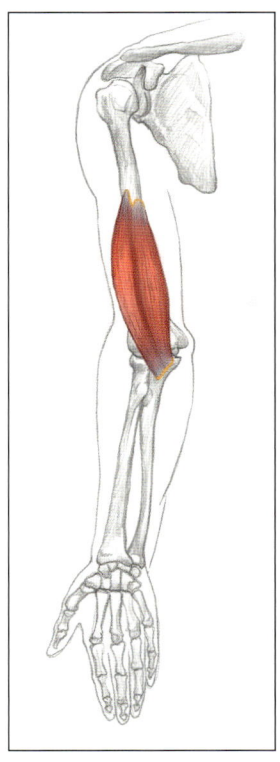

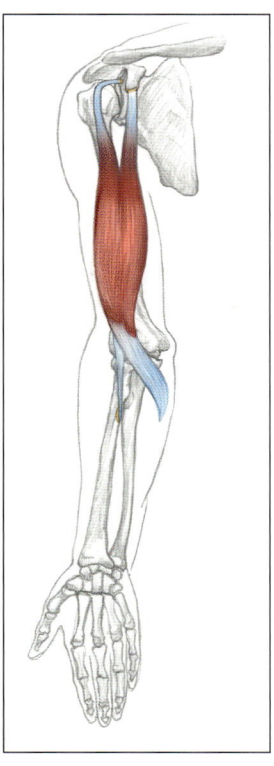

BONES OF THE UPPER ARM: BACK VIEW

Just as in the front view, much of the overall shape of the arm in the back view is determined by the underlying skeletal structure. The *inner and outer epicondyle* (**D** and **E**), are again identifiable, even under layers of muscle. And from this view, the *olecranon*, or elbow (**F**), is also evident.

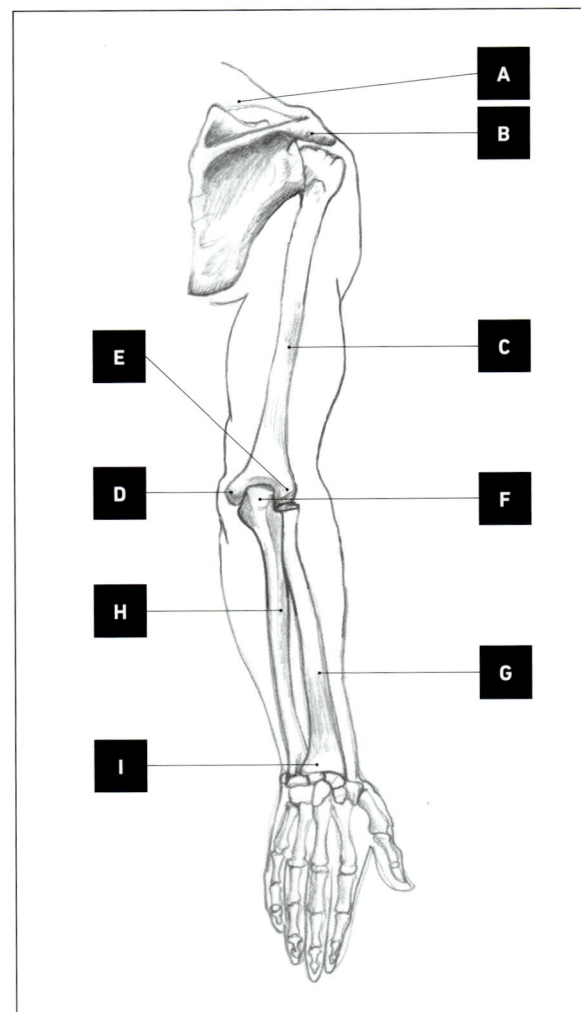

A. Clavicle
B. Acromion process
C. Humerus
D. Inner epicondyle
E. Outer epicondyle
F. Olecranon
G. Radius
H. Ulna
I. Head of radius

MUSCLES OF THE UPPER ARM: BACK VIEW

Muscles work in opposing pairs: Flexors pull, and extensors extend, moving in the opposite direction. When a flexor or extensor muscle becomes active, its opposite becomes passive. From the back view, when the hand is supinated (shown in Figures 1 and 2, right), extensor groups of the lower arm are the most prominent muscles. On the upper arm, the tricep is the most visible extensor.

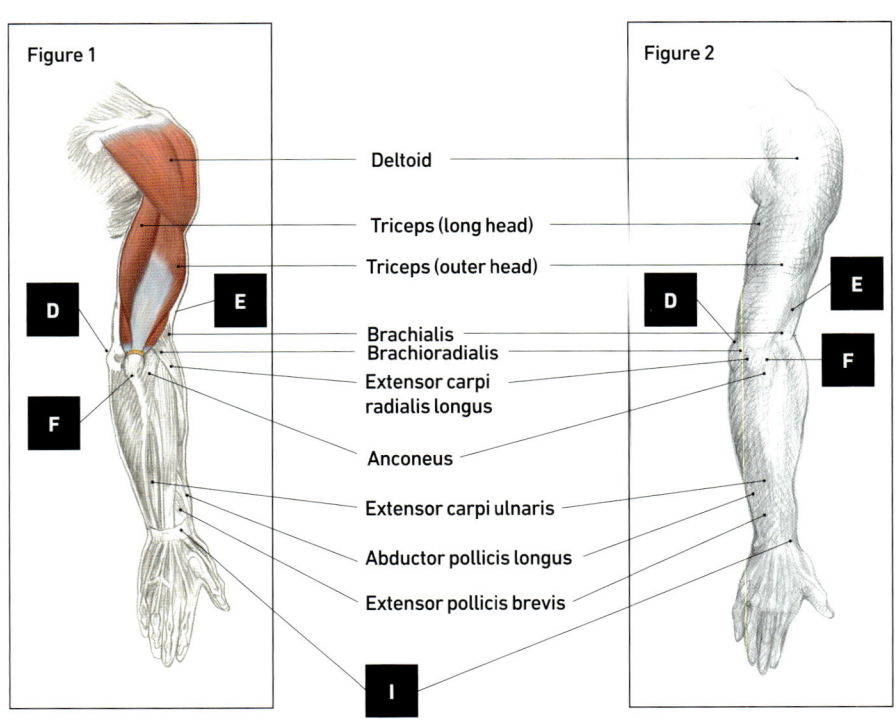

Figure 1

Figure 2

Deltoid
Triceps (long head)
Triceps (outer head)
Brachialis
Brachioradialis
Extensor carpi radialis longus
Anconeus
Extensor carpi ulnaris
Abductor pollicis longus
Extensor pollicis brevis

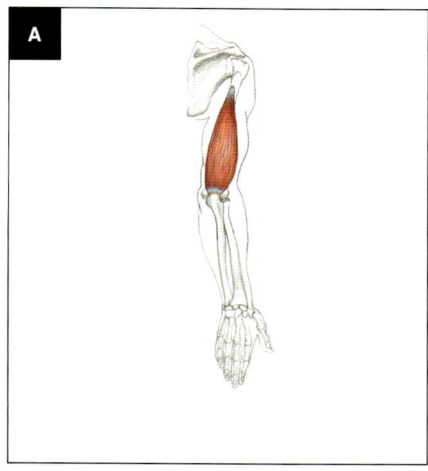

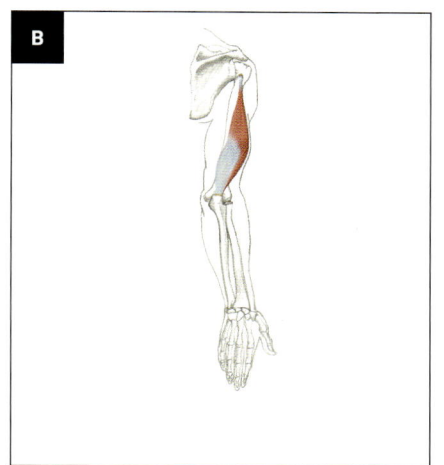

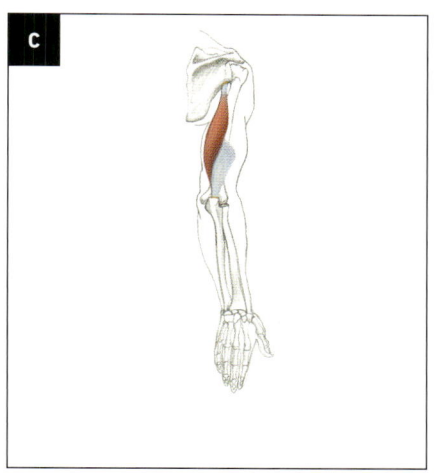

TRICEPS BRACHII

The only visible upper arm muscle on the posterior view is the *triceps brachii*, an extensor muscle with three asymmetrical heads. The medial head, which lies deepest, is rarely visible. The origins and insertions are colored orange.

Origin. Medial head: A large elongated triangular area occupying the lower three-fourths of the back surface of the shaft of the humerus (**A**). Lateral head: Originates just below the head of the humerus and terminates almost halfway down the bone (**B**). Long head: The largest of the three heads, it originates from the infraglenoid tubercle (below the socket of the scapula) (**C**).

Insertion. Distally, all three heads converge onto one *triceps tendon* and insert into the olecranon of the ulna (the elbow).

Action. Powerful extension of the forearm at the elbow joint.

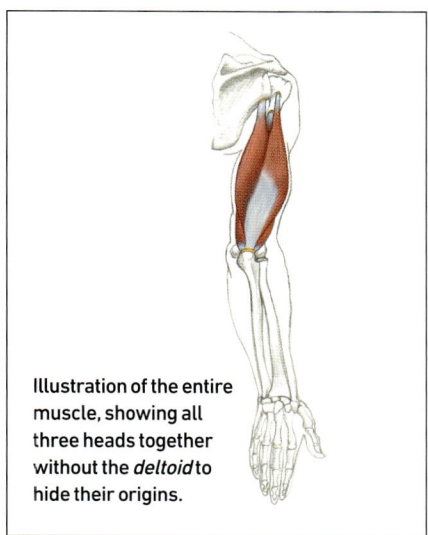

Illustration of the entire muscle, showing all three heads together without the *deltoid* to hide their origins.

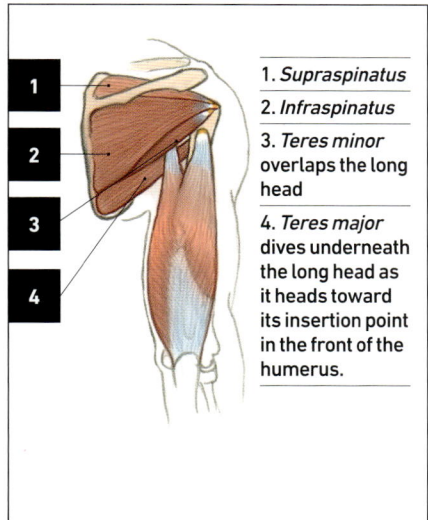

1. *Supraspinatus*
2. *Infraspinatus*
3. *Teres minor* overlaps the long head
4. *Teres major* dives underneath the long head as it heads toward its insertion point in the front of the humerus.

SCAPULAR MUSCLES AND TRICEPS

This illustration shows how two of the scapular muscles interweave with the triceps' long head. Skin and fat soften this overlap, so it is not very obvious on an actual model.

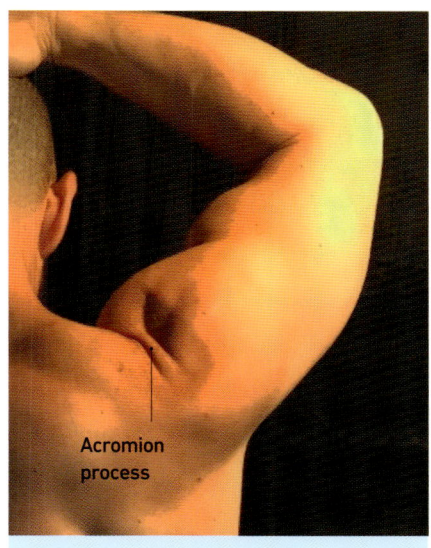

Acromion process

DELTOID CREASE

What is the crease that shows up on top of the shoulder when one's arm is raised? Answer: *The deltoid crease* is a skin fold that develops where the *lateral part of the deltoid* attaches into the top of the *acromion process*.

BONES OF THE ARM: SIDE VIEW

Here the arm is not viewed in full profile; rather, it is seen from an angle that is a combination of a side view and a back view. Because of the angle, the bony landmarks most apparent under the muscle are the *olecranon, outer epicondyle,* and *head of ulna.*

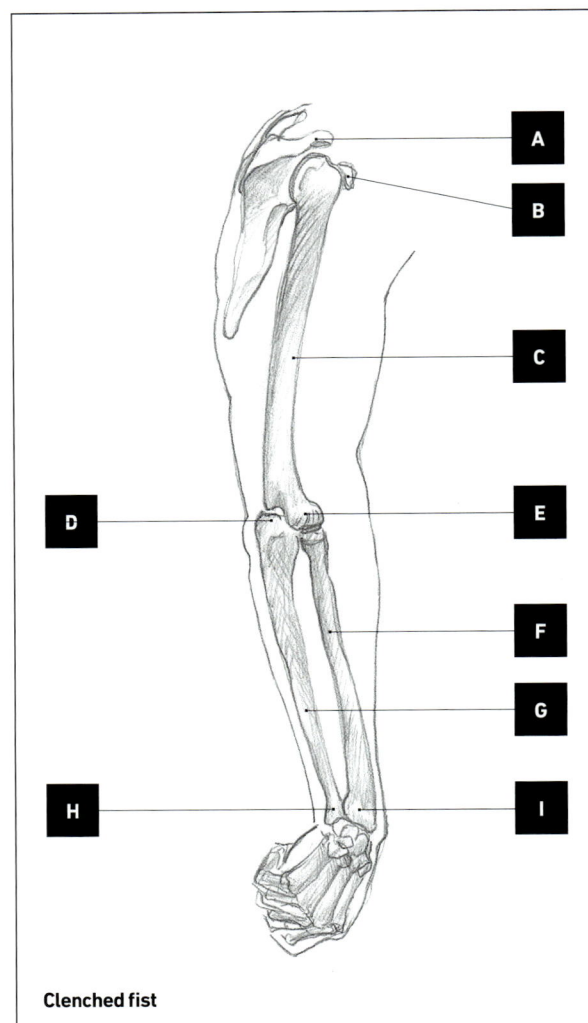

Clenched fist

A. Acromion process
B. Coracoid process
C. Humerus
D. Olecranon
E. Outer epicondyle
F. Radius
G. Ulna
H. Head of ulna
I. Head of radius

MUSCLES OF THE ARM: SIDE VIEW

This view provides a good angle for observing the multi-pennate muscle structure of the *lateral portion of the deltoid* (see page 133).

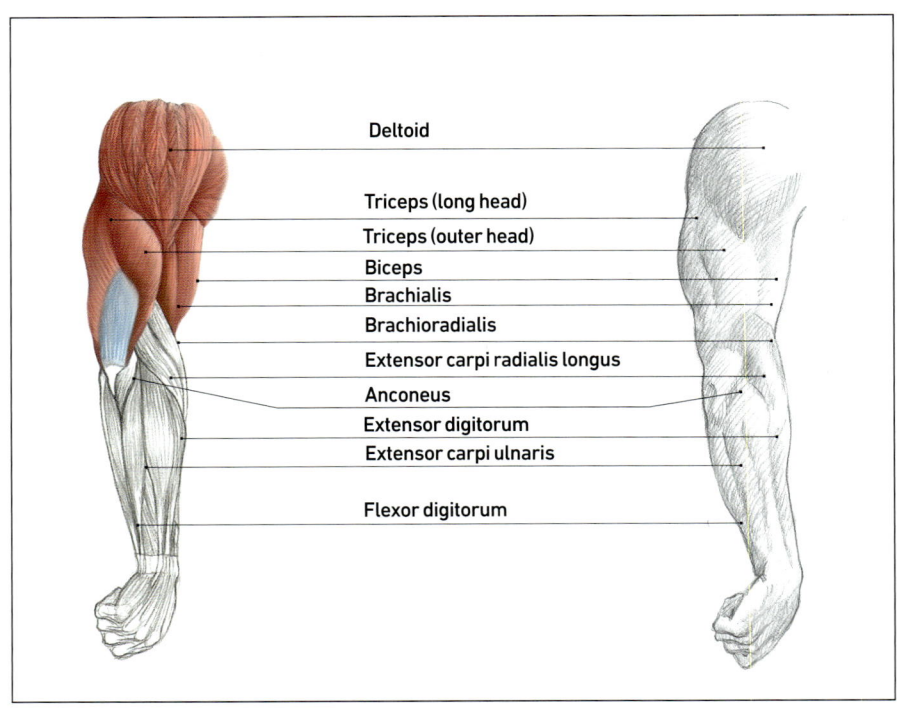

Deltoid

Triceps (long head)
Triceps (outer head)
Biceps
Brachialis
Brachioradialis
Extensor carpi radialis longus
Anconeus
Extensor digitorum
Extensor carpi ulnaris

Flexor digitorum

Upper Arm Muscles Seen from the Side (Lateral)

DELTOID: ACROMIAL (LATERAL) PORTION

As all of the upper arm muscles from the front and back have already been covered, this is a good time to mention and observe a unique aspect of the *lateral (acromial) portion of the deltoid*. While the *anterior and posterior portions* of the *deltoid* muscle are composed of simple parallel fibers, the acromial portion is a multipennate muscle, meaning it has multiple tendons braiding the muscle fibers into a complex pattern. While it is rare to actually see these fibers in minute detail on a model, they do create interesting bumps on the surface.

Origin. *Acromial (lateral) portion—external border of the acromion process of the scapula.*

Insertion. *Deltoid tuberosity* halfway down the outside of the *shaft* of the *humerus*.

Action. Powerfully abducts (raises) the arm laterally.

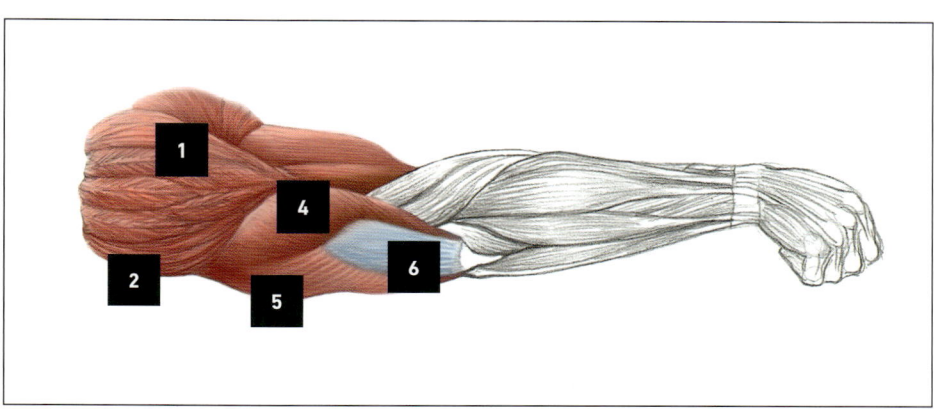

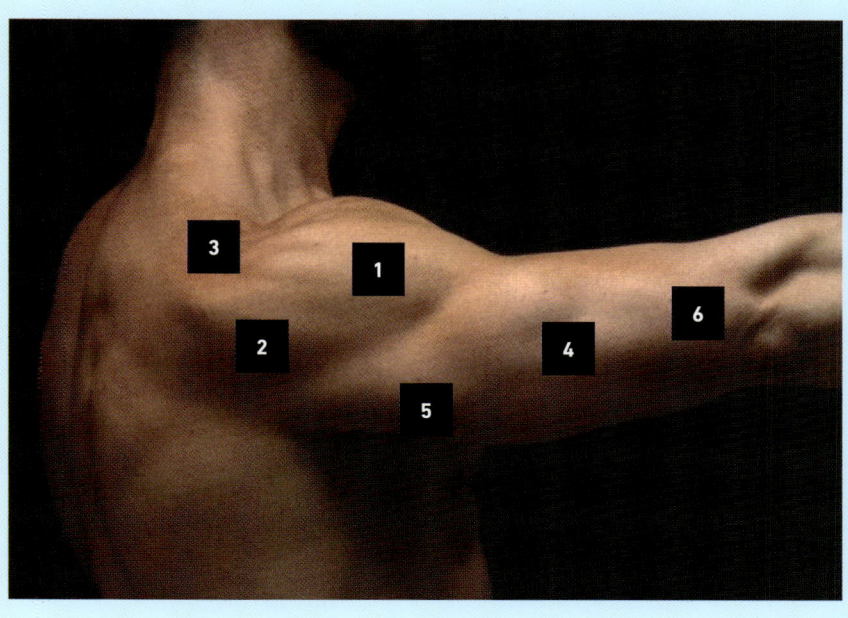

Acromial Portion of the Deltoid
This photograph shows the bumps on the *acromial portion of the deltoid* and other upper arm muscles.

1. Bumps (multipennate fibers) on acromial portion of deltoid

2. *Posterior portion of deltoid*

3. *Acromion process of scapula*

4. Bulge from *lateral head of tricep*

5. *Long head of tricep*

6. Slight bulge of *medial head of tricep muscle*

LOWER ARMS

Muscles of the forearm whose tendons insert into the hand are called *extrinsic* muscles. The muscles of the hand itself are called *intrinsic* muscles. The extrinsic forearm muscles are divided into three main groups: flexors, extensors, and ridge muscles.

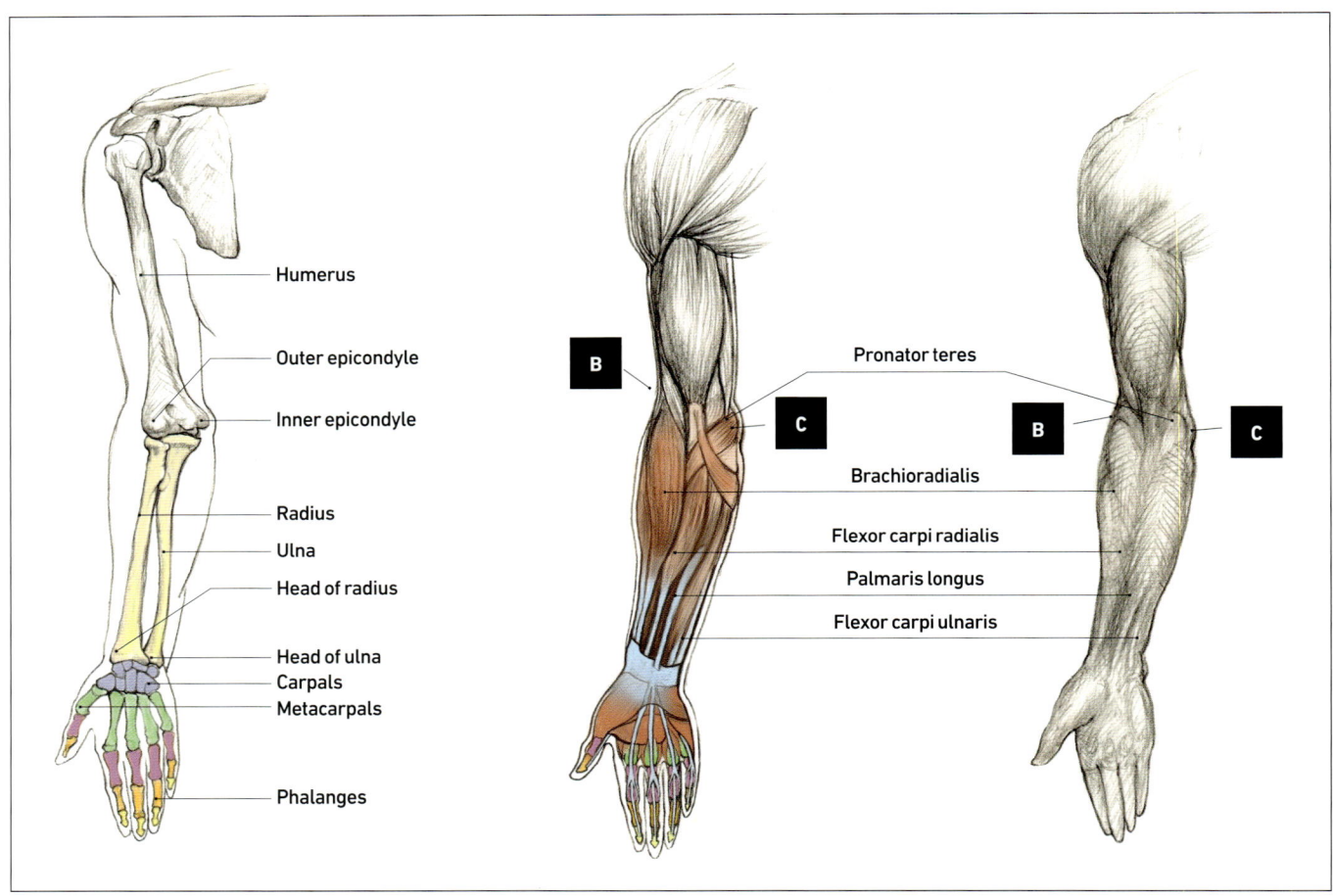

LOWER ARMS: FRONT VIEW

Bones. Several elements of the underlying skeletal structure, such as the outer epicondyle (**B**) and the inner epicondyle (**C**), act as visual landmarks that are identifiable even under layers of muscle and skin.

Flexors. Located on the bottom-side of the arm, this group originates on the inner (medial) epicondyle of the humerus (**C**) and inserts into the palm side of the hand. *Flexor carpi radialis, flexor carpi ulnaris*, and *flexor digitorum superficialis* (hidden by the more prominent *palmaris longus*) both bend the palm and clench the fingers. Flexor tendons can be seen at the wrist, especially the thin *palmaris longus tendon* nearest the center.

INDIVIDUAL FLEXORS OF THE FOREARM: FRONT VIEW

This section covers the origins, insertions, and actions of each of the individual flexors of the forearm.

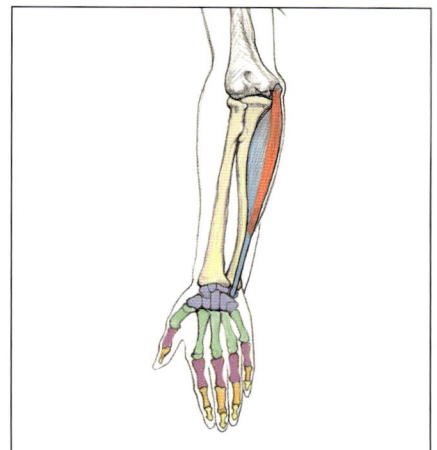

Flexor carpi radialis. Carpi in Latin refers to the bones of the hand, while *radialis* indicates the radial or lateral aspect of the hand.

Origin. Medial epicondyle of humerus.

Insertion. Base of metacarpals 2 and 3.

Action. Pronates forearm; flexes and abducts the hand.

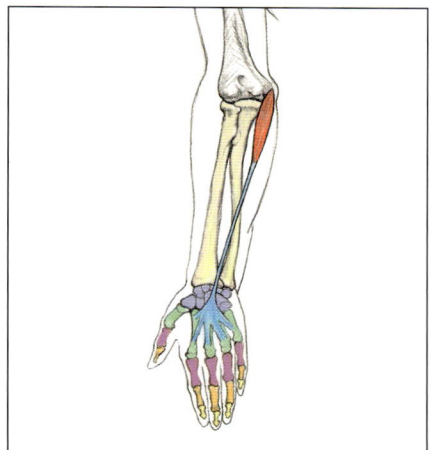

Flexor carpi ulnaris. Much like the flexor carpi radialis muscle, this muscle also inserts at the metacarpal bones but on the ulnar side.

Origin. Medial epicondyle of humerus.

Insertion. Pisiform bone of the wrist.

Action. Flexes and adducts the hand.

Palmaris longus. This muscle's tendon inserts onto the ligamentous structures of the palm of the hand.

Origin. Medial epicondyle of humerus.

Insertion. Palmer aponeurosis fanning out into the palm of the hand.

Action. Pronates forearm and flexes the hand.

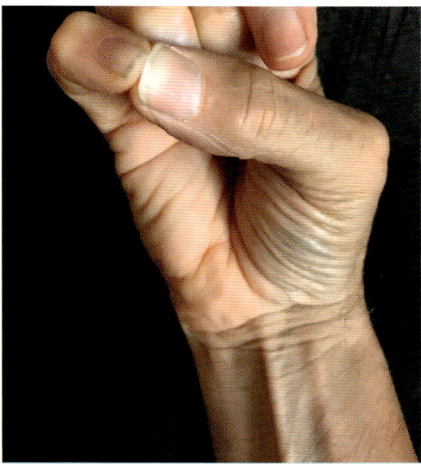

Do You Have This Forearm Muscle?
If you hold your thumb and pinky together and flex your wrist joint, the *palmaris longus* tendon will pop up prominently. If it doesn't show, it means you might not have this muscle at all—not everyone does. Instead, if it's absent, you'll only see two tendons—the *flexor carpi radialis* and *ulnaris tendons*.

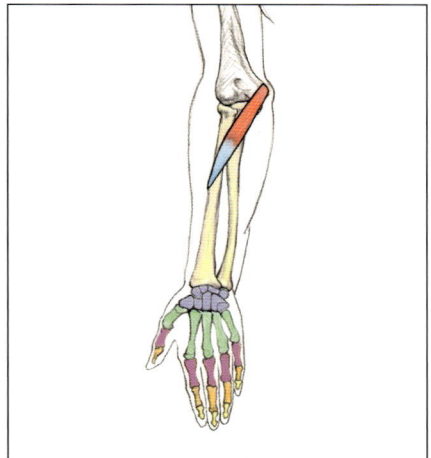

Pronator teres. Unlike most muscles of the forearm, the *pronator teres* does not travel down to reach the hand, but instead inserts onto the radius of the forearm.

Origin. Medial epicondyle of humerus.

Insertion. Anterior and lateral surface of radius.

Action. Pronates the arm (pulls the radius over the ulna) causing the hand to flip over from supination to pronation.

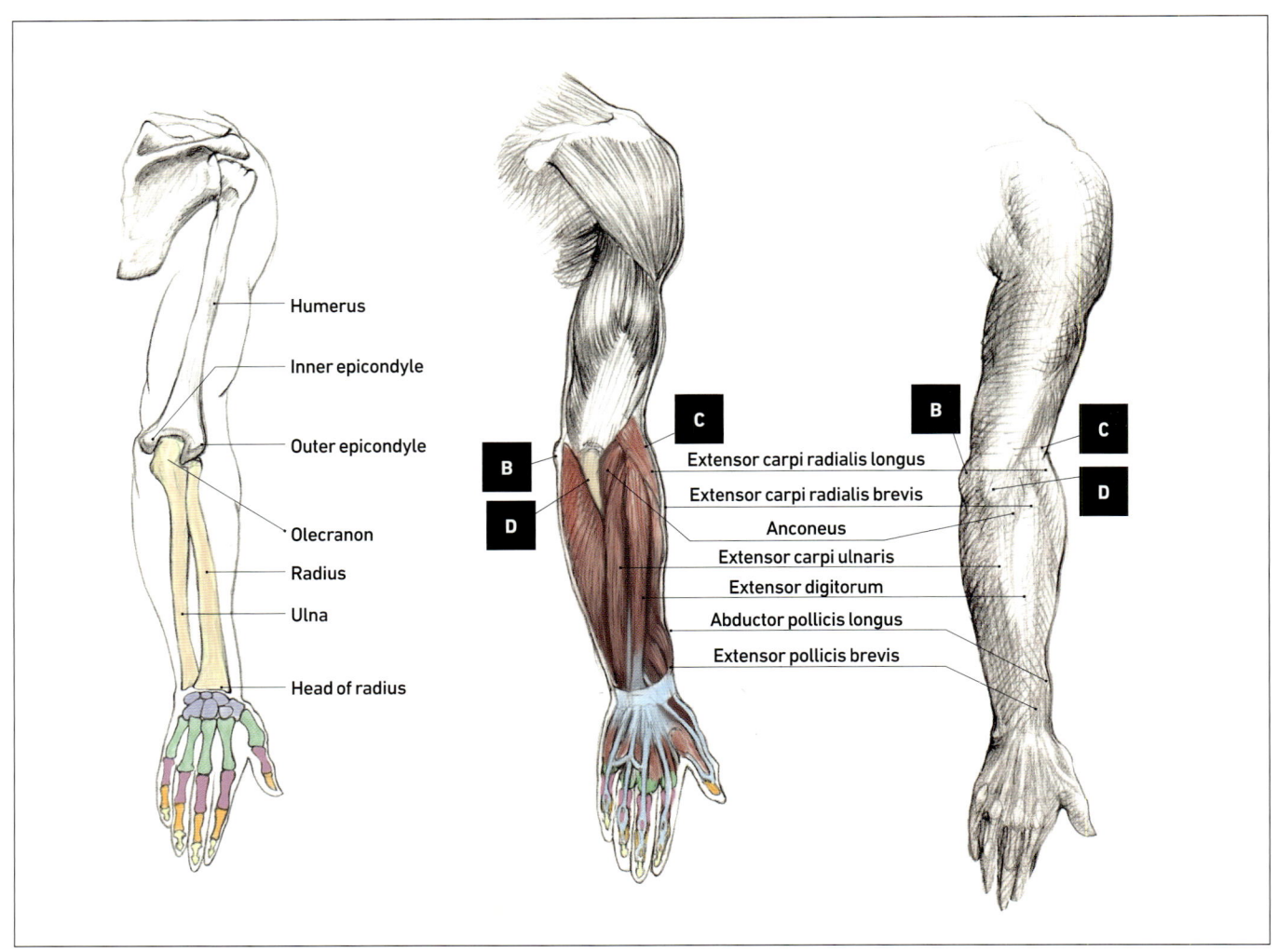

Humerus

Inner epicondyle

Outer epicondyle

Olecranon

Radius

Ulna

Head of radius

C

B

D

Extensor carpi radialis longus

Extensor carpi radialis brevis

Anconeus

Extensor carpi ulnaris

Extensor digitorum

Abductor pollicis longus

Extensor pollicis brevis

B

C

D

BACK VIEW

Bones. Just as with the front view, the *inner and outer epicondyle*, (**B** and **C**), are again identifiable, even under layers of muscle. And from this view, the *olecranon*, or elbow (**D**), is also evident.

Extensors. These muscles straighten the wrist and open the fingers. The main muscles in this group are the *extensor carpi radialis brevis, extensor carpi ulnaris*, and *extensor digitorum*. Located on the top side of the forearm, these muscles

originate on the *outer (lateral) epicondyle of the humerus* (**C**) and travel over the top of the forearm to insert onto the *upper (dorsal) side* of the hand. The two ridge muscles (labeled above), sometimes called "The Twins," (page 139). will be covered in the next section under "Two Ridge Muscles of the Forearm (The Twins)." The two thumb muscles (also shown above), sometimes called "Mini-Twins," are discussed in this section.

INDIVIDUAL EXTENSORS OF THE FOREARM: BACK VIEW

This section covers the origins, insertions, and actions of each of the individual extensors of the forearm.

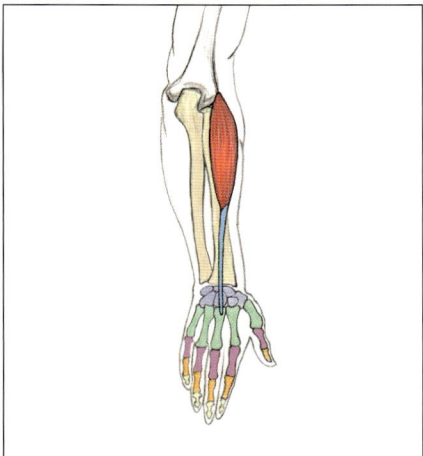

Extensor carpi radialis brevis

Origin. Lateral epicondyle of the humerus.

Insertion. Dorsal surface of metacarpal III (proximal part).

Action. Extends and abducts the hand.

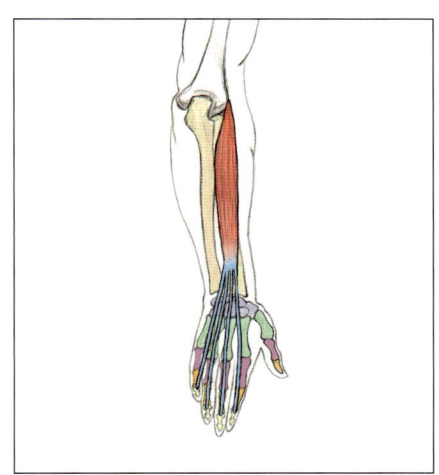

Extensor digitorum

Origin. Lateral epicondyle of the humerus by a common tendon.

Insertion. Dorsal side of the middle and distal phalanges (fingers) 2 through 5. It does not insert into the thumb.

Action. Extends hands and fingers 2 through 5; spreads fingers apart.

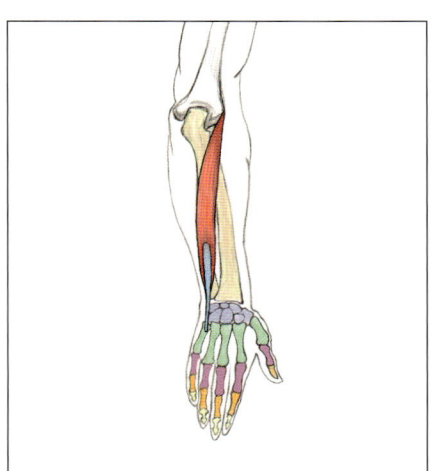

Extensor carpi ulnaris

Origin. Lateral epicondyle of the humerus.

Insertion. Base of metacarpal V.

Action. Abducts hand at the wrist joint.

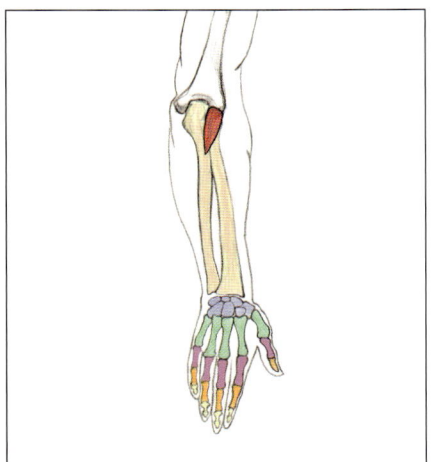

Three Additions to The Extensor Group
Anconeus

Origin. Lateral epicondyle of the humerus.

Insertion. Dorsal surface of ulna.

Action. Extends the forearm.

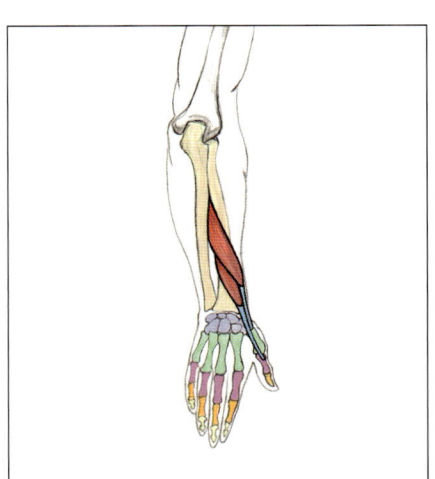

Two Pollicis Muscles of the Forearm (The Mini-Twins). One of my anatomy instructors, Rey Bustos, calls the two *ridge muscles* "Twins" and the *forearm thumb group* near the wrist the "Mini-Twins."

Abductor pollicis longus

Origin. Dorsal surface of ulna and radius; interosseous membrane.

Insertion. Base of metacarpal I.

Action. Abducts and extends the first phalanx; helps to supinate the forearm.

Extensor pollicis brevis

Origin. Dorsal surface of radius; interosseous membrane.

Insertion. Base of first phalanx of thumb.

Action. Abducts and extends the thumb; helps to supinate the forearm.

A. Humerus

B. Outer epicondyle

C. Inner epicondyle

D. Olecranon

E. Radius

F. Ulna

G. Head of ulna

H. Head of radius

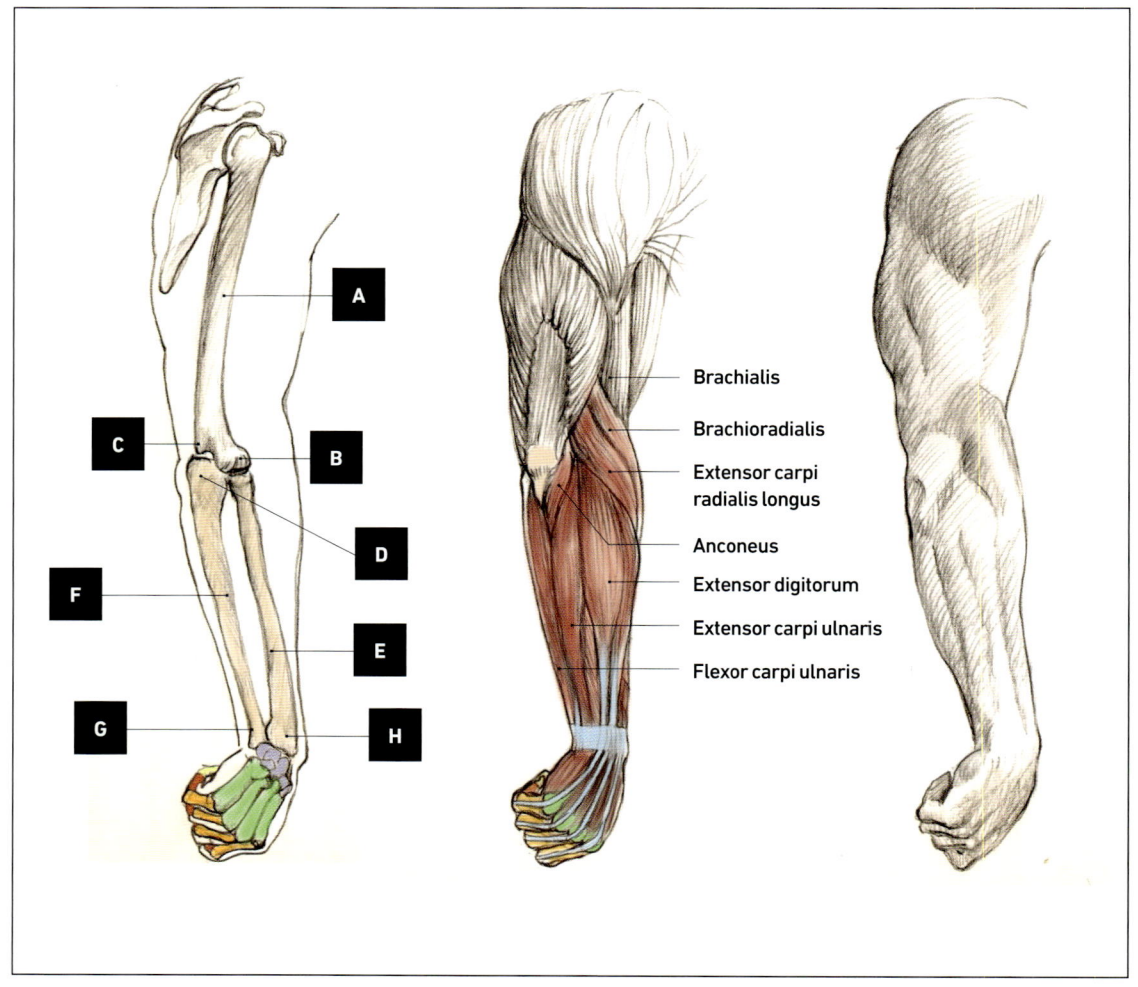

Brachialis

Brachioradialis

Extensor carpi
radialis longus

Anconeus

Extensor digitorum

Extensor carpi ulnaris

Flexor carpi ulnaris

SIDE VIEW

Bones. Seen from this angle, the bony
landmarks most apparent under the
muscles are the olecranon (**D**), outer
epicondyle (**B**), and the head of the *ulna*
(**H**).

Extensors, Flexors, Ridge Muscles. This
view provides a good angle for observing
the *extensors and one flexor muscle* of the
lower arm.

TWO R DGE MUSCLES OF THE FOREARM (THE TWINS)

Located where the upper and lower arms meet, the *brachioradialis and extensor carpi radialis longus* are particularly important because they form the lateral roundish shape between the elbow and forearm. Although these two muscles begin side-by-side, as they descend, the belly of the *extensor carpi radialis longus* is partially covered by the belly of the *brachioradialis*, typically blending them together into a single form.

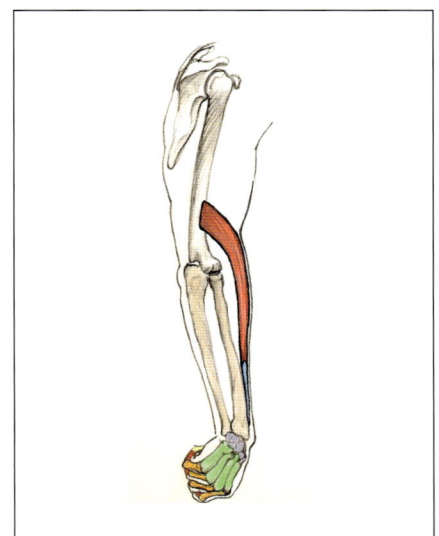

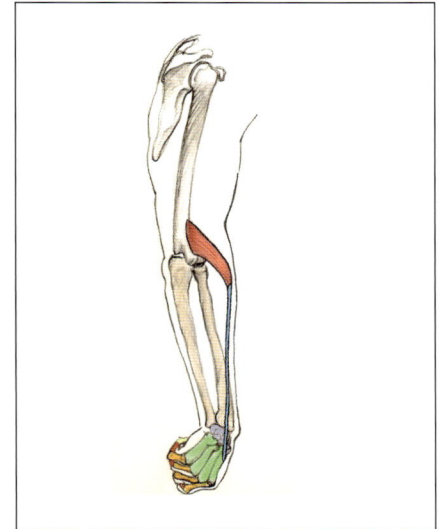

Brachioradialis

Origin. Originates on the *lateral side of the humerus* (**A**), above the *outer epicondyle* (**B**).

Insertion. Styloid process of the radius.

Action. Extends and abducts the hand laterally. Supinates forearm in extension; pronates it in flexion.

Extensor carpi radialis longus

Origin. Originates on the *lateral side of the humerus* (**A**), above *the outer epicondyle* (**B**) underneath the *origin of brachioradialis*.

Insertion. Base of metacarpal II on its dorsal surface.

Action. Extends and abducts the hand laterally. Supinates forearm in extension; pronates it in flexion.

FLEXED FOREARM

Here are some of the most visible posterior view forearm muscles:

(A) Ridge muscle: *The Twins, brachioradialis* and *extensor carpi radialis longus*

(B) *Anconeus*

(C) *Extensor carpi radialis brevis*

(D) Thumb group: the *Mini-Twins, abductor pollicis longus*, and *extensor pollicis brevis*

(E) *Extensor digitorum*

(F) *Extensor carpi ulnaris*

The Twins in context with the extensors showing how the two blend together with *brachioradialis* on top of *extensor carpi radialis longus*.

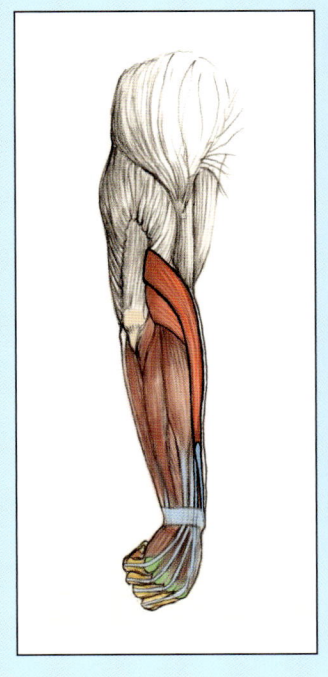

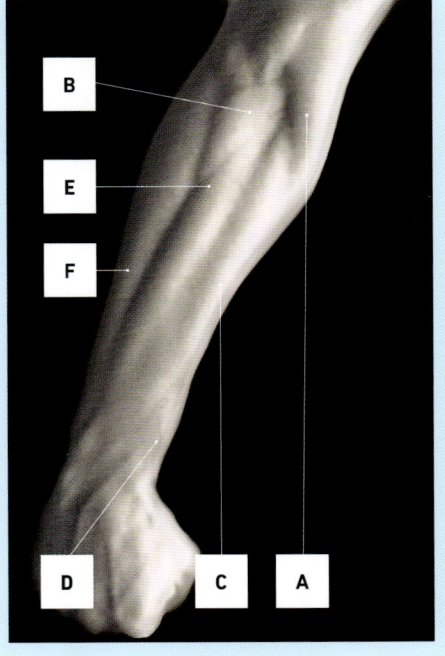

THE HAND AND WRIST

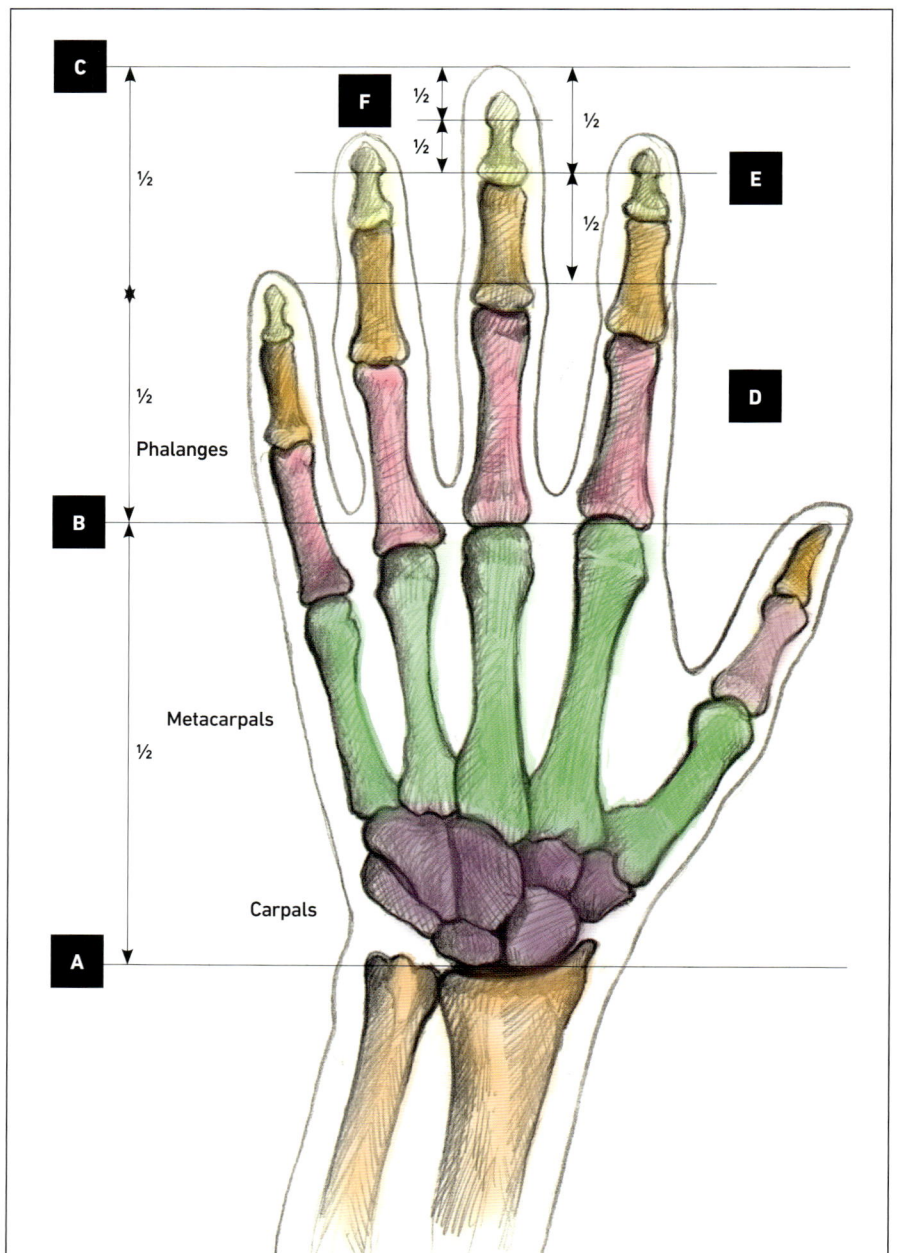

I'd like to start this section with a disclaimer. The skeleton I'm using for the photos and drawings in this book is a real skeleton. The bones are 100 percent accurate, but because they are put together with bolts, nuts, and wires, their positioning may sometimes be a little off. However, once this small flaw is taken into consideration (and corrected in your final drawings), it is still a great representation of how well the joints work together.

Muscles that originate in the hand itself and activate the palms and fingers are called *intrinsic muscles*.

Left hand (dorsal view). The hand's surface form is based mostly on its skeletal shape. The skeleton of the hand consists of *carpals* (the wrist), *metacarpals* (palm), and *phalanges* (fingers). When looking straight down at the hand, a simple way to find the correct proportions is to use the "halve method."

THE HALVE METHOD

The halve method is based on the length of the bones, not the skin. Divide the distance between the end of the carpals (**A**) and the tip of the middle finger (**C**) to find the middle of the hand (**B**), which is also where the heads of the metacarpals (knuckles) are located. To find the length of the three finger joints (**B-C**), divide the distance between B and C to find D. Divide the distance between D and C to find E, the top two joints, and again to find F, the fingernail. Try using this measuring technique on your own hand.

Webbing of the palm (palmer and dorsal views). Notice how your palm, with its webbing, looks longer than the top of your hand. Also notice how your fingers look longer from the dorsal view than they do from the palmar view. This is because the webbing of the palm extends beyond the knuckles (metacarpal heads), nearly halfway to the first joints of the phalanges.

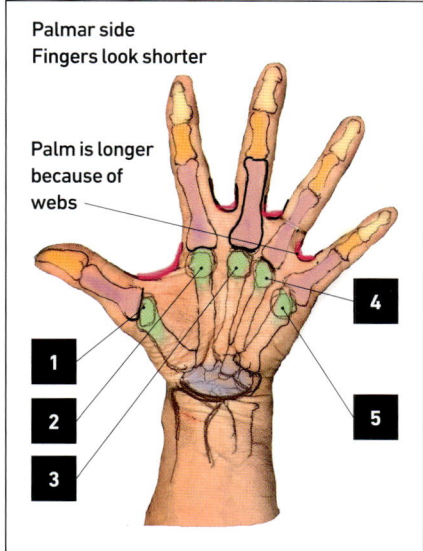

Palmar side
Fingers look shorter

Palm is longer because of webs

1
2
3
4
5

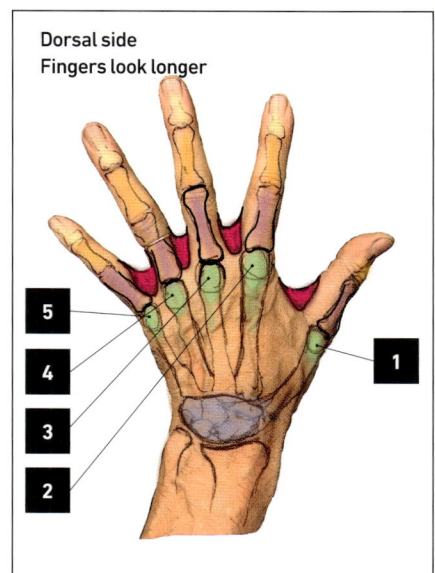

Dorsal side
Fingers look longer

5
4
3
2
1

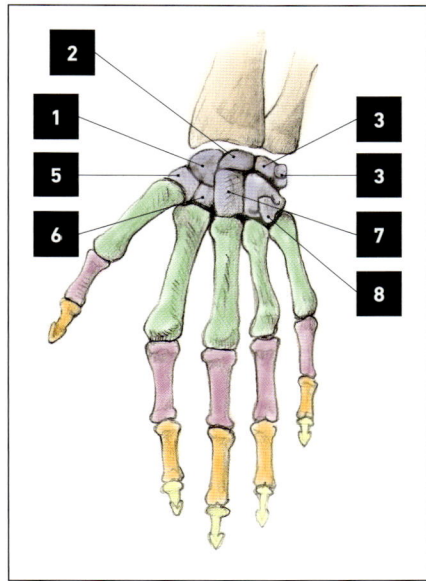

2
1
5
6
3
3
7
8

Bones. The wrist contains eight irregular carpal bones, arranged in two rows of four bones each.

Proximal. *Scaphoid* (**1**), *lunate* (**2**), *triquetral* (**3**), *pisiform* (**4**)
Distal. *Trapezium* (**5**), *trapezoid* (**6**), *capitate* (**7**), *hamate* (**8**).

Here is a good way to remember the names of the eight carpal bones:
Sally **L**eft **T**he **P**arty **T**o **T**ake **C**athy **H**ome

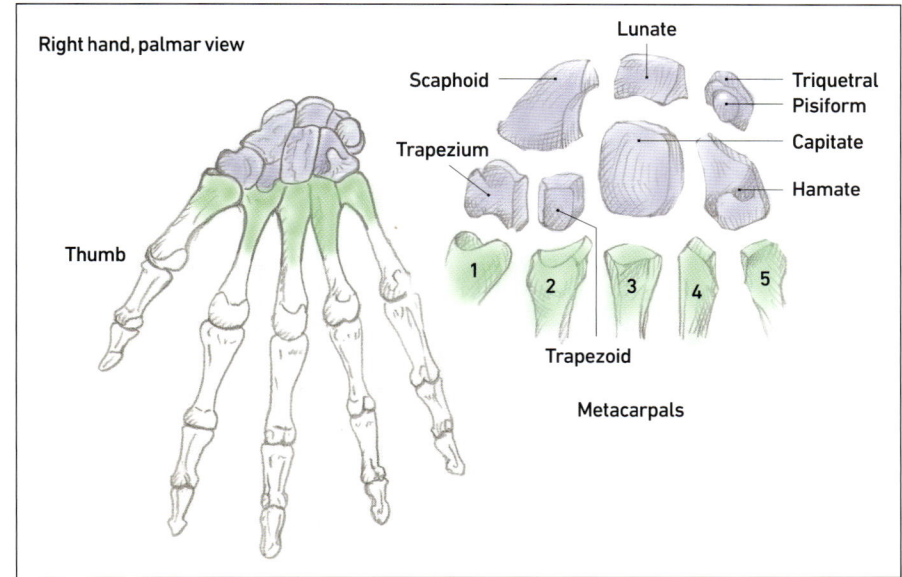

Right hand, palmar view

Scaphoid

Trapezium

Thumb

Lunate

Triquetral
Pisiform

Capitate

Hamate

1   2   3   4   5

Trapezoid

Metacarpals

Right hand (palmar view— above). Carpal bones have essentially flat surfaces. Where they fit together, they form gliding joints, which limit their movements. Numerous small ligaments bind each carpal to each other and to the metacarpals.

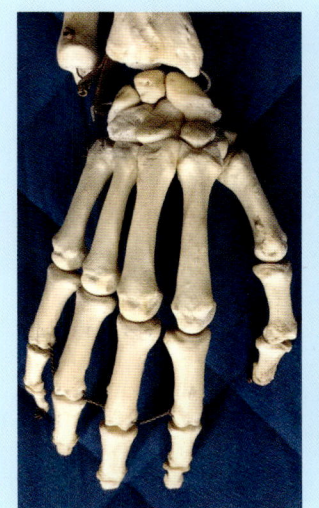

RIGHT HAND DORSAL VIEW
Even though individual carpal bones do not show through the skin, it's still good to know their names for anatomical understanding. However, when it comes to actually drawing the carpal bones, it's better to simplify them as a half-circle, much like the semirounded shape of a half-moon.

Metacarpals. There are five metacarpal bones, beginning with the thumb. Each bone consists of a boxlike proximal base, a shaft, and a rounded distal head. All metacarpals, except the thumb, radiate from an imaginary center point on the distal end of the radius.

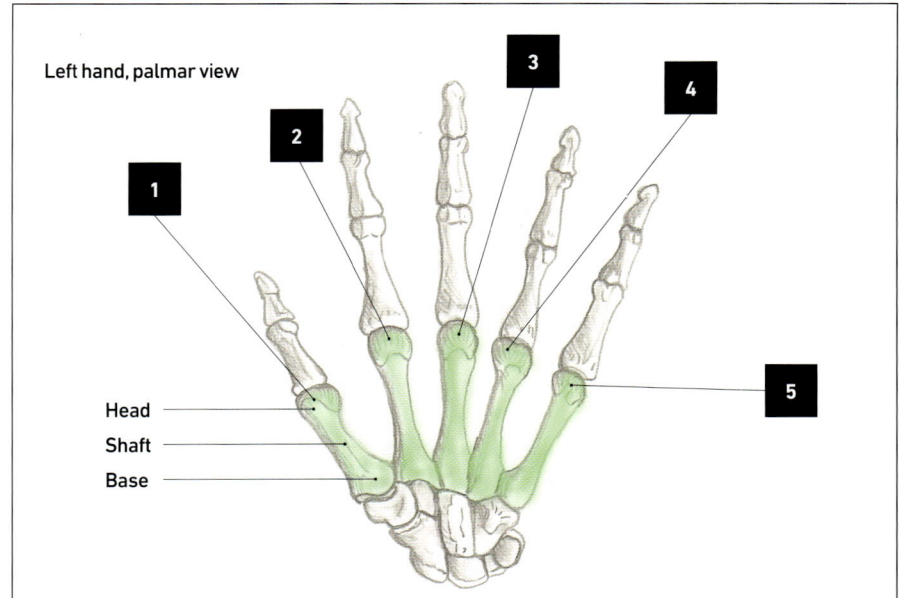

Left hand, palmar view

Head
Shaft
Base

These diagrams show how metacarpals 2 through 5 radiate from an imaginary center point on the distal end of the radius, as well as the placement of metacarpal heads on the palm.

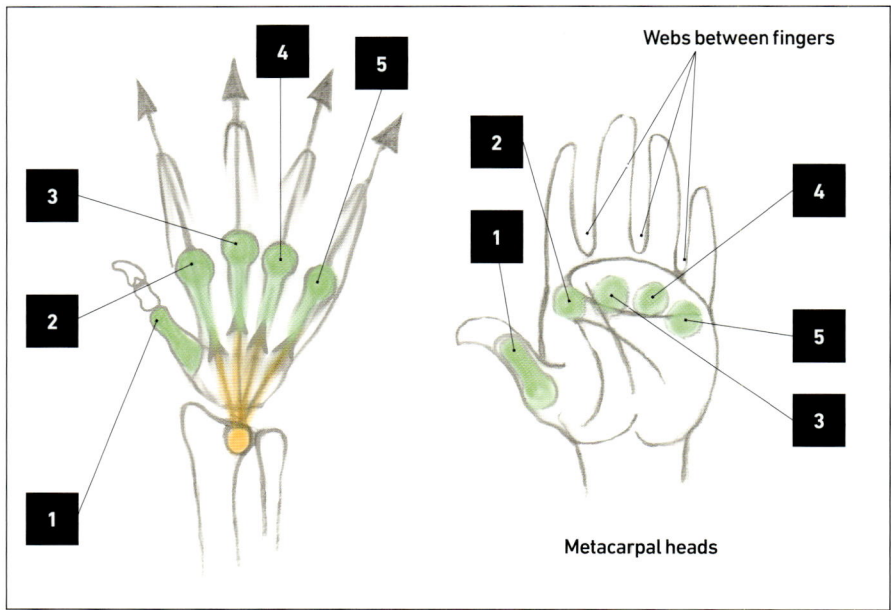

Webs between fingers

Metacarpal heads

Phalanges. All fingers except the thumb have three phalanges. The thumb only has two. The individual bones of each finger are called the *proximal*, *middle*, and *distal phalanges*. Fingers 1 through 5 are called: *thumb* (**1**), *index* (**2**), *middle* (**3**), *ring* (**4**), *little* (**5**).

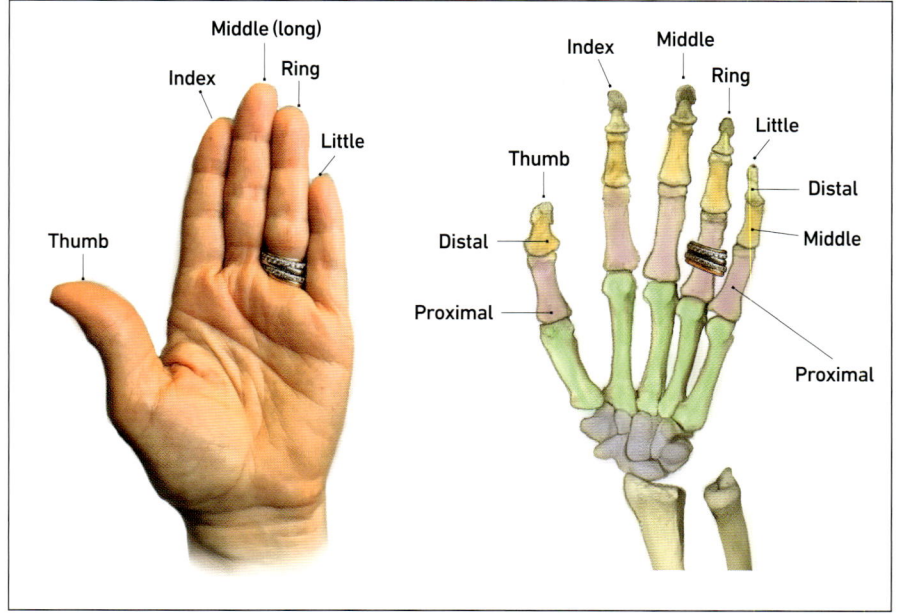

Middle (long)
Index
Ring
Little
Thumb

Index   Middle
             Ring
                  Little
Thumb
                  Distal
Distal
                  Middle
Proximal
                  Proximal

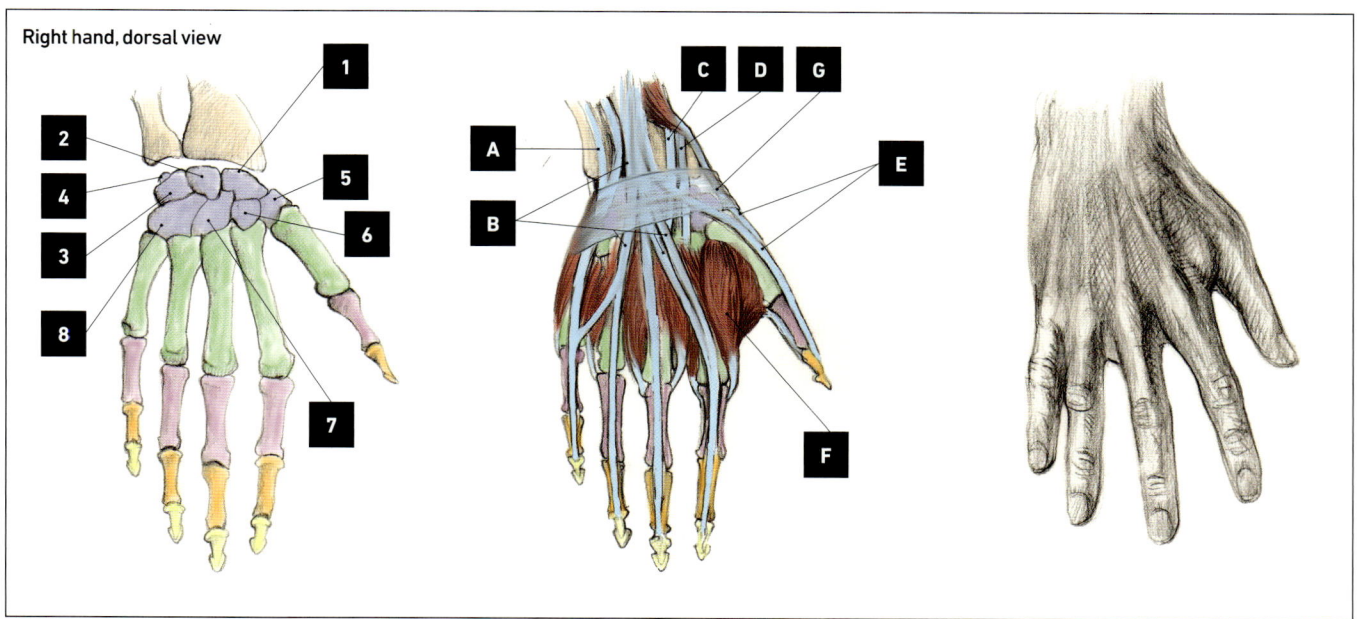

MUSCLES

There are no muscles in the fingers, only tendons, bones, and fat. The muscles and short tendons of the hand (intrinsic musc.es) arise only on the carpals and metacarpals.

Bones. From this view of the hand, all the same bones as above are visible, but the carpal bones appear convex rather than concave. From this angle, the bones have more influence on the shape of the fleshed-out hand.

Muscles tendons. *Extensor carpi ulnaris* (**A**), *extensor digitorum* (**B**), *extensor carpi radialis brevis* (**C**), and *extensor carpi radialis longus* (**D**) are visible forearm tendons that extend into the

hand. These four tendons and the *extensor tendons* of the thumb (**E**) are visible when contracted. The first *dorsal interosseous* (**F**) is the largest of the four dorsal interosseous muscles, and it is the only one that shows its form through the skin's surface; when the thumb is flexed, this muscle appears as a bulging teardrop shape. A wide, thick ligament, the *extensor retinaculum* (**G**), holds the extensor tightly in place.

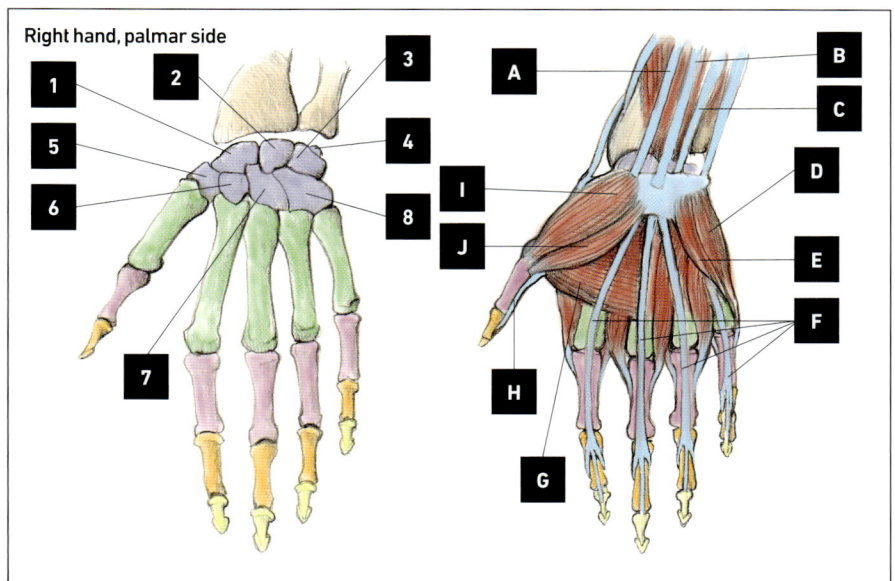

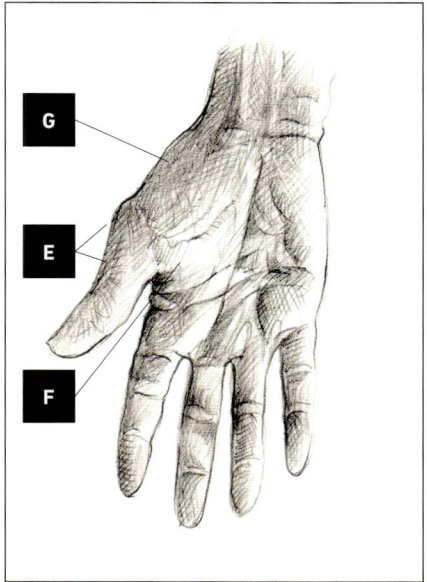

Muscles. The flexor tendons of the forearm muscles, *flexor carpi radialis* (**A**), *palmaris longus* (**B**), *flexor digitorum superficialis* (**C**), and *flexor carpi ulnaris* (**D**), all extend down into the hand. The teardrop-shaped muscle masses, the

thenar eminence abductors of the thumb (**I**, **J**) and the *hypothenar eminence abductor* (**E**) and *flexor* (**F**) of the little finger, are known as the "palmar hand muscles." The *adductor* of the thumb (**G**) lies under the *flexor tendons* (**F**). The

visible creases of the palm result from the way the skin folds over the fat and muscles of the hand.

Right hand, radial side view. Although hand movements are varied and expressive, they are restrained by the borders of the radial and ulnar styloid processes. Hands cannot extend too far forward or flex too far back. The design of the radial and ulnar heads helps to prevent unintentional sprains and tears. Range of motion for an open hand is greater in flexion than it is in extension (90 degrees vs. 70 degrees).

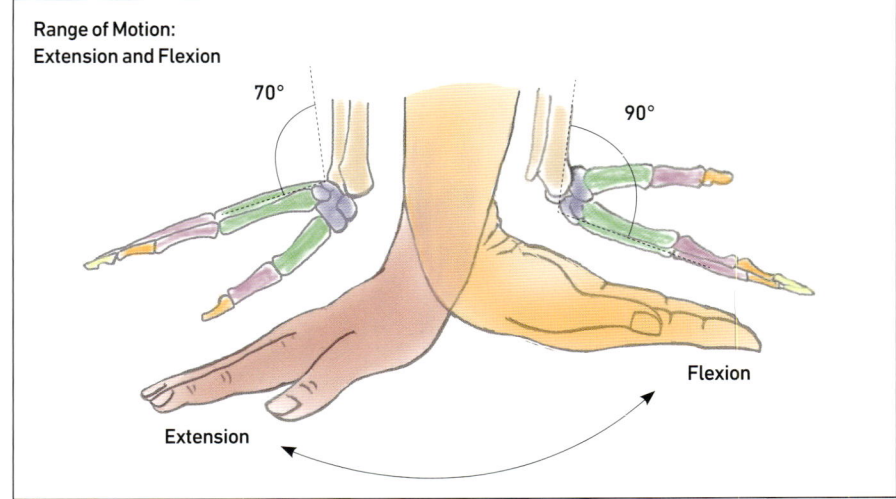

Range of Motion:
Extension and Flexion

70°

90°

Flexion

Extension

Right hand, palmar view. Side-to-side movement is also limited by the styloid processes of the ulna and radius. This, too, helps to avoid wrist sprains. As this diagram shows, radial flexion is more limited than ulnar flexion because the styloid process of the radius sits lower than the head of the ulna.

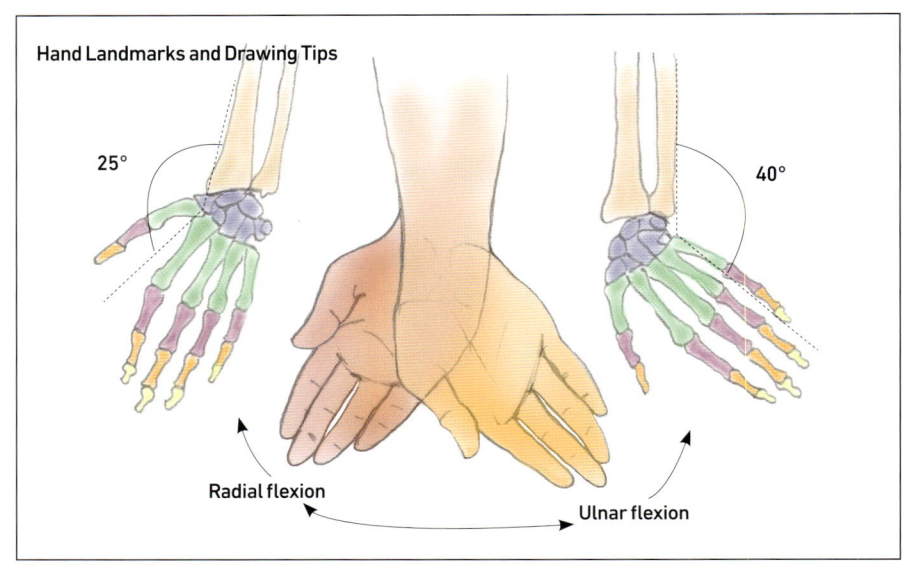

Hand Landmarks and Drawing Tips

25°

40°

Radial flexion

Ulnar flexion

HAND LANDMARKS AND DRAWING TIPS

Flexed hand, palmar view. Form follows function. Because the hand is designed to hold a wide variety of objects, the wrist and entire palm are concave.

(T) Trapezium
(H) Hamate (hook)
(P) Pisiform

Extended hand, palmar view. Carpal protrusions of the *trapezium*, *hamate*, and the pealike *pisiform* bone form the carpal tunnel. The thick ligament called *flexor retinaculum* holds the flexor tendons tightly in place during flexion. When extended, as in this view, the noncontracted flexor tendons are stretched taut.

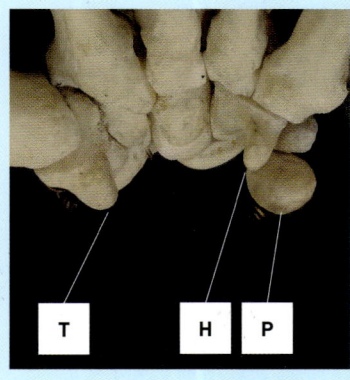

T   H   P

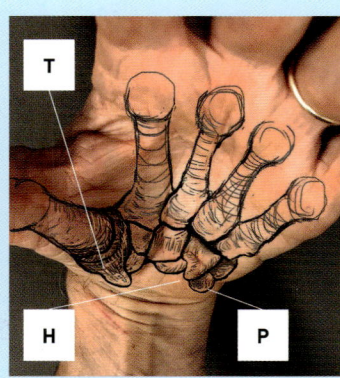

T

H   P

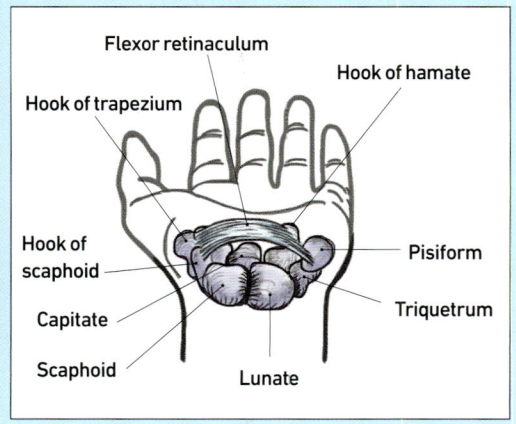

Flexor retinaculum

Hook of trapezium

Hook of hamate

Hook of scaphoid

Pisiform

Capitate

Triquetrum

Scaphoid

Lunate

Palmar muscles. The *thenar eminence* (ball of the thumb) is made up of the *abductor pollicis brevis* and the *flexor pollicis brevis*. It originates on the *scaphoid*, *trapezium*, and *first metacarpal*. The *hypothenar eminence* (muscle mass of the little finger) consists of the *abductor digiti minimi* and *flexor digiti minimi brevis*. Look at your own hand and note how the heads of the metacarpals under the fat pads and the muscle masses form creases in the palms, especially when flexing the fingers and moving the thumb.

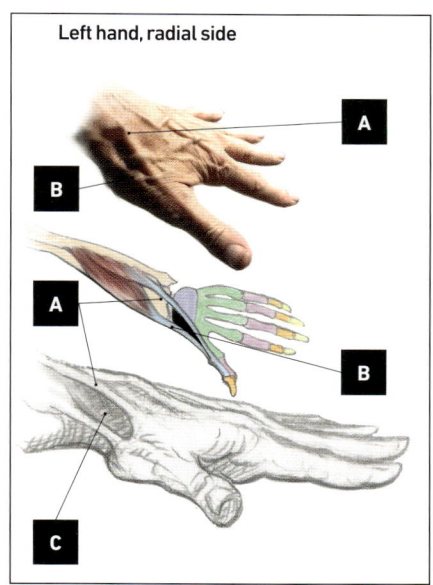

Left hand, radial side

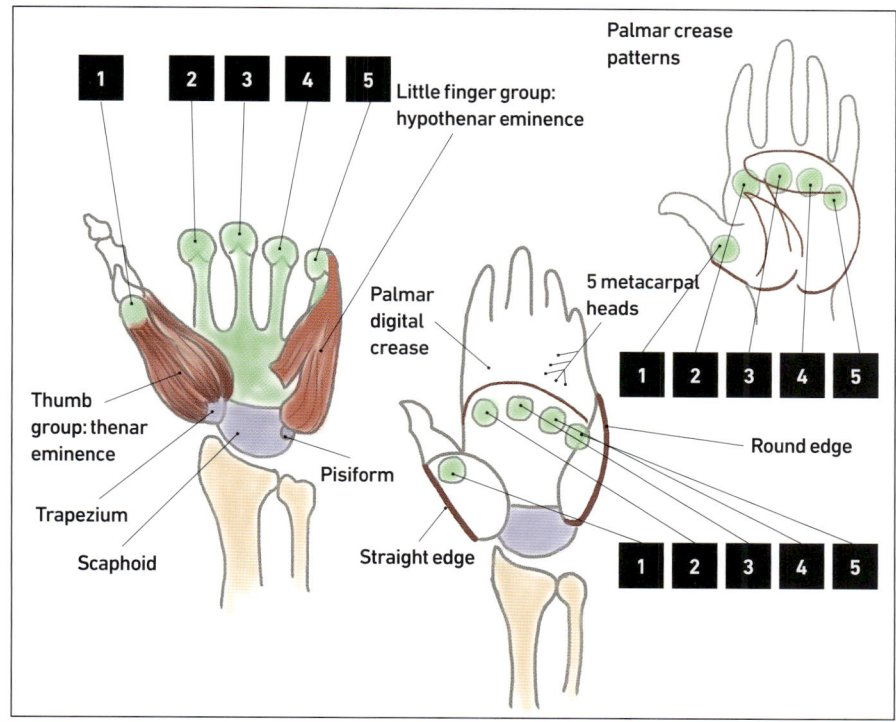

Tendons of the thumb. Fully extend your own thumb and note how the thumb's extensor (**A**) and abductor (**B**) tendons create a hollow (**C**). This hollow landmark is called the "anatomical snuffbox."

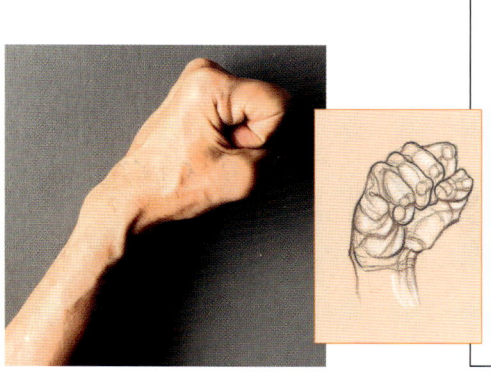

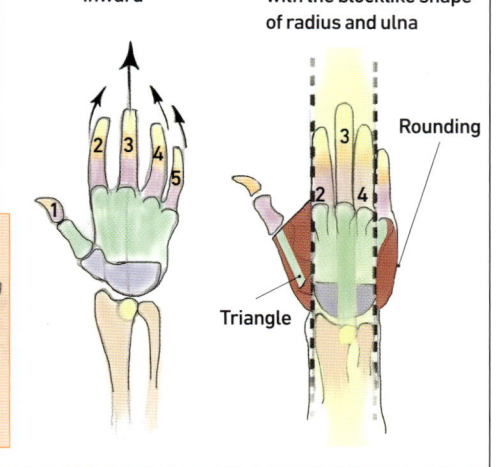

Fingers curve inward

Fingers 2, 3, and 4 line up with the blocklike shape of radius and ulna

Rounding

Triangle

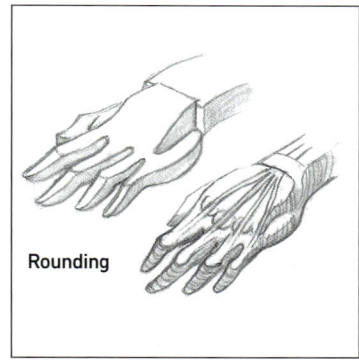

Rounding

Extensor digitorum tendons
Extensor tendons of the fingers bulge at the wrist, creating a slight ramp over the carpal and metacarpal bones.

Drawing a fist
The protruding knuckles are actually the distal heads of the metacarpals. The proximal phalanges (where rings are worn) adjoin the metacarpals at a 90-degree angle. The middle phalanges (where we knock on doors) adjoin the proximal phalanges at 90 degrees. Distal phalanges, the shortest of all, are tightly tucked behind the thumb and into the thenar and hypothenar eminences.

Phalanges
When relaxed, fingers 2, 4, and 5 tend to curve slightly toward the straight middle finger (subtly, unlike this diagram's exaggerated curves). If fingers 2, 3, and 4 are held together, they form a continuation (widthwise) of the boxlike wrist. Hold your own hand in this tight-fingered position and notice how the thumb and little fingers act independently.

JOINTS

Joints are areas where bones are linked together. They have varying degrees of mobility and are classified into three basic types: immovable joints (cranial sutures), slightly movable joints (intervertebral discs), and freely movable joints (synovial joints).

For the purposes of this book, we are only concerned with five types of freely movable joints found in the hands and feet.

Plane joints (e.g., joints of the wrist) glide face to face, limited by their retaining ligaments.

Hinge joints (e.g., joints of the fingers and thumb) can only swing back and forth. Bone movement is restricted to one plane.

Saddle joints (e.g., joint of the thumb) increase the range of hinge joints by permitting 360-degree motion (but no rotation). The saddle joint gets its name because one part of the joint is concave and looks like a saddle. The other bone's end is convex and looks like a rider in a saddle.

Condyloid joints (e.g., joints of the first row of knuckles) increase the extent of the saddle joint by permitting limited circular movement.

Ellipsoid joints (e.g., oval part of wrist) are a modified ball-and-socket where the uniting surfaces are ellipsoidal rather than spherical.

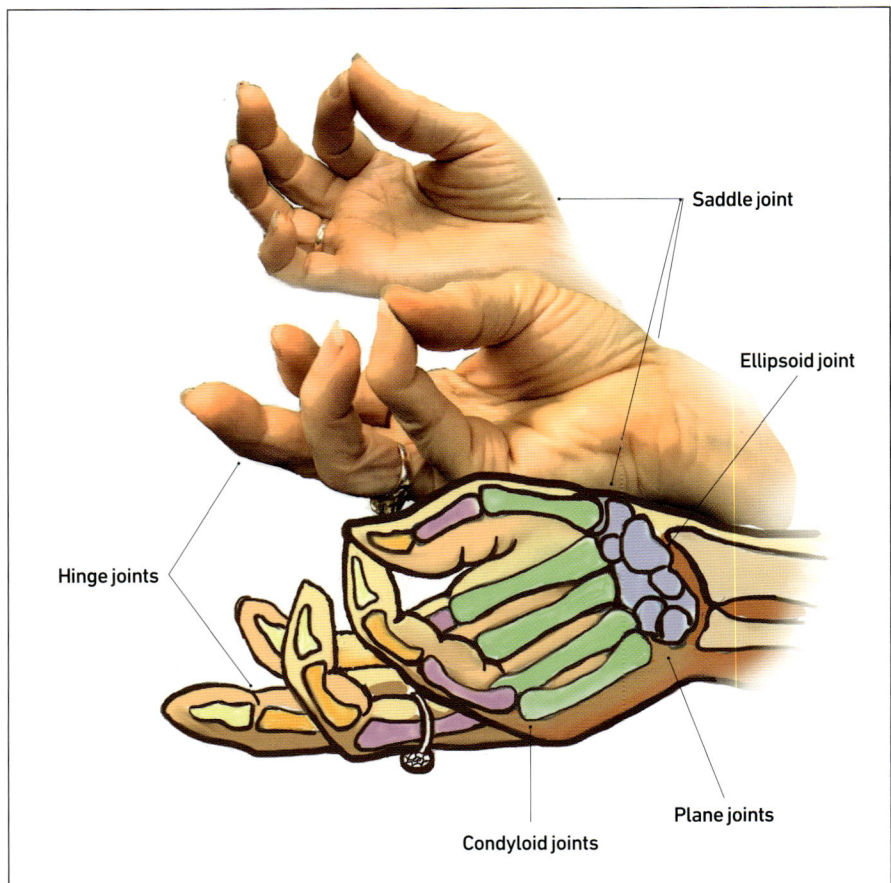

Saddle joint

Ellipsoid joint

Hinge joints

Plane joints

Condyloid joints

THE MOBILE THUMB

With its teardrop muscle and saddle joint, the thumb can move in almost any direction. While the other fingers are also mobile, their lateral movement is diminished by their medial and distal hinge joints, which can only move in one plane. This limitation is compensated for by the knuckle's condyloid joints, where circular movement is possible.

FAT PADS

Except for the thumb, each finger has three fatty finger pads, which act as protective cushions. The thumb has one well-developed pad on its distal phalanx. The finger pads extend past the ends of all of the phalanges in order to protect the tips of the bones. The palm is cushioned by fat in three areas surrounding the central palmar aponeurosis: the *metacarpal heads*, *thenar eminence*, and *hypothenar eminence*.

Palmar creases. The way skin stretches and folds over the fat pads creates permanent creases on the fingers and palms. Creases tell the history of where the hand bends repeatedly, so most joints have corresponding creases, especially as we age.

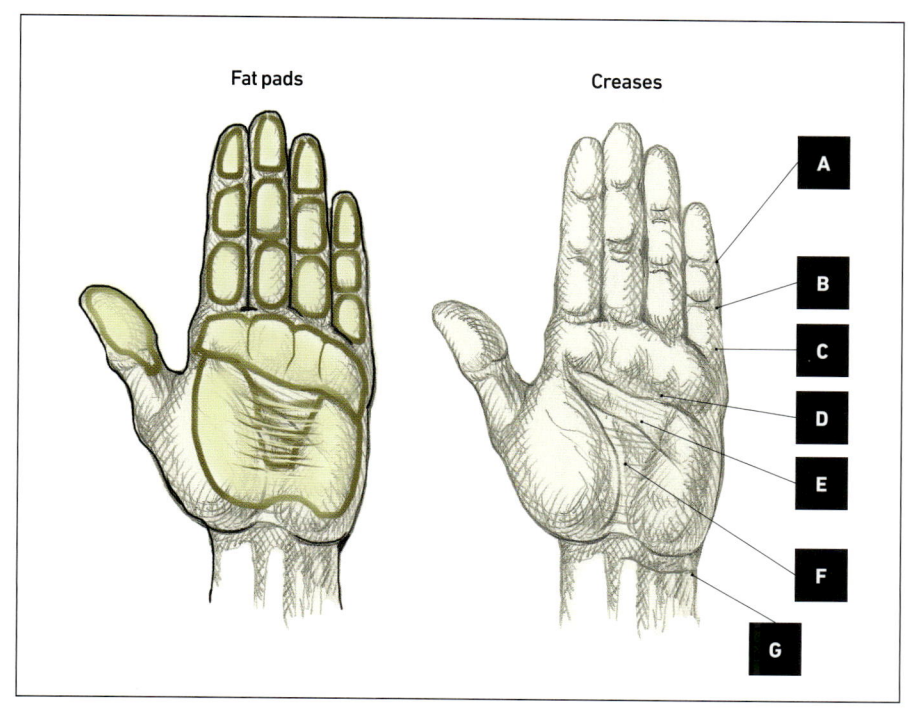

Fat pads

Creases

Phalanges
(**A**) Distal digital crease
(**B**) Middle digital crease
(**C**) Proximal digital crease

Palm and wrist
(**D**) Distal palmar crease (heartline)
(**E**) Proximal palmar crease (headline)
(**F**) Thenar crease (lifeline)
(**G**) Wrist crease

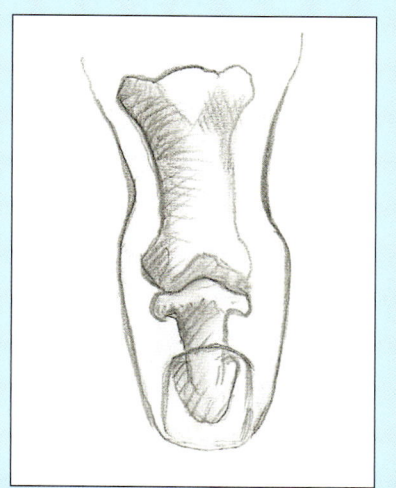

How Fat Pads Work

Finger pads extend slightly past the end of each distal phalanx to protect the bony tips underneath fingernails. Not only do fat pads cushion and protect the finger bones, their "cushiness" also allows us to gently hold objects without dropping them.

Dorsal finger wrinkles. Because the bony dorsal side of the hand has no fat pads, it is not creased like the palmar side. In fact, its "wrinkles," which cover the distal and middle joints, are really just excess skin, all bunched up after years of extension and flexion.

The distal joint wrinkles (**A**) can be simplified into single lines. The middle joint wrinkles (**B**) have an oval pattern that can be drawn with rounded and straight lines. The proximal knuckle wrinkles (**C**) are minor lines because the underlying extensor tendons push up and "smooth out" the loose skin. Check out the knuckle wrinkles on your own extended fingers.

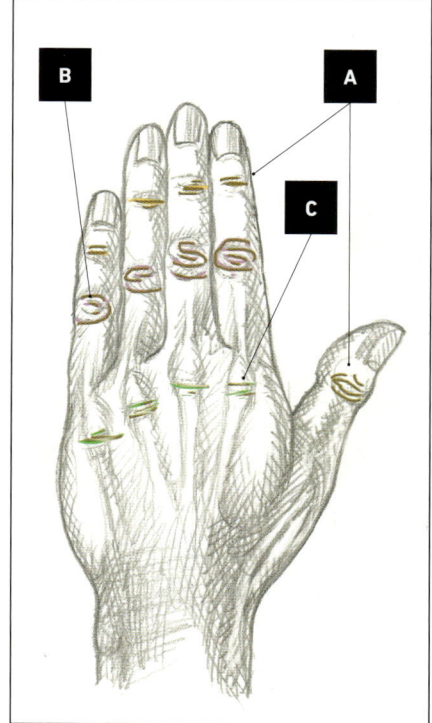

UPPER LEGS

Where does the upper leg actually begin—at the hip or the thigh?

For many artistic anatomists, the upper legs begin at the hip with three visible muscles, the *tensor fascia lata, gluteus medius*, and *gluteus maximus*, collectively called the *outer hip region*. However, in this book I have already grouped the hip muscles with the torso (as most artists do for visual reasons), so our study of the upper legs will begin with the *bones and muscles of the thighs*, not the *hips*. (See page 116 in the Torso chapter to learn about the origins and insertions of the outer hip muscles.)

BONES AND MUSCLES: FRONT VIEW

The thigh of the upper leg contains three muscle groups: the quadriceps, hamstrings, and adductors.

Bones. The femur (**B**), with its great trochanter at the top (**A**) and outer epicondyles (**C**) and inner epicondyles (**D**) at the base, is the heaviest and longest bone of the skeletal system. The kneecap (patella) sits in between the outer epicondyles and inner epicondyles on the patellar surface. The lower leg consists of the thick tibia (**I**) and the slender fibula (**H**). The tibial tuberosity (**F**) and head of the fibula (**G**) are important landmarks at the top, as are the ankle bones (the inner malleolus and outer malleolus) at the bottom.

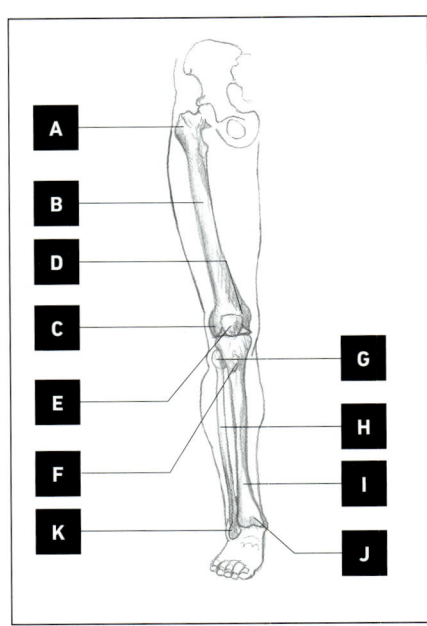

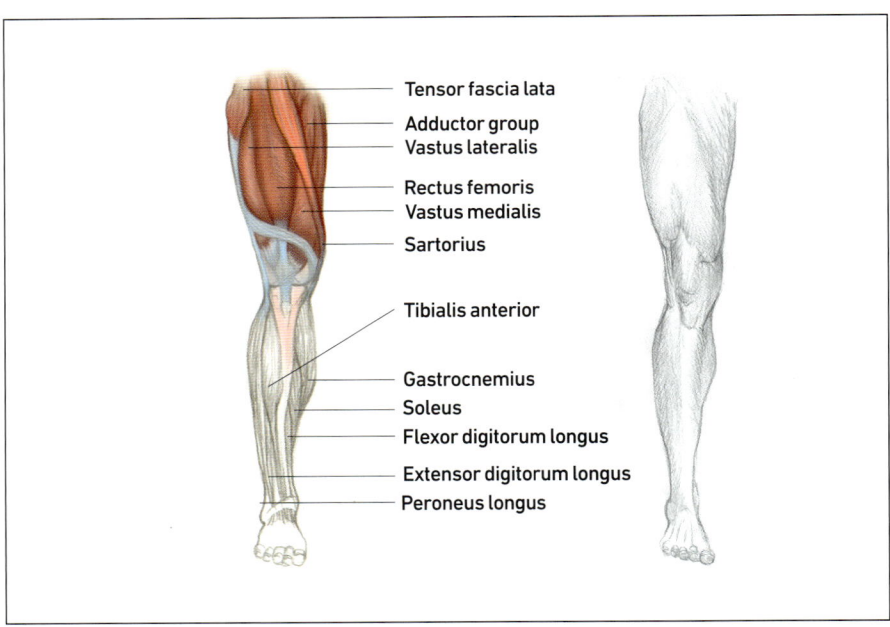

- Tensor fascia lata
- Adductor group
- Vastus lateralis
- Rectus femoris
- Vastus medialis
- Sartorius
- Tibialis anterior
- Gastrocnemius
- Soleus
- Flexor digitorum longus
- Extensor digitorum longus
- Peroneus longus

Muscles. The anterior portion of the upper leg has four major muscle masses: *vastus lateralis*, which attaches to the knee cap (**E**); *rectus femoris*, which engulfs the patella (**E**) and continues toward the tibial tuberosity (**F**); *vastus medialis*, a medial bulge; and the *adductor group* on the inside of the leg. There are also two other masses: the *tensor fascia lata* and the *sartorius*, which originate on the outer hip areas. The *sartorius* is the longest muscle in the body.

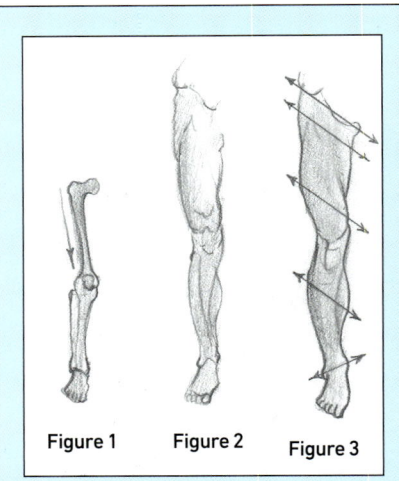

Figure 1   Figure 2   Figure 3

DRAWING TIPS

The legs angle in toward the middle, positioning the body's weight over the gravitational center (see Figures 1 and 2). The muscle masses on the outside of the leg are higher than those on the inside (see Figure 3). The ankles are just the reverse—high inside, low outside.

INDIVIDUAL UPPER LEG MUSCLES: FRONT VIEW

This section provides an overview of the origins, insertions, and actions of each muscle of the upper leg, front view.

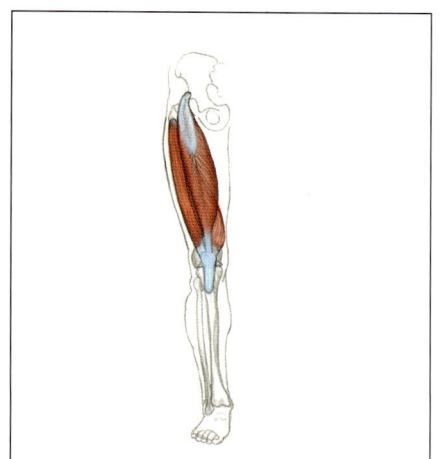

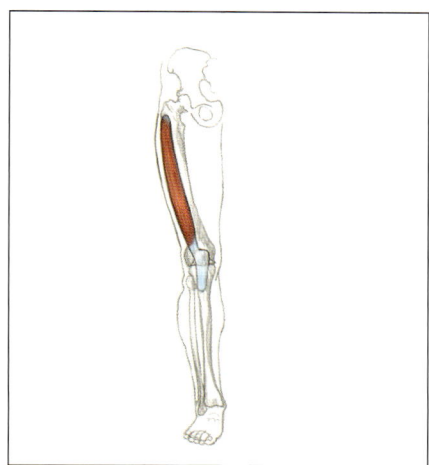

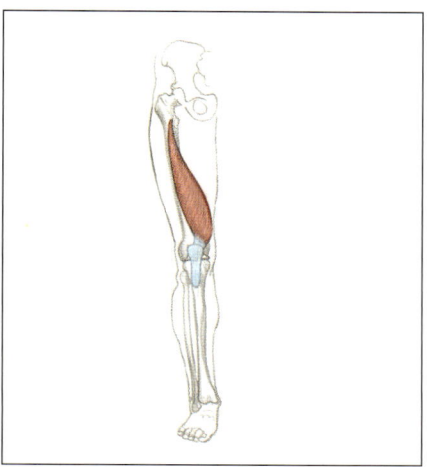

Quadriceps Femoris—Extensor Group of the Thigh

This very large muscle is also one of the strongest muscles of the human body. As indicated by its name, it has four muscles: The *vastus lateralis muscle*, *vastus medialis muscle*, *rectus femoris muscle*, and *vastus intermedius muscle*. Vastus intermedius is hidden beneath the *rectus femoris*, so it is seldom if ever mentioned as a fourth muscle of the group. *Rectus femoris* is the only extensor of the knee joint and is also a hip flexor.

Vastus Lateralis Muscle

Origin. *Great trochanter* and *linea aspera of femur*.

Insertion. Common tendon to patella (quadriceps tendon), continues over patella into fibers of the patellar ligament.

Action. Extends the lower leg at the knee joint.

Vastus Medialis Muscle

Origin. *Linea aspera of femur* at the level of the *lesser trochanter* (also originates from the tendons of the *adductor longus* and *adductor magnus muscles*).

Insertion. Common tendon to patella (quadriceps tendon), continues over patella into fibers of the patellar ligament.

Action. Extends the lower leg at the knee joint and stabilizes the *patella* in its groove between the *femoral condyles*.

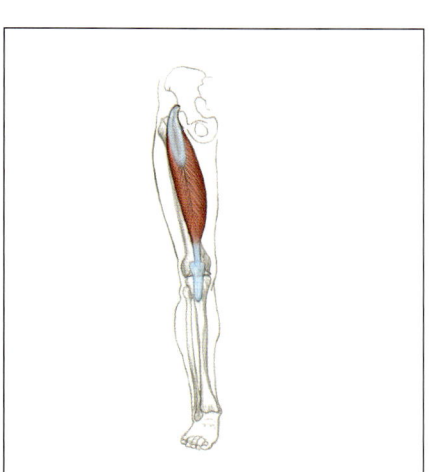

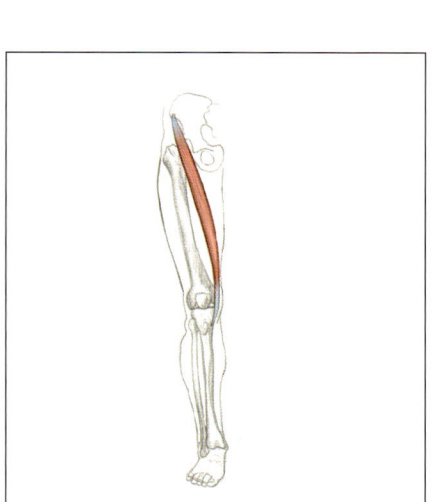

Rectus Femoris Muscle

Origin. *Anterior inferior iliac spine (AIIS)*.

Insertion. Common tendon to patella (quadriceps tendon), continues over patella into fibers of the patellar ligament.

Action. Extends the lower leg at the knee joint. Also *flexes and abducts* the thigh at the hip joint.

Hip Region to the Knee

Sartorius

The *sartorius muscle* is a long, thin muscle responsible for flexion, abduction, and external rotation at the hip joint and flexion and internal rotation at the knee joint.

Origin. *Anterior superior iliac spine (ASIS)*.

Insertion. Behind the *medial epicondyle of the femur* to *tuberosity of tibia* in common with insertions of *gracilis and semimembranosus*.

Action. Flexes and abducts the thigh, rotates it outward and inward.

Tensor Fascia Lata

Origin. *Anterior superior iliac spine—ASIS.*

Insertion. Upper portion of the *iliotibial band (IT band).*

Action. Flexes, abducts, and medially rotates the thigh. Provides tension for the *iliotibial band and stabilizes the knee joint.*

Iliotibial Tract

A long, wide, thin band that lies on the outer surface of the thigh. Technically, it is fascia, not a tendon.

Origin. Begins superiorly at the level of the *great trochanter.*

Insertion. *Lateral condyle of the femur.*

Action. Flexes, abducts, and medially rotates the thigh. Provides tension for the *iliotibial band and stabilizes the knee joint.*

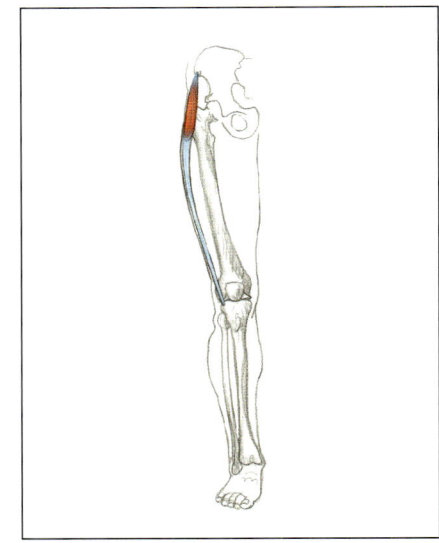

Adductor Group of the Thigh: Three Most Visible Adductors

The adductor muscle group lies on the inside of the thigh. Its superficial muscles are the *gracilis, adductor longus,* and *adductor magnus.* There are other deeper, smaller muscles belonging to this group, but they do not influence surface form. The adductor mass can be visualized as an inverted cone whose internal side is defined by the long, slender shape of the gracilis muscle.

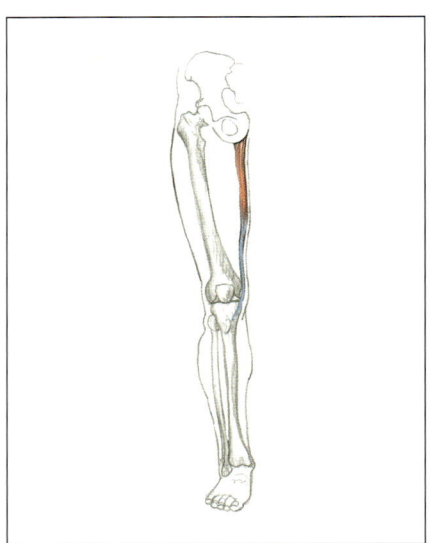

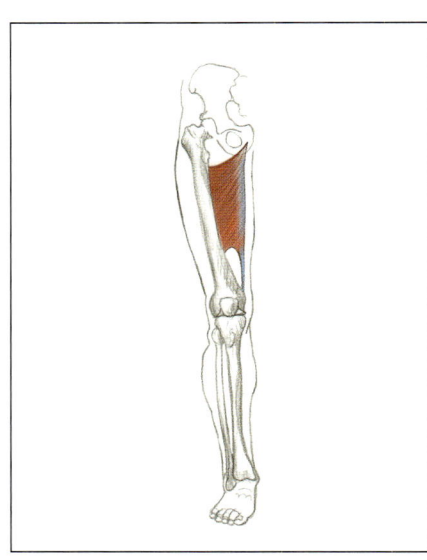

Gracilis

Origin. *Inferior edge* of *pubic arch* between the *pubic symphysis and ischial tuberosity.*

Insertion. *Tuberosity of tibia* below the *medial condyle* and behind the *tendon of sartorius.*

Action. The gracilis muscle is the most superficial and most medial muscle of this group. In addition to facilitating adduction and flexion at the hip joint, it also facilitates flexion and internal rotation at the knee joint.

Adductor Longus

Origin. Small round area just below the *pubic tubercle* and *lateral* to the *pubic symphysis.*

Insertion. *Medial lip of the linea aspera* (vertical line on middle third of the *back of the femur*).

Action. This muscle facilitates both *adduction and flexion of the hip joint* and *medially rotates* the thigh.

Adductor Magnus

Origin. A line beginning on the *lower lateral portion of the ischial tuberosity and ramus of ischium.*

Insertion. *Linea aspera* (line running down the middle of the back of the *femur* beginning at level of the *lesser trochanter*). Also, the *medial epicondyle of femur.*

Action. One of the largest muscles in the human body. The adductor magnus muscle powerfully adducts the thigh and facilitates external rotation and extension of the hip joint.

BONES AND MUSCLES OF THE UPPER LEG: BACK VIEW

Bones. From the back view, the same leg bones that appear in the front view are visible. Their appearance is slightly altered, however, because the bone attachments in the front are designed to allow muscles to extend, and the back attachment is designed for muscles to flex.

Muscles. The upper leg consists of five large muscle masses: the *gluteus maximus and gluteus medius* (already covered under "The Torso, Back View" on page 101), the *adductor group*, and the *vastus externus*, which can be seen peeking out from behind the biceps femoris. Seen from behind, the most prominent muscles of the upper leg are the *hamstring muscle group* (*biceps femoris, semitendinosus*, and *semimembranosus*).

A. Great trochanter
B. Femur
C. Inner condyle
D. Outer condyle
E. Head of the fibula
F. Tibia
G. Fibula
H. Inner malleolus
I. Outer malleolus

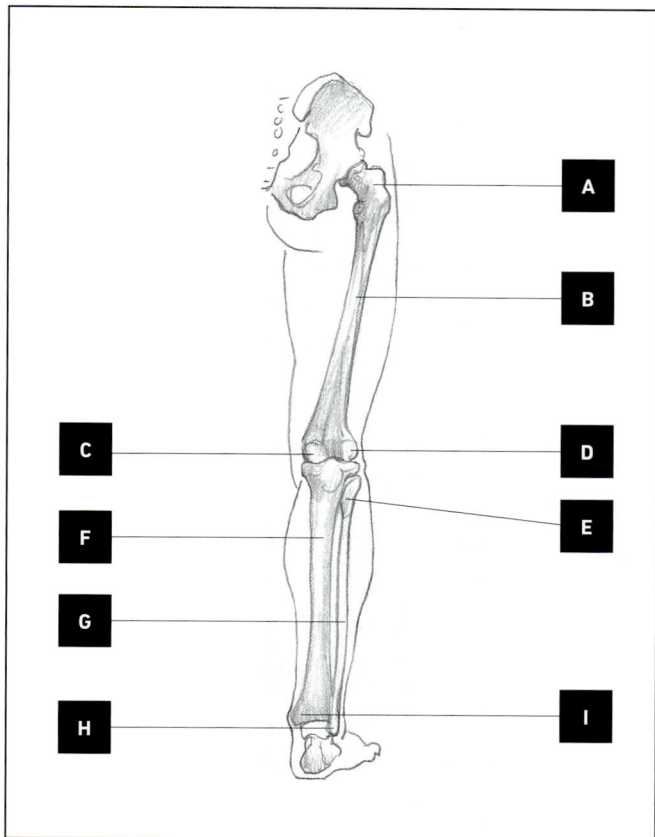

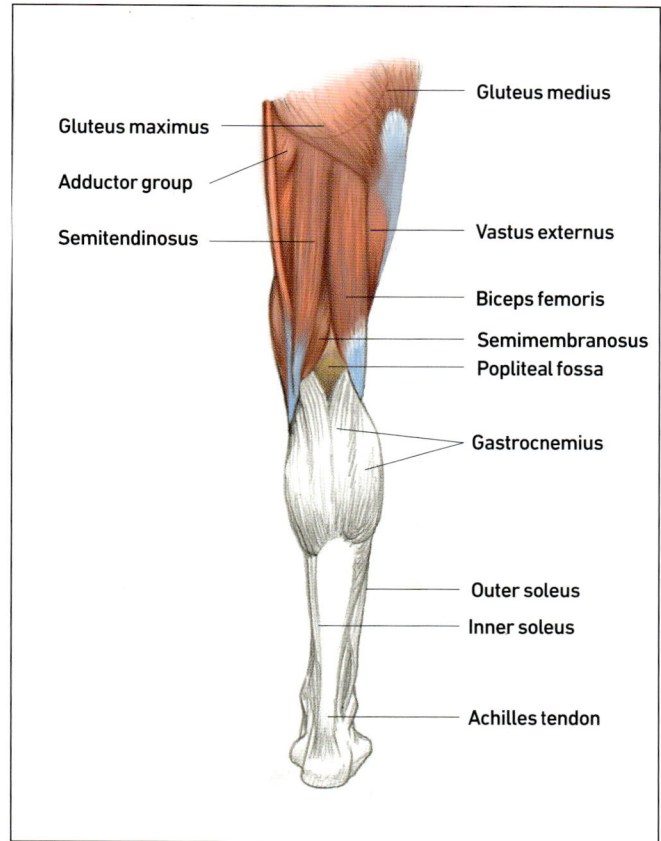

Gluteus maximus
Adductor group
Semitendinosus

Gluteus medius

Vastus externus

Biceps femoris
Semimembranosus
Popliteal fossa

Gastrocnemius

Outer soleus
Inner soleus

Achilles tendon

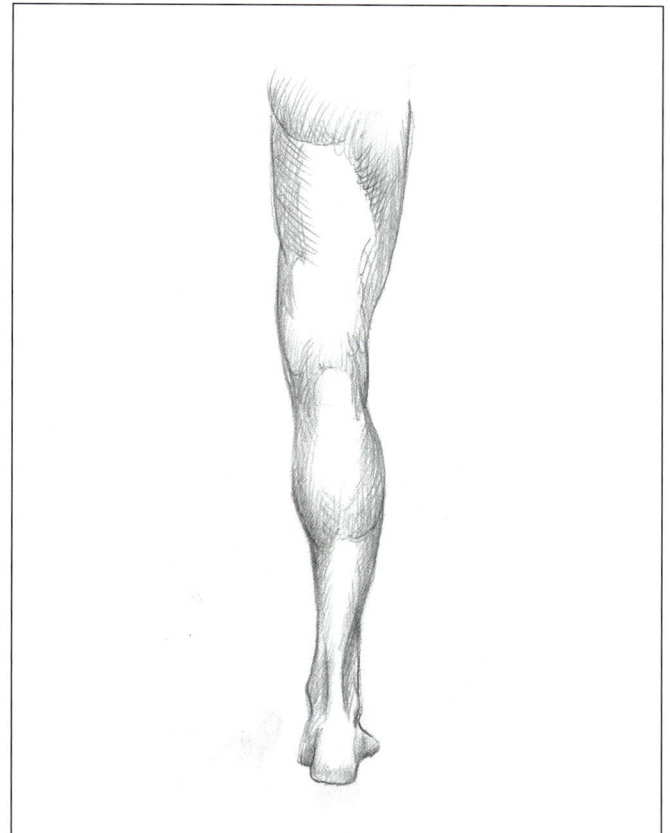

INDIVIDUAL UPPER LEG MUSCLES: BACK VIEW

This section provides an overview of the origins, insertions, and actions of each muscle of the upper leg.

Hamstring Muscle Group

The hamstring muscle group consists of three muscles located on the back of the upper leg: the *biceps femoris*, *semimembranosus*, and *semitendinosus*. The *biceps femoris* has *two heads—a long and a short*. The *hamstring group* contains a total of four *muscular heads* (four forms), all of which eventually insert into the lower leg below the knee joint.

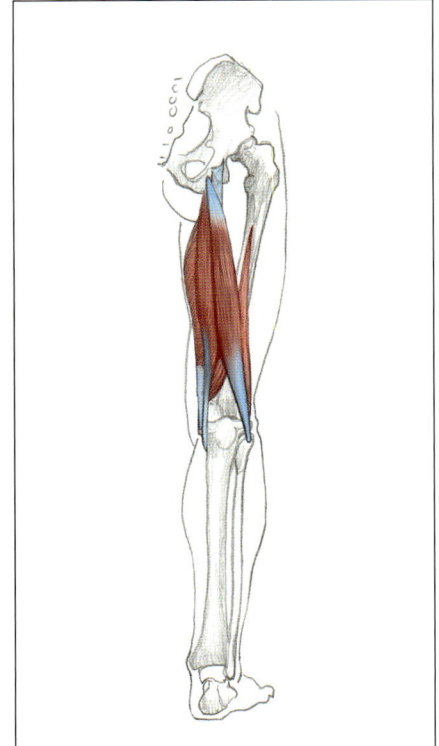

DRAWING TIPS
The hamstring tendons grip below the knee on both sides, almost like a pair of tongs.

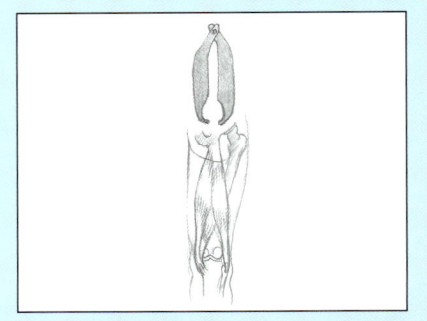

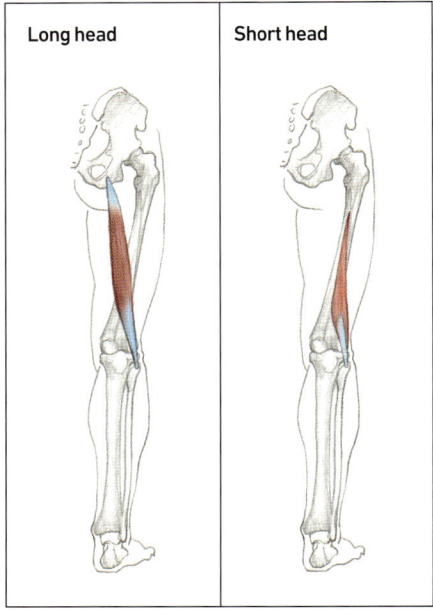

| Long head | Short head |

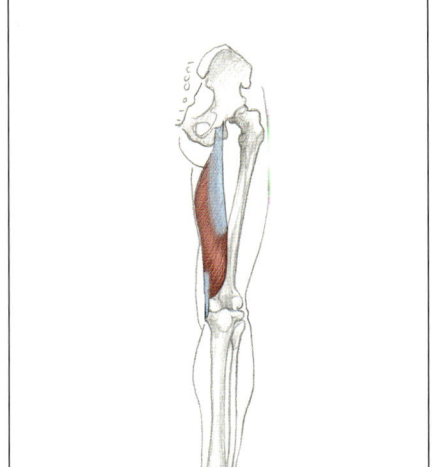

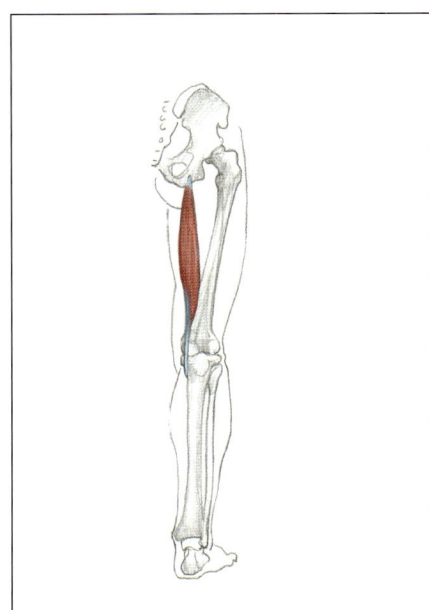

Biceps Femoris

Origin. Two heads.

Long head. *Ischial tuberosity of pelvis.*
Short head. *Linea aspera of femur* (long head partly conceals short head).

Insertion. Both—*head of fibula*.

Action. Both of the heads flex the lower leg at the knee joint and then rotate the tibia laterally. The long head is a two-joint muscle, while the short head is a one-joint muscle. The long head also extends the thigh.

Semimembranosus

Origin. Upper lateral part of the *ischial tuberosity of pelvis* (under and lateral to the origin of (the *biceps femoris*).

Insertion. *Medial condyle of tibia.*

Action. Flexes the lower leg at the knee joint and then medially rotates it, extends thigh at the hip joint.

Semitendinosus

Origin. *Upper lateral part of the ischial tuberosity of pelvis* (in common with the *long head of biceps femoris*).

Insertion. *Tuberosity of tibia* (in common with the *gracilis* behind the *sartorius tendon*).

Action. Flexes the lower leg and then medially rotates it, extends thigh at the hip joint.

BONES AND MUSCLES OF THE UPPER LEG: SIDE VIEW

Bones. Because the long femur (**B**) and large tibia (**H**) carry the weight of the body, they sit directly on top of one another. But in a side-view drawing, the upper and lower leg appear staggered; the front of the shin lines up directly below the iliotibial band muscles and behind the upper-leg masses of the rectus femoris and vastus externus.

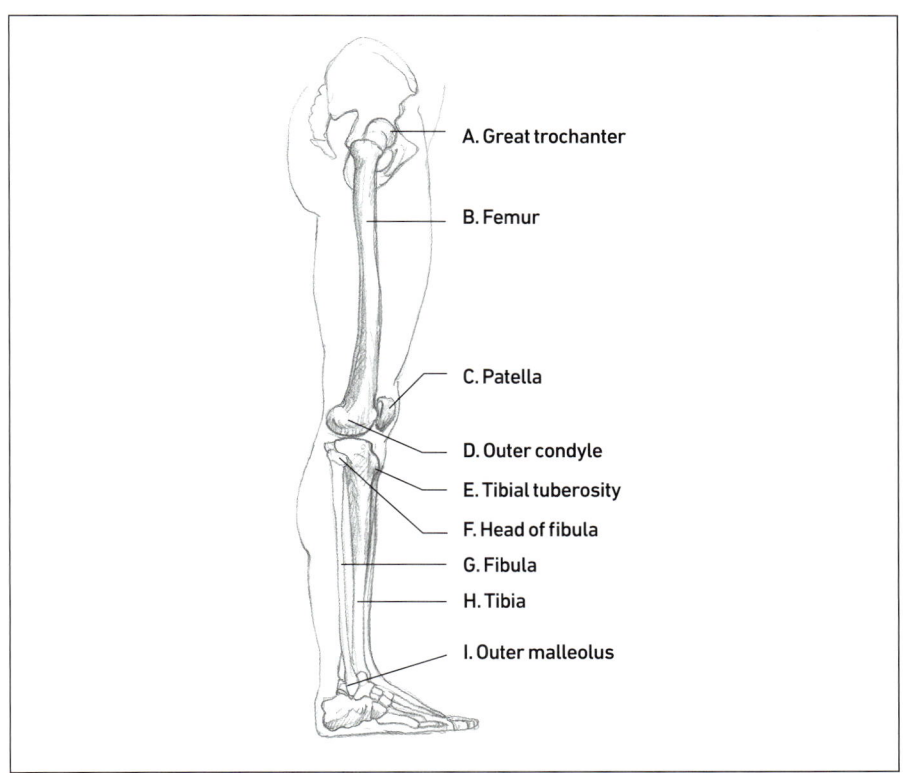

A. Great trochanter
B. Femur
C. Patella
D. Outer condyle
E. Tibial tuberosity
F. Head of fibula
G. Fibula
H. Tibia
I. Outer malleolus

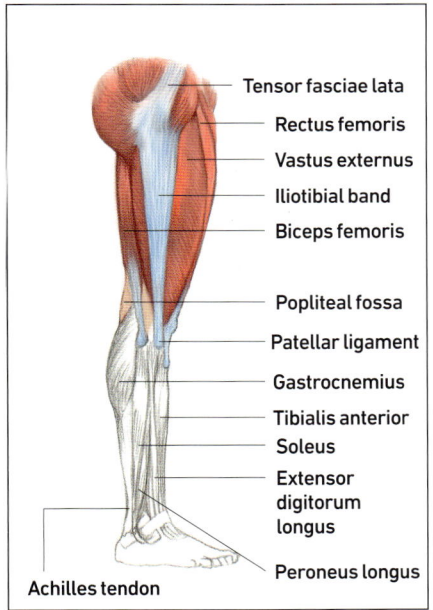

Tensor fasciae lata
Rectus femoris
Vastus externus
Iliotibial band
Biceps femoris
Popliteal fossa
Patellar ligament
Gastrocnemius
Tibialis anterior
Soleus
Extensor digitorum longus
Peroneus longus
Achilles tendon

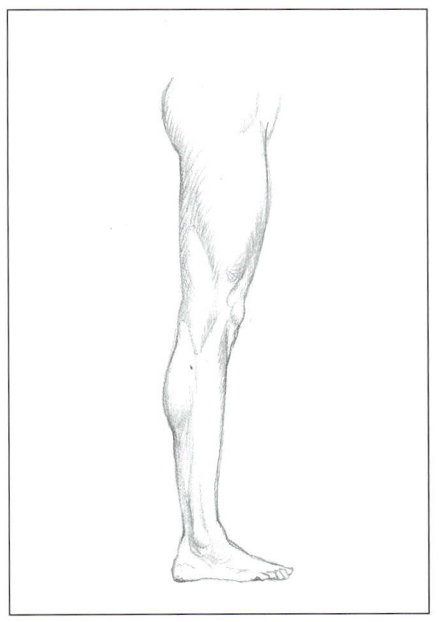

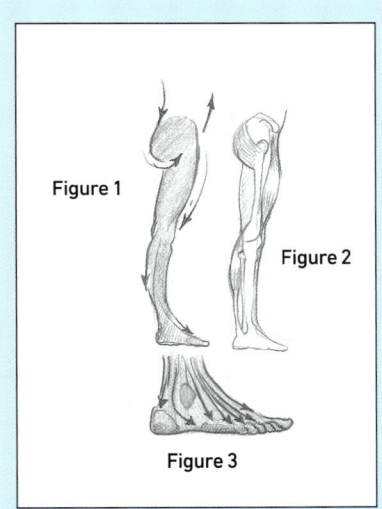

Figure 1
Figure 2
Figure 3

DRAWING TIPS
The six arrows in Figure 1 show the overall gesture of the leg. The upper thigh and lower calf create the gesture (see Figure 2). Figure 3 shows the pattern of tendons in the foot (see page 161).

LOWER LEGS

Just as the *extrinsic muscles* of the forearm send their *tendons* into the hand, *extrinsic muscles* of the lower leg send their *tendons* across the ankle onto the foot. The *extrinsic muscles* of the lower leg originate on the *femur, tibia, or fibula* and insert onto foot bones via *long tendons*. They are divided into three groups: *anterior, posterior, and lateral muscle compartments*.

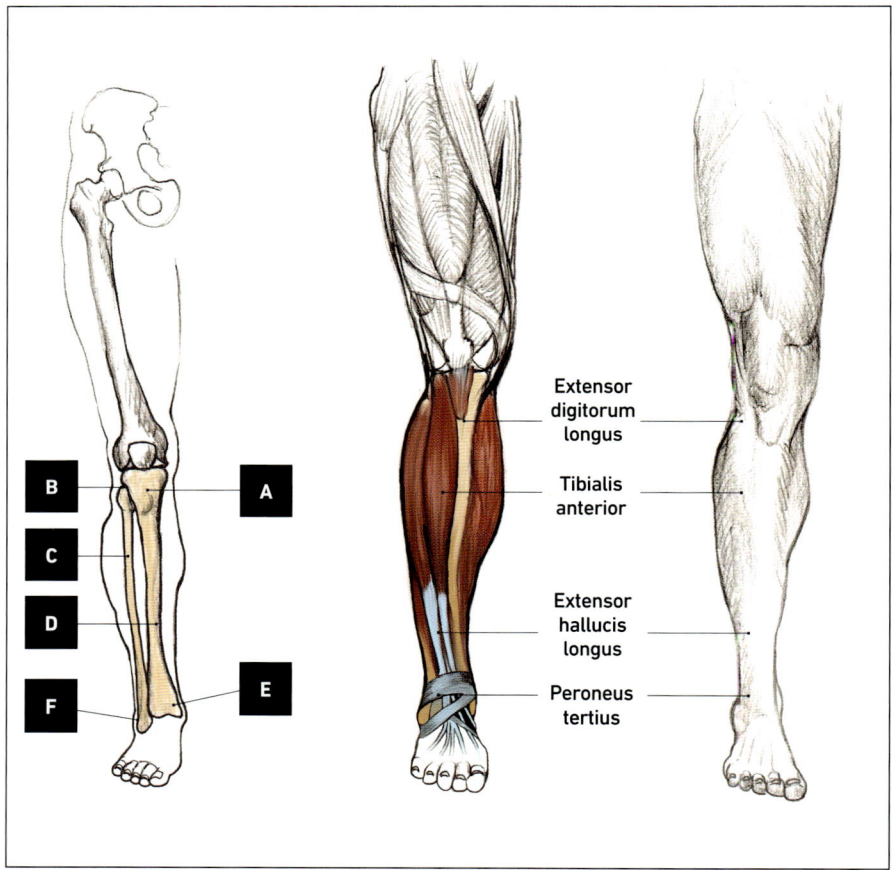

Extensor
digitorum
longus

Tibialis
anterior

Extensor
hallucis
longus

Peroneus
tertius

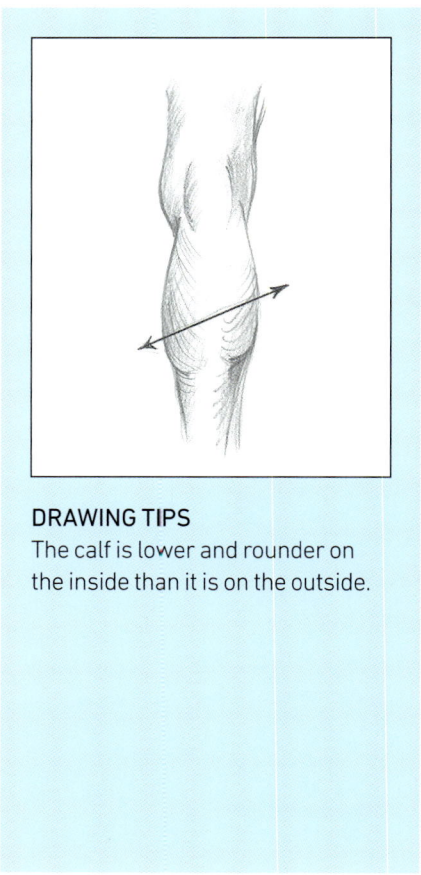

DRAWING TIPS
The calf is lower and rounder on the inside than it is on the outside.

FRONT VIEW (ANTERIOR)

Bones. The lower leg consists of the thick *tibia* (**D**) and the slender *fibula* (**C**). The *tibial tuberosity* (**A**) and *head of the fibula* (**B**) are important landmarks at the top, as are the ankle bones at the bottom, the *inner malleolus* (**E**) and *outer malleolus* (**F**).

Muscles (anterior portion). The anterior portion consists of the *tibialis anterior, extensor digitorum longus, peroneus tertius*, and *extensor hallucis longus*. The tendons of these muscles pass downward on the front of the ankle joint and participate in *dorsiflexion, inversion, eversion*, and *extension* of the toes. The *peroneus tertius* is hidden below the *extensor hallucis longus tendon*, so it is not visible as an individual muscle.

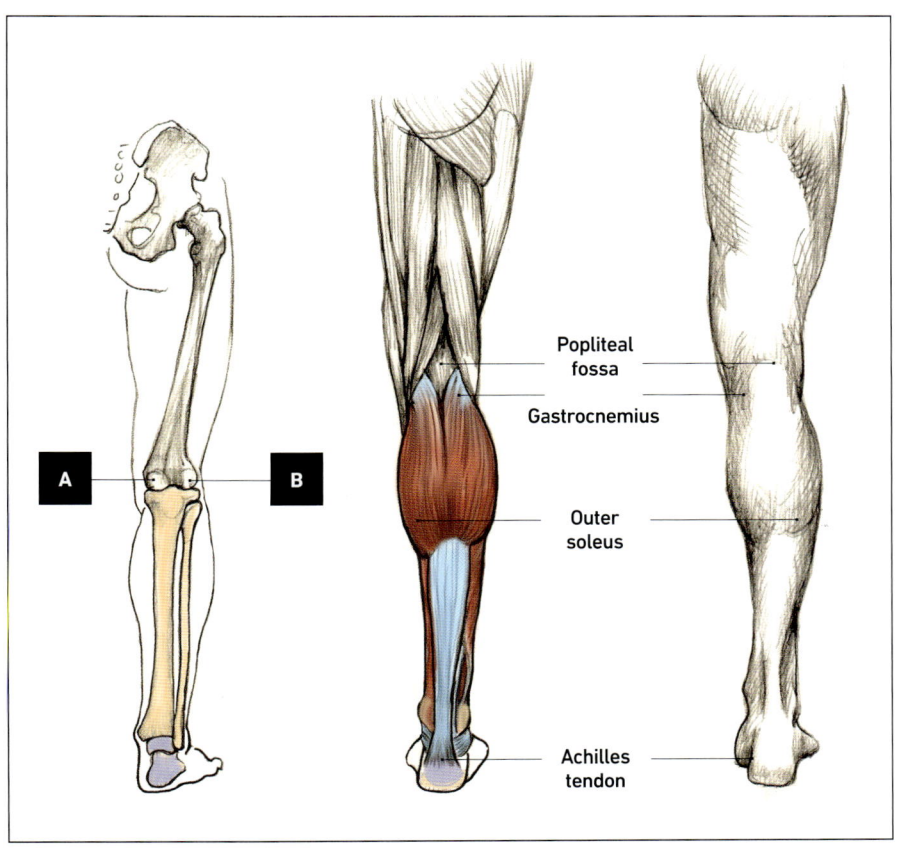

BACK VIEW (POSTERIOR)

Bones. From the back view, the same leg bones that appear in the front view are visible. Their appearance is slightly altered, however, because the bone attachments in the front are designed to allow muscles to extend, and the back attachment is designed for muscles to flex.

Muscles (posterior compartment). The lower leg's *posterior portion* features five masses: three larger ones and two smaller. The larger masses are the two heads of the calf, the *gastrocnemius* and *the Achilles tendon*, which connect to the heel bone. The *two smaller masses are the inner soleus and outer soleus*. Also, notice the hollow area behind the knee where the *calf tendons* originate (**A** and **B**), called the *popliteal fossa*. This fatty hollow makes deep knee bends possible. In opposition to *anterior muscles*, which lift the foot up (*dorsiflexion*), the *posterior muscle group* points the foot down (*plantar flexion*).

Labels in figure: Popliteal fossa, Gastrocnemius, Outer soleus, Achilles tendon; A, B

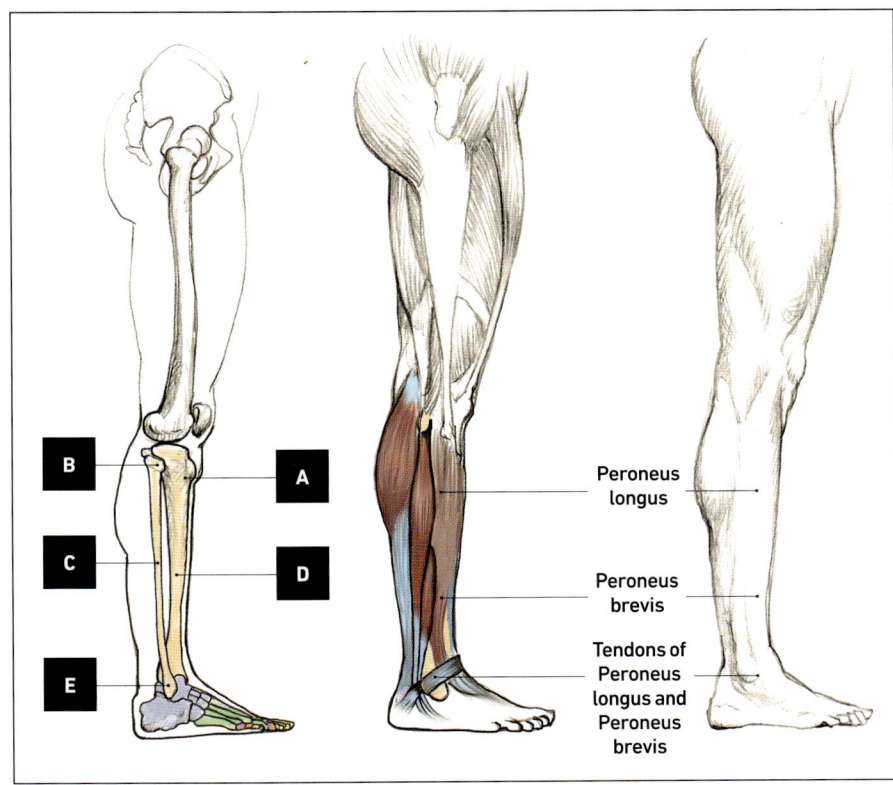

SIDE VIEW (LATERAL)

Bones. From the side view, the *tibial tuberosity* (**A**), *head of the fibula* (**B**), *fibula* (**C**), *tibia* (**D**), and *outer malleolus* (**E**) are visible.

Muscles (lateral). The *lateral portion* consists of the *peroneus longus and peroneus brevis*. The *peroneus longus* arises from the *head and upper shaft of the fibula, inserting onto the bottom of the foot (first metatarsal)*. The *peroneus brevis arises on the lower lateral shaft of the fibula (which is covered by the peroneus longus) and inserts onto the lateral tubercle of the fifth metatarsal* (more on this in the section on the foot). *Tendons from both muscles hook behind the lateral malleolus, and both help to point the foot (plantar flexion).*

Labels in figure: Peroneus longus, Peroneus brevis, Tendons of Peroneus longus and Peroneus brevis; A, B, C, D, E

INDIVIDUAL MUSCLES OF THE LOWER LEG

This section provides an overview of the origins, insertions, and actions of each visible muscle of the lower leg.

The *extrinsic muscles* of the lower leg cross over the ankle joint and move the foot. What follows are the individual muscles of the three compartments of the lower leg: the *anterior, posterior and lateral compartments*. Only the most visible muscles of each compartment are shown here.

Anterior Compartment: Extensor Muscles

These are the three most visible anterior muscles.

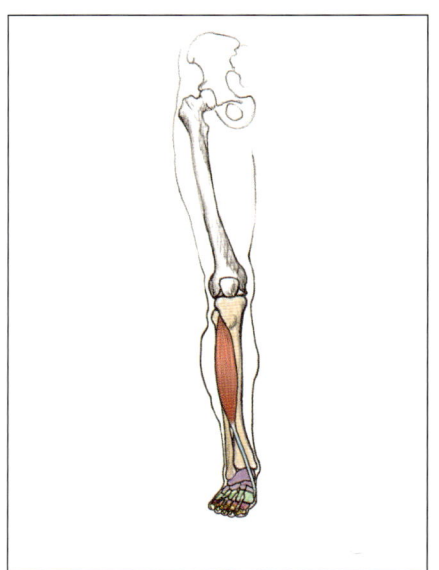

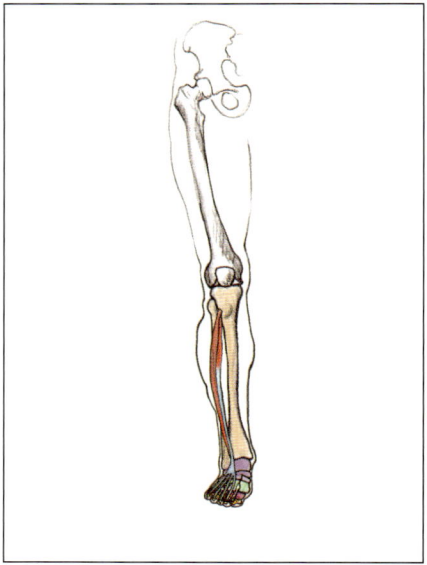

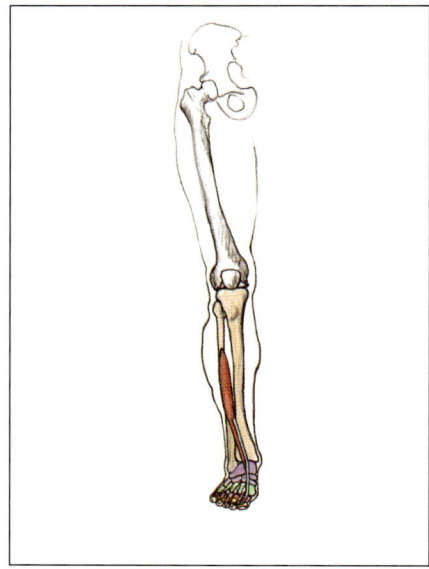

Tibialis Anterior

Origin. The *lateral condyle* and surface of the *tibia*, head and *crest of fibula, interosseus membrane*.

Insertion. Underside of *first cuneiform* and base of the *first metatarsal*.

Action. Raises and inverts the foot.

Extensor Digitorum Longus

Origin. *Lateral condyle of the tibia*, upper three-quarters of the front edge of *fibula, interosseus membrane*.

Insertion. Below and at the front of the ankle by four tendons to the phalanges of toes 2 through 5 (does not go to big toe).

Action. Extends toes 2 through 5, dorsiflexes (raises) the foot at the ankle joint. (Toes 2 through 5 separate when extended and come together when flexed.)

Extensor Hallucis Longus

Origin. Middle of the *medial surface of fibula*.

Insertion. Top of the second phalanx of big toe.

Action. Raises the big toe, assists in dorsiflexion (raising) of the foot.

Posterior Compartment: Flexor Muscles

These are the three most visible posterior muscles.

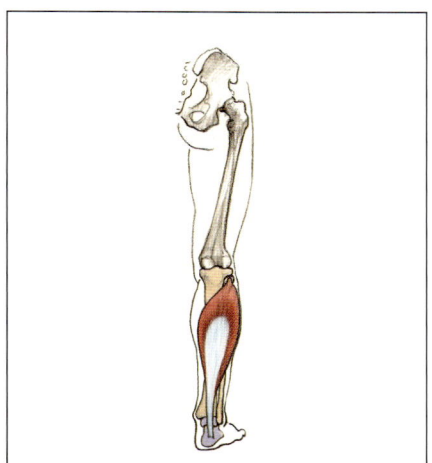

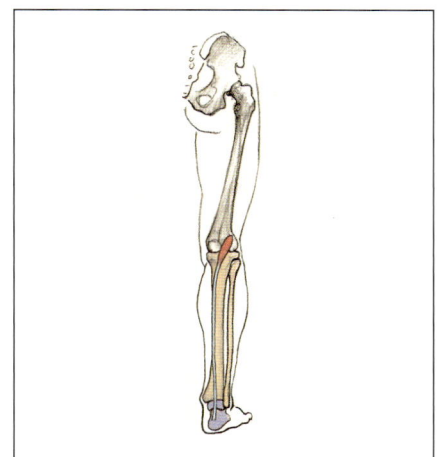

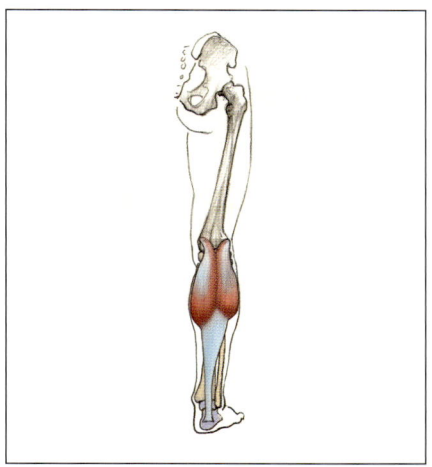

Soleus

The soleus joins the two-headed *gastrocnemius* to form the "calf muscle group."

Origin. Head of the fibula and posterior surface of the fibula and tibia.

Insertion. Via the Achilles tendon (in common with *gastrocnemius*) to the *calcaneus* (heel bone).

Action. Raises the heel when the foot is on the ground and points the foot (plantar flexion) when the foot is free.

Plantaris

This muscle, near the *popliteal fossa*, is only noticeable on well-defined legs.

Origin. Just above the *lateral condyle* (immediately above the origin of the *lateral head of the gastrocnemius*).

Insertion. *Posterior surface of the calcaneus, medial to the insertion of the Achilles tendon.*

Action. Weakly flexes the knee joint and points the foot (plantar flexion) when the foot is free.

Gastrocnemius

The *gastrocnemius* is made up of a lateral head, a medial head, and a single tendon of insertion (*Achilles tendon*) in common with the *soleus*.

Origin (lateral head). Above the lateral condyle of the femur.

Origin (medial head). Above the medial condyle of the femur.

Insertion. Middle part of the *posterior surface of the calcaneus*, in common with the soleus.

Action. Flexes the leg and plantar flexes the foot.

Lateral Compartment: Eversion Muscles

These are the two most visible lateral muscles.

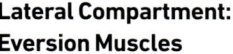

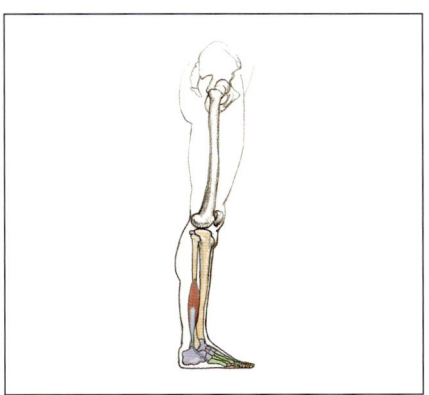

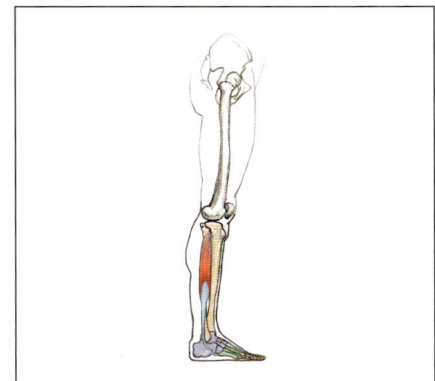

Peroneus Brevis

The peroneus brevis is a long, flat muscle located on the outside of the lower half of the lower leg.

Origin. Lower two-thirds of the *lateral surface of fibula*.

Insertion. Behind the *lateral malleolus* (ankle bone) to the metatarsal bone of the fifth (little) toe.

Action. Everts and plantar flexes (points) the foot.

Peroneus Longus

The elongated muscle belly and tendon of *peroneus longus* sits on the upper half of the leg with its tendon covering *peroneus brevis* on the lower half of the leg.

Origin. *Head and lateral surface* of the upper two-thirds of the *fibula*.

Insertion. *Behind the lateral malleolus* (ankle bone) under the foot into the base of the *metatarsal bone* of the big toe and into the *medial cuneiform (tarsal)* bone.

Action. Flexes the big toe; everts and plantar flexes (points) the foot. Important in maintaining the arch of the foot.

THE FOOT

FOOT MOVEMENTS

Below are some of the main foot movements we use during daily activities.

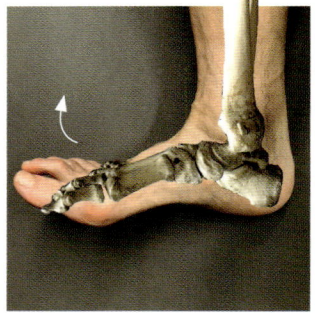

Plantar flexion

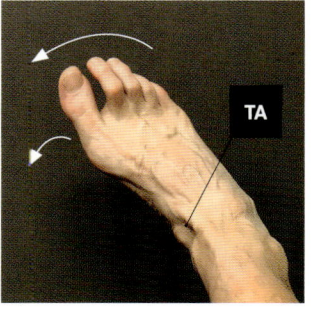

Dorsiflexion

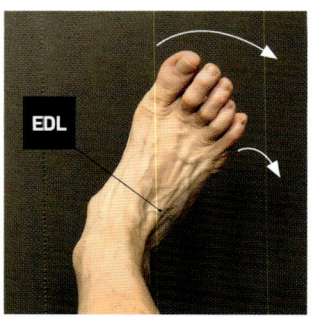

Adduction

Abduction

Plantar flexion. Extension of the ankle pointing the foot down (*gastrocnemius, soleus, Achilles tendon, peroneus longus*, and *peroneus brevis*).

Dorsiflexion. Pointing the foot up (*tibialis anterior*).

Adduction. Foot moves toward the midline of the body (*tibialis anterior*) and *peroneus brevis*).

Abduction. Foot moves away from the midline of the body (*extensor digitorum longus* on top of the foot, and from the lateral side, *peroneus longus* and *oeroneus brevis*).

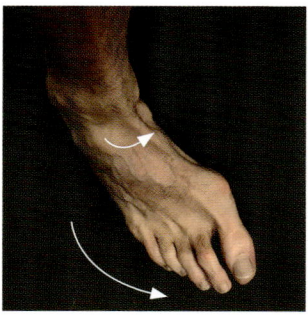

Inversion

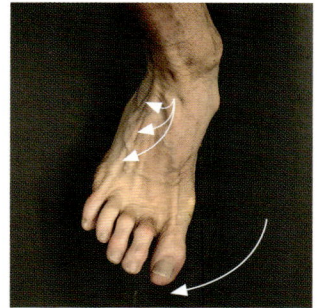

Eversion

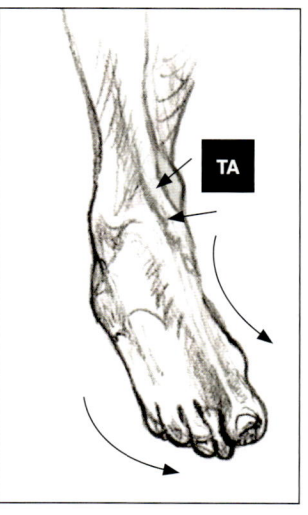

Tibialis anterior

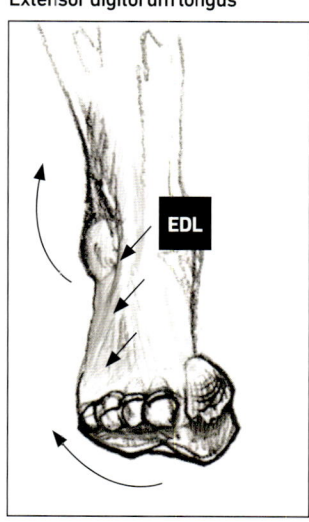

Extensor digitorum longus

Inversion. Pointing the foot toward the midline of the body (*tibialis anterior*).

Eversion. Pointing the foot away from the midline of the body (*extensor digitorum longus*).

ANATOMY OF THE FOOT

The foot is designed as a base of support, as a shock absorber upon impact, and, most importantly, as a propulsor during locomotion. Because many of the foot bones, muscles, and tendons are visible on the surface, knowing these bones and tendons is a great help in drawing the feet.

Bones. Foot bones are very much like hand bones, but their proportions are quite different. Hands are organized from small to large for maximum dexterity, while feet are organized from large to small for maximum stability. Feet are built on a double-arch system, which gives them enough strength and shock absorption to bear the body's weight on any type of surface. Ankle (tarsal) bones are connected to each other with plane joints, which allow just enough movement for feet to flatten and spread out, yet always return to an arch shape.

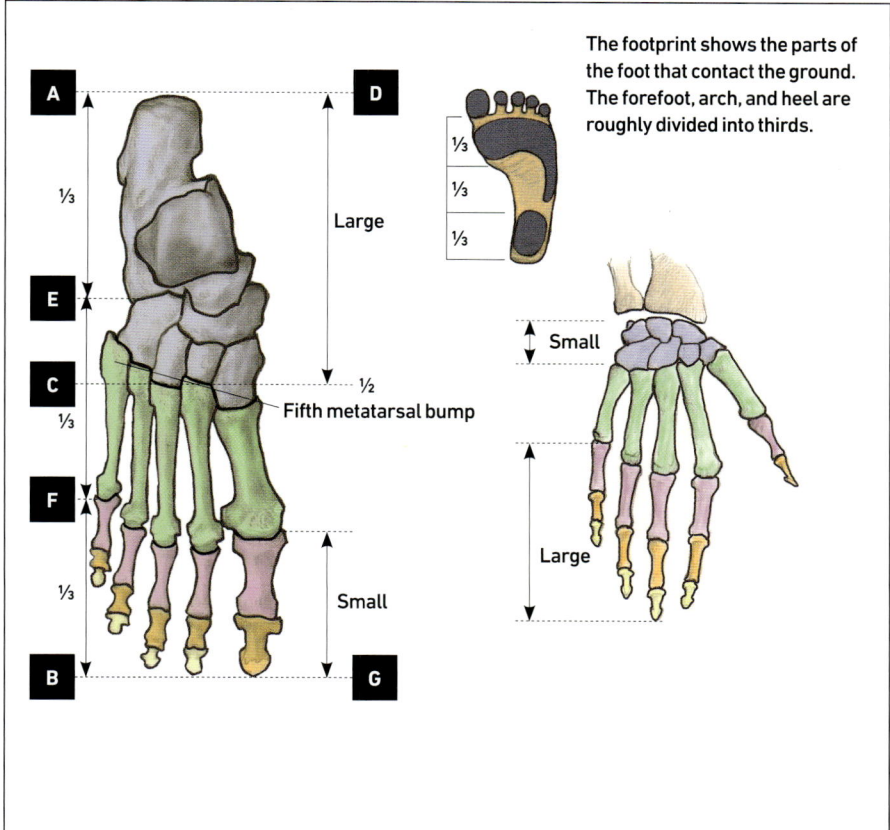

The footprint shows the parts of the foot that contact the ground. The forefoot, arch, and heel are roughly divided into thirds.

PROPORTIONS OF THE FOOT: DORSAL ASPECT

To construct a foot from the dorsal (top) aspect, divide (**A**) and (**B**) to find (**C**), the halfway mark, slightly beyond the "bump" of the fifth metatarsal. The talus bone is a third of the foot's length (**D** to **E**); the cuboid bone to the distal end of the fifth metatarsal is the second third (**E** to **F**); and the proximal interphalangeal joint of the fifth phalange to the end of the big toe is the last third (**F** to **G**).

The seven tarsal bones of the ankle sit in two rows (posterior and anterior) and take up nearly half of the length of the foot.

Posterior (back) row: *calcaneus* (heel bone) (1), *talus* (2), *navicular* (3)

Anterior (front) row: medial cuneiform (4), intermediate cuneiform (5), lateral cuneiform (6), cuboid (7).

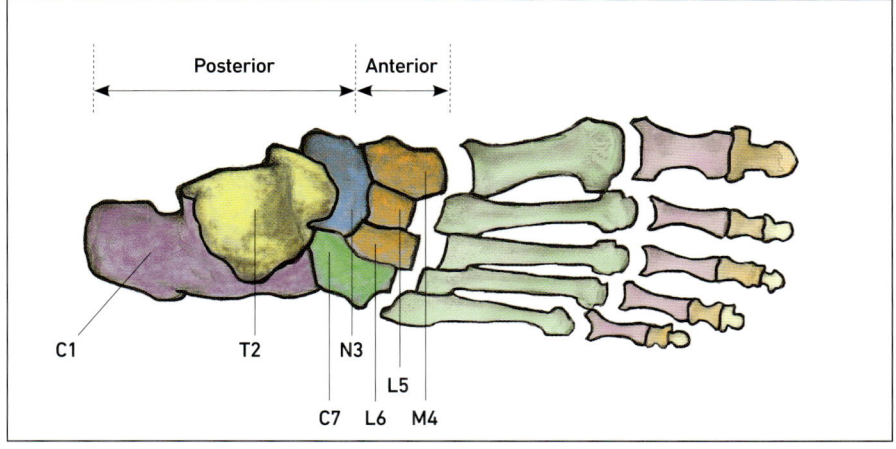

Posterior bones. The posterior bones, the calcaneus and talus, are the largest of the tarsal bones. The navicular bone is visible on the inside of the foot and forms a ball-and-socket joint with the talus, allowing the forefoot a small amount of flexibility.

Anterior bones. The anterior tarsals form a strong transverse arch across the foot yet, with their many plane joints, still allow a reasonable degree of flexibility. Viewed from the front, the anterior tarsal bones resemble an old stone arch with *lateral* and *intermediate cuneiform* bones wedged between *cuboid* and *medial cuneiform bones.*

TARSAL BONES MNEMONIC

Here's a good way to remember the names of the seven tarsal bones:

Tiger **C**ubs **N**eed **MILC**

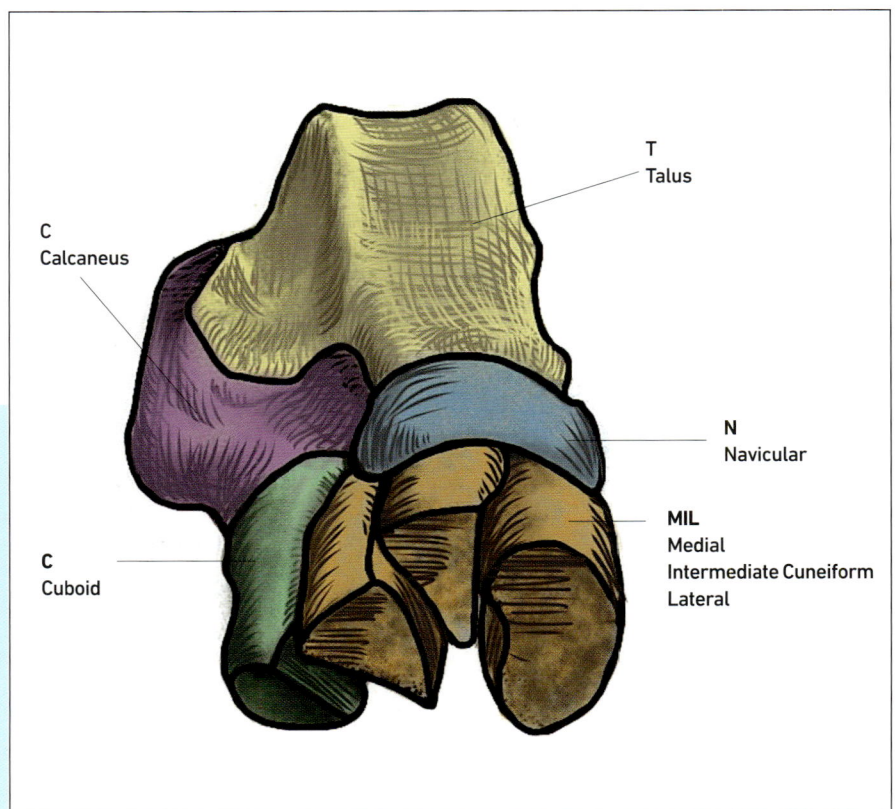

C
Calcaneus

T
Talus

N
Navicular

MIL
Medial
Intermediate Cuneiform
Lateral

C
Cuboid

Metatarsals, Phalanges, and Joints

Metatarsals. Plane joints (**A**) connect tarsal bones to the five metatarsal bones. The metatarsal bones are numbered, starting at the ball of the foot. Each of these bones consists of a boxlike proximal base, a long shaft, and a rounded distal head.

Phalanges. The rounded distal heads of the metatarsals are *ellipsoid joints* (**B**). This type of joint provides great movement to the first (proximal) row of phalanges, which can dorsiflex, plantar flex, adduct, and abduct. The second row of phalanges (intermediate) have *hinge joints* (**C**), which only allow flexion. The third row of phalanges (distal) are also *hinge joints* (**C**) but are modified to allow both flexion and extension. The big toe's proximal and distal phalanges are also connected by a *hinge joint* (**C**) but are limited to plantar flexion only.

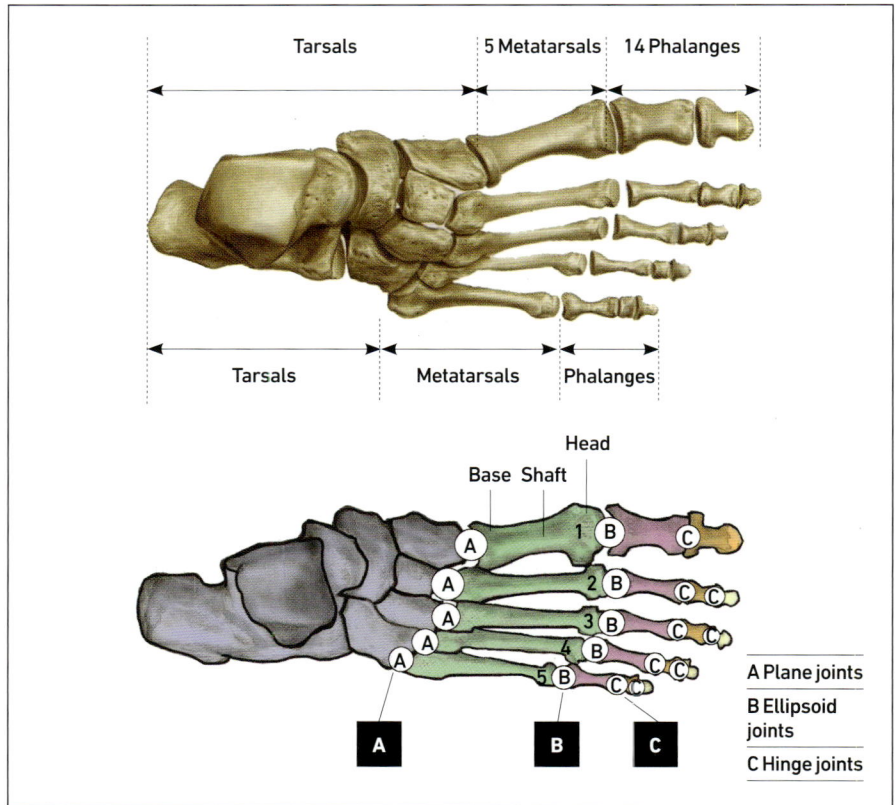

Tarsals | 5 Metatarsals | 14 Phalanges

Tarsals | Metatarsals | Phalanges

Head
Base Shaft

A Plane joints
B Ellipsoid joints
C Hinge joints

A   B   C

Top View (Dorsal)

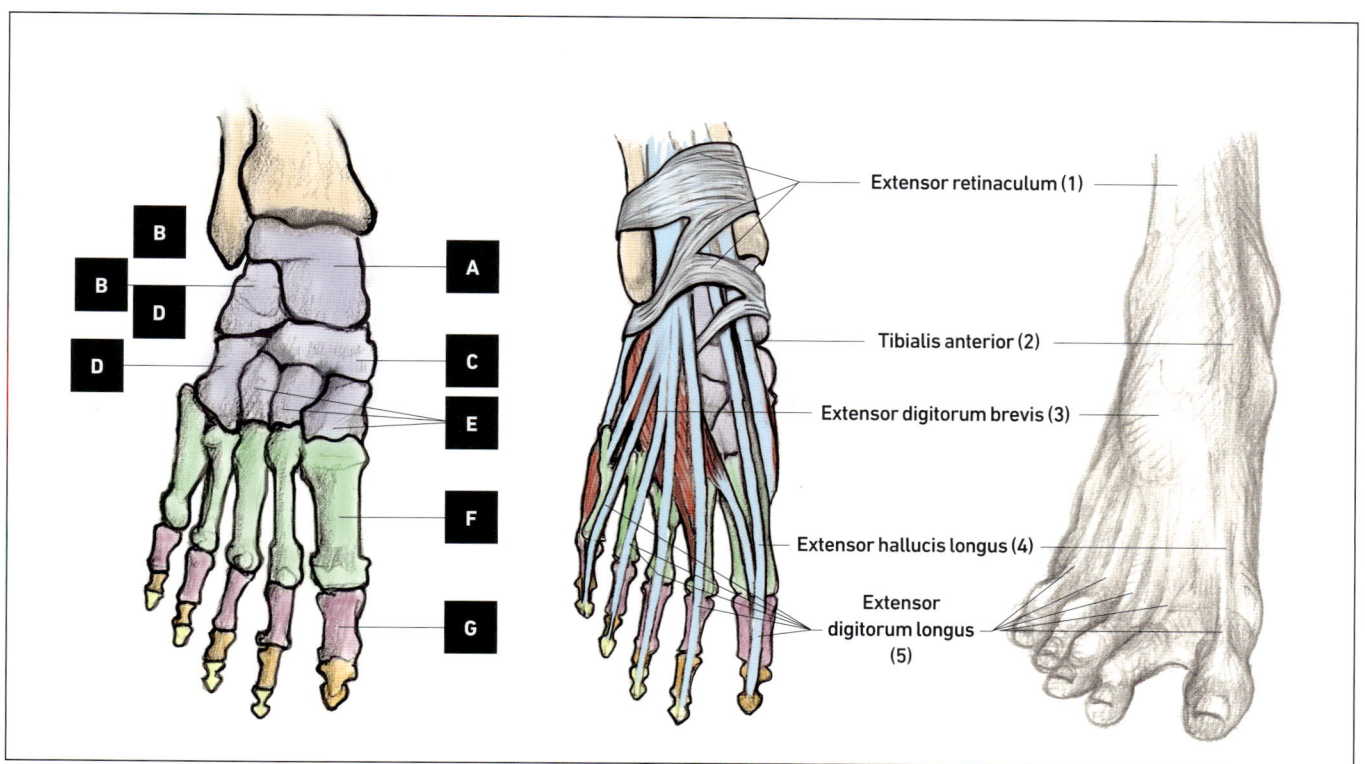

Extensor retinaculum (1)

Tibialis anterior (2)

Extensor digitorum brevis (3)

Extensor hallucis longus (4)

Extensor
digitorum longus
(5)

Bones. As with hands, feet are also composed of three sections: seven tarsal (ankle) bones (**A** to **E**), five metatarsals (**F**), and fourteen phalanges (**G**). Tarsal bones include the ankle, heel, and instep. The metatarsals of the foot, which end at the ball of the foot, are longer and stronger than the metacarpals of the hand. The phalanges of the toes are shorter than those of the fingers and thumb. While the big toe tends to have a slight upward thrust, the four small toes press and grip the ground.

Muscles. When the foot is flexed upward, the following tendons are most evident and are held in place by the *extensor retinaculum* (1): *tibialis anterior* (2), *extensor digitorum brevis* (3), *extensor hallucis longus* (4), and *extensor digitorum longus* (5).

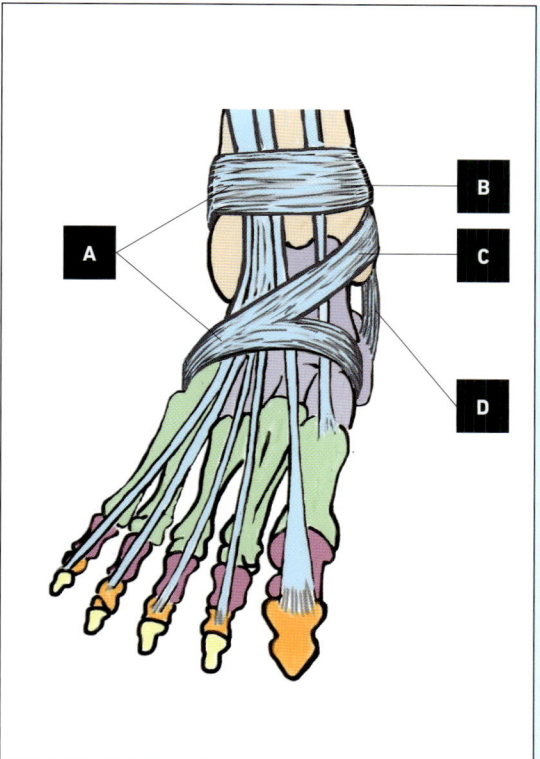

THE RETINACULUM
Retinaculum is a thin band of fascia that holds the tendons in place. The ankle has an *extensor retinaculum* (**A**) and a *flexor retinaculum* (**D**) to help keep the extensor and flexor tendons in place. The extensor retinaculum has a *superior band* (**B**) just above the inner and outer malleoli and a Y-shaped *inferior band* (**C**).

Outside View (Lateral)

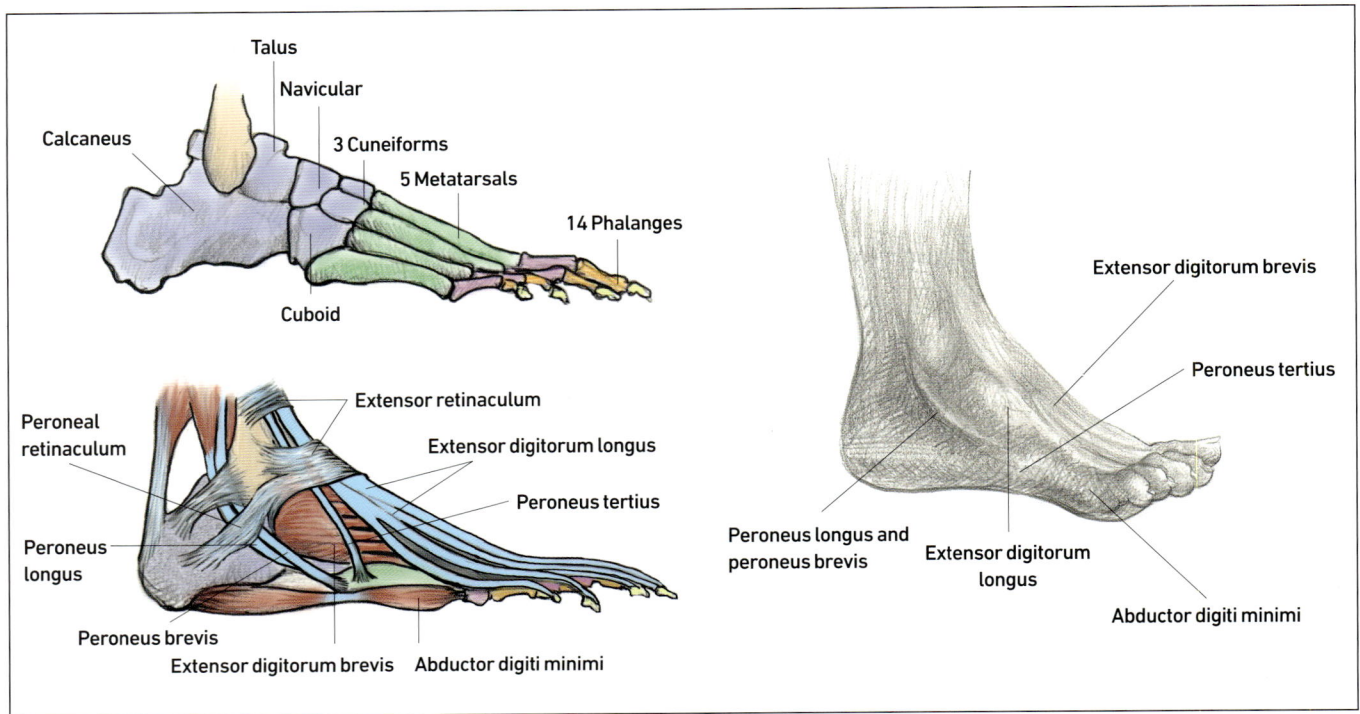

Talus

Navicular

Calcaneus

3 Cuneiforms

5 Metatarsals

14 Phalanges

Cuboid

Extensor retinaculum

Peroneal retinaculum

Extensor digitorum longus

Peroneus tertius

Peroneus longus

Peroneus brevis

Extensor digitorum brevis

Abductor digiti minimi

Extensor digitorum brevis

Peroneus tertius

Peroneus longus and peroneus brevis

Extensor digitorum longus

Abductor digiti minimi

Bones. From this side (lateral) view, the medial cuneiform, first metatarsal, and first phalange (big toe) cannot be seen. All other bones are identified.

Muscles. From the outside view, the two extrinsic tendons that are held in place by the *extensor retinaculum* bands are the *extensor digitorum longus* and *peroneus tertius*. Beneath these muscles, the *extensor digitorum brevis* is evident as an oval-shaped bulge. Another bulge, just behind the little toe, is caused by the *abductor digiti minimi* and runs along the entire lateral edge of the foot.

Hooking behind the lateral ankle bone and held in place by the *peroneal retinaculum* bands are the *peroneus longus* and *peroneus brevis*. During eversion and plantar flexion, their tendons are evident on the outside of the foot.

The *tibialis anterior* is an obvious landmark on the inverted foot (**1**). Dorsiflexion makes visible the *extensor digitorum* (**2**). Plantar flexion shows the tendons of the *peroneus longus* and *brevis* (**3**).

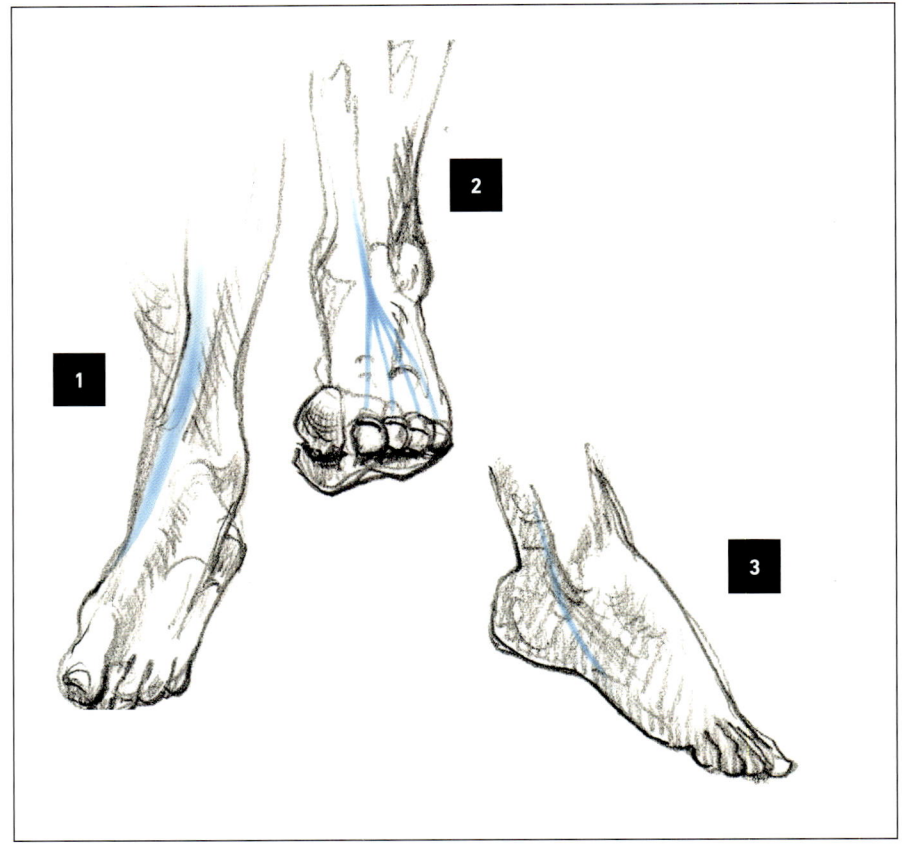

Inside View (Medial)

Bones. As with the outside (lateral) view, some bones cannot be seen. They are the third through the fifth metatarsals, the third cuneiform, and the cuboid bone. All other bones are identified.

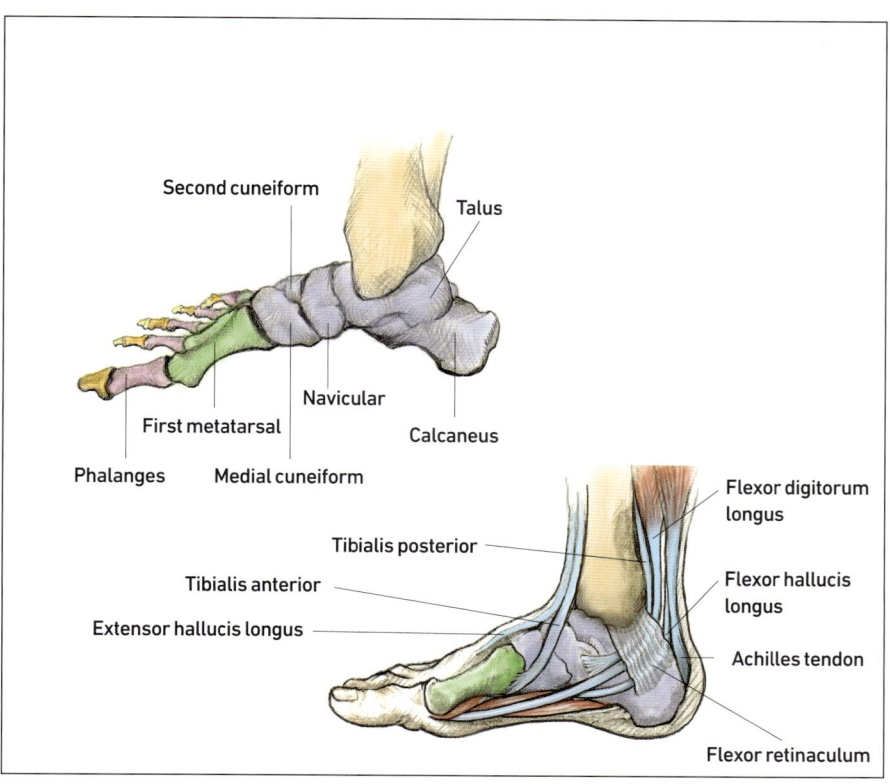

Muscles. The inside (medial) view features mostly extrinsic tendons. Two extensor tendons seen on the top of the foot are the *extensor hallucis longus* and the *tibialis anterior*. Flexor tendons descending from the posterior aspect of the lower leg and inserting into the bottom of the foot are the *tibialis posterior*, *flexor digitorum longus*, and the *flexor hallucis longus*. All are held in place by the *flexor retinaculum*. The *Achilles tendon* drops down from the strong gastrocnemius muscles and is a main actor in plantar flexion.

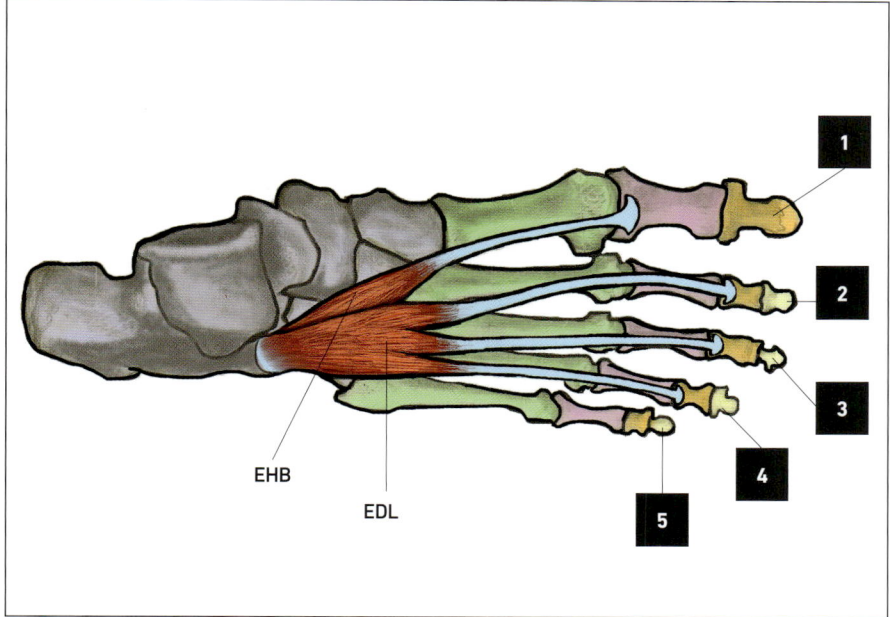

Right foot (dorsal view). The intrinsic foot muscles comprise four layers of small muscles that have both origins and insertions within the foot. On the dorsal (top) side of the foot, there are only two intrinsic muscles, *extensor hallucis brevis* and *extensor digitorum brevis*. They originate on the top of the calcaneus, and their tendons attach onto all four phalanges, except for the baby toe (**5**). Because they originate in the same area, these two muscles appear to be one, but they are actually separate. All other intrinsic muscles originate on the bottom of the foot.

Bottom View (Plantar Aspect)

Palpable bony landmarks. The purpose of these diagrams is to show where the bony landmarks of the skeleton are most palpable on the sole and sides of your foot. Take off your shoes to directly feel the bony landmarks indicated in these drawings. Wherever you cannot feel the bones, it is because the fat pads are doing their job of protecting the muscles and bones.

First, feel just behind the fat pads of your four outer toes. What you feel there are the *proximal interphalangeal joints* of the middle *phalanges* (**1**). Now feel the outside of the *distal phalanx* on your big toe (**2**). It is less protected by fat than its plantar (bottom) side. The prominent head of the *first metatarsal* (ball of the foot) (**3**) and the *navicular bone* (**4**) are both also very easy to feel. The *calcaneus* (heel bone) (**5**), on the other hand, is very well-cushioned, so it can only be felt around its upper areas. On the outside (lateral) of the foot, the *tuberosity* of the *fifth metatarsal* (**6**), one of the most important landmarks when drawing a foot, is highly visible and very easy to feel. The heads of the *metatarsal bones* (**7** and **3**), although not visible, can still be felt under their fat pad coverings. Finally, the *metatarsophalangeal joint* of the *proximal phalanx* (**8**) can been seen and felt even under the attachment of the *abductor digiti minimi* muscles.

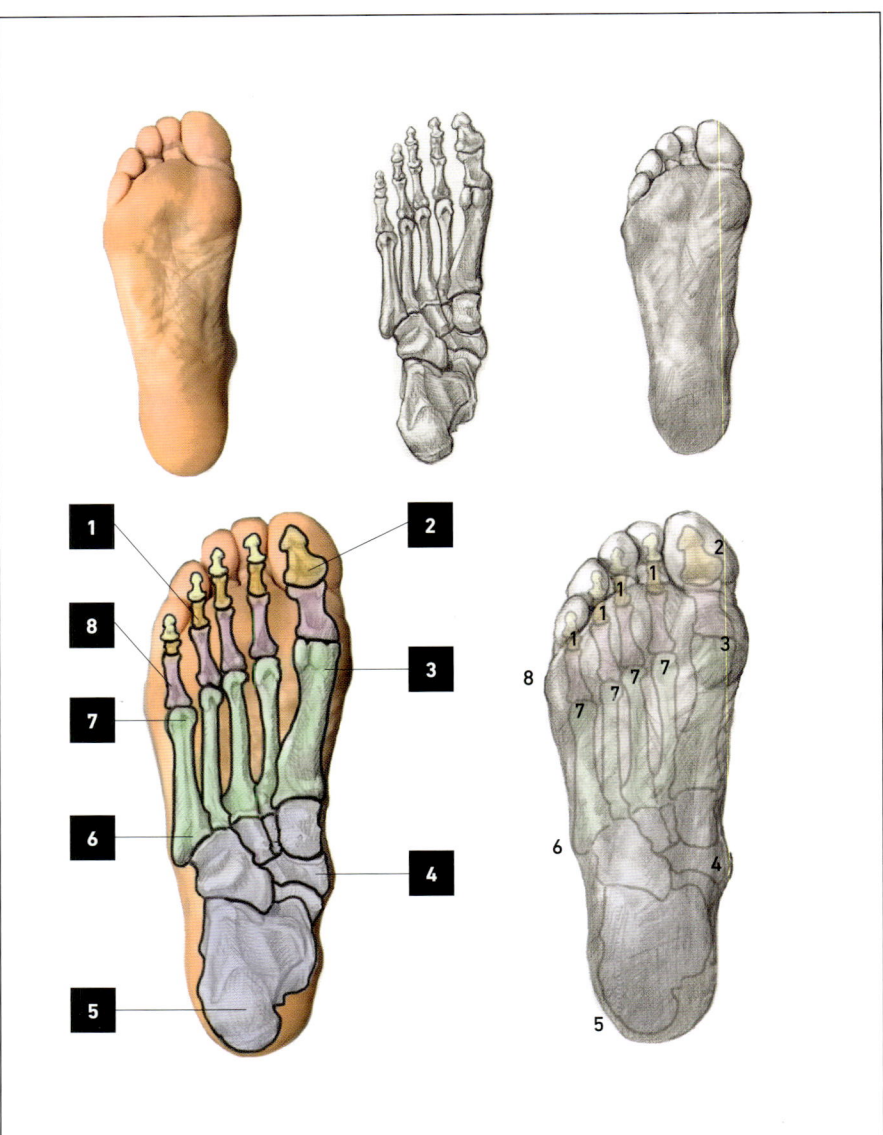

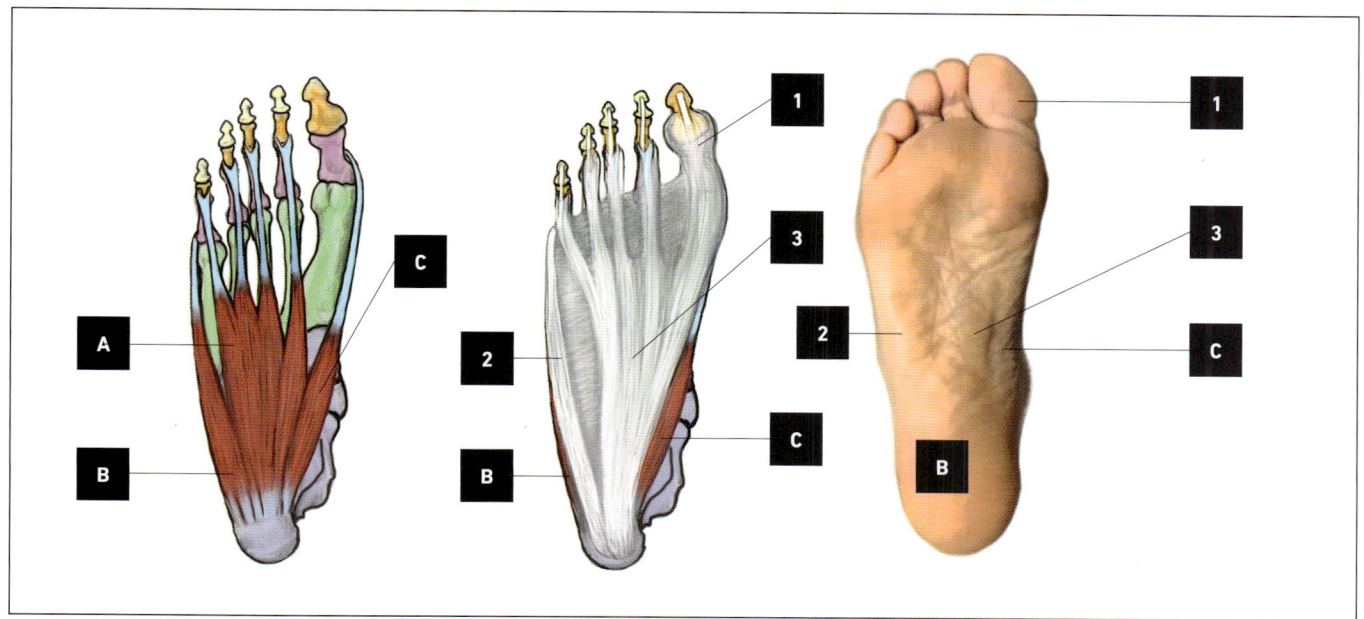

Intrinsic (plantar) foot muscles. The intrinsic muscles in the sole are grouped into four layers: The first layer of muscles is the most superficial to the sole and is located immediately underneath the plantar fascia tendons and fat pads. Most of the other intrinsic muscles are located deep in the sole of the foot. The only muscles regularly seen are in this first layer:

A. *Flexor digitorum brevis*. A large central muscle that flexes the second to fifth toes.

B. *Abductor digiti minimi*. Responsible for flexion and abduction of the fifth toe.

C. *Abductor hallucis*. Abducts the big toes (spreads it outward).

The bulging form of the *abductor digiti minimi* is concealed for the most part by plantar fat, which blends with the form.

Plantar aponeurosis. The plantar aponeurosis is a strong fibrous band of fascia that extends along the bottom of the foot. It lies on top of the foot muscles, passing from the heel toward the toes. It assists in maintaining the longitudinal arches of the foot and provides areas of muscle attachment. The lateral and middle portions of this ligament can be faintly seen on the surface of the foot.

1. *Fibrous digital sheath, first distal phalanx*
2. *Lateral plantar fascia*
3. *Middle plantar eminence*

Surface of the sole (plantar fat pads). The surface of the sole is formed by thick pads of fat and fibrous tissue rather than muscle. Fat pads protect the plantar fascia, bones, muscles, nerves, and blood vessels of the feet by absorbing and dissipating energy from impact when we walk or run.

Phalangeal fat pads cushion the toes. There are three lumps of fat on the big toe. *Metatarsal fat pads* protect the heads of the five metatarsal bones. *Calcaneal fat pads* soften impact on the heel.

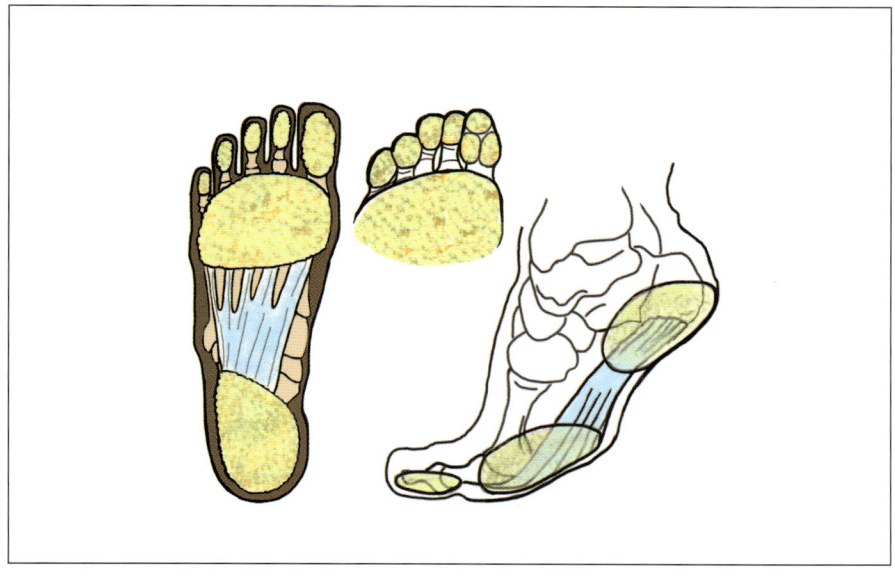

ANATOMY IN PRACTICE: THE LIMBS

CROSS-CONTOURS AS A GUIDE TO SHADING FORM

Once you learn how to incorporate cross-contours into your drawings, you will see an immediate improvement in their dimensionality.

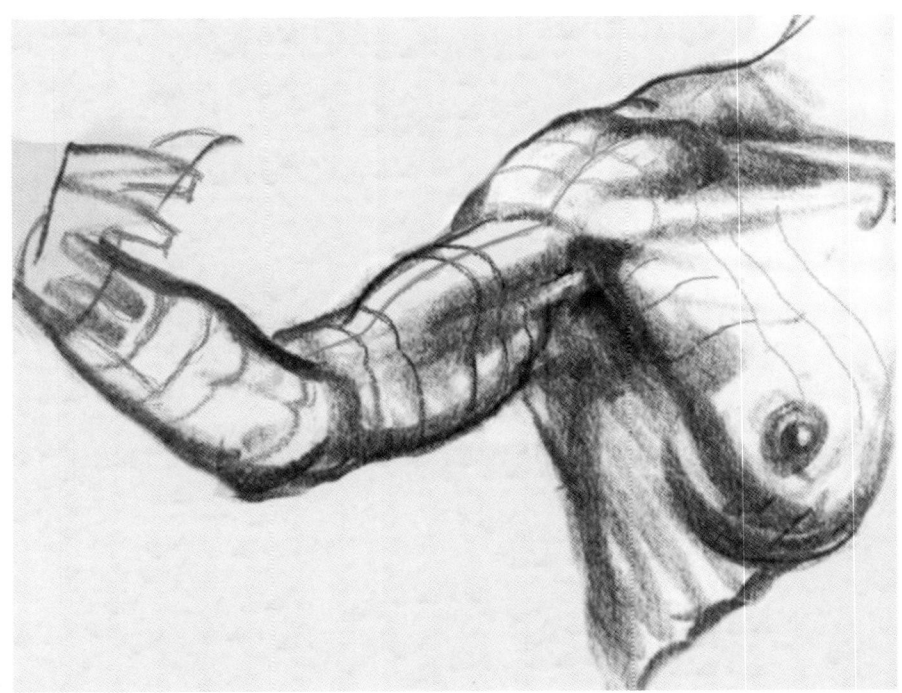

These two drawings show how multiple cross-contours clarify the volumes of arm muscles and breasts. Of course, it's not necessary to always show this many lines, but practicing like this goes a long way toward improving your understanding of volumetric shading. Study old master drawings to see how seamlessly they incorporate these principals into their drawings.

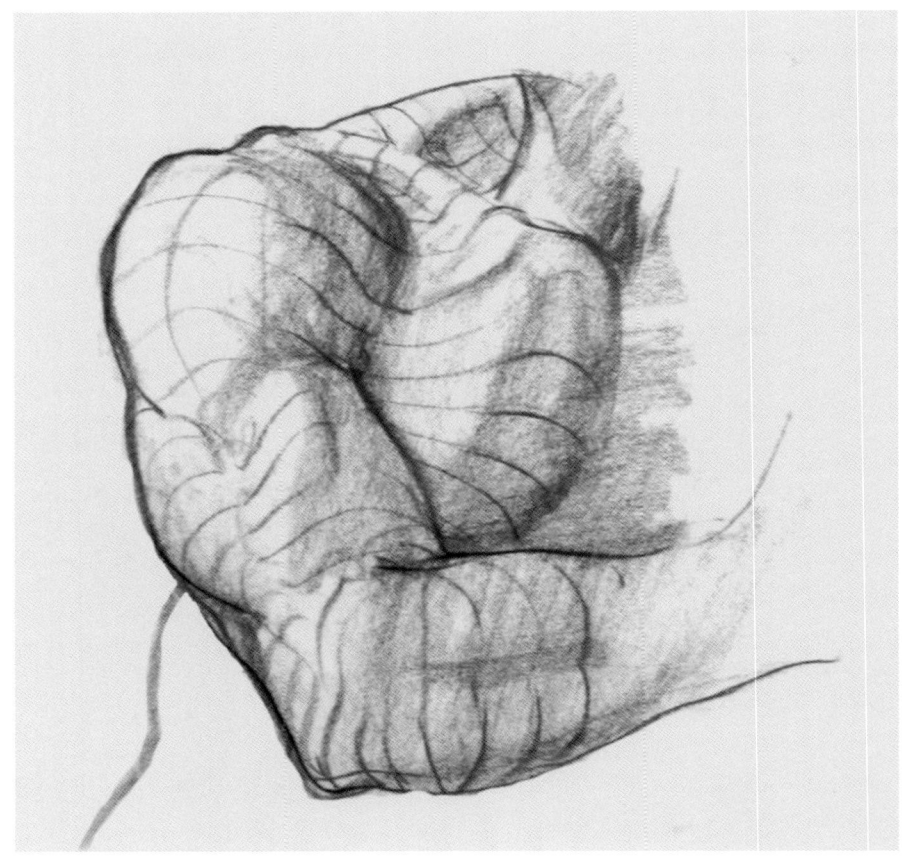

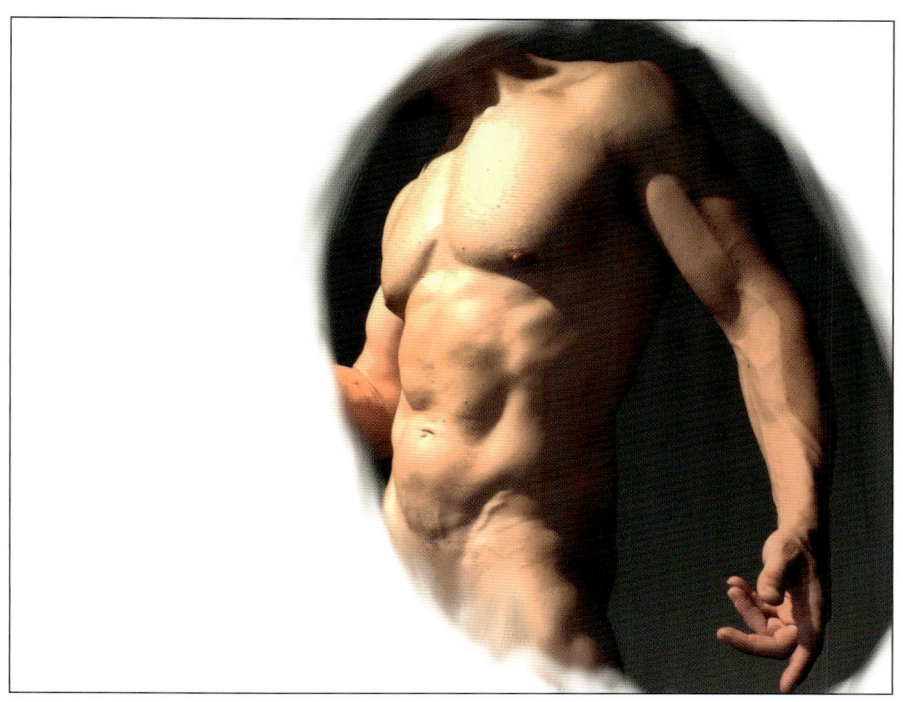

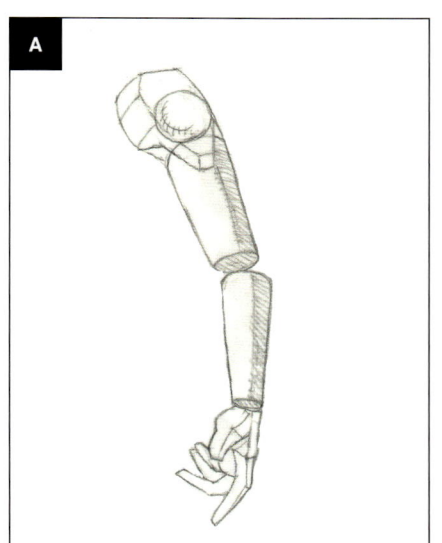

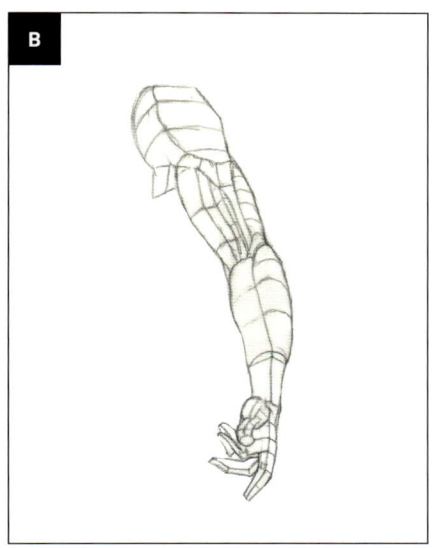

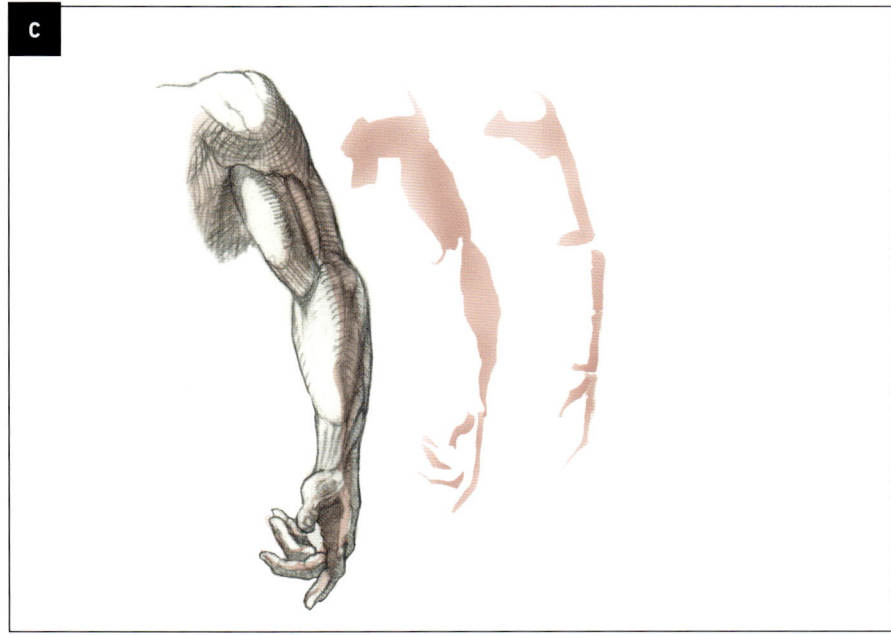

DEVELOPING AN ARM

These graphite drawings do not represent the level of refinement I actually go through when developing an arm, but they do illustrate how I think during the process. The reddish shading represents shadow sides.

A. **Stage 1**. All that matters are correct angles, simple cylinders for the arms, and a block-like shape for the hand. By sticking with these simple forms, I can get the overall proportions and mass without resorting to details.

B. **Stage 2**. Now the basic cylinders are converted into flat muscular front- and side-facing planes. Drawing cross-contours over the volumes helps to give me a better understanding of which stroke directions to emphasize when it's time to shade.

C. **Final stage**. The large masses from the prior stage can now be broken down into actual muscle shapes while still maintaining the same overall sense of volume. Upper arm: *deltoid, biceps, brachialis, triceps*. Lower arm: The entire *flexor group* plus *brachioradialis* and the "Twins," *abductor pollicis longus* and *extensor pollicis brevis*. Note how the crosshatched graphite strokes very deliberately follow the volumes.

FORESHORTENING: STRAIGHTS, C-CURVES, CYLINDERS, AND OVERLAPPING

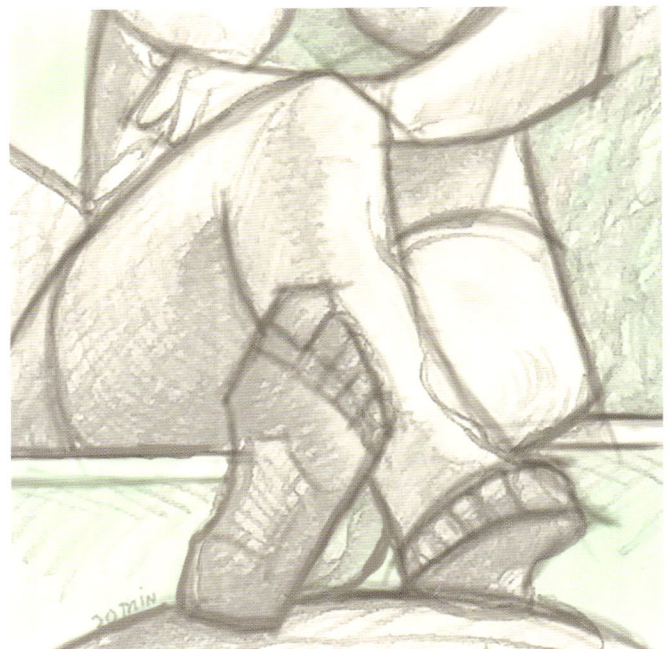

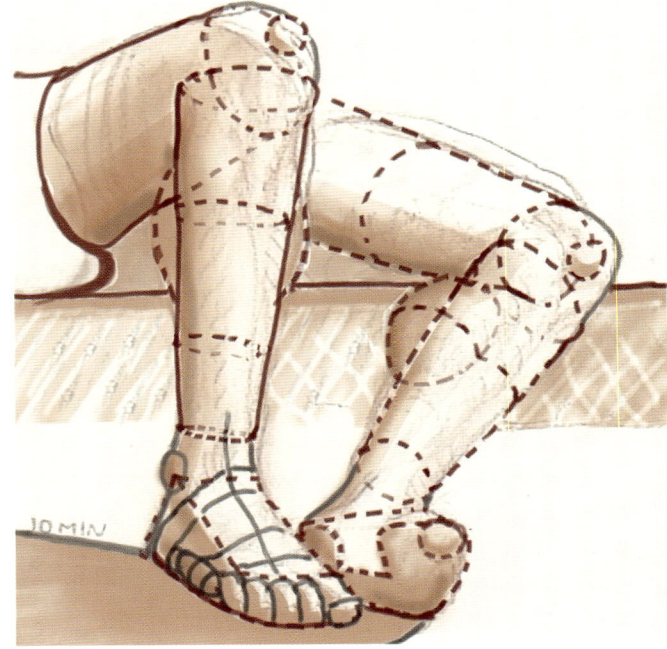

There is another way to begin a foreshortened figure using overlapping lines only. (Left) The extended foot overlaps the bent leg, the knee overlaps the arm, and the arm overlaps the edge of the body. The beauty of overlapping like this is that cylinders needn't be used, and although the drawing looks flat, it will still recede properly and be pleasing to the eye. I kept all the lines graceful by limiting myself to straight and C-curved lines and spent as much time looking at the surrounding space as possible. The green area represents the negative space and frames the figure nicely. Compare it to the same pose below, which is more relaxed and "naturalistic."

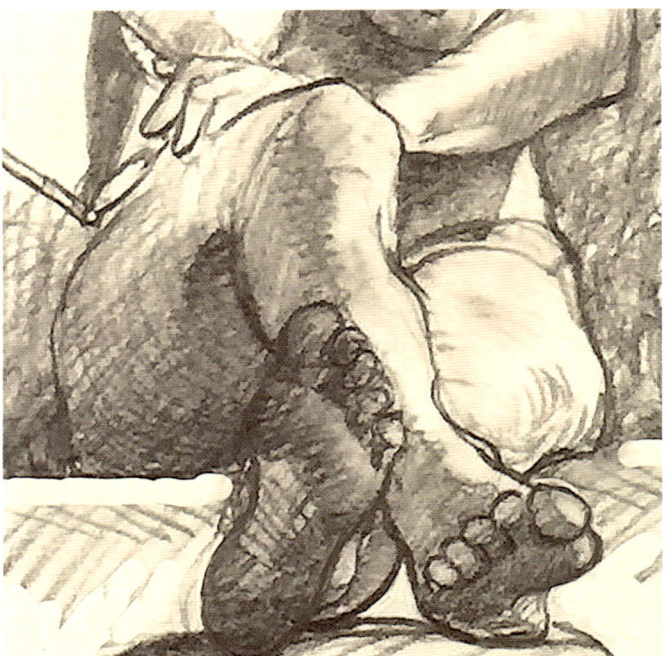

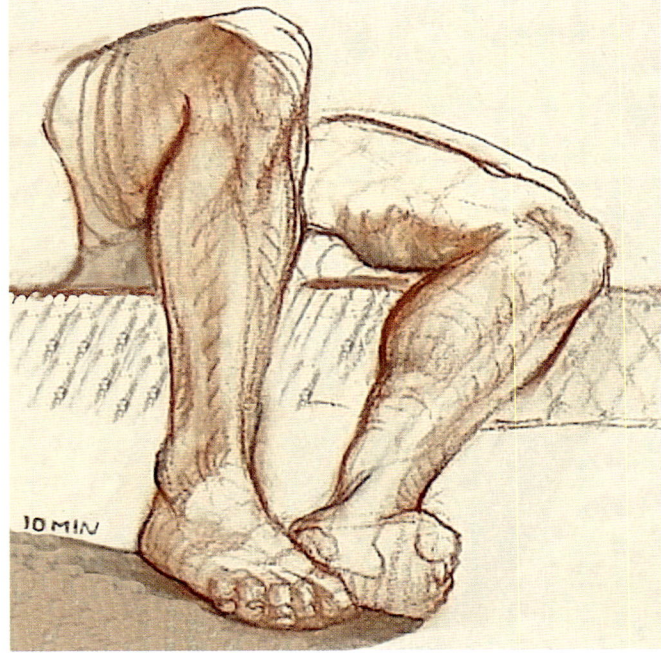

This Conté drawing uses a more traditional combination of cylinders and overlapping, which yields a more naturalistic result. Cross-contours are used to address the foreshortened perspectives during the initial construction stage. They are employed again on the finished sketch but to a much lesser extent and in a more artistic way. The cross-contours I am referring to show up most prominently on the *gastrocnemius* (calf) muscle and are a big part of the reason this leg recedes so well.

STROKE DIRECTION: DEFINING UPPER ARM ANATOMY

As I rendered each of the muscles listed below, it was as if I were modeling in 3D clay. When you try your hand at this, ask yourself, which cross-contour directions will best communicate 3D volumes to my viewers? Once you understand the muscle's dimensionality to your core, then you are ready to apply that feeling to your drawing through the use of thoughtful strokes.

1. *Deltoid—lateral portion*
2. *Triceps brachii—lateral head*
3. *Brachialis*
4. *Biceps brachii*

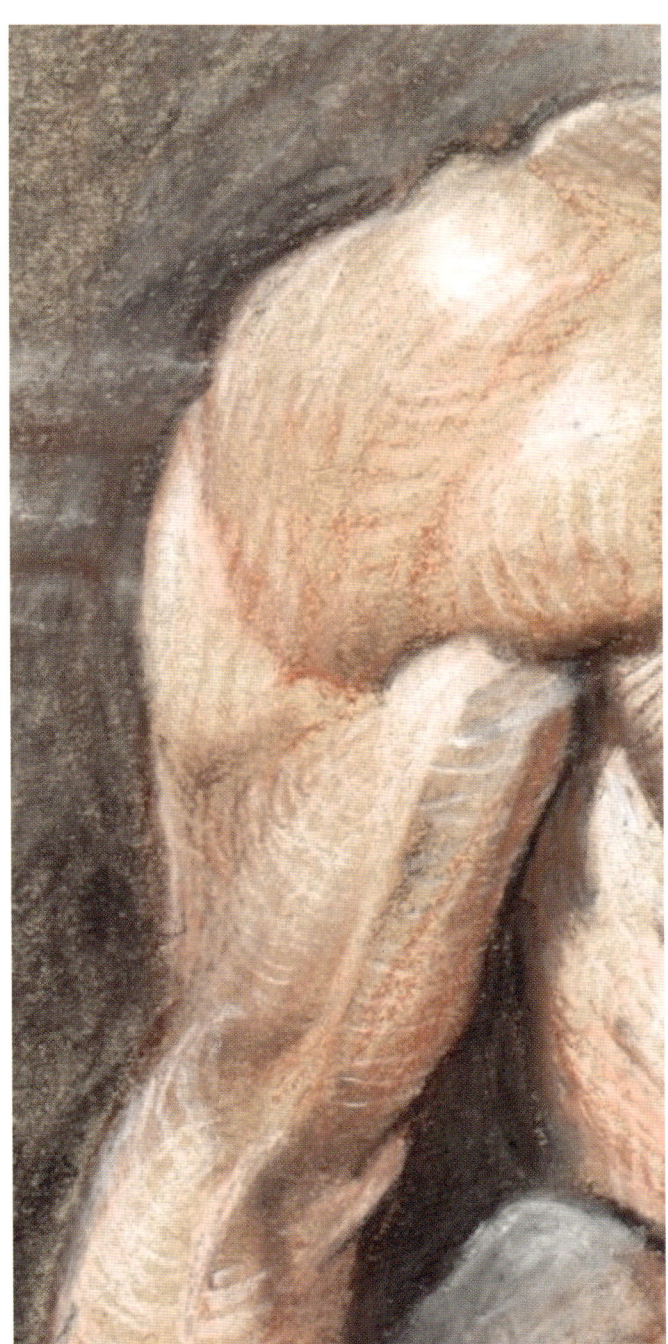

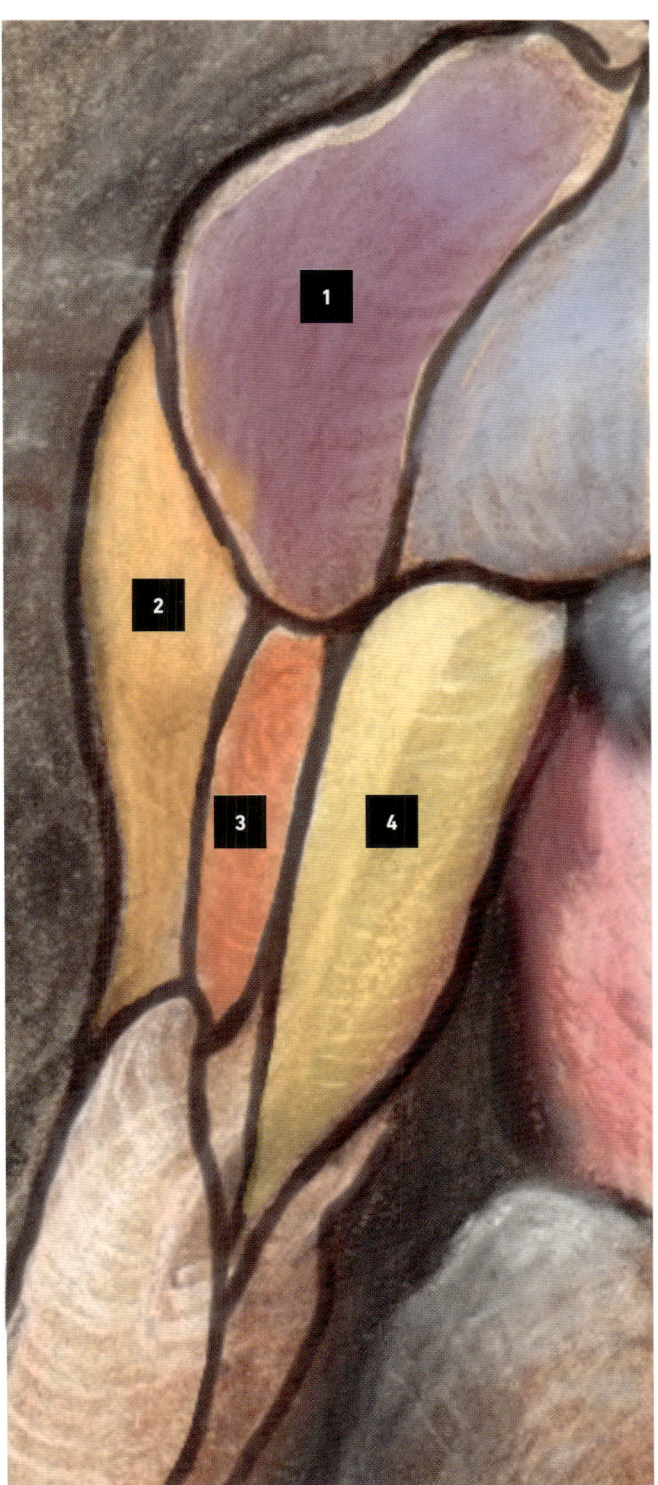

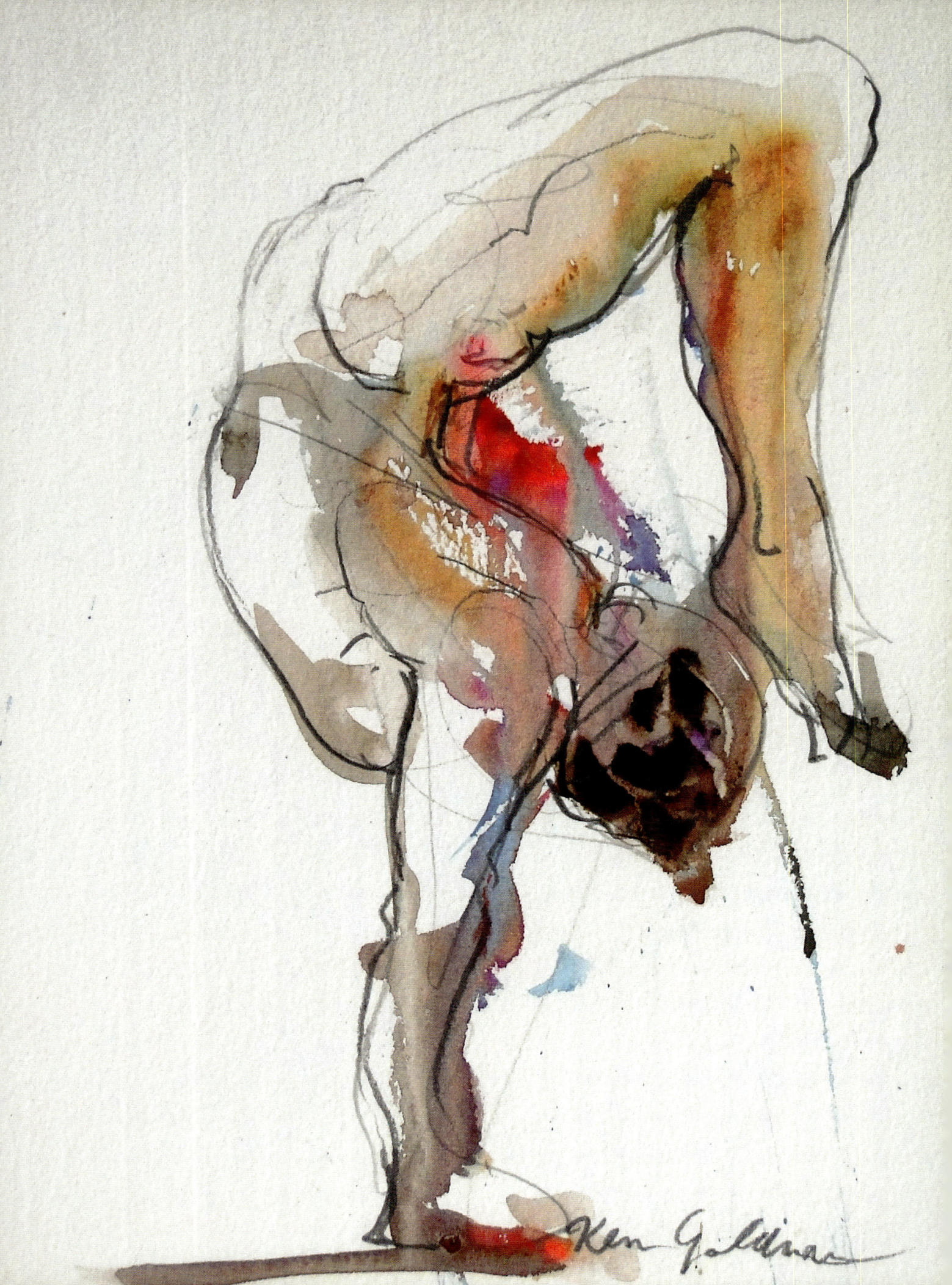

Ken Goldman

CHAPTER 6

MOVEMENT

Sensations of movement in a drawing occur entirely in the eye of a beholder. Just as 3D volumes on a flat piece of paper are an illusion, movement on a paper or canvas is, of course, an illusion too. Any sensation of movement experienced by a viewer is based completely on an artist's ability to construct an engaging composition. The human eye is like a playful kitten. A well composed, interesting drawing is as stimulating to a viewer's eye as a moving ball of yarn is to a kitten.

Ken Goldman, *Acrobatics*, 5-minute watercolor on paper, 12" × 7" (30 × 18 cm)
Some fleeting movements can only be captured with a spontaneous gesture painting.

WHAT IS MOVEMENT?

This chapter covers two types of movement in art:
visual movement and *anatomical movement.*

DEFINITIONS

VISUAL MOVEMENT

Visual movement is a *viewer's perception of movement* in an artwork and is elicited by *an artist's technical and creative skills* in using the *elements and principles of design* in a well composed and innovative way.

ANATOMICAL MOVEMENT

Anatomical movement is any type of physical movement caused by a contraction of any specific muscle or group of muscles. In figure drawing, knowing exactly which muscle is responsible for which movement allows an artist to emphasize or de-emphasize muscular forms and bony landmarks in creative yet properly proportioned ways.

THE ELEMENTS AND PRINCIPLES OF DESIGN

The Seven Elements of Design	The Eight Principles of Design
Line	Contrast
Size	Harmony
Direction	Unity
Color	Dominance
Value	Balance
Shape	Rhythm
Texture	Alternation
	Gradation

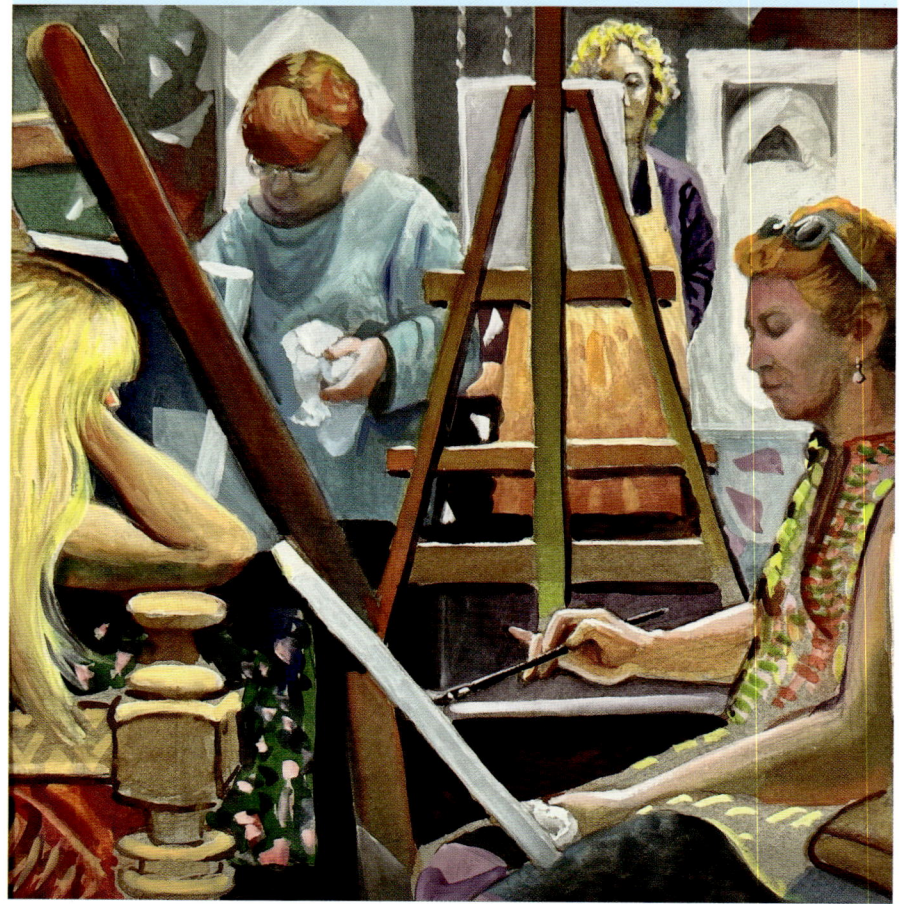

Ken Goldman, *Painting Trio,* watercolor on toned paper, 9" × 9" (23 × 23 cm) (detail)
Elements and principles of design put into practice during a live painting session.

VISUAL MOVEMENT IN DRAWING: THE DYNAMICS OF VISUAL MOVEMENT

Visual movement in drawing is the path, flow, or suggestion of movement that causes a viewer's eyes to follow an intended direction. Elements such as shape, line, and contrast in value are tools used by artists to create focal points of interest within a drawing. These can determine how well an artwork communicates its visual dynamic to a viewer.

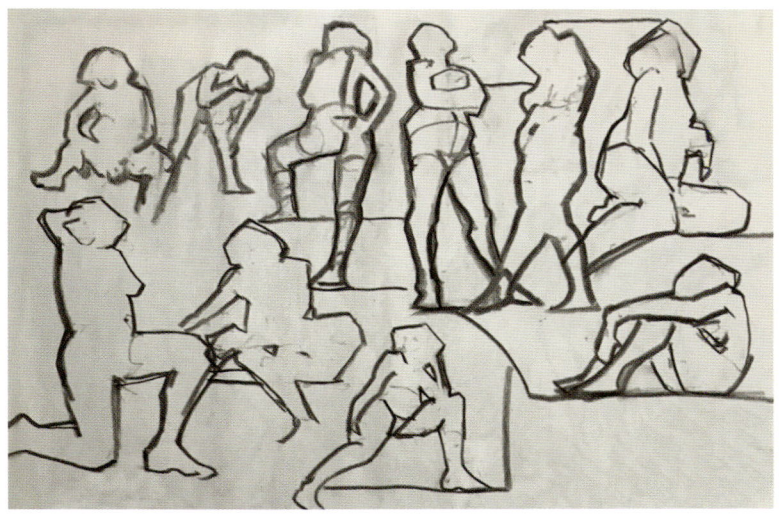

POSITIVE AND NEGATIVE SHAPES

For starters, always try to see the largest overall shapes first, and specifically take note of the surrounding negative spaces that define the figures.

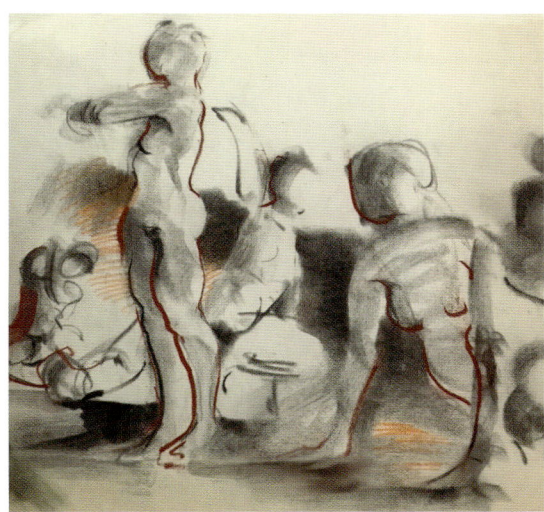

ACCENTS AND VALUES

In these very rough one-minute charcoal silhouettes, a sensation of energy and movement is created by just a few well-placed accent lines and value changes.

GESTURES

In many cases, art models in sketch groups are also dancers, so they know exactly how to incorporate graceful movements into their gestures and can hold them from 30 seconds to 5 minutes. During this short window of time, artists lightly sketch a long line of action into an overall silhouette and then quickly add the head, torso, and limbs using contour lines of varied sizes and values. Here are simplified examples of the steps I follow.

FROM FLAT SILHOUETTE TO 3D FIGURES

1. This is how I see an overall flat silhouette shape.

2. This figure shows the all-important longest line of action, which creates flow.

3 & 4. The addition of overlapping arms, legs, and muscles transforms flat silhouettes into 3D figures.

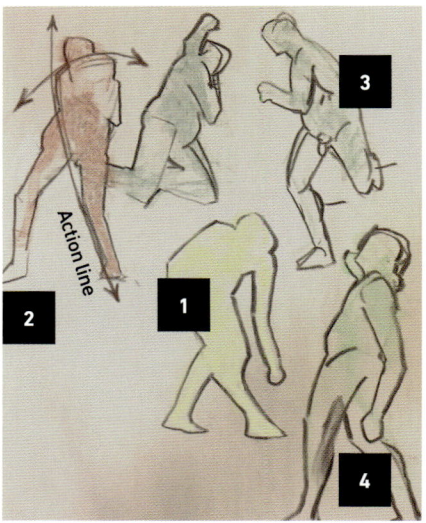

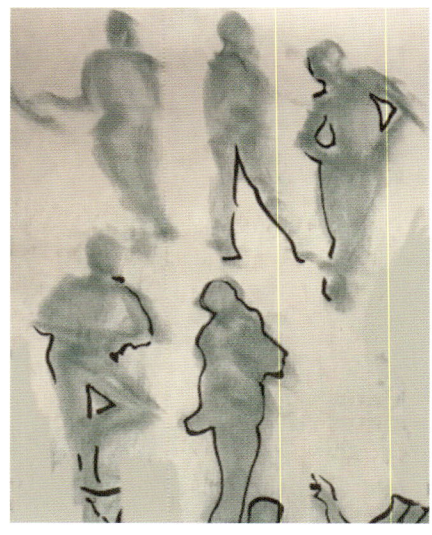

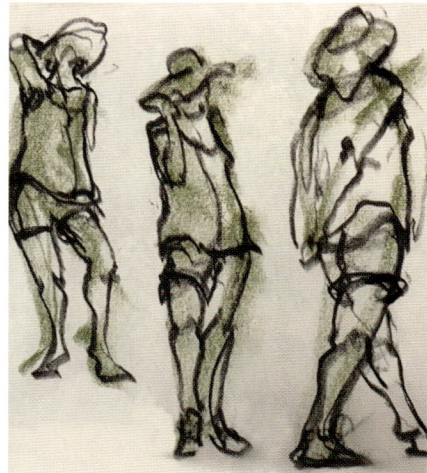

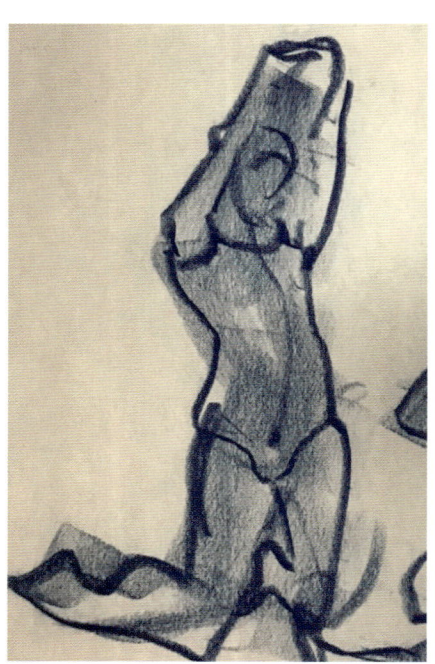

CREATING VOLUME

This two-minute gesture shows the importance of dropping a centerline from the pit of the neck to the *symphysis pubis*. This helps to create a sense of volume.

CONTRAPPOSTO

All three poses contain *contrapposto*, which, in Italian, literally means "counterpose." Hips are weighted heavily onto one leg and the torsos are tilted in opposite directions. Poses like these are dynamic, but with so much weight on one leg, few models can hold them very long.

CAPTURING A POSE'S DYNAMIC ENERGY

Silhouettes drawn with the sides of a pastel capture an overall dynamic but are seldom accurate. It's in the next stage, contour drawing, that proportions are corrected.

PUTTING ANATOMICAL KNOWLEDGE INTO PRACTICE

When does knowledge of anatomy make a difference? Gesture drawing is mostly about expressiveness, but when poses last longer than 20 minutes, artists who do not know anatomy often run out of gas. When artists know about the placement of bony landmarks and the origins and insertions of visible muscles, forms can be drawn with more authority by deliberately beginning a contour line on an origin and ending it on an insertion. Knowing anatomy gives a sense of conviction to figure drawings. Below are two examples.

Charcoal on paper, 4" × 12" (10 × 30 cm)
The goal of a 20-minute life-drawing is to combine the freshness of a gesture with just enough anatomy to make an accurate but not overly detailed sketch. In this reclining pose, the all-important centerline is lightly indicated (**A**). A thin dark line indicates the jutting hip bone (**B**). One medium-thick line indicates the *gastrocnemius muscle* (**C**). A heavy dark line shows that this leg is pressing down against the stand (**D**). The 10th rib is evident because it is being pressed into the flank pad (**E**).

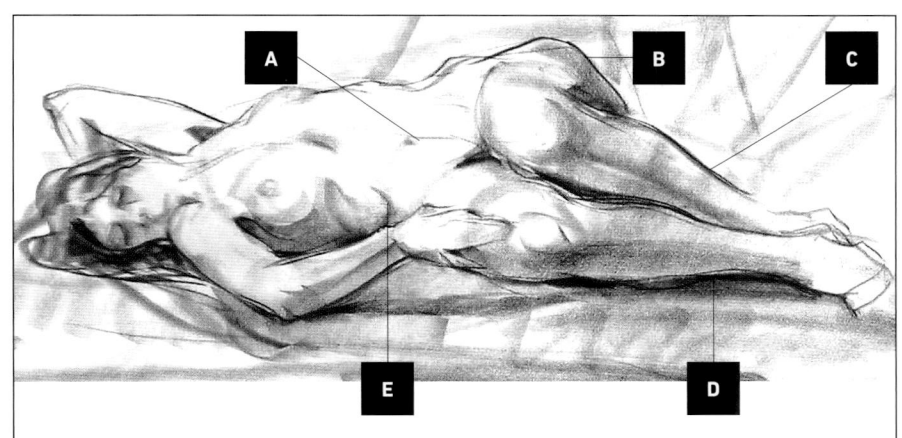

Vine charcoal on Stonehenge paper, 32" × 56" (81 × 142 cm)
This larger drawing took two hours, which left more time for shading and anatomy. With a single line, the roundness of the *gluteus maximus* is made evident (**A**). The rib cage and *latissimus dorsi* overlap the *external oblique* (**B**). The scapula is indicated with a simple dark accent mark (**C**). A light area next to the *lateral epicondyle* separates the box-like shape of the elbow from the rounded extensors of the forearm (**D**). The *styloid process* of the *ulna* is brought out by an adjacent cast shadow (**E**).

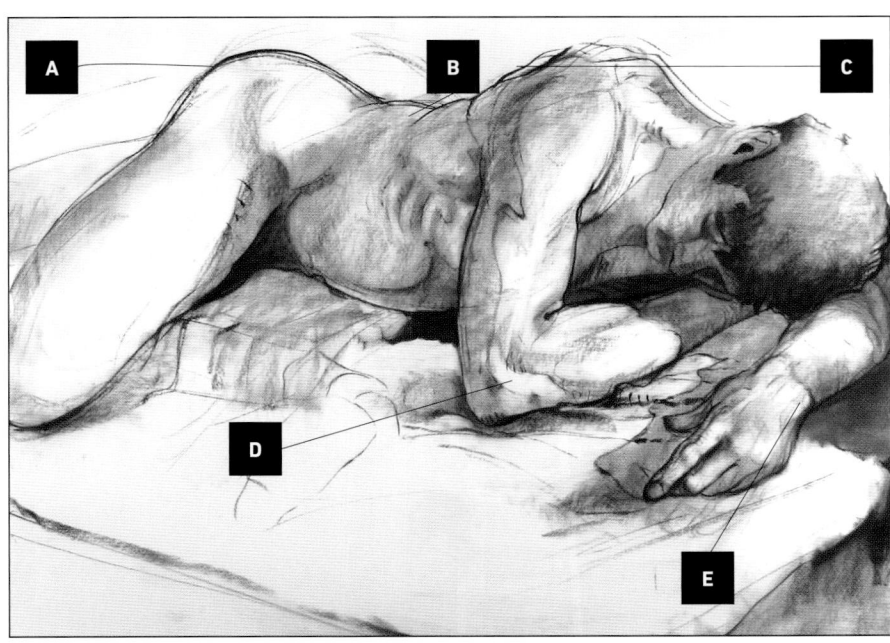

ANATOMICAL MOVEMENT IN DRAWING: THE DYNAMICS OF ANATOMICAL MOVEMENT

The skeleton is very much like a series of multi-shaped levers (bones) rotating around various fulcrums (joints). Each time a muscle or a group of muscles exerts force across a joint, movement occurs. The muscles that cause these movements (by contracting) are called *agonists*, or prime movers. On the other side of these activated levers, inactive muscles called *antagonists* stay relaxed and stretched. There are two other different roles that muscles can play when generating bodily movements, but for lack of space, this section will only deal with agonists and antagonists.

For example: If you hold a weight in your hand and raise your arm *(elbow joint = fulcrum)*, your contracting *bicep* is the *agonist*, while your relaxed *tricep* is the *antagonist*.

AGONISTS AND ANTAGONISTS IN THE UPPER ARM

This illustration of the *biceps and triceps muscles* shows how the role of *agonist* and *antagonist* switches back and forth. During *elbow flexion*, *biceps brachii* is the *agonist* and *triceps brachii* is the *antagonist*. During *elbow extension*, their roles are reversed, and *triceps* becomes the *agonist*.

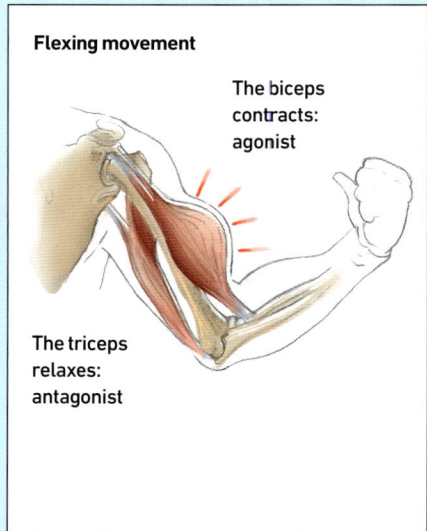

Flexing movement

The biceps contracts: agonist

The triceps relaxes: antagonist

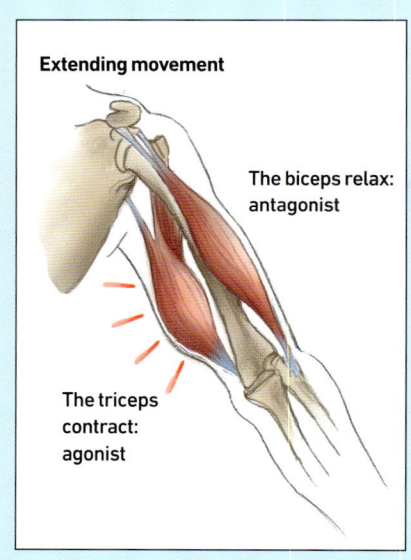

Extending movement

The biceps relax: antagonist

The triceps contract: agonist

AGONISTS AND ANTAGONISTS IN CONTRAPPOSTO

For the rest of this chapter, muscles acting as *agonists* will be colored red and their *antagonists* in blue.

Figure artists try to avoid drawing non-dynamic poses at all costs. In the example below left, a static male back view with four repetitive guidelines is contrasted with a female back view in a much more interesting contrapposto pose, where her four guideline angles are varied between shoulders and hips.

In the *contrapposto* drawing below, as the model's weight-bearing left leg forces her left hip upward, her left *external oblique muscle* acts as an agonist, pulling her rib cage down toward her left hip. If you try getting into this pose yourself, you will see how difficult it is. You will notice that with so much weight on your left leg, you can even lift your right leg without changing your balance point. Try it out. Contrapposto does not feel very natural to hold, but it sure is wonderful to draw. The side-to-side contrast in this pose is emphasized by placing dark accented lines on the pinched (red) side, and lighter, thinner lines on the stretched (blue) side.

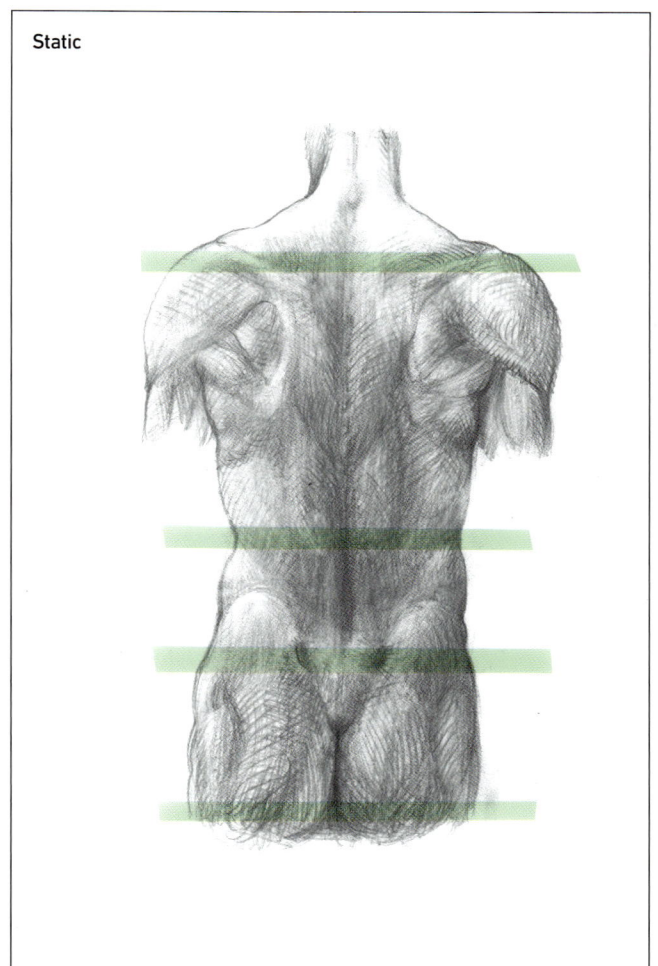

Static

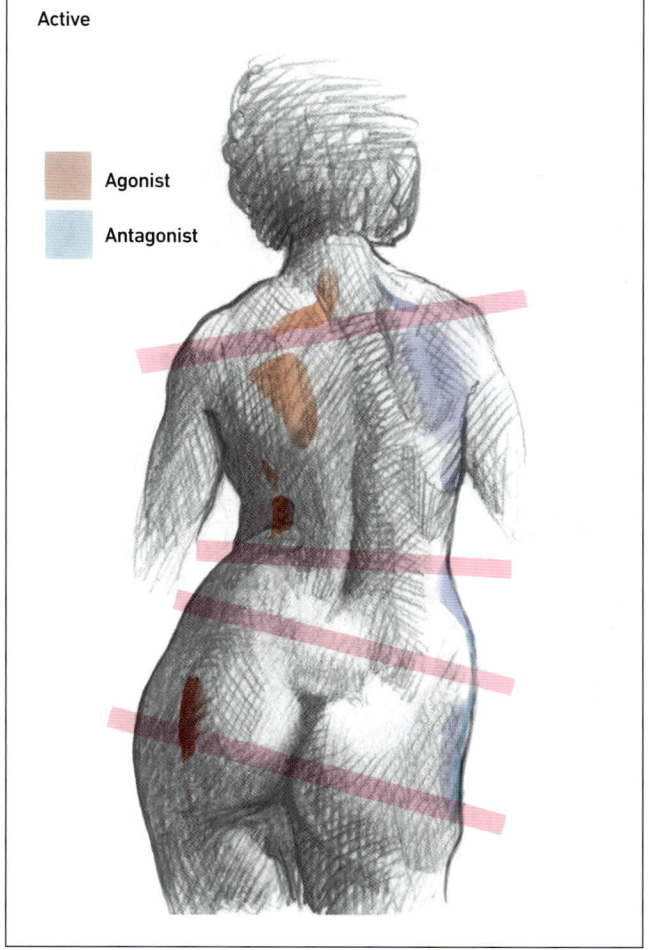

Active

Agonist

Antagonist

AGONISTS AND ANTAGONIST IN DRAMATIC CONTRAPPOSTO

The 20-minute drawing of dramatic contrapposto shown opposite is developed from a two-minute gesture drawing. Knowing which muscles are responsible for which movements helps tremendously when transforming quick sketches into more detailed drawings. An understanding of which muscles contract (*agonists*) and which muscles relax (*antagonists*) gives insight into where a heavier or lighter line should be drawn.

Here are questions to be asked when using a gesture as a basis for a more finished drawing:

Which muscles in the gesture drawing actually cause specific movements?

Which muscles are activated while others are relaxed?

How does the body maintain its dynamic equilibrium?

Which muscles are responsible for balancing?

Which muscles should be accentuated to make a drawing more interesting?

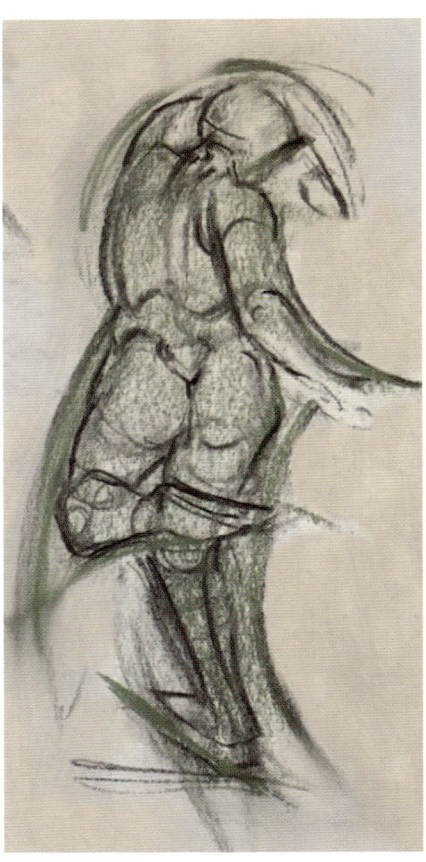

2-minute gesture drawing.

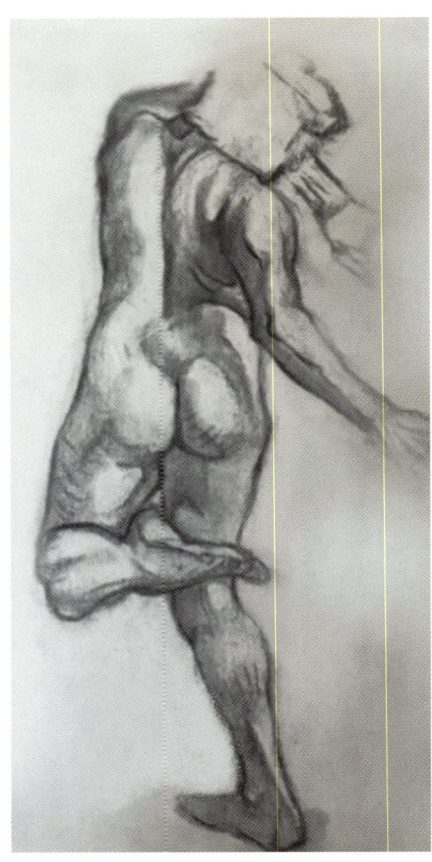

20-minute vine charcoal drawing.

Agonists: Red

Main back muscles. Right side—(twisting): *Trapezius, infraspinatus, teres minor, latissimus dorsi, external oblique*, and *sacrospinalis*.

Main arm muscles. *Deltoid, lateral head of triceps, brachioradialis*, and *extensors* of forearm (lifting).

Main hip muscles. *Gluteus maximus, gluteus medius, tensor fascia lata (contracting)*.

Main leg muscles. *Quadriceps* (lifting leg in front), *iliotibial band* (abducting), *hamstrings* (flexing), *gastrocnemius* and *Achilles tendon* (contracting), and *flexors* on the bottom of the foot (contracting).

Antagonists: Blue

Main back muscles. Left side (relaxing) *latissimus dorsi*.

Main leg muscles. Right leg *adductors* (relaxing), (left leg) *shin muscles—tibialis anterior*, etc. (relaxing).

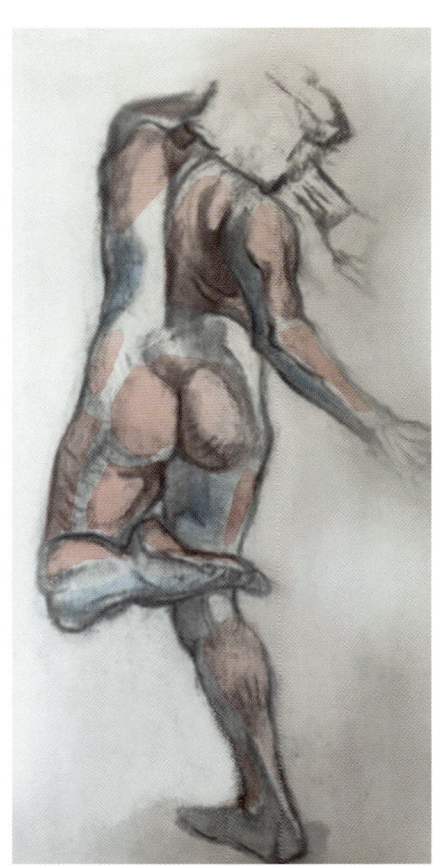

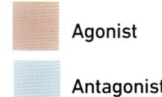

Agonist

Antagonist

MOVEMENT OF THE HEAD AND NECK

Although there are many small neck muscles involved in moving the head, when it comes to knowing and drawing the muscular forms most responsible for head movement, the *sternocleidomastoid and trapezius* are the stars of the show, playing roles as either *agonist* or *antagonist*.

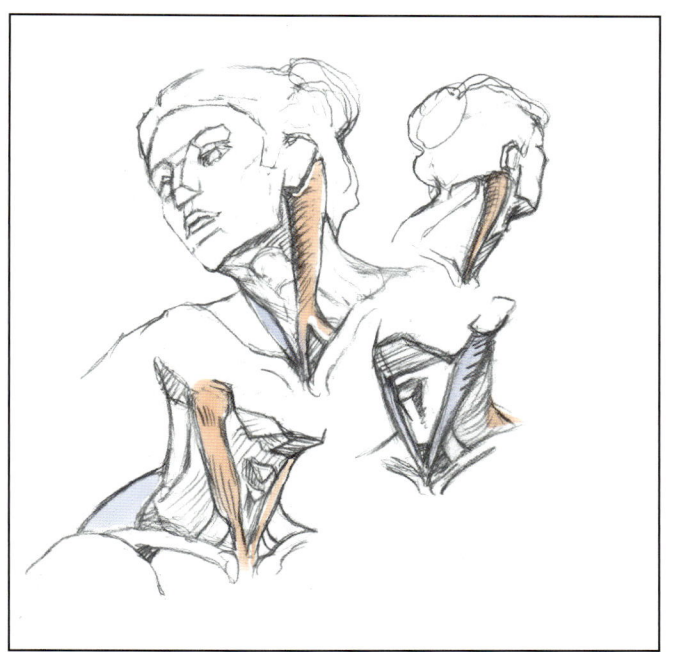

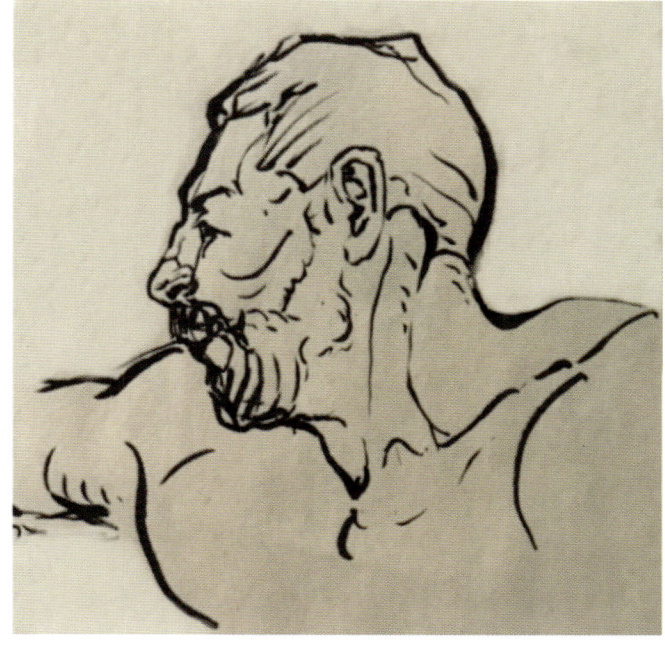

The sternocleidomastoid connects the clavicle to the skull, and the trapezius connects the skull to the scapula. This creates a triangle of muscular efficiency when it comes to moving the head backwards and forward.

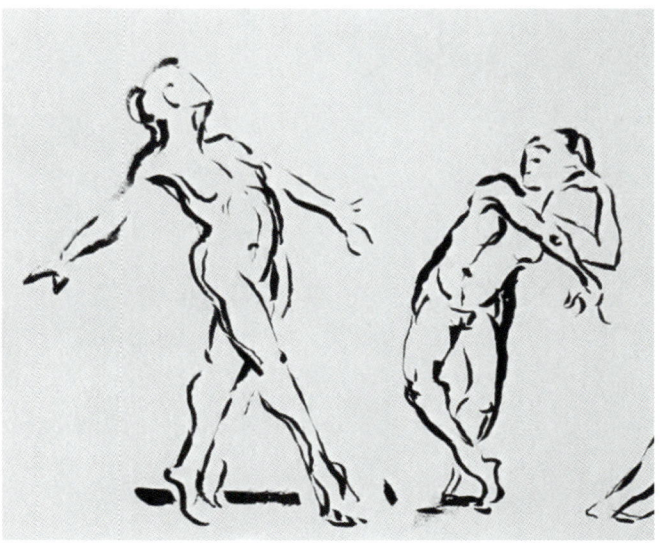

The neck is first and foremost an extension of the spine. This means that head positions are largely determined by the body's movements. Here are two brush-pen gestures showing how necks and heads are influenced by graceful positioning of the torso and limbs.

MOVEMENT OF HANDS AND FEET

CONTOUR DRAWING

Contour drawing is a linear drawing process where depth is achieved through varying line pressure and overlapping rather than through light and dark shading. In these examples, without looking at the page, I moved my pencil only where and when my eye was moving. I only looked at the paper when I lost my concentration or needed to find a new position on the drawing.

Sit down with a small sketchbook, pen, or pencil and pretend that the tip of your pencil is touching the edges of your hand or foot. As much as possible, try not to lift your pencil while focusing mainly on the negative shapes between fingers and toes. Each of your drawings should only take a few minutes but will require a lot of concentration.

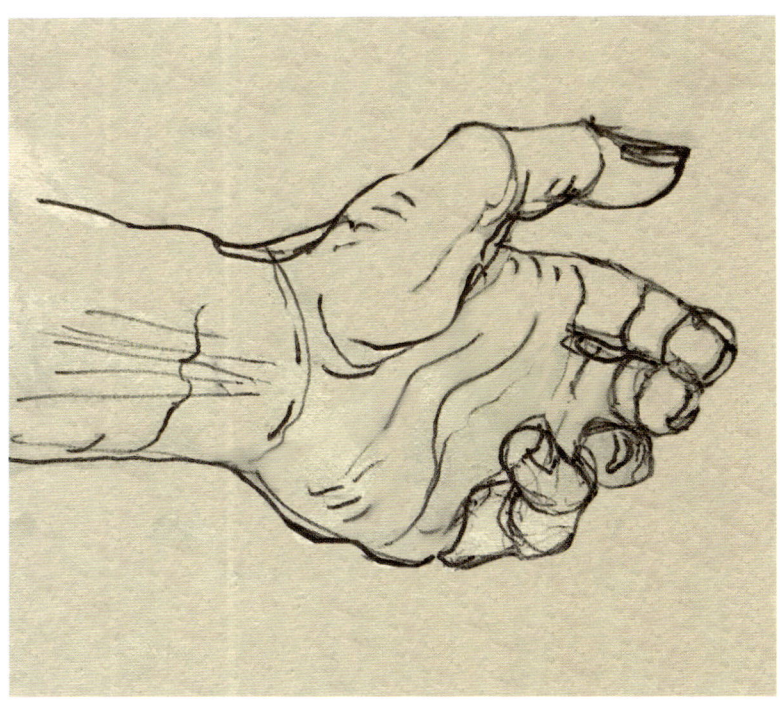
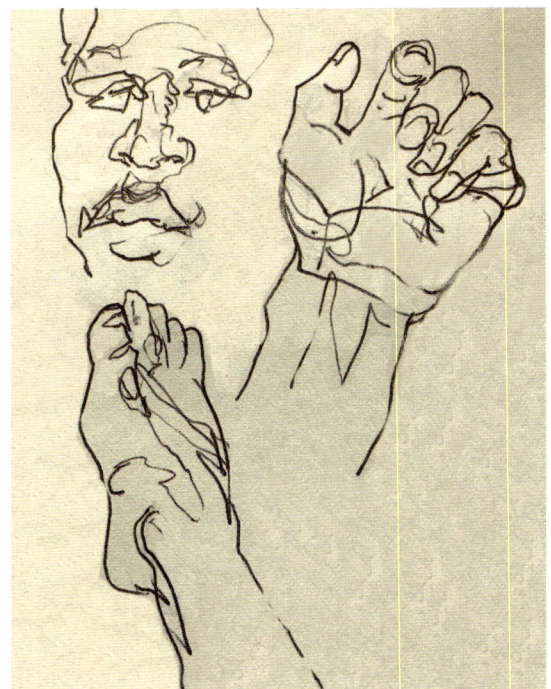
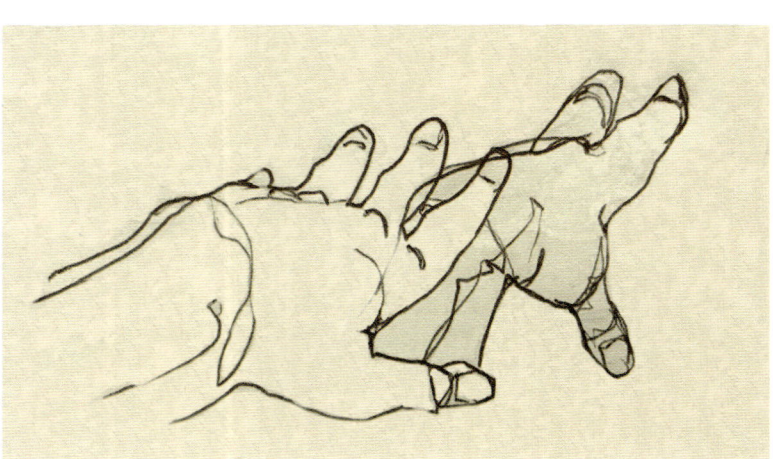
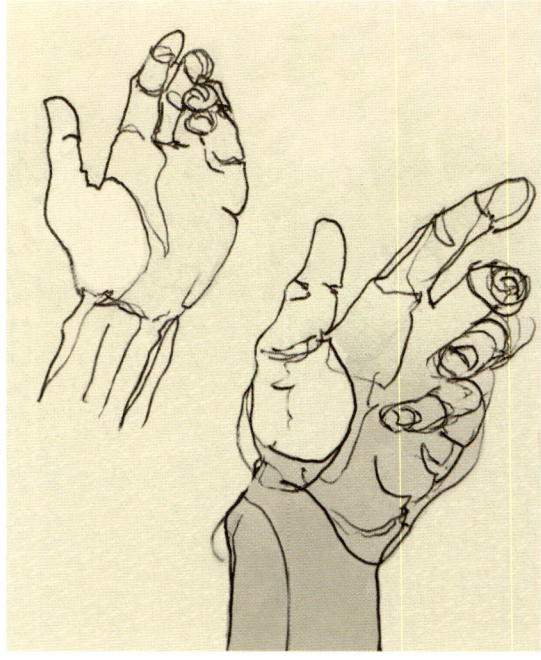

The foot drawings on this page took a little longer than the hands as they include a few anatomical landmarks, such as the extensor tendons, navicular bones, first metatarsal heads (balls of the foot), and a few toe details. Note how I've also indicated the semi-rounded shape of the shin bones and lower-leg muscles with cross-contour lines. Before drawing your own hands and feet, look back at the anatomical section to refresh your memory of which anatomical landmarks you are seeing.

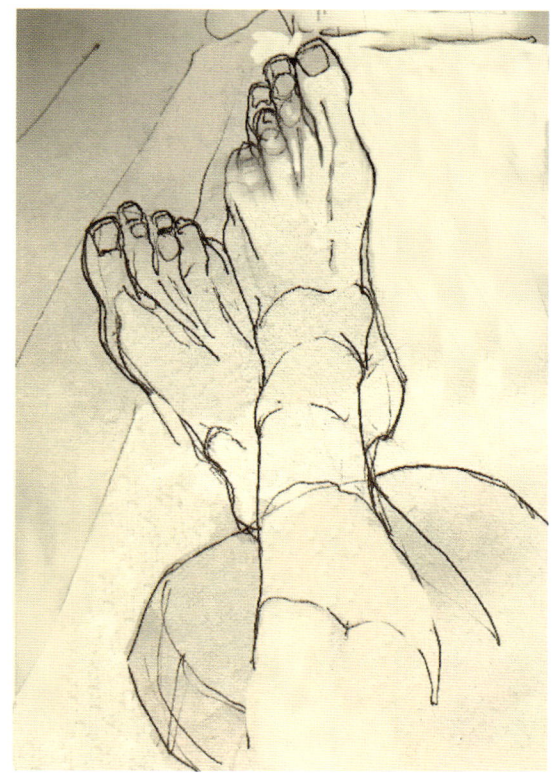

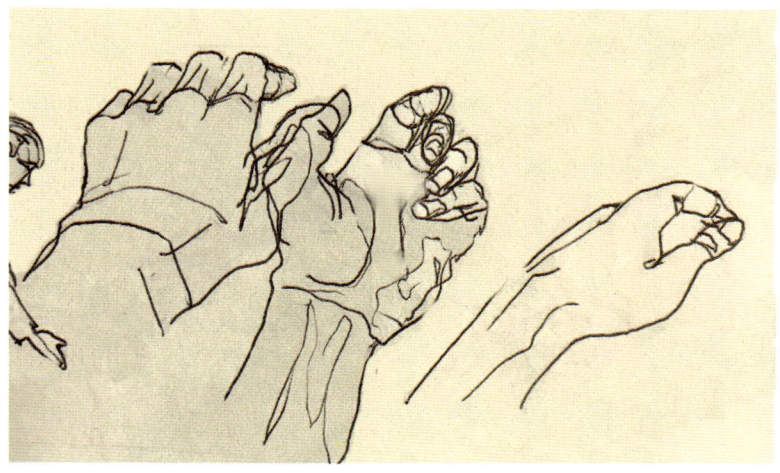

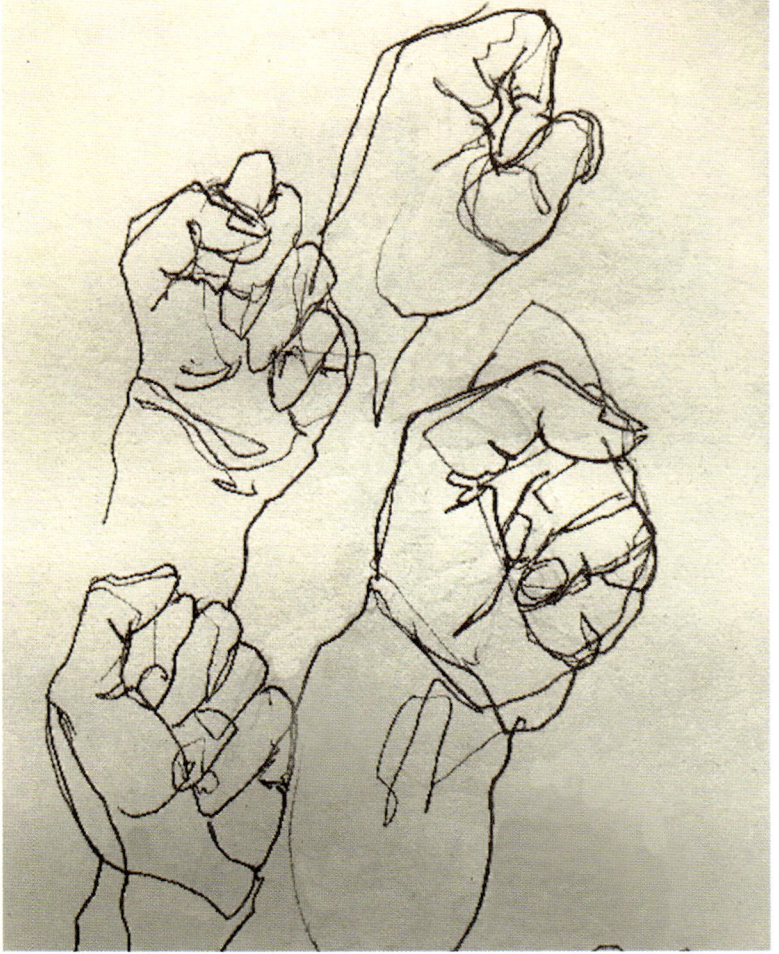

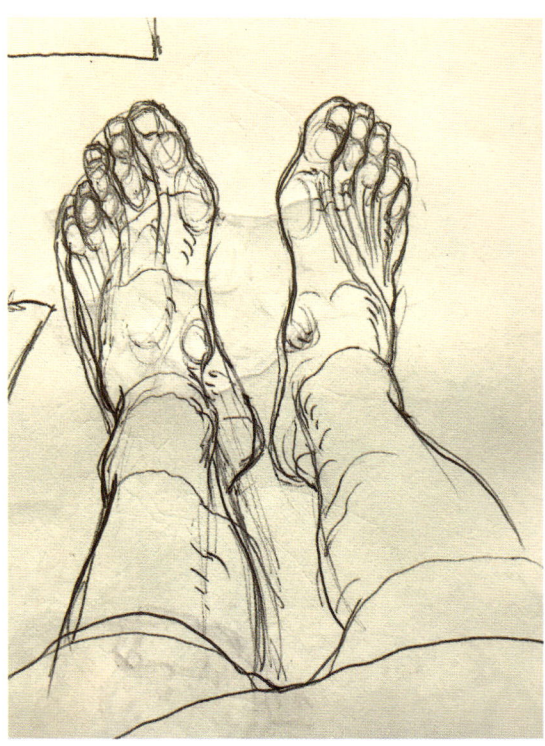

20-MINUTE SKETCHES

All of the hands and feet on this page were drawn with a mechanical 4B graphite pencil and modified with a kneaded eraser. At times, when the poses aren't that great or the hands and feet are totally hidden, it's necessary to find a constructive alternative during the 20-minute pose. On this page, there was one particular pose where the model's hands and feet were completely hidden by drapery. The solution? I ignored the model and drew my own hand instead (**A**).

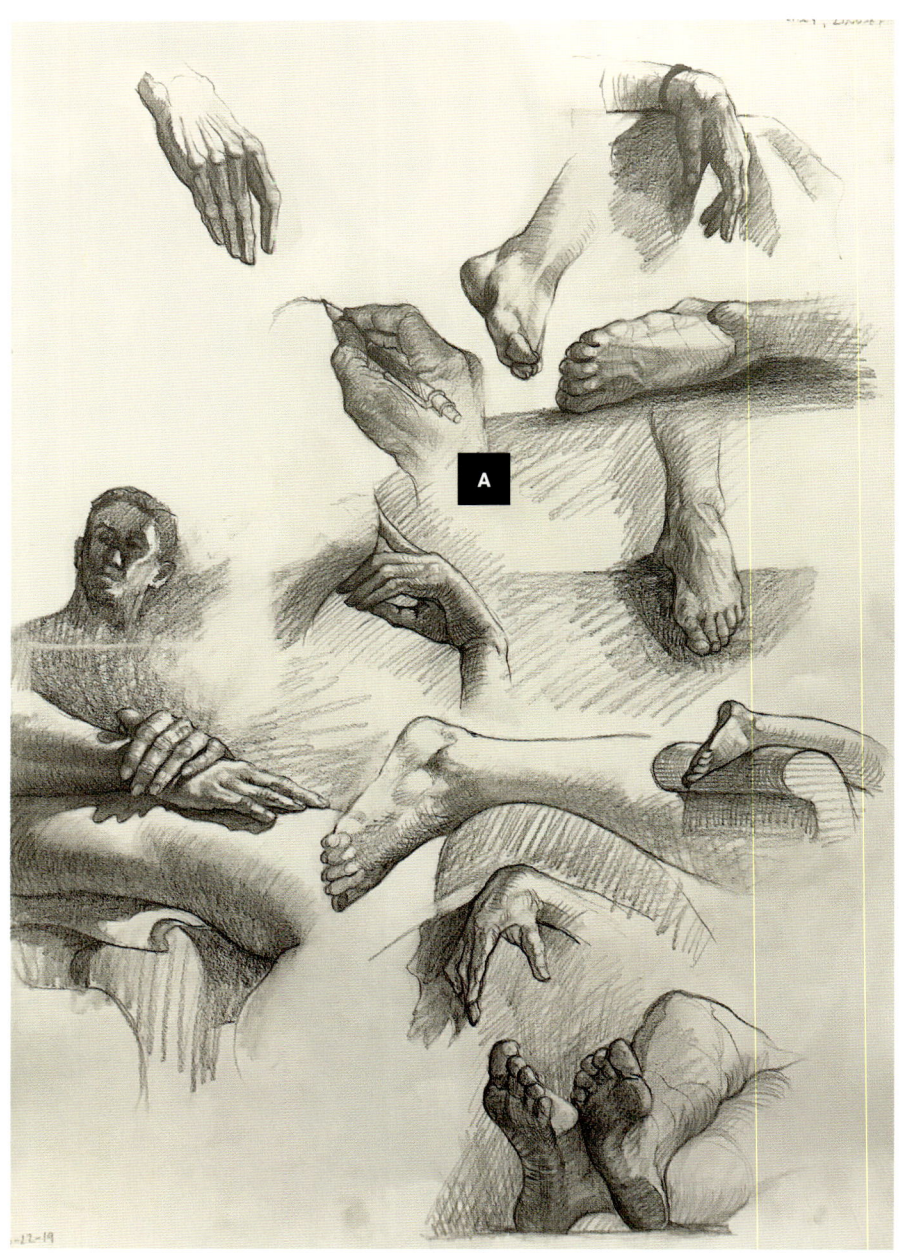

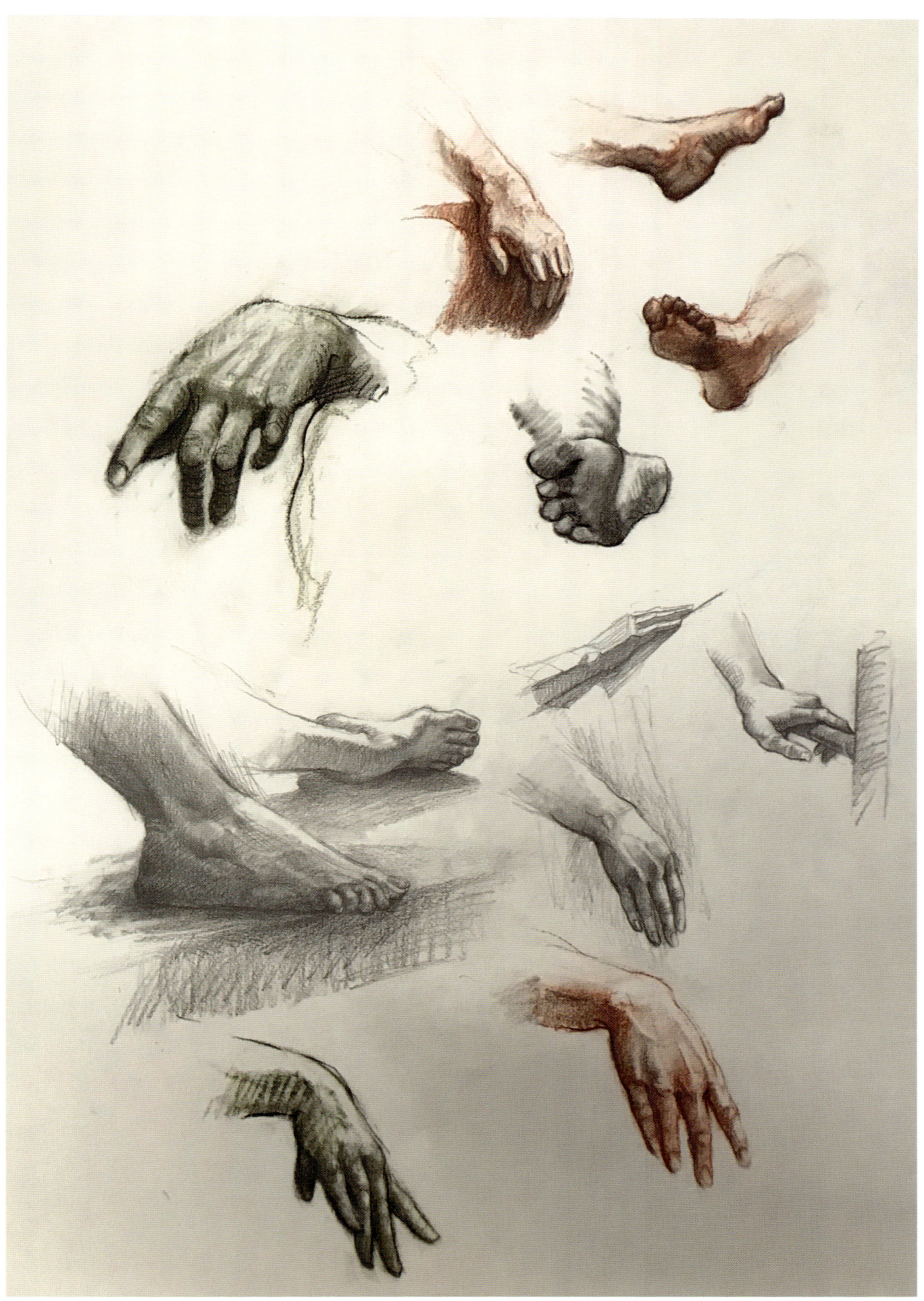

GESTURAL HAND SKETCHES

One of the best ways to practice gesture drawing is to take pictures of hands in many positions (or find them on the web), set a timer (from 1 to 5 minutes) and then, sitting with an 18" × 24" (45.5 × 61 cm) pad of newsprint on your lap, use any of the materials recommended in Chapter 1 and enjoy the challenge.

These 1- and 2-minute gestures were drawn with a blue pastel (for the *silhouettes*) and *vine charcoal*. The mobile thumb (**A**) with its teardrop muscle and *saddle joint* (**B**) can move in almost any direction. The other fingers are mobile, too, but their lateral movement is diminished because *hinge joints* can only move in one plane (**C**). This limitation is compensated for by the knuckle's *condyloid joints*, where circular movement is possible (**D**). If you need a refresher on *joints*, see "Joints" (page 146).

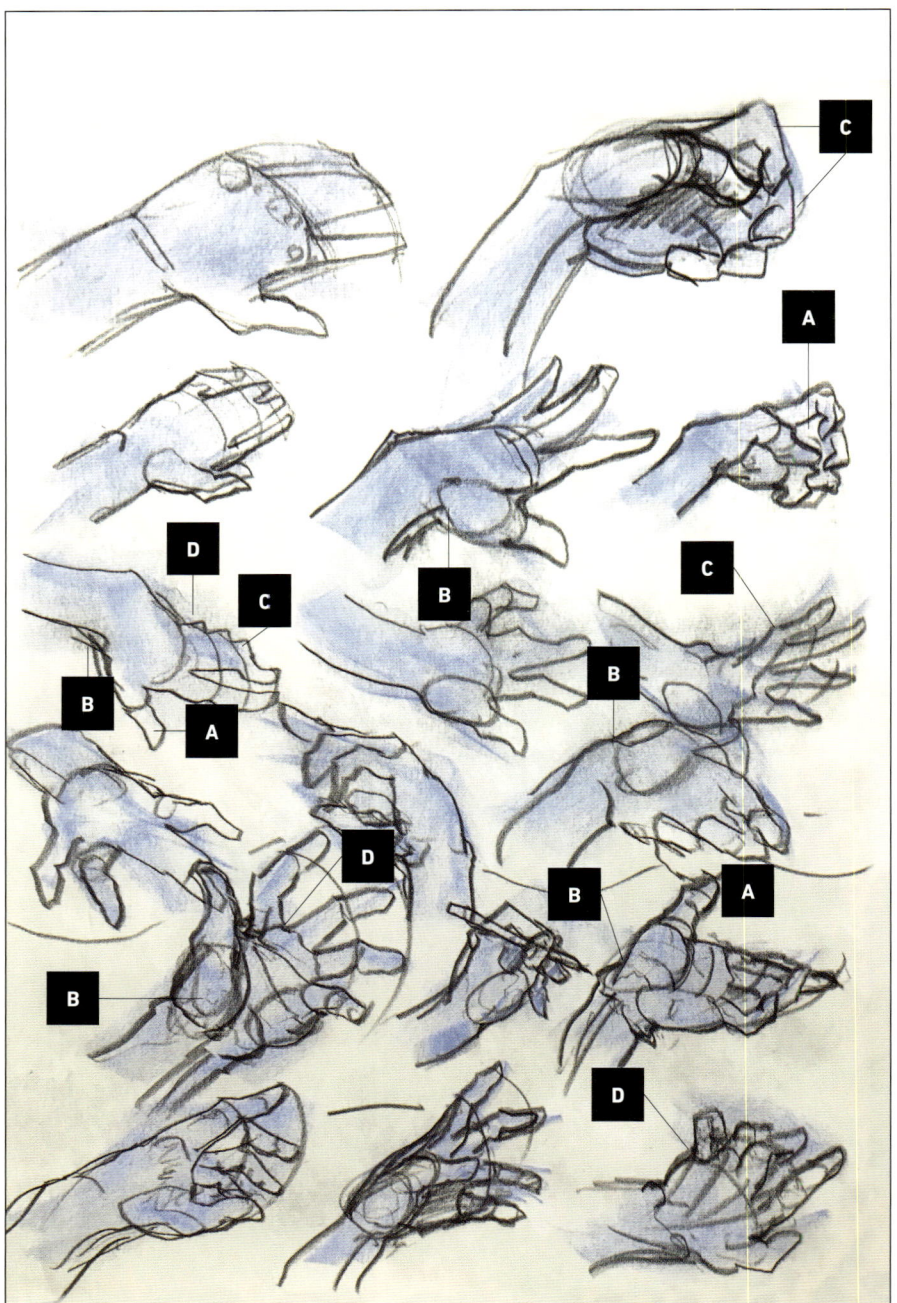

GESTURAL FOOT SKETCHES

Foot gestures are begun exactly like hand gestures—with silhouette first, then broken down into block-like forms. To avoid getting detailed too early, they are begun primarily with straight lines.

The most prominent muscular landmarks on the outside of the foot are the bulging form of extensor digitorum brevis (**A**), parts of extensor digitorum longus (**B**), and the abductor digiti minimi (**C**). The most visible bony landmarks are the ankle bones (**D**), the heel bone (**E**), the ball of the foot (**F**), and the distal head of the fifth metatarsal (**G**). If you need a refresher on feet, see "Anatomy of the Foot," (page 159).

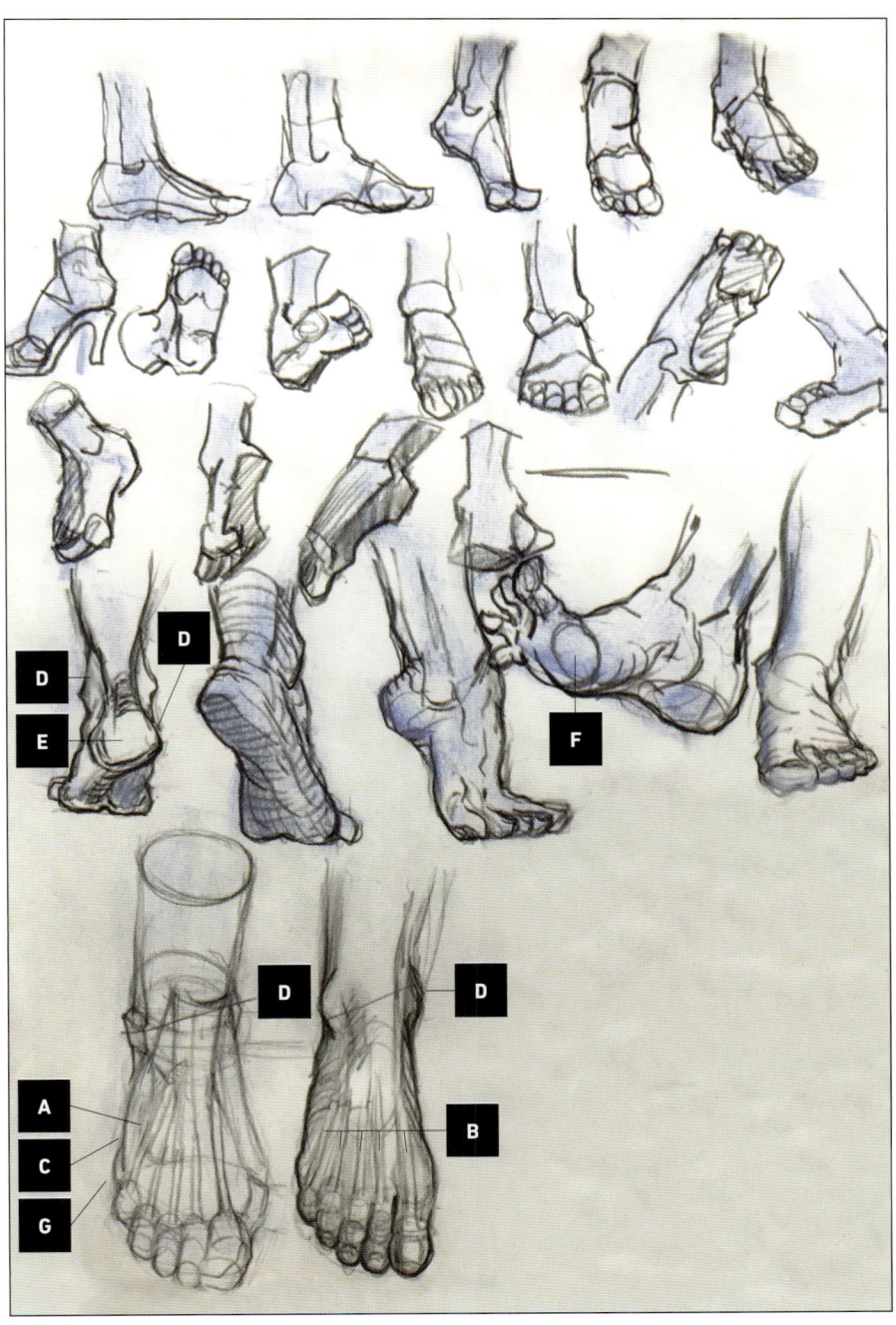

AGONISTS AND ANTAGONISTS IN ACTION

Artists love to draw poses with a strong contraction on one side and a passive long stretch on the other. The muscles that cause contraction are called *agonists*. Their stretched passive counterparts on the other side are called *antagonists*. In the inset drawing, I've colored all *agonists* red and *antagonists* blue. Were this a simple line drawing, I would have placed strong dark accents on the red areas and much lighter thin lines on the passive blue areas.

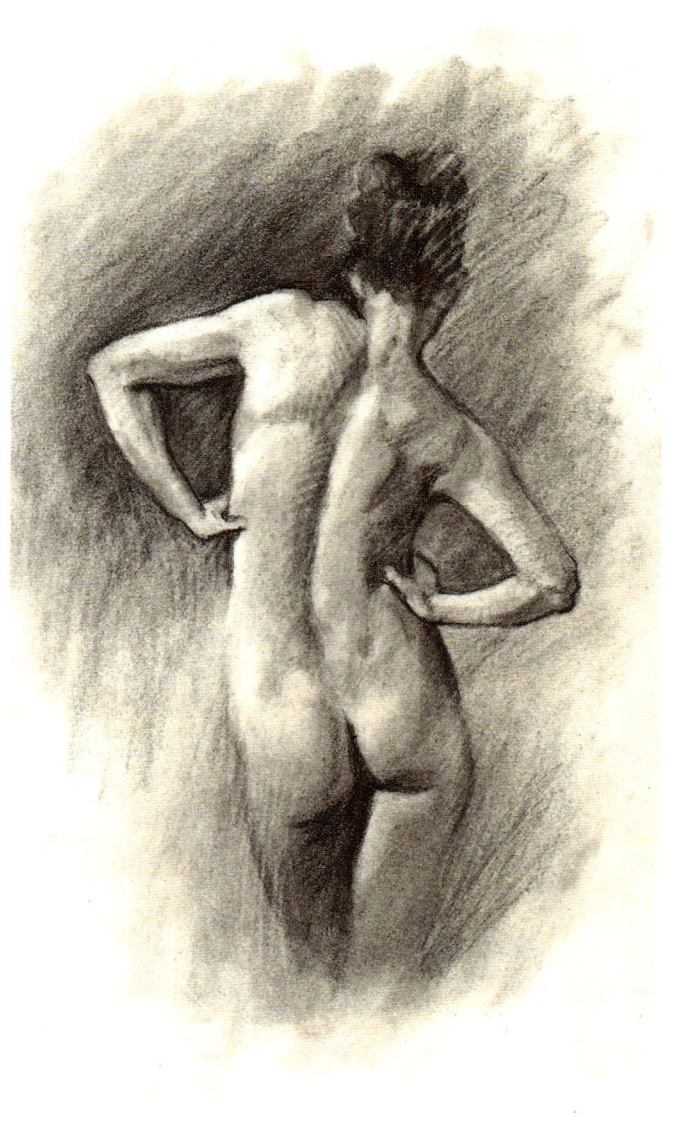

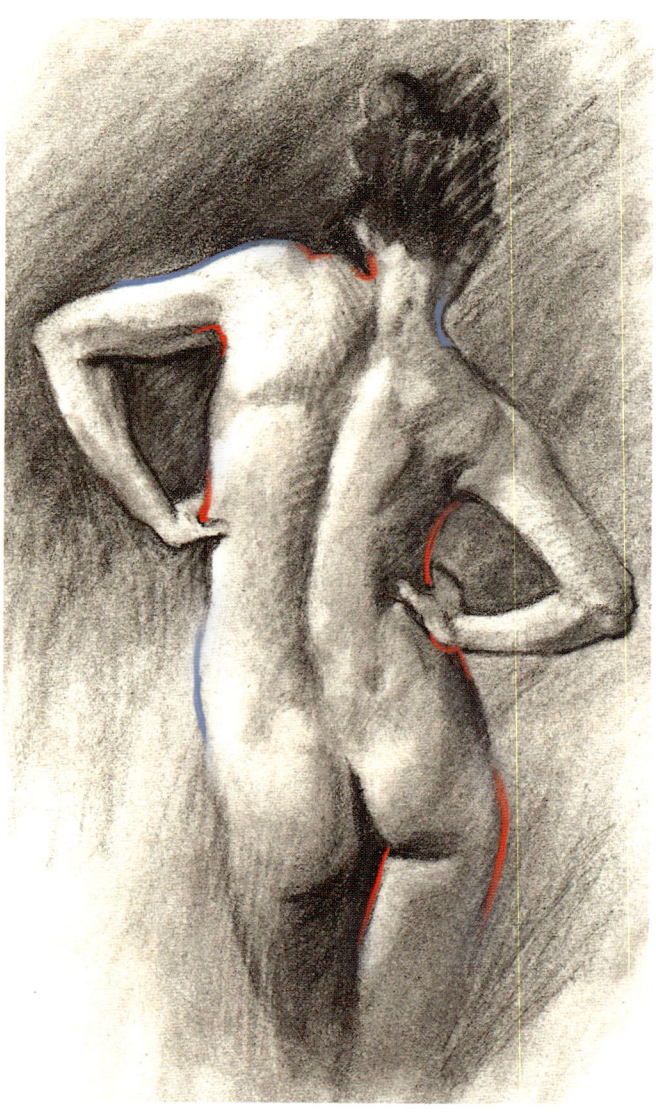

AGONISTS, ANTAGONISTS, AND ACHIEVING BALANCE

There are two types of balance: *static* and *dynamic*. *Static balance* can be defined as the ability to remain standing on one's feet in a controlled manner. *Dynamic balance* is the ability to remain stable during movements or actions that require displacing or moving oneself. For purposes of figure drawing, what both definitions have in common is that a plumbline dropped down from the pit of the neck must fall between the two feet for a model to maintain balance.

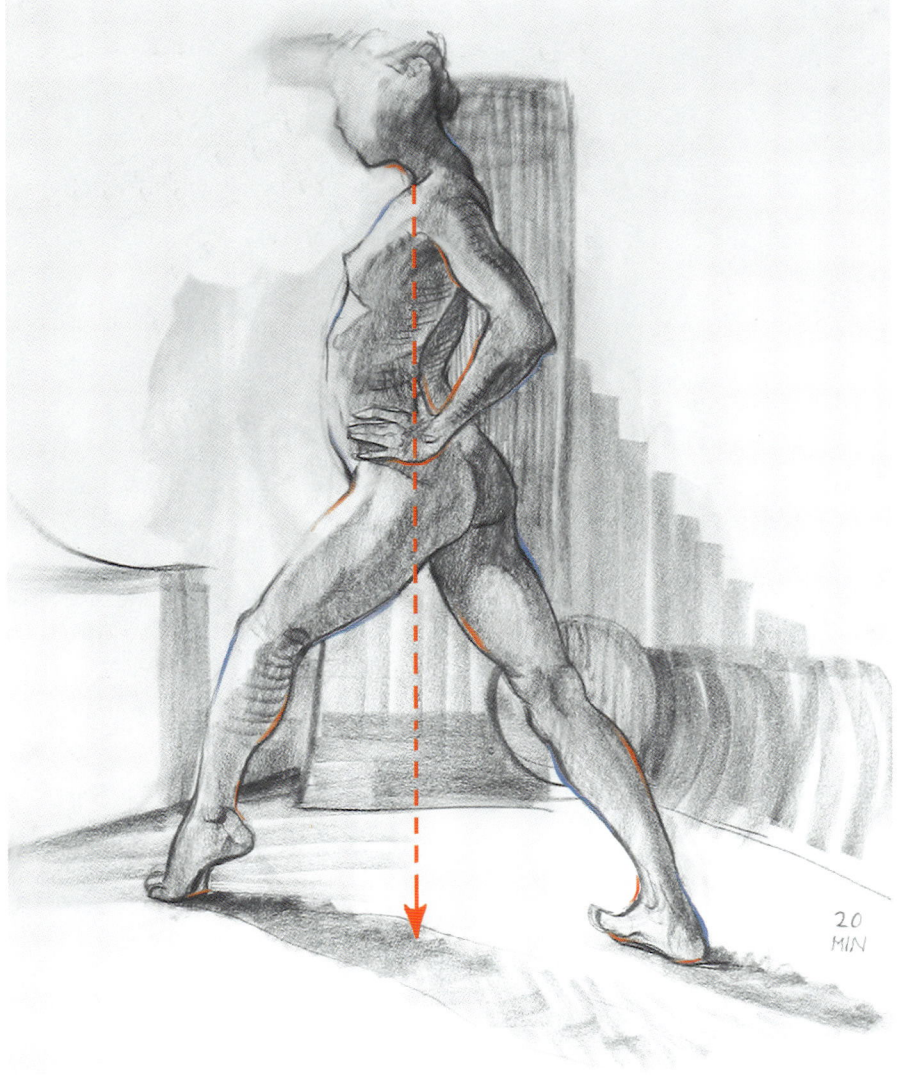

In the drawing below, the upper torso is pulled back because the belly, pelvis, and left leg are thrust forward. This shift of the chest allows the model to maintain *dynamic balance* with the plumb-line landing right between her two feet. Artists must learn to always focus on the relationship of the pit of the neck to the placement of the feet. In this drawing, muscles that act as *agonists* are marked in red, *antagonists* in blue.

20
MIN

DRAWING TECHNIQUES FOR CREATING VISUAL MOVEMENT

RHYTHMIC ACCENT LINES

A *gesture drawing* is usually a quick, simple drawing that captures the essential feeling, energy, movement, and action of a pose. It contains a minimum amount of information but achieves a maximum amount of impact.

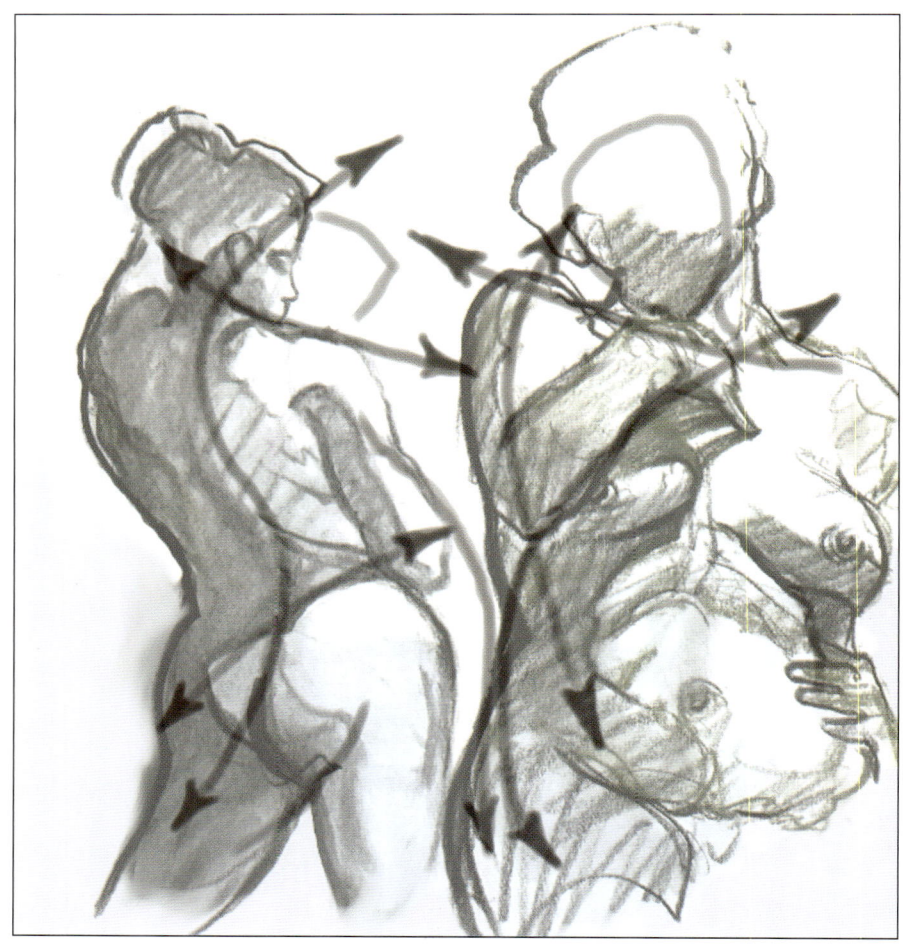

Visual movement is a flow or suggestion of movement that causes a viewer's eyes to follow an intended direction. The directional arrows in these two poses are the rhythmic "flow lines" I sensed and built on as I developed these gestures.

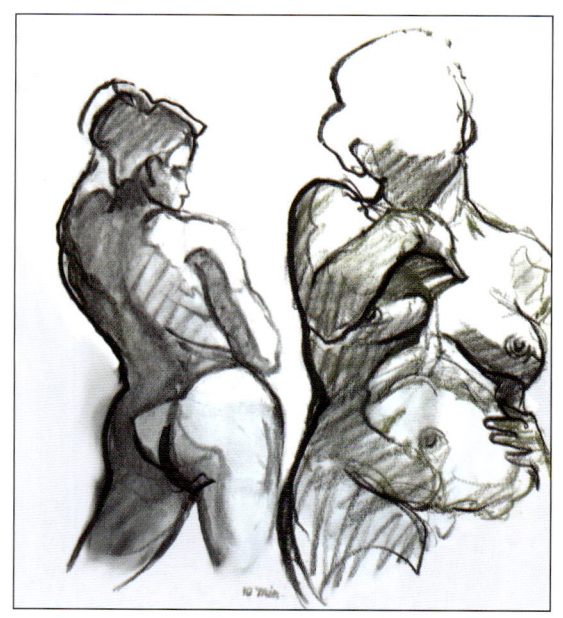

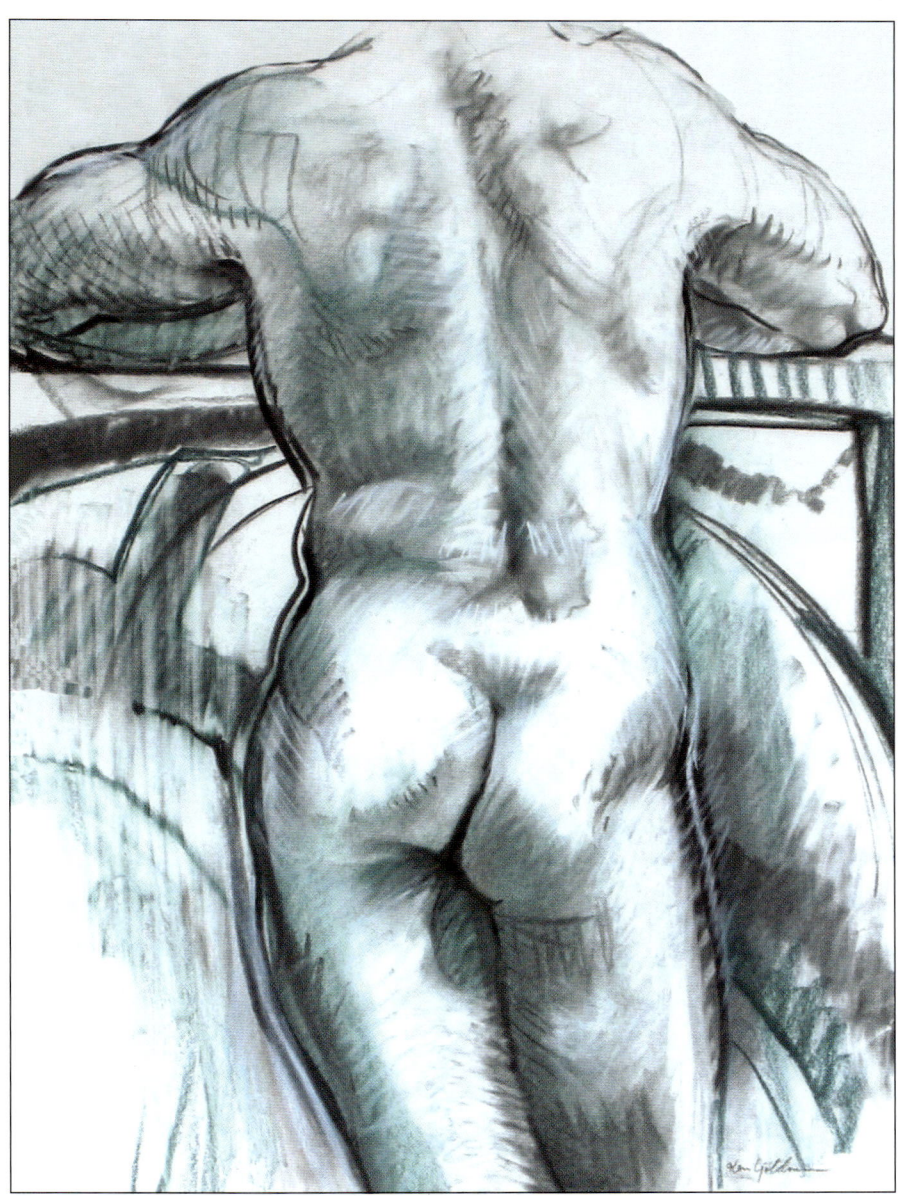

VARIATIONS IN LINE AND TEXTURE

Any sensation of movement experienced by a viewer is based entirely on an artist's ability to construct an engaging composition. Elements such as texture, shape, line, and value contrast are tools used by artists to create such movements within a drawing. This back view has enough of those elements, especially texture and line variation, to stimulate a sense of visual interest in a viewer.

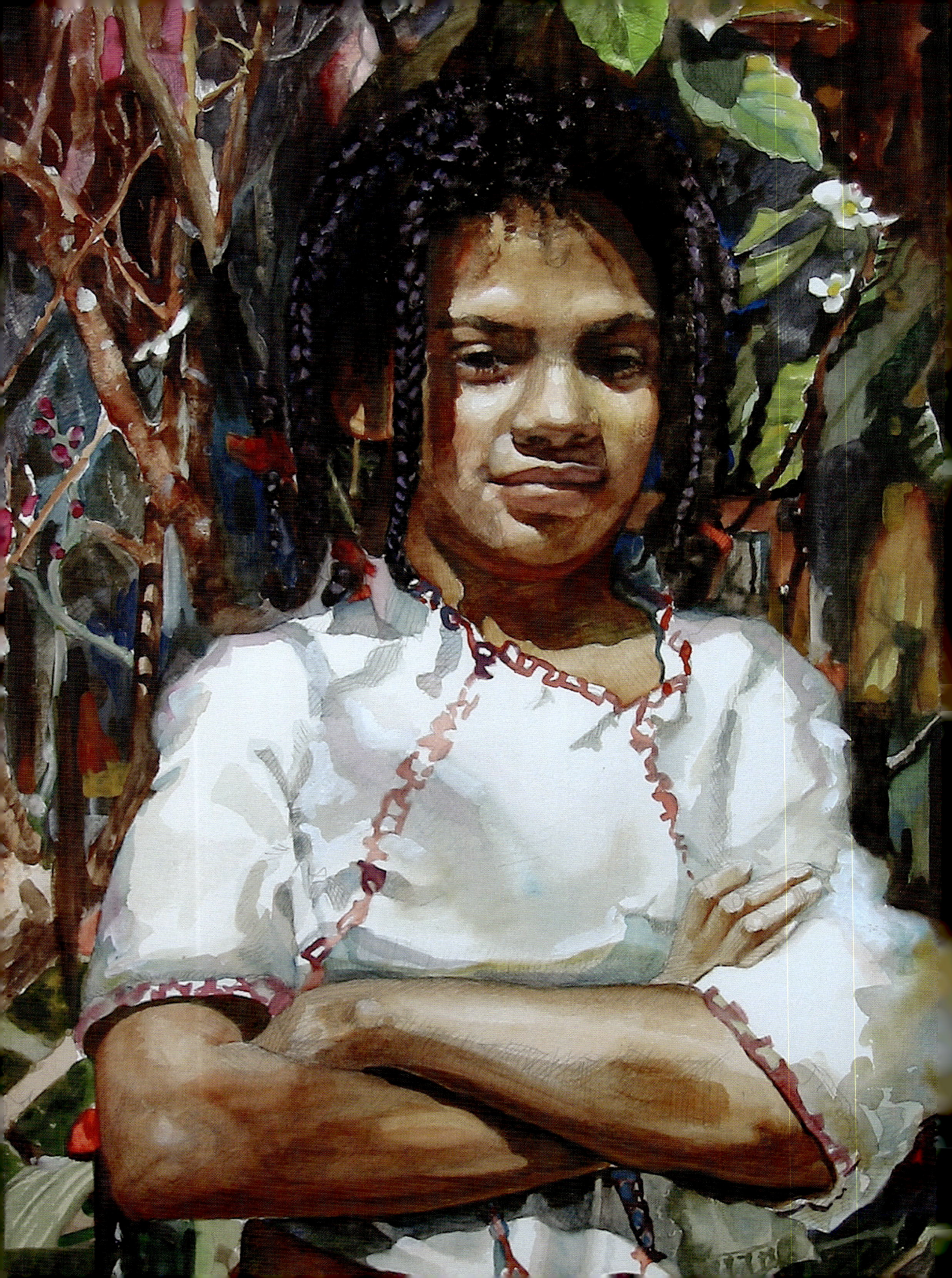

CHAPTER 7

LIGHTING AND BACKGROUND STRATEGIES

There is a very famous saying among experienced artists: Value does all the work while color gets all the credit. Art teachers express this truism about the importance of value when they remind students having trouble choosing colors that "if the value is correct, the color can be anything." But let's get even more basic about the importance of value by discussing degrees of lightness and darkness (the definition of value) in relation to background design strategies and ways in which artists' compositions can elicit a maximum amount of interest.

Ken Goldman, *Sienna*, **watercolor on paper, 22" × 15" (56 × 38 cm)**
When a figure with a simple white blouse is placed against a complex dark background, an interesting visual dynamic is created.

THE FIRST STAGE OF DESIGN

The first stage of designing an impactful composition should be as uninhibited and intuitive as creating a beautiful table setting. Work small and do many thumbnails. Then, when you like a particular composition, analyze it to find out why.

LIGHTING AND DESIGN STRATEGIES

The value scale has maximum impact. Rather than using ten values, which would dilute impact, only four values are necessary, with white and black being accents. Note how a middle-value strip running through the entire scale looks darker next to the light part at the top and lighter next to the darks at the bottom. The strip is the same value throughout and does not actually change at all. This illusion is called "simultaneous contrast" and does not just apply to value contrasts but also to color contrasts.

These six images each have the same range of values as the adjacent scale, and the head in each image contains the exact same values. Which composition do you think is most impactful? A *dark against light* background or a *light against dark* background? Both choices exhibit maximum visual drama, while the other four intermediate combinations show much more nuance.

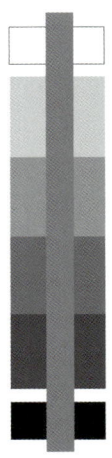
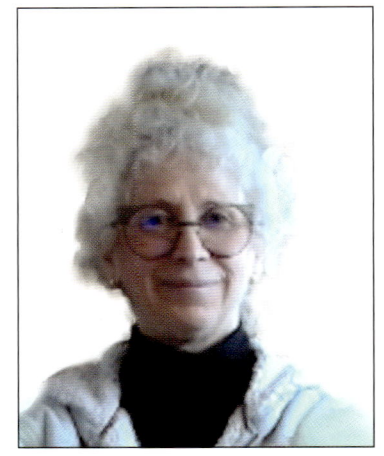
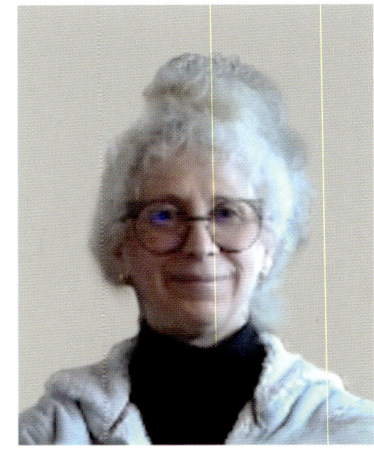
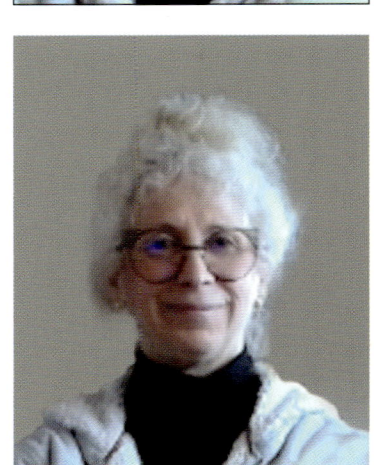
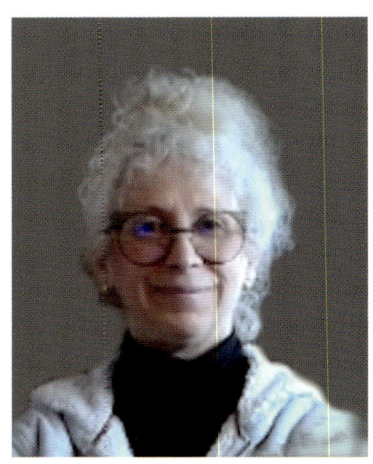
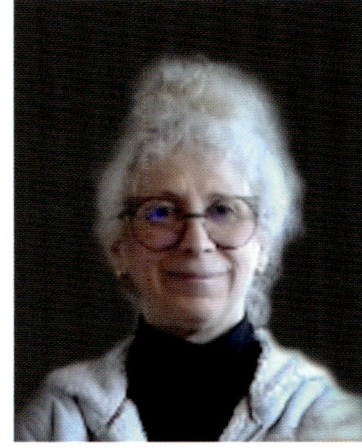
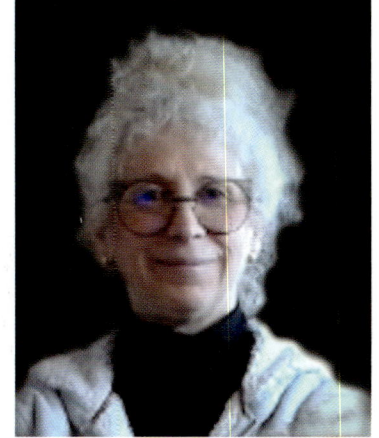

BACKGROUND DESIGN STRATEGIES

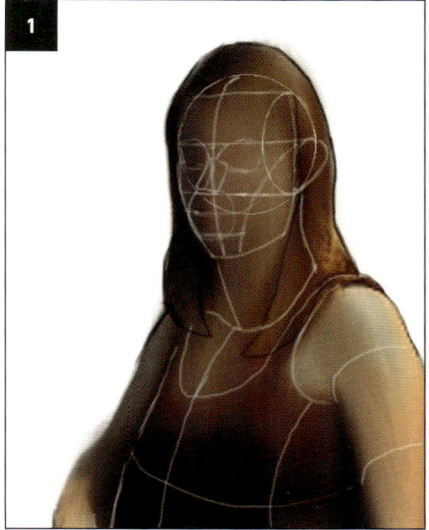

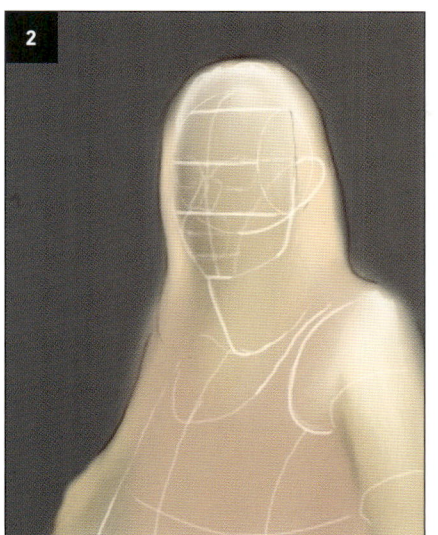

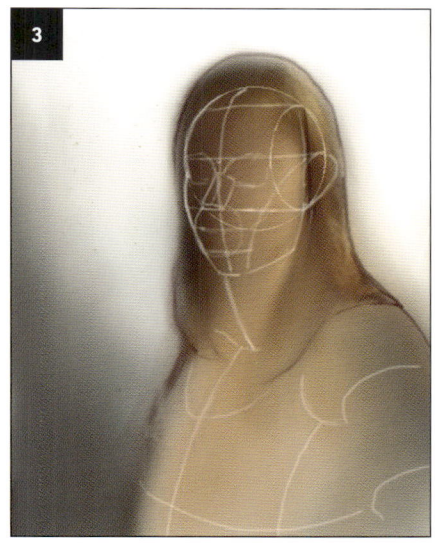

These portrait compositions above (1) and top middle (2) show the impact of *dark against light* and *light against dark*. The composition at top right (3), being *a mixture of both*, is more nuanced.

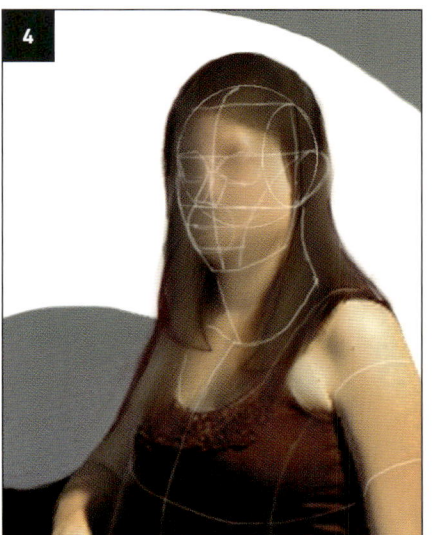

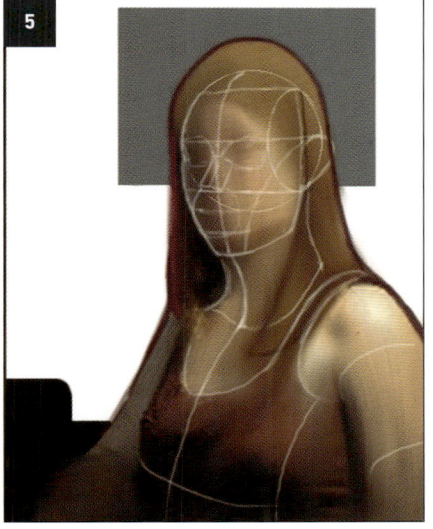

CURVES VS. STRAIGHTS

These two heads above show the difference in feeling that comes about from *compositions emphasizing curves (4)* versus *compositions emphasizing straights (5)*. It's good to practice many small thumbnails like these before you decide on a final direction.

LIGHT AGAINST DARK

Ken Goldman, **Stephanie's Double-Mirrored-Self-Portrait, oil on linen, 30" × 24" (76 × 61 cm)**

This portrait of my wife painting her own self-portrait is a good example of a *light against dark* strategy. When you decide to do a composition like this, make sure the darks dominate and the lights are just bright accents. Always avoid 50/50 proportions.

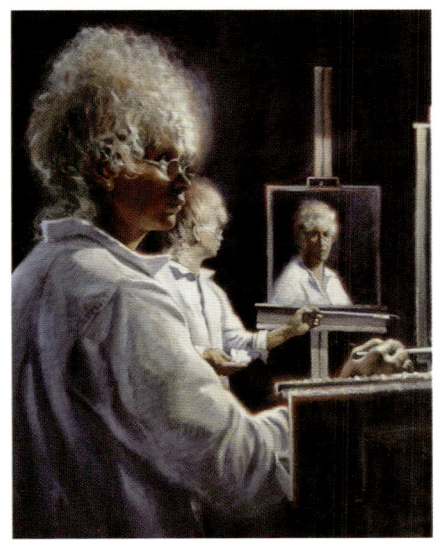

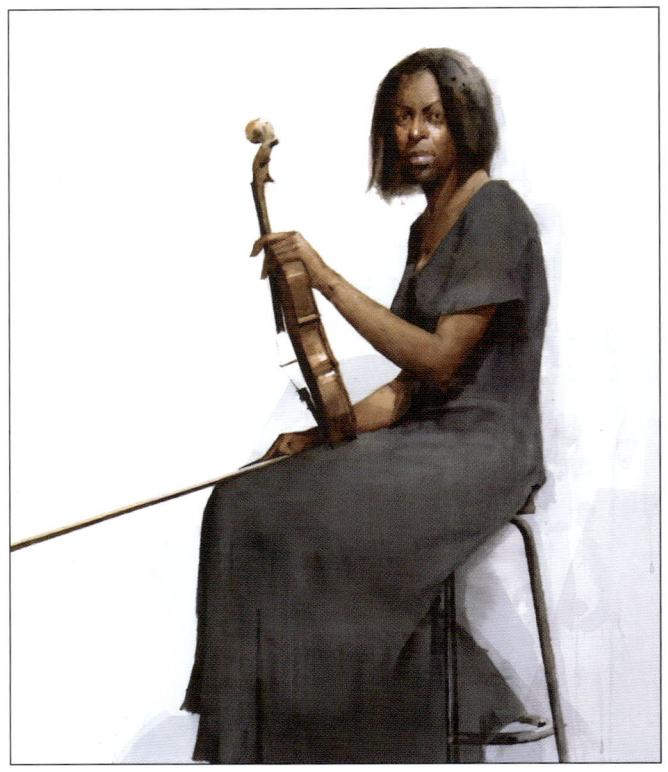

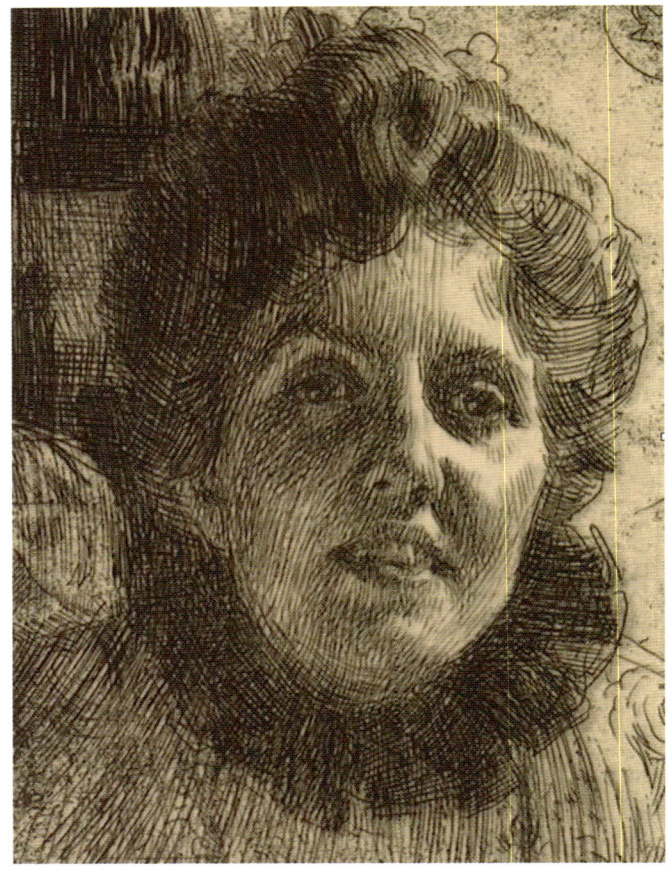

BACKGROUND DESIGN STRATEGIES

This painting by Dean Mitchell shows the power of a simply designed *dark figure against an expansive light background*. Where the figure's edges touch the light background, interesting *negative shapes* are created.

Dean Mitchell, *Melanie*, **watercolor, 30" × 22" (76 × 56 cm)**
deanmitchellstudio.com

This small etching by Anders Zorn is a wonderful example of leaving out extreme dark and light values altogether in favor of a three-value nuanced strategy.

LIGHT

LIGHT GRAY

DARK GRAY

DARK

	ACCENT—WHITE
	L
	LG—1/2 TONE
	DG—SHADOW
	D
	ACCENT—BLACK

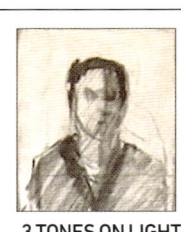

3 TONES ON LIGHT

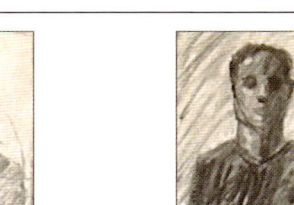

3 TONES ON LIGHT GRAY

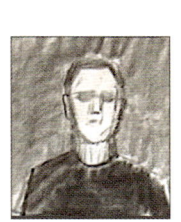

3 TONES ON DARK GRAY

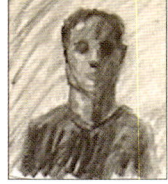

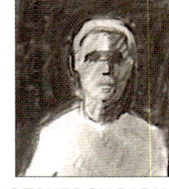

3 TONES ON DARK

6 LIGHTING AND DESIGN STRATEGIES

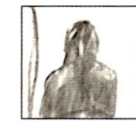 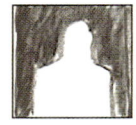 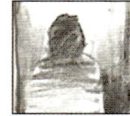 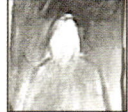 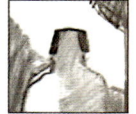 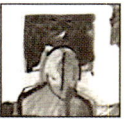

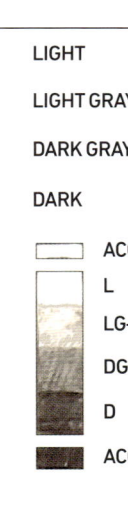

Here is a page of thumbnails I created for one of my classes, showing the importance of pre-planning background strategies. Very little detail is required to get an idea across.

EXPLORING NEW IDEAS: ANATOMICAL EXPRESSIVENESS

Because choice of background plays such a major role in determining what a finished piece of art will look like, it matters very much which value of background is selected: light, medium, or dark.

TWO NOVEL BACKGROUND STRATEGIES

Strategy 1: A Light Background with No Lines

Artist: Wendy Artin (wendyartin.com) One of the best reasons for artists to know specific details of anatomy is so they will also know when to leave those specific details out of a drawing. Degree of finish is of course a matter of personal choice. However, if a viewer is allowed to participate in completing a picture, their interest is increased because they get to finish the untold ending in their own imaginative way. Great wisdom can be expressed in just a few carefully selected words. The same holds true for the visual arts. Here are two masterful examples of figures painted from life by artist Wendy Artin, where, truly, less is more. Negative space in both of these pieces is just as important to the overall composition as the thoughtfully placed, well-proportioned figures. Wendy does not sketch with a pencil before painting. She says, "Each new painting is an adventure. Watercolor can be so quick and full of beautiful surprises—or disasters! I love the way the image can emerge from a puddle of watercolor."

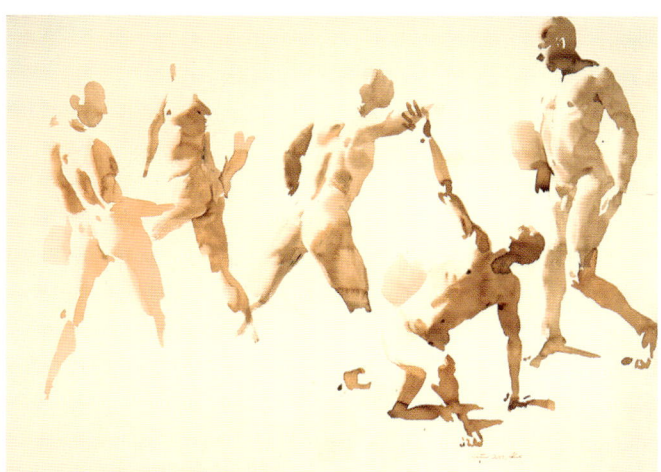

Wendy Artin, **Alex Five Times, watercolor on paper, 13.8" x 19.7" (35 × 50 cm)**
Five figures of one model painted from life. Light areas on the forms merge into the light coming from behind them. Shadow shapes are connected with various degrees of hard, medium, and soft edges.

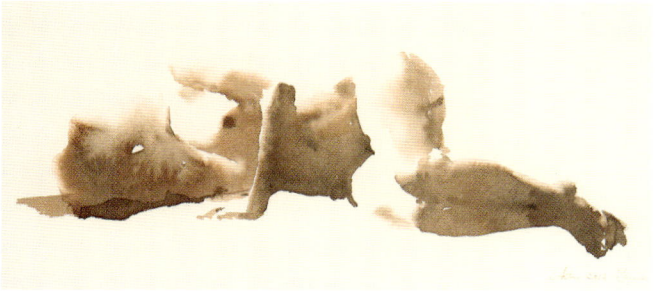

Wendy Artin, **Laura on Side, watercolor on paper, 7.1" x 13.4" (18 × 34 cm)**
Flowing, loose washes are combined with exacting anatomy used in an expressive way.

Strategy 2:
A Dark Background with White Lines

The same principles about negative shapes, hard, medium, and lost edges that hold true for a figure on a light ground also hold true for a figure on a dark ground. Here, the dark negative spaces are just as important to the overall composition as the light spaces are in the previous works on white paper. Specific details of anatomy are not necessary here either because the outer contours are drawn with so much accuracy. Subtle bony landmarks are indicated whenever they count but are not overdone. The expressive inventiveness of this drawing's white lines, semi-opaque white washes, and only three values on such a rich, dark background make this piece a really strong statement.

Stephanie Goldman, **Seated Nude,**
ink and white pen on toned paper,
12" × 9" (30 × 23 cm)
goldmanfineart.com

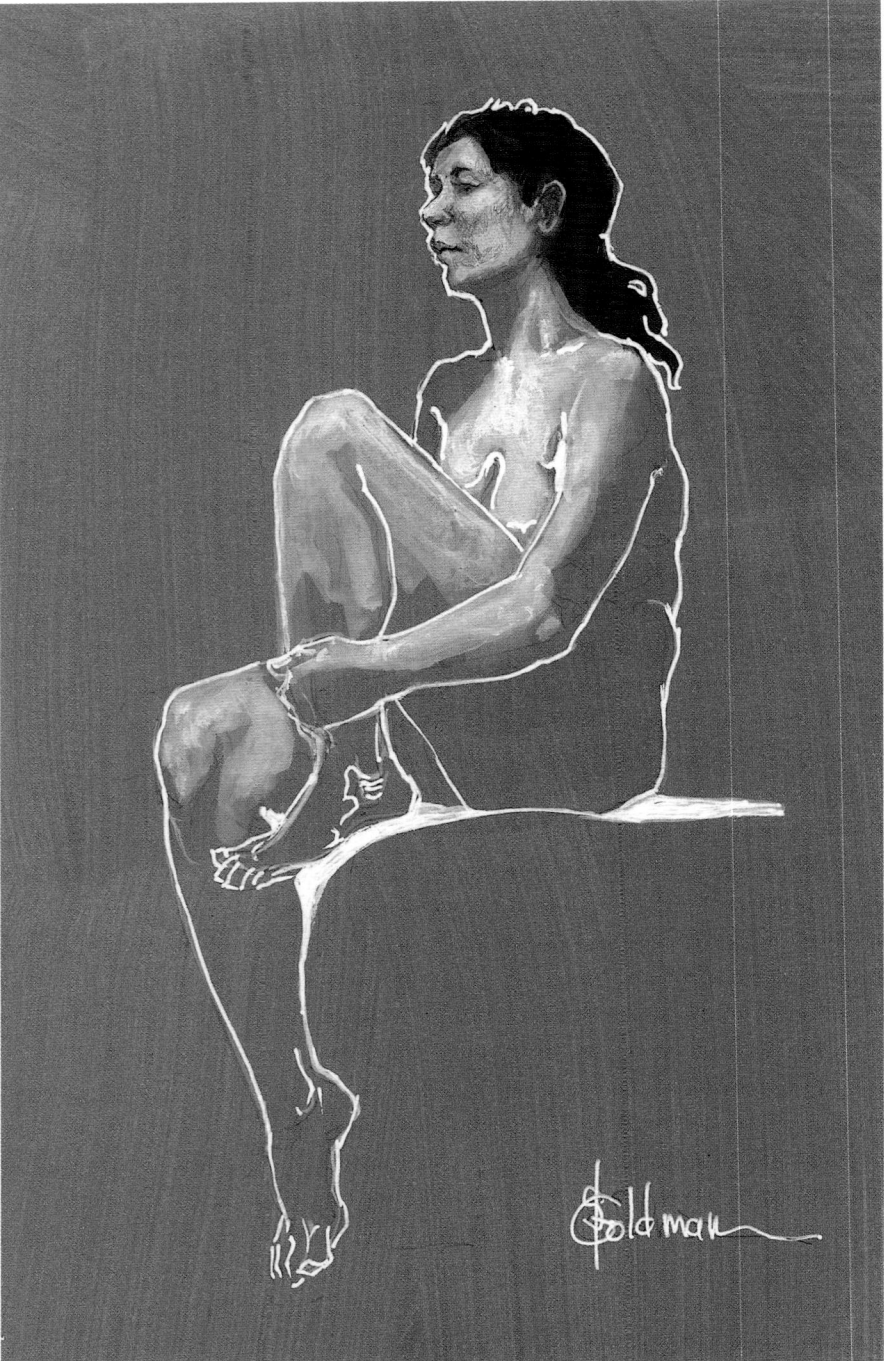

CONCLUSION

When I first began teaching anatomical figure drawing forty years ago, much of the contemporary art world looked down on good draftsmanship as an old-fashioned holdover from a bygone era. Art departments in the 1970s and '80s completely neglected traditional training. It was seen as irrelevant in a rapidly changing art world, where modernism and conceptual art were considered the only art forms worth pursuing. At the time, teaching figure drawing based on realistic human anatomy was a lonely profession.

But this trend seems to have completely run its course now. Once again, good drawing skills are seen as a necessary foundation for artistic training, no matter the style or direction pursued. Based on this renewed interest, traditional art ateliers have sprung up in many parts of the country. If you'd like to further enhance your knowledge of anatomy, I recommend attending an atelier or art workshop near you.

If there are no courses offered in your area, do what artists have done for centuries: Study the works of great masters, such as Michelangelo, Leonardo, Albinus, or, more recently, George Bridgman, Steven Rogers Peck, and Eliot Goldfinger. Study and copy their work diligently, learn their shorthand strokes, and see how they solved the same drawing issues you face in your own work. With each attempt, you will go a little further and learn a little more. And remember that this journey is not about making perfect drawings; it's about making each drawing you create better than the one before it, while still having a good time.

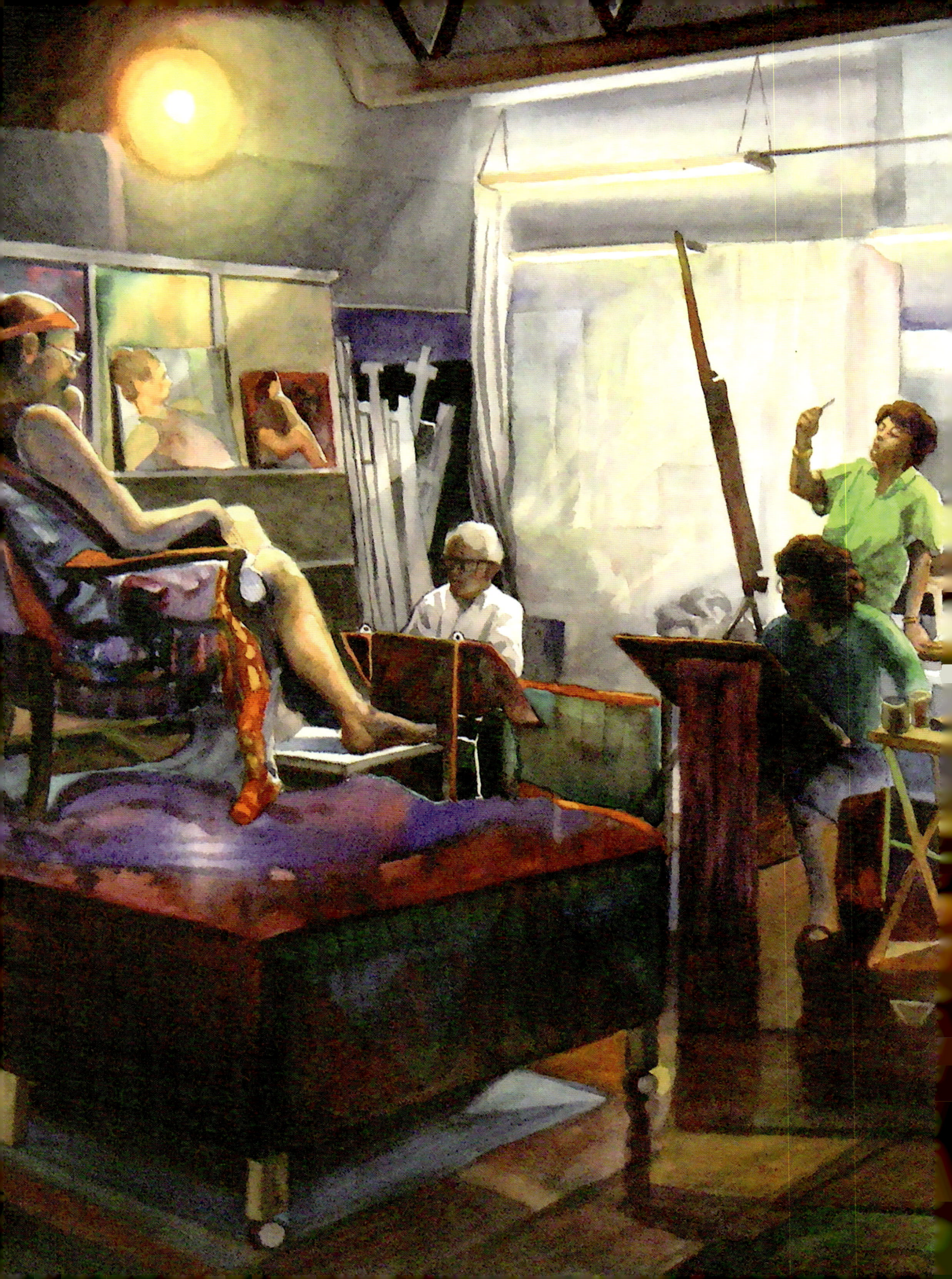

RESOURCES

SUPPLIES

Brush Pens
pentel.com

Charcoal Pencils
generalpencil.com
prang.com

Conté Pencils and Chalk
conteaparis.com/en

Cutting Tools
xacto.com/knives-blades.html

Pads and Paper
us.canson.com
strathmoreartist.com

BOOKS

Bridgman, George. *Constructive Anatomy*. New York: Dover Publications Inc., 1973.

Goldfinger, Eliot. *Human Anatomy for Artists*. Oxford: Oxford University Press, 1991.

Hale, Robert Beverly. *Anatomy Lessons from the Great Masters*. New York: Watson-Guptill, 2000.

Hamm, Jack. *Drawing the Head and Figure*. New York: TarcherPerigee, 1982.

Peck, Stephen Rogers. *Atlas of Human Anatomy for the Artist*. Oxford: Oxford University Press, 1982.

ONLINE RESOURCES

Body Worlds: bodyworlds.com

Kenhub: kenhub.com

Los Angeles Academy of Figurative Art: laafa.edu

New Masters Academy: nma. art and youtube.com/user/ NewMastersAcademy

LEARN MORE ABOUT KEN GOLDMAN

goldmanfineart.com/ken-goldman

Ken Goldman, *Life Drawing Class*, **watercolor and pastel on paper, 22" × 30" (56 × 76 cm) (detail)**
The intense concentration of students in my life drawing class (measuring, rendering, and working hard) inspired me to compose this painting of them.

ACKNOWLEDGMENTS

First and foremost, I am eternally grateful to my artist mother, Maxine, who wanted all her children to not only become happy, fulfilled human beings, but, if possible, to become artists as well. As a part of that desire, she took me and my older brother, Robert, to our first nude life drawing class in 1963, when we were only thirteen and fourteen years old, to "be sure we would both know about the beauty and wonder of the male and female figure" and that "nakedness was not a dirty thing." My brother and I now feel that this early education in being reverential toward the human figure, clothed or nude, was the spark that lit the fire that made us both want to become professional fine artists for life.

I am also forever grateful to my generous father, who worked tirelessly to be sure his family could do all the artistic things we believed in. Not only was Dad extremely wise, business-savvy, and kind, he also possessed the broadest shoulders of any man I've ever known. He supported a wife and four children without ever complaining and taught us that work should always be fun or, at least, a great learning experience.

In the late '60s and early 70s, I mostly drew and painted birds and animals to the exclusion of all other subjects.

I am extremely grateful to my artist brother Robert for throwing down the gauntlet by suggesting that "no great artist, past or present, has ever been worth their salt unless they could draw the human figure." I am also grateful that Robert introduced me to my second life drawing class in the mid '70s. After that, I never looked back. Since 1985, I have been blessed to be married to Stephanie, my best friend, love of my life, co-worker, and wonderful artist, who loves to draw, paint, and study art just as much as I do. She is a constant inspiration to me.

As for my favorite anatomy instructors, I was fortunate enough to study in person with Terence Coyle, assistant to the late anatomist Robert Beverly Hale; Vern Wilson of the Pasadena Art Center (the kindest art teacher I've ever known); Daniel Green at the Art Students League; and Burt Silverman at the National Academy of Design. I thank all of them for their inspirational instruction.

When it comes to learning from anatomy books, I've garnered the most from *Atlas of Human Anatomy for the Artist* by Stephen Rogers Peck, *Anatomy Lessons from the Great Masters* by Robert Beverly Hale, *Human Anatomy for Artists* by Eliot Goldfinger, *Constructive Anatomy* by George Bridgman, and for great figure drawing "quick tips and hirts," *Drawing the Head and Figure* by Jack Hamm. I heartily recommend these books to all of you.

I am also extremely grateful to Quarto and Rockport Publishers acquiring editor Joy Aquilino, designer Hailey Toohey, editorial project manager Liz Weeks, and their teams, for turning all of my long hours of drawing and writing into a well-designed, readable book. However, none of the illustrations in this book would have been possible without the use of live models. Firstly, I would like to thank Chris Getsla, Spencer Jeffreys, and Minerva Neal for agreeing to pose for Expressions of Emotion and Head Structure. Then, for the rest of the anatomy in this book, I was fortunate that good friend and professional art model Yoni Baker, Bakermodel.com, was also available. Yoni is well known throughout the country for his creative poses, excellent musculature, and easy-going demeanor.

Finally, I'd like to acknowledge Walter Foster Publishing, whose books I not only read as a child in the '50s, but for whom, since 1990, I've written many instructional books on anatomy, portraiture, figure drawing, charcoals, pastels, and acrylics.

I used to copy skulls from Walter Foster's book on anatomy in the mid '50s, so it was an interesting twist of fate that a talent scout from Walter Foster saw me doing a pastel demo in 1989 and asked if I would do a book for them. *Portraits in Pastel* was my first book, published in 1990 (no such thing as computer cut and paste then . . . all done with handwritten notes and an old-fashioned typewriter). Since then, I've cone lots more books with Walter Foster.

ABOUT THE AUTHOR

Ken Goldman is an internationally known artist, author, teacher, and art juror. A recipient of numerous awards, Goldman has exhibited widely in various group shows and solo exhibitions in The Netherlands, Paris, Italy, Greece, China, Colombia, Mexico, New York, Boston, and Washington, D.C. In California, Goldman has shown at the Oceanside Museum of Art, the Fisher Museum of Art, the Frederick R. Weisman Museum, and the Autry Museum of the American West. Goldman's work has also been exhibited throughout China at the Shanghai International Biennale, two Shenzhen international biennales, and five universities: Jimei, Quanzhou, Tsinghua, Qingdao, and the Shanghai University.

Goldman's work is included in the permanent collections of the San Diego Museum of Art; the Hilbert Museum of California Art; North Carolina's Hickory Museum of Fine Art; the Zuo Wen Museum in Qingdao, China; the San Diego Natural History Museum; and the San Diego Watercolor Society. In 2018, Goldman curated exhibitions for the Oceanside Museum of Art titled "National Watercolor Society: Southern California Inspirations, Past and Present" and in 2020, at the Hilbert Museum of California Art, "National Watercolor Society: The First 100 Years."

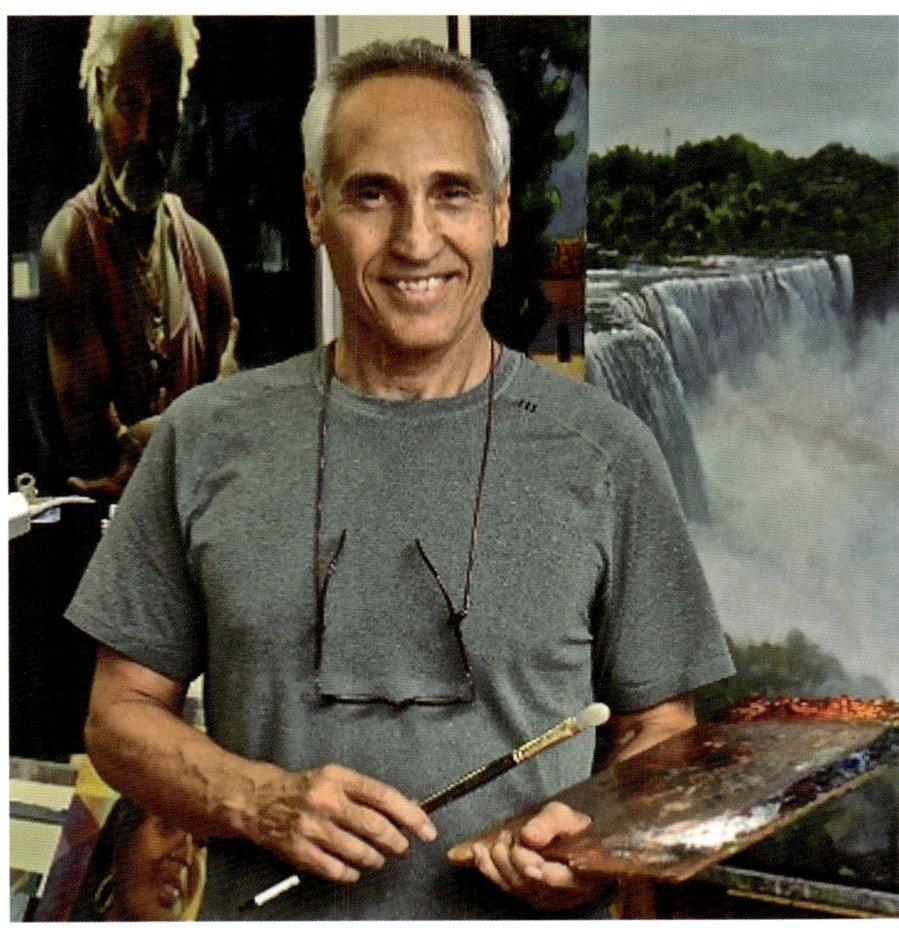

The author of sixteen instructional books on pastels, acrylics, charcoal, and artistic anatomy, Goldman has also been featured in several magazines, including *The Art of Watercolour; Southwest Art; International Artist; Watercolor Magic; Splash* 12, 13, and 19; and *The Artist's Magazine.*

Goldman is a past president of the National Watercolor Society and is represented by CaliforniaWatercolor.com Gallery. Please visit goldmanfineart.com/ken-goldman for more information.

INDEX

OTHER TITLES IN THE *FOR ARTISTS* SERIES FROM ROCKPORT PUBLISHERS

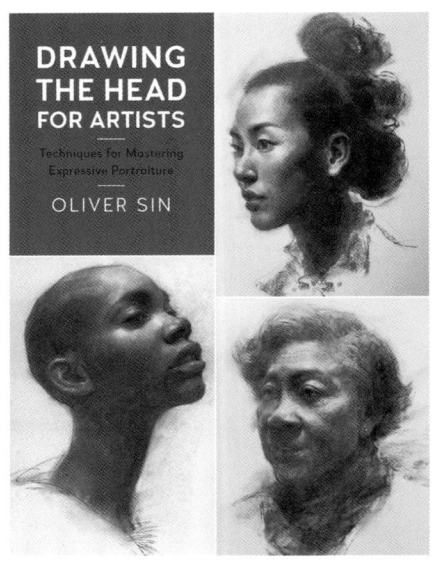

Drawing the Head for Artists
978-1-63159-692-6

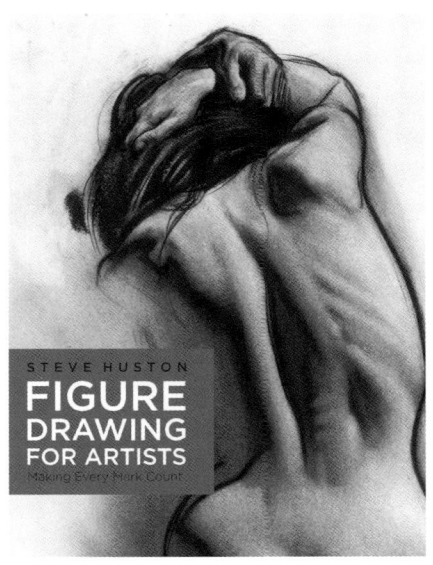

Figure Drawing for Artists
978-1-63159-065-8

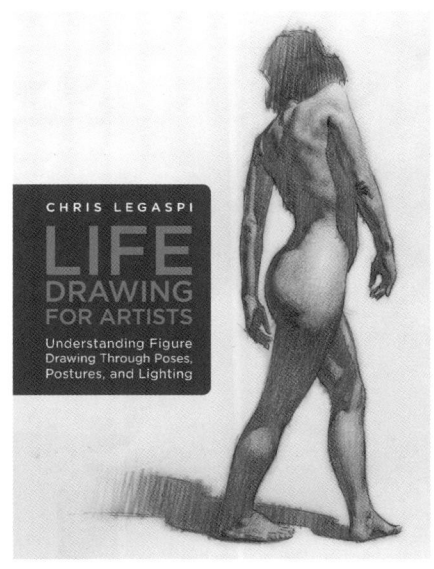

Life Drawing for Artists
978-1-63159-801-2

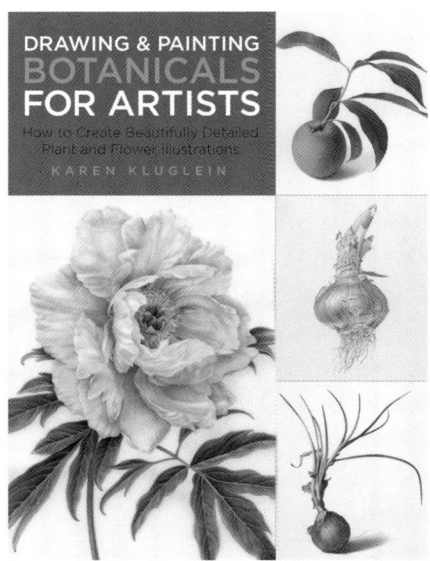

Drawing and Painting Botanicals for Artists
978-1-63159-857-9

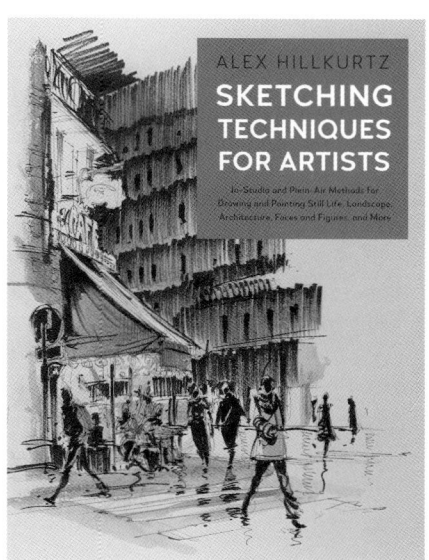

Sketching Techniques for Artists
978-1-63159-923-1

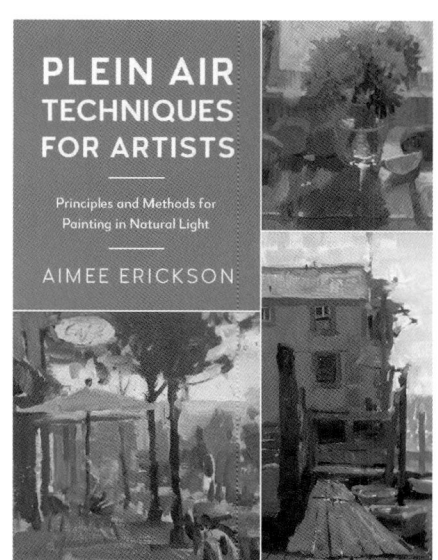

Plein Air Technique for Artists
978-0-76037-935-6

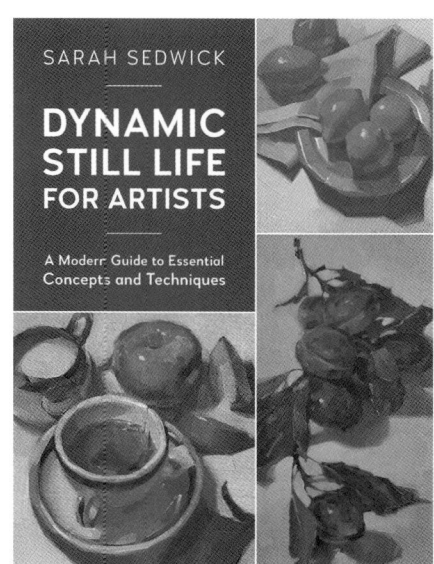

Dynamic Still Life for Artists
978-0-76037-700-0

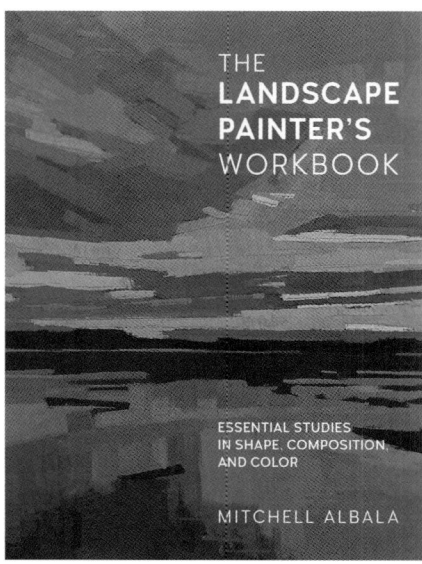

The Landscape Painter's Workbook
978-0-76037-135-0

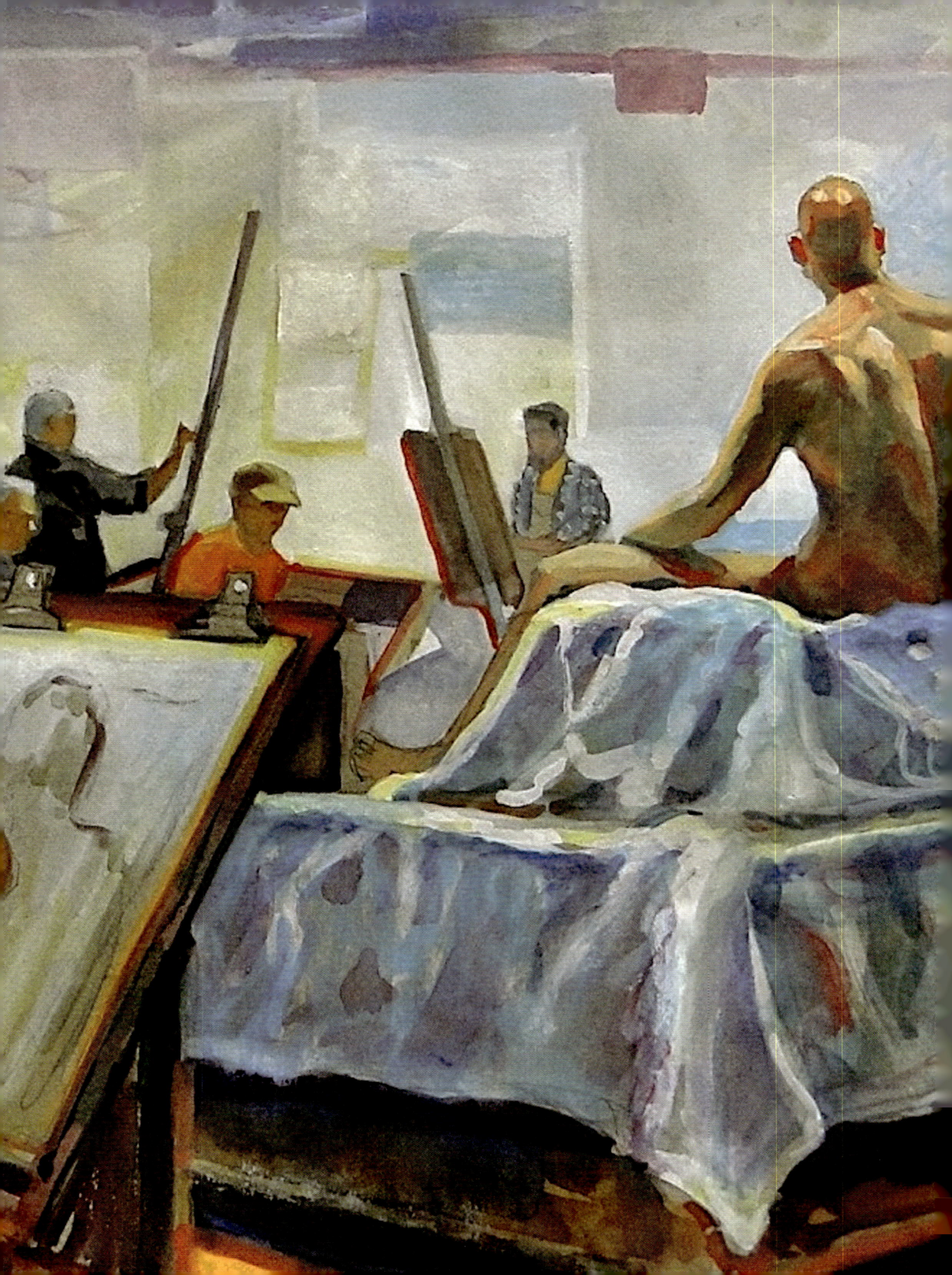